325 HOT & SPICY CURRIES

325 HOT & SPICY CURRIES

Authentic curry dishes from around the world: step-by-step recipes shown in more than 325 mouth-watering photographs

MRIDULA BALJEKAR

southwater

This edition is published by Southwater
an imprint of Anness Publishing Ltd,
Blaby Road, Wigston, Leicestershire LE18 4SE
info@anness.com

www.southwaterbooks.com; www.annesspublishing.com

If you like the images in this book and would like to investigate using them for publishing, promotions or advertising, please visit our website www.practicalpictures.com for more information.

Publisher: Joanna Lorenz
Editor: Joy Wotton
Jacket Design: Nigel Partridge
Production Controller: Steve Lang
Design: SMI

ETHICAL TRADING POLICY
At Anness Publishing we believe that business should be conducted in an ethical and ecologically sustainable way, with respect for the environment and a proper regard to the replacement of the natural resources we employ.

As a publisher, we use a lot of wood pulp in high-quality paper for printing, and that wood commonly comes from spruce trees. We are therefore currently growing more than 750,000 trees in three Scottish forest plantations: Berrymoss (130 hectares/320 acres), West Touxhill (125 hectares/305 acres) and Deveron Forest (75 hectares/185 acres). The forests we manage contain more than 3.5 times the number of trees employed each year in making paper for the books we manufacture.

Because of this ongoing ecological investment programme, you, as our customer, can have the pleasure and reassurance of knowing that a tree is being cultivated on your behalf to naturally replace the materials used to make the book you are holding.

Our forestry programme is run in accordance with the UK Woodland Assurance Scheme (UKWAS) and will be certified by the internationally recognized Forest Stewardship Council (FSC). The FSC is a non-government organization dedicated to promoting responsible management of the world's forests. Certification ensures forests are managed in an environmentally sustainable and socially responsible way. For further information about this scheme, go to www.annesspublishing.com/trees

A CIP catalogue record for this book is available from the British Library.

Recipes in this book have previously appeared in other books published by Lorenz Books.

PUBLISHER'S NOTE
Although the advice and information in this book are believed to be accurate and true at the time of going to press, neither the authors nor the publisher can accept any legal responsibility or liability for any errors or omissions that may have been made nor for any inaccuracies nor for any loss, harm or injury that comes about from following instructions or advice in this book.

Notes
Bracketed terms are intended for American readers.
For all recipes, quantities are given in both metric and imperial measures and, where appropriate, in standard cups and spoons. Follow one set of measures, but not a mixture, because they are not interchangeable.
Standard spoon and cup measures are level. 1 tsp = 5ml, 1 tbsp = 15ml, 1 cup = 250ml/8fl oz.
Australian standard tablespoons are 20ml. Australian readers should use 3 tsp in place of 1 tbsp for measuring small quantities.
American pints are 16fl oz/2 cups. American readers should use 20fl oz/2.5 cups in place of 1 pint when measuring liquids.
Electric oven temperatures in this book are for conventional ovens. When using a fan oven, the temperature will probably need to be reduced by about 10–20°C/20–40°F. Since ovens vary, you should check with your manufacturer's instruction book for guidance.
The nutritional analysis given for each recipe is calculated per portion (i.e. serving or item), unless otherwise stated.
If the recipe gives a range, such as Serves 4–6, then the nutritional analysis will be for the smaller portion size, i.e. 6 servings.
The analysis does not include optional ingredients, such as salt added to taste.
Medium (US large) eggs are used unless otherwise stated.
Vegetable ghee has been used in the recipes, but ghee made from butter can be used instead.

Main front cover image shows Lahore-style Lamb– for recipe, see page 100

Contents

Introduction

Curries are perfect for modern living with their emphasis on fresh ingredients, speedy preparation and exciting flavours. Besides offering fabulous tastes, Indian and South-east

Asian cooking can be extremely healthy with their focus on fresh food and good-quality ingredients – it is even thought that garlic and root ginger, essential ingredients in many curries, contain properties that may help to combat heart diseases and stomach ulcers respectively.

The word curry is generally believed to be an anglicized version of the south Indian word *kaari*, and in India, the word refers to a sauce or gravy used as an accompaniment to moisten rice or to make bread more enjoyable. Other theories suggest that the word *cury* has existed in English in the context of cooking since the 14th century, and that it was originally derived from the French verb *cuire* (to cook).

India has long been known as the spice bowl of the world, and South-east Asia, too, has its own important place in the international history of the spice trade. The use of spices was an established way of life in these sun-drenched, monsoon-fed lands long before traders and merchants, including Arabs, English, Dutch, Portuguese and Spanish, were lured by the value of these exotic ingredients.

Traditionally, curry in India is accompanied by rice or breads, in South-east Asia by rice or noodles. Curried meat and fish are usually served in small quantities, surrounded by inviting little side dishes, such as pickles, chutneys, salads and sambals, flavoured with fresh herbs and chillies, yogurt or soy sauce, and used as seasonings.

Exotic spiced sauces, or curries, have been used for thousands of years to liven up the daily staples of rice, noodles and bread. Turmeric, cumin, coriander, cardamom, chilli, fenugreek and many other pungent spices and scented flavourings have been used to contribute magical tastes and aromas to dishes all over the world. It is the careful blending and combining of these various spices, herbs and other aromatics, often into a mixed powder or blended into a paste to which other ingredients are then added, that defines much of the art of creating mouthwatering curries.

Many of the spices, herbs and aromatics used in this book are readily available. Cumin, coriander, cardamom, garlic, turmeric, cinnamon, ginger, chilli and peppercorns are available in most stores and supermarkets, whether in the form of dried and ground powder, as seeds, or fresh and whole. Some ingredients may be harder to buy – mango powder, asafoetida, galangal and fennel, as well as fresh leaves such as curry leaves, kaffir lime leaves and fenugreek – however, there are many Asian speciality stores

where these ingredients can be bought or you can look for them online or through mail order.

Spicy food is universally popular, and you will find here an inspiring range of dishes from many countries around the world including the Indian Subcontinent, Malaysia, Burma, Thailand, Singapore, Vietnam, Korea, China, Africa and the Caribbean. Discover how to make over 325 authentic curry dishes in this easy-to-use guide, which offers an incredible range of some of the greatest curries of the world. All the classic dishes are here, from Prawn Korma, Rogan Josh and Balti Lamb with Yogurt & Spices to Mussaman Beef, Chicken Dopiaza and Onion Bhajias, but there are many unusual contemporary dishes to try too, including Tamarind-laced Vegetables and Chicken with Green Mango.

The recipes are divided into accessible chapters on Appetizers and Light Bites; Fish and Shellfish; Chicken and Poultry; Meat and Game; Vegetarian Curries; Rices and Biryanis; Rice Side Dishes and Breads; Side Dishes; Chutneys and Relishes; and Salads. With every deliciously tempting curry recipe clearly explained in steps with a photograph of the finished dish, you can be certain to find a curry dish that is perfect for you, whatever your mood or occasion.

Monkfish Soup with Red Thai Spices

This light and creamy coconut soup provides a base for a colourful fusion of red-curried tender monkfish chunks and flat rice noodles.

Serves 4

175g/6oz flat rice noodles
30ml/2 tbsp vegetable oil
2 garlic cloves, chopped
15ml/1 tbsp red curry paste
450g/1lb monkfish fillet, cut into
    bitesize pieces
300ml/½ pint/1¼ cups
    coconut cream

750ml/1¼ pints/3 cups hot
    chicken stock
45ml/3 tbsp Thai fish sauce
15ml/1 tbsp palm sugar
    (jaggery)
60ml/4 tbsp roasted peanuts,
    roughly chopped
4 spring onions (scallions),
    shredded lengthways
50g/2oz/½ cup beansprouts
large handful of fresh Thai
    basil leaves
salt and ground black pepper
1 fresh red chilli, seeded and cut
    lengthways into slivers,
    to garnish

1 Soak the noodles in a bowl of boiling water for 10 minutes, or according to the packet instructions. Drain.

2 Heat the oil in a wok or pan over high heat. Add the garlic and cook for 2 minutes. Stir in the curry paste and cook for 1 minute, until fragrant.

3 Add the monkfish and stir-fry over high heat for about 4–5 minutes, until just tender. Pour the coconut cream and chicken stock into the pan.

4 Stir the fish sauce and sugar into the pan, and bring the mixture just to the boil. Add the drained noodles and cook for 1–2 minutes, until tender.

5 Stir half the peanuts, half the spring onions, half the beansprouts and the Thai basil leaves into the pan. Season with salt and black pepper to taste.

6 Ladle the soup into deep individual soup bowls and sprinkle over the remaining peanuts. Garnish with the remaining spring onions, beansprouts and the slivers of red chilli.

Curried Salmon Soup

A hint of mild curry paste really enhances the flavour of this tasty soup, without making it too spicy. Grated creamed coconut adds a luxury touch, while helping to amalgamate the flavours.

Serves 4

50g/2oz/¼ cup butter
2 onions, roughly chopped
10ml/2 tsp mild curry paste
150ml/¼ pint/⅔ cup
    white wine

300ml/½ pint/1¼ cups double
    (heavy) cream
50g/2oz/½ cup creamed coconut,
    grated or 120ml/4fl oz/½ cup
    coconut cream
2 potatoes, about 350g/12oz,
    cubed
450g/1lb salmon fillet,
    skinned and cut into
    bitesize pieces
60ml/4 tbsp chopped fresh
    flat-leaf parsley
salt and ground black pepper

1 Melt the butter in a large pan, add the onions and cook for about 3–4 minutes until beginning to soften. Stir in the curry paste. Cook for 1 minute more.

2 Add 475ml/16fl oz/2 cups water, the wine, cream and creamed coconut or coconut cream, with seasoning. Bring to the boil, stirring until the coconut has dissolved.

3 Add the potatoes and simmer, covered, for about 15 minutes or until they are almost tender. Do not allow them to break down into the liquid.

4 Add the fish and cook gently so as not to break it up for about 2–3 minutes until just cooked. Add the parsley and adjust the seasoning. Serve immediately.

Cook's Tip
There is a wide choice of curry pastes available. Select a concentrated paste for this recipe, rather than a 'cook-in-sauce' type of product. If you cannot find a suitable paste, cook 5ml/1 tsp curry powder in a pan with a little melted butter over low heat and use that mixture instead.

Red Monkfish Energy 379kcal/1589kJ; Protein 25.5g; Carbohydrate 41.2g, of which sugars 4.7g; Fat 12g, of which saturates 2g; Cholesterol 18mg; Calcium 49mg; Fibre 0.9g; Sodium 111mg.
Curried Salmon Energy 837kcal/3466kJ; Protein 26.3g; Carbohydrate 16.6g, of which sugars 3.6g; Fat 71.8g, of which saturates 41.2g; Cholesterol 186mg; Calcium 74mg; Fibre 0.9g; Sodium 158mg.

Chicken Soup with Curry Paste

This is an example of a distinctly Eurasian dish – a delicious spicy chicken soup made with freshly made curry paste.

Serves 4–6

1 chicken, about 1kg/2¼lb
2 cinnamon sticks
5ml/1 tsp black peppercorns
5ml/1 tsp fennel seeds
5ml/1 tsp cumin seeds
15ml/1 tbsp ghee or vegetable oil with a little butter
15–30ml/1–2 tbsp brown mustard seeds

a handful of fresh curry leaves
salt and ground black pepper
2 limes, quartered, to serve

For the curry paste
40g/1½oz fresh root ginger, peeled and chopped
4 garlic cloves, chopped
4 shallots, chopped
2 lemon grass stalks, trimmed and chopped
4 dried red chillies, soaked to soften, drained, seeded and the pulp scraped out
15–30ml/1–2 tbsp Indian curry powder

1 To make the curry paste, grind the ginger with the garlic, shallots and lemon grass, using a mortar and pestle, food processor or blender. Add the chilli pulp and curry powder, blend again, and set aside.

2 Put the chicken and the chicken feet, if using, in a deep pan with the cinnamon sticks, peppercorns, fennel and cumin seeds. Add enough water to just cover, and bring it to the boil.

3 Reduce the heat and cook gently for about 1 hour, until the chicken is cooked. Remove the chicken from the broth, skin it and shred the meat. Strain the broth, discarding the spices.

4 In a pan or wok, heat the ghee or oil and butter. Stir in the mustard seeds and, once they begin to pop and give off a nutty aroma, add the curry paste. Fry the paste until fragrant, then pour in the strained broth.

5 Bring the broth to the boil and season to taste with salt and pepper. Add the curry leaves and shredded chicken, and ladle the soup into bowls. Serve with wedges of lime to squeeze into the soup.

Aubergine Soup with Beef and Lime

This tasty soup can be made with aubergines, green jackfruit or any of the squash family. The quantity of rice should be greater than the soup, as the soup is meant to moisten and flavour the rice.

Serves 4

30ml/2 tbsp palm, groundnut (peanut) or corn oil
150g/5oz lean beef, cut into thin strips
500ml/17fl oz/generous 2 cups coconut milk
10ml/2 tsp sugar
3–4 Thai aubergines (eggplants) or 1 large aubergine, cut into wedges

3–4 kaffir lime leaves
juice of 1 lime
salt

For the spice paste
4 shallots, chopped
4 red chillies, seeded and chopped
25g/1oz fresh root ginger, chopped
15g/½oz fresh turmeric, chopped or 2.5ml/½ tsp ground turmeric
2 garlic cloves, chopped
5ml/1 tsp coriander seeds
2.5ml/½ tsp cumin seeds
3 candlenuts or macadamia nuts

To serve
cooked rice
1 lime, quartered
chilli sambal

1 To make the spice paste, using a mortar and pestle, grind all the ingredients together to form a textured paste, or process them together in an electric blender or food processor.

2 Heat the oil in a wok or heavy pan, stir in the spice paste and fry until fragrant.

3 Add the beef, stirring to coat it well in the spice paste, then add the coconut milk and sugar. Bring the liquid to the boil, then reduce the heat and simmer gently for 10 minutes.

4 Add the aubergine wedges and kaffir lime leaves to the pan and cook gently for a further 5–10 minutes, until tender but not mushy. Stir in the lime juice and season with salt to taste.

5 Ladle the soup into individual warmed bowls and serve with bowls of cooked rice to spoon the soup over, wedges of lime to squeeze on the top and a chilli sambal.

Chicken Soup Energy 264kcal/1093kJ; Protein 20.7g; Carbohydrate 1.6g, of which sugars 1g; Fat 19.4g, of which saturates 6.3g; Cholesterol 112mg; Calcium 19mg; Fibre 0.5g; Sodium 104mg.
Aubergine Soup Energy 224kcal/938kJ; Protein 12.1g; Carbohydrate 14.6g, of which sugars 12.6g; Fat 13.6g, of which saturates 3.2g; Cholesterol 22mg; Calcium 79mg; Fibre 3g; Sodium 181mg.

Curried Lamb Samosas

Filo pastry is perfect for making samosas. Once you've mastered folding them, you'll be amazed at how quick they are to make. These lamb samosas have a simple filling that is tasty and quick to make – perfect for party fare.

Makes 12
25g/1oz/2 tbsp butter
225g/8oz/1 cup minced
    (ground) lamb
30ml/2 tbsp mild curry paste
12 sheets of filo pastry,
    wrapped in a damp dish towel
salt and ground black pepper

1 Heat a little of the butter in a large heavy pan and add the lamb. Fry for 5–6 minutes, stirring occasionally until the meat is evenly browned all over. Stir in the curry paste and cook for 1–2 minutes. Season and set aside. Preheat the oven to 200°C/400°F/Gas 6.

2 Melt the remaining butter in a pan. Cut the pastry sheets in half lengthways. Brush one strip of pastry with butter, then lay another strip on top and brush with more butter.

3 Place a spoonful of lamb in the corner of the strip and fold over to form a triangle at one end. Keep folding over in the same way to form a triangular shape.

4 Brush with butter and place on a baking sheet. Repeat using the remaining pastry and filling. Bake in the oven for about 10–15 minutes until golden. Serve immediately.

Variation

For Cashew Nut Samosas, mix together 225g/8oz cooked and mashed potato, 15ml/1 tbsp chopped cashew nuts, 5ml/1 tsp coconut milk powder, 1/2 chopped green chilli, 5ml/ 1 tsp mustard seeds, 5ml/1 tsp cumin seeds, 15ml/1 tbsp chopped fresh coriander (cilantro) and 5ml/1 tsp soft light brown sugar. Use this mixture to fill the samosas in place of the lamb filling. If you like, the mustard and cumin seeds can be dry-roasted first.

Spiced Savoury Biscuits

These biscuits are ideal for serving with drinks.

Makes 20–30
150g/5oz/1 1/4 cups plain
    (all-purpose) flour
10ml/2 tsp curry powder
115g/4oz/1/2 cup butter
75g/3oz/3/4 cup grated
    Cheddar cheese
10ml/2 tsp poppy seeds
5ml/1 tsp black onion seeds
1 egg yolk
cumin seeds, to garnish

1 Grease two large baking sheets. Sift the flour and curry powder into a mixing bowl. Rub in the butter until the mixture resembles breadcrumbs, then stir in the cheese and seeds.

2 Stir the egg yolk into the mixture and mix until a firm dough forms. Wrap the dough in a piece of clear film (plastic wrap) and chill in the refrigerator for 30 minutes.

3 Roll out the dough on a floured surface to a thickness of about 3mm/1/8in. Cut into shapes with a cookie cutter, place on the baking sheets and sprinkle with the cumin seeds. Chill them in the refrigerator for about 15 minutes.

4 Preheat the oven to 190°C/375°F/Gas 5. Bake for about 20 minutes until they are crisp and golden. Serve warm or cold.

Peanut Crackers

These snacks are popular across South-east Asia.

Serves 4–5
225g/8oz/2 cups plus 30ml/
    2 tbsp rice flour
5ml/1 tsp baking powder
5ml/1 tsp ground turmeric
5ml/1 tsp ground coriander
300ml/1/2 pint/1 1/4 cups
    coconut milk
115g/4oz/3/4 cup unsalted
    peanuts, coarsely chopped
2–3 macadamia nuts, ground
2–3 garlic cloves, crushed
corn oil, for shallow frying
salt and ground black pepper
chilli sambal, for dipping

To season
5ml/1 tsp paprika
salt

1 Put the rice flour, baking powder, turmeric and coriander into a bowl. Make a well in the centre, pour in the coconut milk and stir to combine. Beat well to make a smooth batter.

2 Add the peanuts, macadamia nuts and garlic to the bowl and mix well together. Season with salt and black pepper and then set the mixture aside for 30 minutes.

3 In a small bowl, mix the paprika with a little salt.

4 Heat a thin layer of oil in a wok and drop in a spoonful of batter for each cracker. Work in batches, flipping the crackers over when the lacy edges become crispy and golden brown. Drain on kitchen paper and transfer them to a basket.

5 Sprinkle the paprika mixture over the crackers and toss them lightly. Serve immediately while still warm and crisp with some chilli sambal for dipping.

Curried Lamb Samosas Energy 101kcal/423kJ; Protein 5g; Carbohydrate 10.4g, of which sugars 0.2g; Fat 4.6g, of which saturates 2.3g; Cholesterol 19mg; Calcium 37mg; Fibre 1g; Sodium 37mg.
Spiced Savoury Biscuits Energy 59kcal/244kJ; Protein 1.3g; Carbohydrate 4g, of which sugars 0.1g; Fat 4.2g, of which saturates 2.7g; Cholesterol 18mg; Calcium 29mg; Fibre 0.2g; Sodium 49mg.
Peanut Crackers Energy 403kcal/1679kJ; Protein 9.7g; Carbohydrate 42.2g, of which sugars 4.6g; Fat 21.3g, of which saturates 3.4g; Cholesterol 0mg; Calcium 44mg; Fibre 2.5g; Sodium 69mg.

Fish Cakes with Cucumber Relish

These wonderful, small fish cakes are a very familiar and popular appetizer in Thailand and increasingly throughout South-east Asia.

Makes about 12
8 kaffir lime leaves
300g/11oz cod fillet, cut
  into chunks
30ml/2 tbsp red curry paste
1 egg
30ml/2 tbsp Thai fish sauce
5ml/1 tsp sugar
30ml/2 tbsp cornflour (cornstarch)

15ml/1 tbsp chopped fresh
  coriander (cilantro)
50g/2oz/½ cup green beans,
  thinly sliced
vegetable oil, for deep-frying

For the cucumber relish
60ml/4 tbsp coconut or rice vinegar
50g/2oz/¼ cup sugar
60ml/4 tbsp water
1 head pickled garlic
1cm/½in piece fresh root
  ginger, chopped
1 cucumber, cut into thin batons
4 shallots, thinly sliced

1 To make the cucumber relish, mix the coconut or rice vinegar, sugar and water in a pan. Heat gently, stirring constantly until the sugar has dissolved. Remove from the heat and leave to cool.

2 Place the garlic and ginger in a mixing bowl. Add the cucumber and shallots. Mix in the vinegar and stir lightly to combine. Cover and set aside.

3 Reserve two or three kaffir lime leaves for the garnish and thinly slice the remaining leaves. Put the fish, curry paste and egg in a food processor and blend to a smooth paste. Transfer to a bowl and stir in the fish sauce, sugar, cornflour, sliced kaffir lime leaves, coriander and green beans. Shape the mixture into thick cakes.

4 Heat the oil in a deep-frying pan or wok to 190°C/375°F or until a cube of bread, added to the oil, browns in about 45 seconds. Fry the fish cakes, a few at a time, for 4–5 minutes, until cooked and evenly brown. Lift out and drain on kitchen paper.

5 Keep each batch hot in a low oven, while frying successive batches. Garnish with the reserved kaffir lime leaves and serve with the cucumber relish.

Goan Fish Cakes

Goan fish and shellfish are skilfully prepared with spices to make cakes of all shapes and sizes, while the rest of India makes fish kebabs.

Makes 20
450g/1lb skinned haddock or cod
2 potatoes, peeled, boiled and
  coarsely mashed
4 spring onions (scallions),
  finely chopped

4 fresh green chillies,
  finely chopped
5cm/2in piece fresh root
  ginger, crushed
a few coriander (cilantro) and
  mint sprigs, chopped
2 eggs
breadcrumbs, for coating
vegetable oil, for shallow-frying
salt and ground black pepper
lemon wedges and chilli sauce,
  to serve

1 Place the skinned fish in a lightly greased steamer and steam gently until cooked (test with a fork – the flesh should flake easily). Remove the steamer from the stove but leave the fish on the steaming tray until cool.

2 When the fish is cool, crumble it coarsely into a large bowl, using a fork. Mix in the mashed potatoes, spring onions, chillies, crushed ginger, chopped coriander and mint, and one of the eggs. Season to taste with salt and pepper.

3 Shape the mixture into about 20 cakes. Beat the remaining egg and place on a plate. Place the breadcrumbs on a separate plate. Dip the cakes in the egg, then into the breadcrumbs. Heat the oil in a frying pan and fry the cakes until brown on all sides. Serve immediately as an appetizer or as a side dish, with the lemon wedges and chilli sauce.

> **Variations**
> • To make a quicker version of these fish cakes, used canned tuna in brine and omit step 1. Make sure the tuna is thoroughly drained before use.
> • Although haddock or cod are used in this recipe, you can substitute them with other less expensive firm white fish, such as coley or whiting.

Fish Cakes Energy 86kcal/361kJ; Protein 6.2g; Carbohydrate 8.1g, of which sugars 5.4g; Fat 3.4g, of which saturates 0.5g; Cholesterol 27mg; Calcium 16mg; Fibre 0.2g; Sodium 2040mg.
Goan Fish Cakes Energy 80kcal/336kJ; Protein 5.5g; Carbohydrate 4.4g, of which sugars 0.3g; Fat 4.6g, of which saturates 0.6g; Cholesterol 27mg; Calcium 11mg; Fibre 0.2g; Sodium 43mg.

Split Pea or Lentil Fritters

These delicious spicy fritters are an Indian speciality.

Serves 4–6

250g/9oz/generous 1 cup yellow split peas or red lentils, soaked overnight
3–5 garlic cloves, chopped
30ml/2 tbsp roughly chopped fresh root ginger
120ml/4fl oz/½ cup chopped fresh coriander (cilantro) leaves
2.5–5ml/½–1 tsp ground cumin
1.5–2.5ml/¼–½ tsp ground turmeric
large pinch of cayenne pepper or ½–1 fresh green chilli, chopped
2.5ml/½ tsp salt
2.5ml/½ tsp ground black pepper
120ml/4fl oz/½ cup gram flour
5ml/1 tsp baking powder
30ml/2 tbsp couscous
2 large or 3 small onions, chopped
vegetable oil, for frying
lemon wedges and fresh chilli, to serve

1 Drain the split peas or lentils, reserving a little of the soaking water. Put the chopped garlic and ginger in a food processor or blender and process until finely minced (ground). Add the drained peas or lentils, 15–30ml/1–2 tbsp of the reserved soaking water and the coriander, and process to form a paste.

2 Add the cumin, turmeric, cayenne or chilli, the salt and pepper, the gram flour, baking powder and couscous to the mixture and combine. The mixture should form a thick batter. If it seems too thick, add a spoonful of the soaking water. Add a little more flour or couscous if it is too watery. Mix in the onions.

3 Heat the oil in a wide, deep frying pan, to a depth of about 5cm/2in, until it is hot enough to brown a cube of bread in 30 seconds. Using two spoons, form the mixture into two-bitesize balls and slip each one gently into the hot oil. Cook until golden brown on the underside, then turn and cook the second side until golden brown.

4 Remove the fritters from the hot oil with a slotted spoon and drain well on kitchen paper. Transfer the fritters to a baking sheet and keep them warm in a preheated oven until all the mixture is cooked. Serve the fritters hot or at room temperature with lemon wedges and chopped fresh chilli.

Spicy Corn Patties

When it comes to snack food, these spicy fried patties are a must. Serve with chilli sambal on the side to give that extra fiery kick to these tasty snacks.

Serves 4

2 fresh corn on the cob
3 shallots, chopped
2 garlic cloves, chopped
25g/1oz galangal or fresh root ginger, chopped
1–2 chillies, seeded and chopped
2–3 candlenuts or macadamia nuts, ground
5ml/1 tsp ground coriander
5ml/1 tsp ground cumin
15ml/1 tbsp coconut oil
3 eggs
45–60ml/3–4 tbsp grated fresh coconut or desiccated (dry unsweetened shredded) coconut
2–3 spring onions (scallions), white parts only, finely sliced
corn or groundnut (peanut) oil, for shallow frying
1 small bunch fresh coriander (cilantro) leaves, chopped
salt and ground black pepper
1 lime, quartered, for serving
chilli sambal, for dipping

1 Put the corn on the cob into a large pan of water, bring to the boil and boil for about 8 minutes. Drain the cobs and scrape all the corn off the cob and put aside. Discard the cobs.

2 Using a mortar and pestle, grind the shallots, garlic, galangal or ginger, and chillies to a paste. Add the candlenuts or macadamia nuts, ground coriander and cumin and beat well together.

3 Heat the coconut oil in a heavy pan, stir in the spice paste and stir-fry until the paste becomes fragrant and begins to colour. Transfer the paste on to a plate and leave to cool.

4 Beat the eggs in a bowl. Add the coconut and spring onions and beat in the corn and the spice paste. Season to taste.

5 Heat a thin layer of corn oil in a heavy frying pan. Working in batches, drop spoonfuls of the corn mixture into the oil and fry the patties for 2–3 minutes, until golden brown on both sides.

6 Drain the patties on kitchen paper and arrange them on a serving dish on top of the coriander leaves. Serve hot or cool with wedges of lime and a chilli sambal for dipping.

Split Pea Fritters Energy 360kcal/1511kj; Protein 14.1g; Carbohydrate 51.3g, of which sugars 8.3g; Fat 12.3g, of which saturates 1.4g; Cholesterol 0mg; Calcium 119mg; Fibre 5.3g; Sodium 26g.
Corn Patties Energy 368kcal/1531kj; Protein 10.8g; Carbohydrate 18.1g, of which sugars 8.2g; Fat 28.7g, of which saturates 9.7g; Cholesterol 143mg; Calcium 68mg; Fibre 4.1g; Sodium 196mg.

Spiced Beef and Potato Puffs

These crisp, golden pillows of pastry filled with spiced beef and potatoes are delicious served straight from the wok. The light pastry puffs up in the hot oil and contrasts enticingly with the fragrant spiced beef.

Serves 4

15ml/1 tbsp sunflower oil
½ small onion, finely chopped
3 garlic cloves, crushed
5ml/1 tsp fresh root ginger, grated
1 red chilli, seeded and chopped
30ml/2 tbsp hot curry powder
75g/3oz minced (ground) beef
115g/4oz mashed potato
60ml/4 tbsp chopped fresh coriander (cilantro)
2 sheets ready-rolled, fresh puff pastry
1 egg, lightly beaten
vegetable oil, for deep-frying
salt and ground black pepper
fresh coriander (cilantro) leaves, to garnish
tomato ketchup, to serve

1 Heat the oil in a wok, then add the onion, garlic, ginger and chilli. Stir-fry over medium heat for 2–3 minutes. Add the curry powder and beef and stir-fry over high heat for 4–5 minutes, or until the beef is browned and just cooked through, then remove from the heat.

2 Transfer the beef mixture to a large bowl and add the mashed potato and chopped fresh coriander. Stir well, then season with salt and pepper and set aside.

3 Lay the pastry sheets on a clean, dry surface and cut out eight rounds, using a 7.5cm/3in pastry (cookie) cutter. Place a large spoonful of the beef mixture in the centre of each pastry round. Brush the edges of the pastry with the beaten egg and fold each round in half to enclose the filling. Press and crimp the edges with the tines of a fork to seal.

4 Fill a wok or large heavy pan one-third full of vegetable oil and heat to 190°C/375°F or until a cube of bread, added to the oil, browns in about 45 seconds.

5 Deep-fry the puffs, in batches, for 2–3 minutes until golden brown. Drain on kitchen paper and garnish with fresh coriander leaves. Serve with tomato ketchup for dipping.

Chickpea Cakes with Tahini

These spicy little cakes are equally good hot or cold. For a more substantial snack, tuck them into pitta bread with salad.

Serves 4

2 x 425g/15oz cans chickpeas
2 garlic cloves, crushed
1 bunch spring onions (scallions), white parts only, chopped
10ml/2 tsp ground cumin
10ml/2 tsp ground coriander
1 fresh green chilli, seeded and finely chopped
30ml/2 tbsp chopped fresh coriander (cilantro)
1 small egg, beaten
30ml/2 tbsp plain (all-purpose) flour
seasoned flour, for shaping
vegetable oil, for shallow-frying
salt and ground black pepper
lemon wedges and fresh coriander, to garnish

For the tahini and lemon dip
30ml/2 tbsp tahini
juice of 1 lemon
2 garlic cloves, crushed

1 Drain the chickpeas thoroughly. Transfer them into a blender or food processor and process until smooth. Add the garlic, spring onions, cumin and ground coriander. Process again.

2 Scrape the mixture into a bowl and stir in the chilli, fresh coriander, egg and flour. Mix well and season with salt and pepper. If the mixture is very soft add a little more flour. Chill for about 30 minutes to firm the mixture.

3 Make the dip. Mix the tahini, lemon juice and garlic in a bowl, adding a little water if the sauce is too thick. Set aside.

4 Using floured hands, shape the chickpea mixture into 12 cakes. Heat the oil in a frying pan and fry the cakes in batches for about 1 minute on each side, until crisp and golden. Drain well on kitchen paper and serve immediately with the dip and lemon and coriander garnish.

Variation
Another quick and easy dipping sauce is made by mixing yogurt with a little chopped chilli and fresh mint.

Spiced Beef Puffs Energy 408kcal/1695kJ; Protein 9g; Carbohydrate 24.2g, of which sugars 1.8g; Fat 31.8g, of which saturates 4.2g; Cholesterol 67mg; Calcium 46mg; Fibre 0.5g; Sodium 202mg.
Chickpea Cakes Energy 342kcal/1433kJ; Protein 15.9g; Carbohydrate 28.1g, of which sugars 1.8g; Fat 19.5g, of which saturates 2.6g; Cholesterol 48mg; Calcium 171mg; Fibre 7.9g; Sodium 358mg.

Rice Cakes with Dipping Sauce

These cakes are easy to make and will last for weeks in an airtight container.

Serves 4–6
175g/6oz/1 cup Thai jasmine rice
350ml/12fl oz/1½ cups water
oil, for deep-frying and greasing

For the spicy dipping sauce
6–8 dried chillies
2.5ml/½ tsp salt
2 shallots, chopped
2 garlic cloves, chopped
4 coriander (cilantro) roots
10 white peppercorns
250ml/8fl oz/1 cup coconut milk
5ml/1 tsp shrimp paste
115g/4oz minced (ground) pork
115g/4oz cherry tomatoes, chopped
15ml/1 tbsp Thai fish sauce
15ml/1 tbsp palm sugar
   (jaggery) or light muscovado
   (brown) sugar
30ml/2 tbsp tamarind juice
   (tamarind paste mixed with
   warm water)
30ml/2 tbsp coarsely chopped
   roasted peanuts
2 spring onions (scallions), chopped

1 Make the sauce. Snap off the chilli stems, scrape out the seeds and soak the chillies in warm water for 20 minutes. Drain and put in a mortar. Sprinkle over the salt and crush. Add the shallots, garlic, coriander and peppercorns. Pound to a paste.

2 Pour the coconut milk into a pan and bring to the boil. Stir in the pounded chilli paste and cook for 2–3 minutes. Stir in the shrimp paste and cook for 1 minute more.

3 Add the pork and cook for 5–10 minutes, then stir in the tomatoes, fish sauce, sugar and tamarind juice. Simmer, stirring occasionally, until the sauce thickens, then stir in the chopped peanuts and spring onions. Set aside to cool.

4 Preheat the oven to the lowest setting. Grease a baking sheet. Wash the rice and put it in a pan, add the water and cover. Bring to the boil, then simmer gently for 15 minutes. Spoon the cooked rice on to the baking sheet and press it down. Leave in the oven to dry out overnight.

5 Break the rice into bitesize pieces. Heat the oil in a wok or deep-fryer. Deep-fry the cakes, in batches, for about 1 minute, until they puff up. Remove and drain. Serve with the sauce.

Spicy Potato Pancakes

Although called a pancake, these crispy spiced cakes are more like a traditional Indian bhaji. They make an ideal appetizer for a meal.

Makes 10
300g/11oz potatoes
25ml/1½ tsp garam masala or
   curry powder
4 spring onions (scallions),
   finely chopped
1 large (US extra large) egg
   white, lightly beaten
30ml/2 tbsp sunflower or
   olive oil
salt and ground black pepper
Indian chutney and relishes,
   to serve

1 Peel and grate the potatoes into a large bowl. Using your hands, squeeze the excess liquid from the grated potatoes and pat dry with kitchen paper.

2 Place the dry, grated potatoes in a separate bowl and add the spices, spring onions, egg white and seasoning. Stir to combine the ingredients.

3 Heat a large, non-stick frying pan over medium heat and add the vegetable oil.

4 Drop tablespoonfuls of the potato on to the pan and flatten out with the back of a spoon (you will need to cook the pancakes in two batches).

5 Cook the first batch for a few minutes and then flip over the pancakes. Cook for a further 3 minutes. Remove them from the pan and keep them warm in a preheated low oven while you cook the remaining batch.

6 Drain the pancakes well on kitchen paper and serve immediately with chutney and relishes.

> **Cook's Tip**
> *Don't grate the potatoes too soon before you intend to use them as the flesh will quickly turn brown.*

Rice Cakes Energy 361kcal/1508kJ; Protein 11.7g; Carbohydrate 42g, of which sugars 8.8g; Fat 16g, of which saturates 2.9g; Cholesterol 19mg; Calcium 38mg; Fibre 0.8g; Sodium 359mg.
Potato Pancakes Energy 50kcal/210kJ; Protein 1.3g; Carbohydrate 5.8g, of which sugars 0.5g; Fat 2.6g, of which saturates 0.3g; Cholesterol 0mg; Calcium 8mg; Fibre 0.4g; Sodium 11mg.

Curry-spiced Pakoras

These delicious batter balls make a wonderful snack with this fragrant chutney.

Makes 25
15ml/1 tbsp sunflower oil
20ml/4 tsp cumin seeds
5ml/1 tsp black mustard seeds
1 small onion, finely chopped
10ml/2 tsp grated fresh
 root ginger
2 green chillies, seeded and
 chopped
600g/1lb 5oz potatoes, cooked
200g/7oz fresh peas
juice of 1 lemon
90ml/6 tbsp chopped fresh
 coriander (cilantro) leaves
115g/4oz/1 cup gram flour

25g/1oz/¼ cup self-raising
 (self-rising) flour
40g/1½oz/⅓ cup rice flour
large pinch of turmeric
10ml/2 tsp crushed
 coriander seeds
350ml/12fl oz/1½ cups water
vegetable oil, for frying
salt and ground black pepper

For the chutney
105ml/7 tbsp coconut cream
200ml/7fl oz/scant 1 cup natural
 (plain) yogurt
50g/2oz mint leaves,
 finely chopped
5ml/1 tsp golden caster
 (superfine) sugar
juice of 1 lime

1 Heat a wok over medium heat and add the sunflower oil. When hot, fry the cumin and mustard seeds for 1–2 minutes. Add the onion, ginger and chillies to the wok and cook for 3–4 minutes. Add the cooked potatoes and peas and stir-fry for a further 5–6 minutes. Season, then stir in the lemon juice and coriander leaves. Leave the mixture to cool slightly, then divide into 25 portions. Shape each portion into a ball with your hands and chill in the refrigerator.

2 To make the chutney, place all the ingredients in a blender and process until smooth. Season, then chill. To make the batter, put the gram flour, self-raising flour and rice flour in a bowl. Season and add the turmeric and coriander seeds. Gradually whisk in the water to make a smooth batter.

3 Fill a wok one-third full of oil and heat to 180°C/350°F. Working in batches, dip the chilled balls in the batter, then drop into the oil and deep-fry for 1–2 minutes, or until golden. Drain on kitchen paper, and serve immediately with the chutney.

Onion Bhajias

Makes 20–25
2 large onions, sliced thinly
225g/8oz/2 cups gram flour
2.5ml/½ tsp chilli powder
5ml/1 tsp ground turmeric
5ml/1 tsp baking powder
1.5ml/¼ tsp asafoetida

2.5ml/½ tsp each nigella, fennel,
 cumin and onion seeds, crushed
2 fresh green chillies, finely chopped
50g/2oz/2 cups fresh coriander
 (cilantro), chopped
vegetable oil, for deep-frying
salt

1 In a bowl mix together the flour, chilli powder, turmeric, baking powder and asafoetida. Add salt to taste. Add the seeds, onion, chillies fresh coriander. Mix well. Add enough cold water to make a paste, then stir in more water to make a thick batter.

2 Heat the oil and drop spoonfuls of the mixture into the oil, and fry until golden. Drain on kitchen paper and serve hot.

Onion Pakoras

Serves 4–5
675g/1½lb onions, thinly sliced
5ml/1 tsp salt
5ml/1 tsp ground coriander
5ml/1 tsp ground cumin
2.5ml/½ tsp ground turmeric
1 green chilli, seeded and chopped
45ml/3 tbsp chopped fresh
 coriander (cilantro)

90g/3½oz/¾ cup gram flour
2.5ml/½ tsp baking powder
vegetable oil, for deep-frying

To serve
lemon wedges (optional)
fresh coriander (cilantro) sprigs,
 chutney or a yogurt dip

1 Toss the onions in the salt. Leave to stand for 45 minutes. Rinse the onions, then squeeze out any excess moisture.

2 Place the onions in a bowl. Add the spices, gram flour and baking powder. Mix well. Shape the mixture into 12–15 pakoras.

3 Heat the oil and deep-fry the pakoras until golden brown. Drain each batch on kitchen paper. Serve with lemon, coriander and chutney or a yogurt cucumber dip.

Onion Bhajias Energy 72kcal/301kJ; Protein 1.2g; Carbohydrate 8.8g, of which sugars 1.3g; Fat 3.8g, of which saturates 0.4g; Cholesterol 0mg; Calcium 23mg; Fibre 0.7g; Sodium 2mg.
Onion Pakora Energy 207kcal/861kJ; Protein 5.4g; Carbohydrate 19.8g, of which sugars 8.2g; Fat 12.3g, of which saturates 1.4g; Cholesterol 0mg; Calcium 84mg; Fibre 4.3g; Sodium 14mg.
Curry-spiced Pakoras Energy 126kcal/525kJ; Protein 4.1g; Carbohydrate 8.3g, of which sugars 2.6g; Fat 8.8g, of which saturates 5.2g; Cholesterol 0mg; Calcium 35mg; Fibre 1.3g; Sodium 16mg.

Quick-fried Spicy Prawns

Serves 4

450g/1lb large raw prawns (shrimp)
2.5cm/1in fresh root ginger, grated
2 garlic cloves, crushed
5ml/1 tsp hot chilli powder
5ml/1 tsp ground turmeric
10ml/2 tsp black mustard seeds

4 green cardamom pods, seeded
50g/2oz/¼ cup ghee or butter
120ml/4fl oz/½ cup coconut milk
salt and ground black pepper
30–45ml/2–3 tbsp chopped fresh
   coriander (cilantro), to garnish
naan bread, to serve

1 Peel and devein the prawns. Put in a bowl and mix with the spices.

2 Heat a wok until hot. Add the ghee or butter. Add the prawns and stir-fry for about 1–1½ minutes until pink. Stir in the coconut milk and simmer for 3–4 minutes until the prawns are cooked.

3 Season to taste. Sprinkle with the chopped fresh coriander and serve immediately, with naan bread.

Hot Spiced Clams

Serves 3–4

500g/1¼lb small clams, scrubbed
1 small onion, finely chopped
1 celery stick, sliced
2 garlic cloves, finely chopped
2.5cm/1in piece fresh root
   ginger, grated
30ml/2 tbsp olive oil

1.5ml/¼ tsp chilli powder
5ml/1 tsp ground turmeric
30ml/2 tbsp chopped fresh parsley
30ml/2 tbsp dry white wine
salt and ground black pepper
celery leaves, to garnish
fresh bread, to serve

1 Place the onion, celery, garlic and ginger in a large pan, pour in the oil, and add the spices and parsley and stir-fry gently for about 5 minutes. Add the clams to the pan and cook for 2 minutes.

2 Add the wine to the pan, then cover and cook gently for 2–3 minutes, shaking occasionally, until the shells have opened.

3 Season to taste. Discard any clams whose shells remain closed, then serve immediately with fresh bread and celery leaves.

Spicy Shrimp and Scallop Satay

This dish is succulent, spicy and very moreish. Serve with rice and a salad or pickled vegetables and lime.

Serves 4

250g/9oz shelled shrimp or
   prawns (shrimp), deveined
   and chopped
250g/9oz shelled scallops, chopped
30ml/2 tbsp potato, tapioca or
   rice flour
5ml/1 tsp baking powder
12–16 wooden, metal, lemon
   grass or sugar cane skewers
1 lime, quartered, to serve

For the spice paste

2 shallots, chopped
2 garlic cloves, chopped
2–3 red chillies, seeded
   and chopped
25g/1oz galangal or fresh root
   ginger, chopped
15g/½oz fresh turmeric, chopped
   or 2.5ml/½ tsp ground turmeric
2–3 lemon grass stalks,
   finely chopped
15–30ml/1–2 tbsp palm or
   groundnut (peanut) oil
5ml/1 tsp shrimp paste
15ml/1 tbsp tamarind paste
5ml/1 tsp palm sugar (jaggery)

1 First make the spice paste. Using a mortar and pestle, pound the shallots, garlic, chillies, galangal or ginger, turmeric and lemon grass together to form a coarse paste.

2 Heat the oil in a wok or large, heavy frying pan, stir in the paste and fry until it becomes fragrant and begins to colour. Add the shrimp paste, tamarind and sugar and continue to cook, stirring, until the mixture darkens. Put aside and leave to cool.

3 In a bowl, pound the shrimps or prawns and scallops together to form a paste, or blend them together in an electric blender or food processor. Beat in the spice paste, followed by the flour and baking powder, and beat until combined. Put the mixture in the refrigerator for about 1 hour. If using wooden skewers, soak them in water for about 30 minutes.

4 Meanwhile, prepare the barbecue, or, if you are using the grill (broiler), preheat 5 minutes before you start cooking. Using your fingers, scoop up lumps of the shellfish paste and wrap it around the skewers. Place each skewer on the barbecue or under the grill and cook for 3 minutes on each side, until golden brown. Serve with the lime wedges.

Quick-fried **Prawns** Energy 382kcal/1590kJ; Protein 40.8g; Carbohydrate 1g, of which sugars 0.9g; Fat 23.8g, of which saturates 3.4g; Cholesterol 439mg; Calcium 254mg; Fibre 1.9g; Sodium 440mg.
Spiced Clams Energy 126kcal/526kJ; Protein 12.5g; Carbohydrate 4.5g, of which sugars 2.2g; Fat 6g, of which saturates 0.9g; Cholesterol 50mg; Calcium 69mg; Fibre 0.6g; Sodium 906mg.
Spicy Shrimp Energy 220kcal/922kJ; Protein 27.1g; Carbohydrate 11.5g, of which sugars 1g; Fat 7.3g, of which saturates 1g; Cholesterol 151mg; Calcium 99mg; Fibre 1.5g; Sodium 249mg.

Pan-fried Baby Squid with Moroccan Spices

Baby squid needs very little cooking and tastes wonderful with this spicy sweet and sour sauce, which teams turmeric and ginger with honey and lemon juice.

Serves 4

8 baby squid, prepared,
  with tentacles
5ml/1 tsp ground turmeric

15ml/1 tbsp smen (see Cook's
  Tip) or olive oil
2 garlic cloves, finely chopped
15g/½oz fresh root ginger,
  peeled and finely chopped
5–10ml/1–2 tsp clear honey
juice of 1 lemon
10ml/2 tsp harissa
salt
small bunch of fresh coriander
  (cilantro), chopped, to garnish

1 Gently pat dry the squid bodies with kitchen paper, inside and out, and dry the tentacles. Sprinkle the squid bodies and tentacles with the ground turmeric.

2 Heat the smen or olive oil in a large, heavy frying pan and stir in the garlic and ginger.

3 Just as the ginger and garlic begin to colour, add the squid and tentacles and fry quickly on both sides over a high heat. (Take care to not overcook the squid, otherwise it will become rubbery and unpleasant.)

4 Add the honey, lemon juice and harissa to the pan and stir to form a thick, spicy, caramelized sauce.

5 Season the mixture with salt, sprinkle with the chopped coriander and serve immediately.

Cook's Tip
Smen is a pungent, aged butter used widely in Moroccan cooking. It can also served with chunks of warm, fresh bread and is used to enhance other dishes including couscous and some tagines and stews.

Steamed Mussels in Coconut Milk

Mussels steamed in coconut milk and fresh aromatic herbs are quick and easy to prepare and great for a relaxed dinner with friends.

Serves 4

1.6kg/3½lb mussels
15ml/1 tbsp sunflower oil
6 garlic cloves, roughly chopped
15ml/1 tbsp finely chopped fresh
  root ginger

2 large red chillies, seeded and
  finely sliced
6 spring onions (scallions),
  finely chopped
2 limes
400ml/14fl oz/1⅔ cups
  coconut milk
45ml/3 tbsp light soy sauce
5ml/1 tsp caster (superfine) sugar
a large handful of chopped
  coriander (cilantro)
salt and ground black pepper

1 Scrub the mussels in cold water. Scrape off any barnacles with a knife, then pull out and discard the fibrous beard visible between the hinge on any of the shells. Discard any mussels that are not tightly closed, or that fail to close when tapped.

2 Heat a wok over high heat and then add the oil. Stir in the garlic, ginger, chillies and spring onions and stir-fry over medium to high heat for 30 seconds.

3 Grate the rind of the limes into the ginger mixture, then squeeze both fruit and add the juice to the wok with the coconut milk, soy sauce and sugar. Stir to mix.

4 Bring the mixture to the boil, then add the mussels. Return to the boil, cover and cook briskly for 5–6 minutes, or until all the mussels have opened. Discard any unopened mussels.

5 Remove the wok from the heat and stir in the chopped coriander. Season the mussels well with salt and pepper. Ladle into warmed bowls and serve immediately.

Cook's Tip
For a supper with friends, take the wok straight to the table. There's something irresistible about eating straight from the pan.

Baby Squid Energy 154kcal/647kJ; Protein 19.8g; Carbohydrate 5.8g, of which sugars 4.3g; Fat 5.9g, of which saturates 1g; Cholesterol 281mg; Calcium 54mg; Fibre 1g; Sodium 144mg.
Steamed Mussels Energy 160kcal/679kJ; Protein 21.5g; Carbohydrate 6.7g, of which sugars 6.7g; Fat 5.5g, of which saturates 1g; Cholesterol 48mg; Calcium 272mg; Fibre 0.2g; Sodium 630mg.

Ginger and Chilli Steamed Fish Custards

These pretty little custards make an unusual and exotic appetizer for a dinner party. The pandanus leaves impart a distinctive flavour – but don't be tempted to eat them once the custards are cooked: they are inedible.

Serves 4
2 eggs
200ml/7fl oz/scant 1 cup coconut cream
60ml/4 tbsp chopped fresh coriander (cilantro)
1 red chilli, seeded and sliced
15ml/1 tbsp finely chopped lemon grass

2 kaffir lime leaves, finely shredded
30ml/2 tbsp red Thai curry paste
1 garlic clove, crushed
5ml/1 tsp finely grated fresh root ginger
2 spring onions (scallions), finely sliced
300g/11oz mixed firm white fish fillets (cod, halibut or haddock), skinned
200g/7oz raw tiger prawns (shrimp), peeled and deveined
4–6 pandanus (screwpine) leaves
salt and ground black pepper
shredded cucumber, steamed rice and soy sauce, to serve

1 Beat the eggs in a bowl, then stir in the coconut cream, coriander, chilli, lemon grass, lime leaves, curry paste, garlic, ginger and spring onions. Finely chop the fish and roughly chop the prawns and add to the egg mixture. Stir well and season.

2 Grease four ramekins and line them with the pandanus leaves. Divide the fish mixture between the lined ramekins, then arrange in a bamboo steamer.

3 Pour 5cm/2in water into a wok and bring to the boil. Suspend the steamer over the water, cover, reduce the heat to low and steam for 25–30 minutes, or until cooked through. Serve with shredded cucumber, steamed rice and soy sauce.

Cook's Tip
Pandanus leaves are available from Asian markets.

Cumin-scented Chicken

Serves 4
45ml/3 tbsp cumin seeds
45ml/3 tbsp vegetable oil
2.5ml/½ tsp black peppercorns
4 green cardamom pods
2 fresh green chillies, finely chopped
2 garlic cloves, crushed
2.5cm/1in piece fresh root ginger, grated

5ml/1 tsp ground coriander
10ml/2 tsp ground cumin
2.5ml/½ tsp salt
8 chicken pieces, such as thighs and drumsticks, skinned
5ml/1 tsp garam masala
cucumber raita, garnished with fresh coriander (cilantro) and chilli powder, to serve (optional)

1 Preheat a large pan over medium heat and dry-roast 15ml/1 tbsp of the cumin seeds for 1–2 minutes. Set aside.

2 Heat the oil in a large pan and fry the remaining cumin seeds, peppercorns and cardamoms for about 2 minutes. Add the chillies, garlic and ginger and fry for 2 minutes. Add the coriander and cumin with the salt, and cook, stirring constantly for a further 1–2 minutes.

3 Add the chicken pieces to the pan, stir thoroughly. Cover the pan with a lid and cook over low heat for 20–25 minutes. Add the garam masala and reserved dry-roasted cumin seeds to the pan, and cook for a further 5 minutes. Place the spice-coated chicken pieces on a serving plate and serve immediately with cucumber raita, if you like.

Chicken Naan Pockets

Serves 4
45ml/3 tbsp natural (plain) yogurt
7.5ml/1½ tsp garam masala
5ml/1 tsp chilli powder
5ml/1 tsp salt
45ml/3 tbsp lemon juice
15ml/1 tbsp chopped fresh coriander (cilantro)
1 fresh green chilli, chopped
450g/1lb/3¼ cups chicken, skinned, boned and cubed

15ml/1 tbsp vegetable oil (optional)
8 onion rings
2 tomatoes, quartered
½ white cabbage, shredded

To serve
4 naans or pitta breads, slit
lemon wedges
2 small tomatoes, halved
mixed salad leaves
fresh coriander (cilantro)

1 In a large bowl, mix together the yogurt, garam masala, chilli powder, salt, lemon juice, coriander and chilli. Pour the marinade over the chicken pieces and leave to marinate for about 1 hour.

2 When the chicken has marinated, preheat the grill (broiler) to very hot, then lower the heat to medium.

3 Place the chicken in a flameproof dish and grill (broil) for 15–20 minutes until tender and cooked through, turning the chicken pieces at least twice. If you like, baste the chicken pieces with the oil while cooking.

4 Remove from the heat and fill each naan or pitta bread with the chicken and then with the onion rings, tomatoes and cabbage. Serve immediately with the lemon wedges, tomatoes, salad leaves and fresh coriander.

Fish Custards Energy 150kcal/632kJ; Protein 26.2g; Carbohydrate 2.8g, of which sugars 2.7g; Fat 3.9g, of which saturates 1g; Cholesterol 227mg; Calcium 100mg; Fibre 0.6g; Sodium 234mg.
Cumin-scented Chicken Energy 269kcal/1126kJ; Protein 20.3g; Carbohydrate 22.9g, of which sugars 9.5g; Fat 11.6g, of which saturates 1.5g; Cholesterol 40mg; Calcium 136mg; Fibre 2.4g; Sodium 82mg.
Chicken Naan Pockets Energy 410kcal/1733kJ; Protein 35.8g; Carbohydrate 51.3g, of which sugars 8.5g; Fat 8.2g, of which saturates 1.3g; Cholesterol 83mg; Calcium 227mg; Fibre 3.6g; Sodium 629mg.

Turkey Sosaties with a Curried Sweet-and-Sour Sauce

These South African kebabs are simply delicious.

Serves 4
15ml/1 tbsp sunflower oil
1 onion, finely chopped
1 garlic clove, crushed
2 bay leaves
juice of 1 lemon
30ml/2 tbsp curry powder
60ml/4 tbsp apricot jam
60ml/4 tbsp apple juice
salt
675g/1½lb turkey fillet
60ml/4 tbsp crème fraîche

1 Heat the oil in a pan. Add the onion, garlic and bay leaves and cook over a low heat for 10 minutes until the onions are softened but not browned.

2 Add the lemon juice, curry powder, apricot jam and apple juice to the pan. Season with salt to taste. Cook gently for about 5 minutes. Leave to cool.

3 Cut the turkey into 2cm/¾in cubes and add to the marinade. Mix well until the turkey is well coated. Cover the bowl with clear film (plastic wrap) and leave in a cool place to marinate for at least 2 hours or overnight in the refrigerator.

4 Thread the marinated turkey pieces on to skewers, allowing the excess marinade to run back into the bowl. Grill (broil) or cook the sosaties on a barbecue for 6–8 minutes, turning several times, until cooked.

5 Meanwhile, transfer the marinade to a pan and simmer over low heat for 2 minutes to warm through. Stir in the crème fraîche and serve with the sosaties.

Cook's Tip
Soaking bamboo skewers for about 30 minutes in a large bowl of warm water before use ensures that they won't scorch when placed under the grill.

Pineapple Chicken Kebabs

This chicken dish has a delicate tang and the meat is very tender. The pineapple not only tenderizes the chicken but also gives it a slight sweetness.

Serves 6
225g/8oz can pineapple
  chunks
5ml/1 tsp ground cumin
5ml/1 tsp ground coriander
5ml/1 tsp chilli powder
2.5ml/½ tsp crushed garlic
5ml/1 tsp salt
30ml/2 tbsp natural (plain)
  low-fat yogurt
15ml/1 tbsp chopped fresh
  coriander (cilantro)
few drops of orange food
  colouring (optional)
275g/10oz boneless chicken,
  skinned and cubed
½ red (bell) pepper, seeded
½ yellow or green (bell)
  pepper, seeded
1 large onion
6 cherry tomatoes
15ml/1 tbsp vegetable oil
salad leaves, to serve

1 Drain the pineapple juice into a bowl. Reserve eight large chunks of pineapple and squeeze the juice from the remaining chunks into the bowl and set aside. You should have about 120ml/4fl oz/½ cup pineapple juice.

2 In a large bowl, mix together the spices, garlic, salt, yogurt, fresh coriander and food colouring, if using. Pour in the reserved pineapple juice and mix well to combine.

3 Add the chicken to the yogurt and spice mixture, cover and leave to marinate in a cool place for about 1–1½ hours. Cut the peppers and onion into bitesize chunks.

4 Preheat the grill (broiler) to medium. Arrange the chicken pieces, vegetables and reserved pineapple chunks alternately on six metal or wooden skewers (wooden skewers should be soaked in water for 30 minutes before use to prevent them from burning under the grill).

5 Brush the kebabs lightly with the oil, then place the skewers on a flameproof dish or in a grill pan, turning the chicken pieces and basting with the marinade regularly, for about 15 minutes until cooked through. Serve with salad leaves.

Turkey Sosaties Energy 325kcal/1381kJ; Protein 59.4g; Carbohydrate 12.2g, of which sugars 12.1g; Fat 4.8g, of which saturates 1.9g; Cholesterol 125mg; Calcium 18mg; Fibre 0g; Sodium 162mg.
Chicken Kebabs Energy 135kcal/565kJ; Protein 13.2g; Carbohydrate 13.6g, of which sugars 10.3g; Fat 3.5g, of which saturates 0.6g; Cholesterol 32mg; Calcium 31mg; Fibre 1.7g; Sodium 35mg.

Chicken Satay with a Spicy Peanut Sauce

One of the classic spicy foods of the East.

Serves 4
4 skinless chicken breast fillets
10ml/2 tsp soft light brown sugar

For the marinade
5ml/1 tsp cumin seeds
5ml/1 tsp fennel seeds
7.5ml/1½ tsp coriander seeds
6 shallots, chopped
1 garlic clove, crushed
1 lemon grass stalk, root trimmed
3 macadamia nuts
2.5ml/½ tsp ground turmeric

For the peanut sauce
4 shallots, sliced
2 garlic cloves, crushed
1cm/½in cube shrimp paste
6 cashew nuts or almonds
2 lemon grass stalks, trimmed, and the lower 5cm/2in portion finely sliced
45ml/3 tbsp sunflower oil
5–10ml/1–2 tsp chilli powder
400ml/14fl oz can coconut milk
60–75ml/4–5 tbsp tamarind water
15ml/1 tbsp soft light brown sugar
175g/6oz/½ cup crunchy peanut butter

1 Cut the chicken breast fillets into thin strips, about the size of a finger. Sprinkle with the sugar and set aside.

2 Make the marinade. Dry-fry the spices, then grind to a powder. Put the shallots in a food processor and add the garlic. Add the lower 5cm/2in of the lemon grass to the processor with the nuts, ground spices and turmeric. Process to a paste and place in a bowl with the chicken. Stir well, cover and leave for 4 hours.

3 Process the shallots for the sauce with the garlic and shrimp paste. Add the nuts and the lemon grass. Process to a purée and fry in hot oil for 2–3 minutes. Add the chilli powder and cook for 2 minutes more.

4 Stir in the coconut milk and bring to the boil. Reduce the heat and stir in the tamarind water and sugar. Add the peanut butter and simmer until thick. Preheat the grill (broiler).

5 Thread the chicken on to 16 skewers. Grill (broil) for 5 minutes until golden and tender. Serve with the peanut sauce.

Chicken Tikka

This extremely popular Indian first course is quick and easy to cook and tastes absolutely delectable. This dish can also be served as part of a spicy buffet.

Serves 6
450g/1lb boneless chicken, skinned and cubed
5ml/1 tsp crushed fresh root ginger
5ml/1 tsp crushed garlic
5ml/1 tsp chilli powder
1.5ml/¼ tsp ground turmeric
5ml/1 tsp salt
150ml/¼ pint/⅔ cup natural (plain) low-fat yogurt
60ml/4 tbsp lemon juice
15ml/1 tbsp chopped fresh coriander (cilantro)
15ml/1 tbsp vegetable oil

For the garnish
mixed salad leaves
1 small onion, cut into rings
lime wedges
fresh coriander (cilantro)

1 In a medium bowl, mix together the chicken pieces, ginger, garlic, chilli powder, turmeric and salt.

2 Stir in the yogurt, lemon juice and fresh coriander and leave to marinate for at least 2 hours.

3 Place in a grill (broiler) pan or in a flameproof dish lined with foil and baste with the oil.

4 Preheat the grill to medium. Grill (broil) the chicken for 15–20 minutes until cooked, turning and basting several times. Serve on a bed of mixed salad leaves, garnished with onion rings, lime wedges and coriander.

Cook's Tips
• *To make the turning and basting of the meat easier, thread the chicken pieces on to skewers before placing under the grill (broiler) or on top of a barbecue. If you are using wooden skewers, soak them in cold water for 30 minutes prior to using to prevent them from burning under the grill.*
• *This dish also makes a great main course for four people. Serve with a little more salad and some pickles.*

Chicken Satay Energy 48kcal/200kJ; Protein 4.8g; Carbohydrate 2.2g, of which sugars 2.1g; Fat 2.2g, of which saturates 0.4g; Cholesterol 13mg; Calcium 3mg; Fibre 0.1g; Sodium 105mg.
Chicken Tikka Energy 415kcal/1730kJ; Protein 46g; Carbohydrate 2g, of which sugars 0.2g; Fat 24.8g, of which saturates 8.5g; Cholesterol 203mg; Calcium 21mg; Fibre 0.5g; Sodium 172mg.

Chicken Kofta Balti with Pepper and Onion Paneer

This appetizer looks elegant served in small karahis.

Serves 6
For the koftas
450g/1lb boneless chicken, skinned and cubed
5ml/1 tsp crushed garlic
5ml/1 tsp shredded fresh root ginger
7.5ml/1½ tsp ground coriander
7.5ml/1½ tsp chilli powder
7.5ml/1½ tsp ground fenugreek
1.5ml/¼ tsp ground turmeric
5ml/1 tsp salt

30ml/2 tbsp chopped fresh coriander (cilantro)
2 fresh green chillies, chopped
600ml/1 pint/2½ cups water
corn oil, for frying
fresh mint sprigs

For the paneer mixture
1 medium onion, sliced
1 red (bell) pepper, seeded and cut into strips
1 green (bell) pepper, seeded and cut into strips
175g/6oz paneer, cubed
175g/6oz/1½ cups corn

1 Put all the kofta ingredients, apart from the oil, into a medium pan. Bring to the boil slowly over medium heat, and cook, stirring, until all the liquid has evaporated. Remove from the heat and leave to cool slightly. Put the mixture into a food processor or blender and process for 2 minutes.

2 Transfer the mixture to a large mixing bowl. Taking a little of the mixture at a time, shape it into 12 small balls. Heat the corn oil in a karahi, wok or deep pan over high heat. Reduce the heat slightly and drop the koftas carefully into the oil. Move them around gently to ensure that they cook evenly.

3 When the koftas are lightly browned, remove them from the oil with a slotted spoon and drain well on kitchen paper. Set aside and keep warm in a low oven.

4 Heat the oil still remaining in the karahi, and flash-fry all the ingredients for the paneer mixture. This should take about 3 minutes over a high heat. Divide the paneer mixture evenly between six individual karahis. Add two koftas to each serving, and garnish with mint sprigs.

Lamb Kebabs

First introduced by the Muslims, kebabs have now become a favourite Indian dish and are often sold at open stalls; the wonderful aroma of the spicy meat wafting down the street is guaranteed to stop passers-by in their tracks to buy one.

Serves 8
For the kebabs
900g/2lb lean minced (ground) lamb
1 large onion, roughly chopped
5cm/2in piece fresh root ginger, chopped
2 garlic cloves, crushed
1 fresh green chilli, finely chopped

5ml/1 tsp chilli powder
30ml/2 tbsp chopped fresh coriander (cilantro)
5ml/1 tsp garam masala
10ml/2 tsp ground coriander
5ml/1 tsp ground cumin
5ml/1 tsp salt
1 egg
15ml/1 tbsp natural (plain) low-fat yogurt
15ml/1 tbsp vegetable oil
mixed salad, to serve

For the raita
250ml/8fl oz/1 cup natural (plain) low-fat yogurt
½ cucumber, finely chopped
30ml/2 tbsp chopped fresh mint
1.5ml/¼ tsp salt

1 Put all the ingredients for the kebabs, except the yogurt and oil, into a food processor or blender and process until the mixture binds together. Spoon into a large bowl, cover and leave to marinate for 1 hour.

2 To make the raita, mix together all the ingredients and chill for at least 15 minutes in a refrigerator.

3 Preheat the grill (broiler). Divide the lamb mixture into eight equal portions with lightly floured hands and mould into long sausage shapes. Thread the meat on to metal skewers and chill in the refrigerator for at least 1 hour.

4 Brush the kebabs lightly with the yogurt and oil and cook under a hot grill for 8–10 minutes, turning occasionally, until brown all over. Serve the kebabs on a bed of mixed salad, accompanied by the raita.

Chicken Kofta Energy 253kcal/1056kJ; Protein 24.7g; Carbohydrate 10.8g, of which sugars 6.7g; Fat 12.6g, of which saturates 2.2g; Cholesterol 57mg; Calcium 71mg; Fibre 1.8g; Sodium 471mg.
Lamb Kebabs Energy 339kcal/1409kJ; Protein 22.6g; Carbohydrate 2.7g, of which sugars 2.4g; Fat 26.5g, of which saturates 7.9g; Cholesterol 86mg; Calcium 16mg; Fibre 0.7g; Sodium 102mg.

Chargrilled Lamb with Cumin

Small pieces of tender, spicy lamb are wrapped in flat breads with red onion, parsley and lemon juice.

Serves 4–6
2 onions, grated
7.5ml/1½ tsp salt
2 garlic cloves, crushed
10ml/2 tsp cumin seeds, crushed
900g/2lb boneless shoulder of
 lamb, trimmed and cut into
 bitesize pieces

For the flat breads
225g/8oz/2 cups strong white
 bread flour
50g/2oz/¼ cup wholemeal
 (whole-wheat) flour
5ml/1 tsp salt

To serve
1 large red onion, cut in half
 lengthways and sliced
1 large bunch of fresh flat leaf
 parsley, roughly chopped
2–3 lemons, cut into wedges

1 Sprinkle the onions with the salt and leave for 15 minutes. Place a sieve (strainer) over a bowl, put in the onions and press down to extract the juice. Discard the onions left in the sieve, then mix the garlic and cumin seeds into the onion juice and toss in the lamb. Cover and leave to marinate for 3–4 hours.

2 Meanwhile, prepare the dough for the breads. Sift the flours and salt into a bowl. Make a well in the middle and gradually add 200ml/7fl oz/scant 1 cup lukewarm water, drawing in the flour from the sides. Knead the dough until firm and springy.

3 Divide the dough into 24 pieces and knead each one into a ball. Place on a floured surface and cover with a damp cloth. Leave to rest for 45 minutes while you get the barbecue ready.

4 Just before cooking, roll each ball of dough into a wide, thin circle. Dust them with flour, and keep them covered.

5 Thread the meat on to metal skewers and cook on the barbecue for 2–3 minutes on each side. At the same time, cook the flat breads on a hot griddle or other flat pan, flipping them over as they begin to go brown and buckle. Pile up on a plate.

6 Slide the meat off the skewers on to the flat breads. Sprinkle onion and parsley over and squeeze lemon juice over the top.

Curried Lamb and Potato Cakes

An unusual variation on burgers or rissoles, these little spicy lamb triangles are easy to make. They are really good served hot as part of a buffet, but they can also be eaten cold as a snack or taken on picnics.

Makes 12–15
450g/1lb new or small,
 firm potatoes
3 eggs

1 onion, grated
30ml/2 tbsp chopped
 fresh parsley
450g/1lb finely minced (ground)
 lean lamb
115g/4oz/2 cups fresh
 breadcrumbs
vegetable oil, for frying
salt and ground black pepper
sprigs of fresh mint,
 to garnish
pitta bread and herby green
 salad, to serve

1 Cook the potatoes in a large pan of boiling salted water for 20 minutes or until tender, then drain and leave to cool.

2 Beat the eggs in a large bowl. Add the onion, parsley and seasoning and beat together.

3 When the potatoes are cold, grate them coarsely and stir evenly into the egg mixture, together with the minced lamb. Knead the mixture well for 3–4 minutes until all the ingredients are thoroughly blended together.

4 Take a handful of the lamb mixture and roll it into a ball. Repeat this process until all the meat is used.

5 Roll the balls in the breadcrumbs and then mould them into fairly flat triangular shapes, about 13cm/5in long. Coat them in the breadcrumbs again.

6 Heat a 1cm/½in layer of oil in a large frying pan over medium heat. When the oil is hot, fry the potato cakes for 8–12 minutes until golden brown on both sides, turning occasionally. Drain on kitchen paper.

7 Serve the cakes immediately, garnished with mint and accompanied by pitta bread and salad.

Chargrilled Lamb Energy 433kcal/1821kJ; Protein 34.3g; Carbohydrate 37.1g, of which sugars 4.4g; Fat 17.5g, of which saturates 7.9g; Cholesterol 114mg; Calcium 83mg; Fibre 2.5g; Sodium 460mg.
Lamb Cakes Energy 181kcal/760kJ; Protein 10.8g; Carbohydrate 13.9g, of which sugars 1.1g; Fat 9.6g, of which saturates 2.8g; Cholesterol 76mg; Calcium 31mg; Fibre 0.8g; Sodium 128mg.

Shammi Kebabs

These Indian treats are derived from the kebabs of the Middle East. They can be served either as appetizers or side dishes with a raita or chutney.

Serves 5–6

2 onions, finely chopped
250g/9oz lean lamb, boned and cubed
50g/2oz/¼ cup chana dhal (yellow lentils) or yellow split peas
5ml/1 tsp cumin seeds
5ml/1 tsp garam masala
4–6 fresh green chillies
5cm/2in piece fresh root ginger, grated
175ml/6fl oz/¾ cup water
a few fresh coriander (cilantro) and mint leaves, chopped, plus extra coriander sprigs to garnish
juice of 1 lemon
15ml/1 tbsp gram flour
2 eggs, beaten
vegetable oil, for shallow-frying
salt

1 Put the first seven ingredients and the measured water into a large pan with a pinch of salt, and bring to the boil. Simmer, covered, until the meat and dhal are cooked. Remove the lid and continue to cook for a few more minutes, to reduce the excess liquid. Set aside to cool.

2 Transfer the cooled meat mixture to a food processor or blender and process well until the mixture turns into a rough, gritty paste. You can use a mortar and pestle, if you prefer.

3 Put the paste into a large mixing bowl and add the chopped coriander and mint leaves, lemon juice and gram flour. Knead well with your fingers for a good couple of minutes, to ensure that all ingredients are evenly distributed through the mixture, and any excess liquid has been thoroughly absorbed. When the colour appears even throughout, and the mixture has taken on a semi-solid, sticky rather than powdery consistency, the kebabs are ready for shaping into portions.

4 Divide the kebab mixture into 10–12 equal portions and use your hands to roll each into a ball, then flatten slightly. Chill in the refrigerator for 1 hour. Dip the kebabs in the beaten egg and shallow-fry each side until golden brown. Pat dry on kitchen paper and serve immediately.

Sumac-spiced Burgers with Relish

The sharp-sweet red onion relish works perfectly with these tasty burgers, which are based on Middle-Eastern style lamb. Serve the burgers and relish with pitta bread and tabbouleh or a green salad.

Serves 4

25g/1oz/3 tbsp bulgur wheat
500g/1¼lb minced (ground) lamb
1 small red onion, finely chopped
2 garlic cloves, finely chopped
1 green chilli, seeded and finely chopped
5ml/1 tsp ground cumin seeds
2.5ml/½ tsp ground sumac
15g/½oz chopped fresh parsley
30ml/2 tbsp chopped fresh mint
olive oil, for frying
salt and ground black pepper

For the relish

2 red (bell) peppers, halved
2 red onions, cut into 5mm/¼in thick slices
75–90ml/5–6 tbsp virgin olive oil
350g/12oz cherry tomatoes, chopped
½–1 fresh red or green chilli, seeded and finely chopped
30ml/2 tbsp chopped mint
30ml/2 tbsp chopped parsley
15ml/1 tbsp chopped oregano
2.5–5ml/½–1 tsp each ground toasted cumin and sumac
juice of ½ lemon
caster (superfine) sugar, to taste

1 Pour 150ml/¼ pint/⅔ cup hot water over the bulgur wheat and leave to stand for 15 minutes, then drain.

2 Place the bulgur wheat in a bowl and add the minced lamb, onion, garlic, chilli, cumin, sumac, parsley and mint. Mix together thoroughly, then season with 5ml/1 tsp salt and plenty of black pepper. Form the mixture into eight burgers and set aside while you make the red onion relish.

3 Grill (broil) the peppers, until the skin chars and blisters. Peel off the skin, dice and place in a bowl. Brush the onions with oil and grill until browned. Chop. Add the onions, tomatoes, chilli, mint, parsley, oregano and 2.5ml/½ tsp each of the cumin and sumac to the peppers. Stir in 60ml/4 tbsp oil and 15ml/1 tbsp of the lemon juice and salt, pepper and sugar to taste. Set aside.

4 Heat a frying pan over a high heat and grease with oil. Cook the burgers for 5–6 minutes on each side. Serve immediately.

Shammi Kebabs Energy 207kcal/861kJ; Protein 12.8g; Carbohydrate 7.7g, of which sugars 1g; Fat 14.1g, of which saturates 3.6g; Cholesterol 95mg; Calcium 40mg; Fibre 1.1g; Sodium 65mg.
Sumac Burgers Energy 537kcal/2228kJ; Protein 27.2g; Carbohydrate 19g, of which sugars 13.4g; Fat 39.6g, of which saturates 11.1g; Cholesterol 96mg; Calcium 83mg; Fibre 4.2g; Sodium 105mg.

Karahi Prawns and Fenugreek

The black-eyed beans, prawns and paneer in this recipe ensure that it is rich in protein. The combination of both ground and fresh fenugreek makes this a very fragrant and delicious dish.

Serves 4–6

60ml/4 tbsp corn oil
2 medium onions, sliced
2 medium tomatoes, sliced
7.5ml/1½ tsp crushed garlic
5ml/1 tsp chilli powder
5ml/1 tsp grated fresh
   root ginger
5ml/1 tsp ground cumin
5ml/1 tsp ground coriander
5ml/1 tsp salt
150g/5oz paneer, cubed
5ml/1 tsp ground fenugreek
1 bunch fresh fenugreek leaves
115g/4oz cooked
   prawns (shrimp)
2 fresh red chillies, sliced
30ml/2 tbsp chopped fresh
   coriander (cilantro)
50g/2oz/⅓ cup canned
   black-eyed beans
   (peas), drained
15ml/1 tbsp lemon juice

1 Heat the oil in a karahi, wok or deep pan. Lower the heat slightly and add the onions and tomatoes. Fry for about 3–5 minutes until the onions begin to soften.

2 Add the garlic, chilli powder, ginger, ground cumin, ground coriander, salt, paneer and the ground and fresh fenugreek. Lower the heat and stir-fry for about 2 minutes.

3 Add the prawns, red chillies, fresh coriander and black-eyed beans, and mix well. Toss over the heat for a further 3–5 minutes, or until the prawns are heated through. Sprinkle with the lemon juice and serve.

Cook's Tips
• Paneer is a type of cheese made with the curds from boiling milk which has been acidified with lemon juice. If you cannot locate paneer, tofu or halloumi makes a good substitute.
• When preparing fresh fenugreek, use the leaves whole, but remove and discard the stalks because they will impart a bitter flavour to the dish.

Sizzling Balti Prawns in Hot Sauce

This sizzling prawn dish is cooked in a fiery hot and spicy sauce. This sauce not only contains chilli powder, but is further enhanced by the addition of ground fresh green chillies mixed with other spices.

Serves 4

2 medium onions or 1 large
   onion, roughly chopped
30ml/2 tbsp tomato
   purée (paste)
5ml/1 tsp ground coriander
1.5ml/¼ tsp ground turmeric
5ml/1 tsp chilli powder
2 fresh green chillies
45ml/3 tbsp chopped fresh
   coriander (cilantro)
30ml/2 tbsp lemon juice
5ml/1 tsp salt
45ml/3 tbsp corn oil
16 cooked king prawns
   (jumbo shrimp)
sliced green chillies,
   to garnish (optional)

1 Put the onions, tomato purée, ground coriander, turmeric, chilli powder, 2 whole green chillies, 30ml/2 tbsp of the fresh coriander, the lemon juice and salt into the bowl of a food processor. Process for about 1 minute. If the mixture seems too thick, add a little water to loosen it.

2 Heat the oil in a karahi, wok or deep pan. Lower the heat slightly and add the spice mixture. Fry the mixture for about 3–5 minutes or until the sauce has thickened slightly.

3 Add the cooked prawns to the pan and stir-fry briefly over a medium heat until heated through.

4 As soon as the prawns are heated through, transfer them to a serving dish. Garnish with the rest of the fresh coriander and the sliced green chillies, if using. Serve immediately.

Cook's Tips
• Take care not to overcook the prawns when heating them through or they will become tough.
• If the heat of this dish seems extreme, offer a cooling raita to moderate the piquant flavour.

Karahi Prawns Energy 151kcal/629kJ; Protein 8.5g; Carbohydrate 10.1g, of which sugars 6.6g; Fat 8.7g, of which saturates 1.7g; Cholesterol 41mg; Calcium 72mg; Fibre 1.8g; Sodium 445mg.
Sizzling Balti Prawns Energy 161kcal/668kJ; Protein 13.6g; Carbohydrate 0.8g, of which sugars 0.1g; Fat 11.5g, of which saturates 1.7g; Cholesterol 146mg; Calcium 60mg; Fibre 0.2g; Sodium 143mg.

Parsi Prawn Curry

Serves 4–6
60ml/4 tbsp vegetable oil
1 medium onion, finely sliced
6 garlic cloves, finely crushed
5ml/1 tsp chilli powder
7.5ml/1½ tsp turmeric
15ml/1 tbsp tamarind
1 large onion, finely chopped
5ml/1 tsp mint sauce
15ml/1 tbsp demerara
 (raw) sugar
450g/1lb fresh king prawns (jumbo
 shrimp), peeled and deveined
75g/3oz/3 cups fresh coriander
 (cilantro), chopped
salt

1 Heat the oil in a frying pan and fry the onion until it becomes soft, stirring frequently. In a bowl, mix the garlic, chilli powder and turmeric with a little water to form a paste. Add to the onion and simmer for 3 minutes.

2 To make the tamarind juice, mix the tamarind pulp with 45ml/3 tbsp water in a small bowl. Discard any seeds or pulp. Add the tamarind juice to the pan with the mint sauce, sugar and salt, and simmer for 3 minutes.

3 Add the prawns to the mixture with a small amount of water and stir-fry until the prawns turn bright orange-pink. When the prawns are cooked, add the fresh coriander and stir-fry over high heat to thicken the sauce. Serve immediately.

Prawn Korma

Serves 4
50g/2oz/½ cup blanched almonds
500g/1¼lb raw peeled king
 prawns (jumbo shrimp)
30ml/2 tbsp lemon juice
2.5ml/½ tsp ground turmeric
15ml/1 tbsp white poppy seeds
15ml/1 tbsp sesame seeds
150g/5oz/⅔ cup natural
 (plain) yogurt, whisked
7.5ml/1½ tsp gram flour
60ml/4 tbsp sunflower or olive oil
1 large onion, finely chopped
10ml/2 tsp ginger purée (paste)
10ml/2 tsp garlic purée (paste)
1 chilli, seeded and finely chopped
1.5–2.5ml/¼–½ tsp chilli powder
5ml/1 tsp salt, or to taste
15ml/1 tbsp toasted flaked
 (sliced) almonds, to garnish

1 Soak the almonds in 150ml/¼ pint/⅔ cup boiling water for 20 minutes. Meanwhile, in a large bowl, mix the prawns, lemon juice and turmeric together. Set aside.

2 Grind the seeds in a blender until they are finely ground. Whisk the yogurt and gram flour together and set aside.

3 In a heavy pan, heat the oil over medium heat and add the onion. Fry gently for 5–6 minutes until soft and translucent.

4 Add the ginger and garlic, the ground poppy and sesame seeds, and the chilli powder. Cook for 2–3 minutes, stirring constantly, then add the prawns, salt and yogurt. Reduce the heat to low, cover the pan with a lid and cook for 3–4 minutes.

5 Purée the almonds with the water in which they were soaked in a food processor or blender, and add to the prawns. Stir well and cook for 5–6 minutes. Transfer the korma to a serving dish and garnish with the almonds before serving.

Stir-fried Chilli-garlic Prawns

These spice-coated prawns make a mouthwatering appetizer or light lunch, when served with a salad, or they can be transformed into a main meal with the addition of naan bread.

Serves 4
15ml/1 tbsp vegetable oil
3 garlic cloves, roughly halved
3 tomatoes, chopped
2.5ml/½ tsp salt
5ml/1 tsp crushed dried
 red chillies
5ml/1 tsp lemon juice
mango chutney, to taste
1 fresh green chilli, chopped
16–20 peeled, cooked king
 prawns (jumbo shrimp)
fresh coriander (cilantro) sprigs
 and chopped spring onions
 (scallions), to garnish

1 In a wok, karahi or large heavy pan, heat the vegetable oil over a low heat and fry the garlic halves gently for 5–6 minutes until they are tinged with golden brown.

2 Add the chopped tomatoes, salt, crushed red chillies, lemon juice, mango chutney and the chopped fresh chilli to the pan. Stir well until all the ingredients are well combined.

3 Add the prawns to the pan, then raise the heat and stir-fry briskly, mixing the prawns with the other ingredients until they are thoroughly heated through.

4 Transfer the prawns in the sauce to a warm serving dish and garnish with fresh coriander sprigs and chopped spring onions. Serve the prawns immediately.

Variation
This dish can be also be made with other seafood. Substitute the same quantity of mussels or scallops for the prawns (shrimp).

Cook's Tip
Take care not to let the garlic burn during the frying in step 1, otherwise it will impart a bitter taste to the rest of the dish.

Parsi Prawn Curry Energy 204kcal/852kJ; Protein 23.4g; Carbohydrate 8.8g, of which sugars 6.6g; Fat 8.6g, of which saturates 1g; Cholesterol 244mg; Calcium 145mg; Fibre 1.6g; Sodium 244mg.
Prawn Korma Energy 143kcal/601kJ; Protein 20.4g; Carbohydrate 5.4g, of which sugars 2.7g; Fat 4.8g, of which saturates 0.7g; Cholesterol 195mg; Calcium 168mg; Fibre 0.6g; Sodium 230mg.
Stir-fried Prawns Energy 118kcal/495kJ; Protein 17.9g; Carbohydrate 3g, of which sugars 3g; Fat 3.9g, of which saturates 0.5g; Cholesterol 195mg; Calcium 83mg; Fibre 0.4g; Sodium 234mg.

Grilled Prawns with Fried Spices

Serves 4
45ml/3 tbsp natural (plain) yogurt
5ml/1 tsp paprika
5ml/1 tsp grated fresh root ginger
16–20 peeled, cooked king prawns
  (jumbo shrimp), thawed if
  frozen
15ml/1 tbsp vegetable oil
3 onions, sliced
2.5ml/½ tsp fennel seeds,
  finely crushed
2.5cm/1in piece cinnamon stick
5ml/1 tsp crushed garlic
5ml/1 tsp chilli powder
1 yellow (bell) pepper, seeded
  and roughly chopped
1 red (bell) pepper, seeded and
  roughly chopped
salt
15ml/1 tbsp fresh coriander
  (cilantro) leaves, to garnish

1 Blend together the yogurt, paprika, ginger and salt to taste. Add to the prawns and leave to marinate for 45 minutes.

2 Heat the oil in a large pan and fry the onions with the fennel and cinnamon over medium heat, stirring occasionally, until the onions have softened. Lower the heat and stir in the garlic and chilli. Add the peppers and stir-fry for 3–5 minutes.

3 Remove the pan from the heat and transfer the onion and spice mixture to a warm serving dish, discarding the cinnamon stick. Set the dish aside.

4 Preheat the grill (broiler) to high. Put the prawns in a flameproof dish and place under the grill to achieve a chargrilled effect. Add the prawns to the onion and spice mixture, and garnish with fresh coriander leaves. Serve immediately.

Prawn and Spinach Pancakes

Serve these delicious filled pancakes hot. Try to use red onions, although they are not essential.

Makes 4–6
175g/6oz/1½ cups plain
  (all-purpose) flour
2.5ml/½ tsp salt
3 eggs
350ml/12fl oz/1½ cups
  semi-skimmed (low-fat) milk
15g/½oz/1 tbsp low-fat margarine

For the filling
30ml/2 tbsp vegetable oil
2 medium red onions, sliced

2.5ml/½ tsp garlic pulp
2.5cm/1in piece fresh root
  ginger, shredded
5ml/1 tsp chilli powder
5ml/1 tsp garam masala
5ml/1 tsp salt
2 tomatoes, sliced
225g/8oz frozen leaf spinach,
  thawed and drained
115g/4oz cooked prawns (shrimp)
30ml/2 tbsp chopped fresh
  coriander (cilantro)

For the garnish
1 tomato, quartered
fresh coriander (cilantro) sprigs
lemon wedges

1 To make the pancakes, sift the flour and salt together. Beat the eggs and add to the flour, beating constantly. Gradually stir in the milk. Leave to stand for 1 hour.

2 Heat the oil in a large frying pan and fry the onions over a medium heat until golden. Add the garlic, ginger, chilli powder, garam masala and salt, followed by the tomatoes and spinach. Add the prawns and fresh coriander. Cook for 5–7 minutes or until any excess water has been absorbed. Keep warm.

3 Heat about 2.5ml/½ tsp of the low-fat margarine in a 25cm/10in non-stick frying pan. Pour in about one-quarter of the pancake batter, tilting the pan so the batter spreads well, coats the bottom of the pan and is evenly distributed.

4 When bubbles appear on top, flip it over using a spatula and cook for a further minute or so. Transfer to a plate and keep warm. Cook the remaining pancakes in the same way.

5 Fill the pancakes with the spinach and prawns, and garnish with the tomato and coriander. Serve warm with lemon wedges.

Ginger Prawn and Mangetout Stir-fry

Serves 4
15ml/1 tbsp oil
2 medium onions, diced
15ml/1 tbsp tomato purée (paste)
5ml/1 tsp Tabasco sauce
5ml/1 tsp lemon juice
5ml/1 tsp grated fresh root ginger
5ml/1 tsp crushed garlic
5ml/1 tsp chilli powder
5ml/1 tsp salt
15ml/1 tbsp chopped fresh
  coriander (cilantro)
175g/6oz/1½ cups frozen cooked
  peeled prawns (shrimp),
  thawed
12 mangetouts (snow peas),
  cut in half

1 Heat the oil in a karahi, wok or heavy pan and fry the onions for 6–8 minutes until golden brown.

2 Mix the tomato purée with 30ml/2 tbsp water in a bowl. Add the Tabasco sauce, lemon juice, ginger and garlic, chilli powder and salt. Stir well until combined.

3 Lower the heat, pour the sauce over the onions and stir-fry for a few seconds until well mixed in.

4 Add the coriander, prawns and mangetouts to the pan and stir-fry for about 5–7 minutes, or until the sauce has reduced and thickened. Serve immediately.

Prawn Pancakes Energy 268kcal/1127kJ; Protein 14g; Carbohydrate 33g, of which sugars 8.1g; Fat 10g, of which saturates 2.4g; Cholesterol 136mg; Calcium 229mg; Fibre 2.9g; Sodium 174mg.
Grilled King Prawns Energy 118kcal/495kJ; Protein 17.9g; Carbohydrate 3g, of which sugars 3g; Fat 3.9g, of which saturates 0.5g; Cholesterol 195mg; Calcium 83mg; Fibre 0.4g; Sodium 234mg.
Ginger Prawn Stir-fry Energy 125kcal/524kJ; Protein 17.6g; Carbohydrate 5.2g, of which sugars 3.6g; Fat 3.4g, of which saturates 0.4g; Cholesterol 171mg; Calcium 96mg; Fibre 1.3g; Sodium 436mg.

Prawn and Cauliflower Curry

This is a basic fisherman's curry. Simple to make, it would usually be eaten from a communal bowl.

Serves 4

450g/1lb raw tiger prawns (jumbo shrimp), peeled, deveined and cleaned
juice of 1 lime
15ml/1 tbsp vegetable oil
1 red onion, roughly chopped
2 garlic cloves, roughly chopped
2 Thai chillies, seeded and finely chopped
1 cauliflower, broken into florets
5ml/1 tsp sugar
2 star anise, dry-fried and ground
10ml/2 tsp fenugreek, dry-fried and ground
450ml/¾ pint/2 cups coconut milk
1 bunch fresh coriander (cilantro), chopped, to garnish
salt and ground black pepper

1 In a bowl, toss the prawns in the lime juice and set aside. Heat a wok or heavy pan and add the oil. Stir in the onion, garlic and chillies. As they brown, add the cauliflower to the pan. Stir-fry for 2–3 minutes.

2 Stir the sugar and spices into the pan. Add the coconut milk, stirring to make sure it is thoroughly combined. Reduce the heat and simmer for 10–15 minutes, or until the liquid has reduced and thickened a little.

3 Add the prawns and lime juice and cook for 1–2 minutes, or until the prawns turn pink. Season to taste, and sprinkle with coriander. Serve immediately.

Cook's Tip
To devein prawns, make a shallow cut down the back of the prawn, lift out the thin, black vein and discard, then rinse the prawns thoroughly under cold running water.

Variation
Other popular combinations include prawns (shrimp) with butternut squash or pumpkin.

Yellow Prawn Curry

This South-east Asian speciality lives up to its name with an intense turmeric yellow colour that matches the strong flavours.

Serves 4

30ml/2 tbsp coconut or palm oil
2 shallots, finely chopped
2 garlic cloves, finely chopped
2 red chillies, seeded and finely chopped
25g/1oz fresh turmeric, finely chopped, or 10ml/2 tsp ground turmeric
25g/1oz fresh root ginger, finely chopped
2 lemon grass stalks, finely sliced
10ml/2 tsp coriander seeds
10ml/2 tsp shrimp paste
1 red (bell) pepper, seeded and finely sliced
4 kaffir lime leaves
about 500g/1¼lb fresh prawns (shrimp), shelled and deveined
400g/14oz can coconut milk
salt and ground black pepper
1 green chilli, seeded and sliced, to garnish

To serve
cooked rice
4 fried shallots or fresh chillies, seeded and sliced lengthways

1 Heat the oil in a wok or heavy frying pan. Stir in the shallots, garlic, chillies, turmeric, ginger, lemon grass and coriander seeds and fry until the fragrant aromas are released.

2 Stir in the shrimp paste and cook for 2–3 minutes. Add the red pepper and lime leaves and stir-fry for a further 1 minute.

3 Add the prawns to the pan. Pour in the coconut milk, stirring to combine, and bring to the boil. Cook for 5–6 minutes until the prawns are cooked. Season with salt and pepper to taste.

4 Spoon the prawns on to a warmed serving dish and sprinkle with the sliced green chilli to garnish. Serve with rice and fried shallots or the fresh chillies on the side.

Variation
Big, juicy prawns are delectable in this dish, but you can easily substitute them with scallops, squid or mussels, or a combination of all three, depending on what is available.

Prawn Curry Energy 157kcal/664kJ; Protein 24.7g; Carbohydrate 10.4g, of which sugars 9.4g; Fat 2.2g, of which saturates 0.6g; Cholesterol 219mg; Calcium 169mg; Fibre 2.7g; Sodium 351mg.
Yellow Curry Energy 230kcal/965kJ; Protein 26.4g; Carbohydrate 16g, of which sugars 13.5g; Fat 7.2g, of which saturates 1g; Cholesterol 263mg; Calcium 226mg; Fibre 2.7g; Sodium 519mg.

Bengali Prawn Curry

The Bay of Bengal provides enormous quantities of fish and shellfish. This fragrant curry features delectable tiger prawns.

Serves 4

675g/1½lb raw tiger prawns (jumbo shrimp)
4 dried red chillies
50g/2oz/1 cup desiccated (dry unsweetened shredded) coconut
5ml/1 tsp black mustard seeds
1 large onion, chopped
45ml/3 tbsp vegetable oil
4 bay leaves
2.5cm/1in piece fresh root ginger, chopped
2 garlic cloves, crushed
15ml/1 tbsp ground coriander
5ml/1 tsp chilli powder
5ml/1 tsp salt
4 tomatoes, finely chopped
plain boiled rice, to serve

1 Peel the prawns. Run a sharp knife along the back of each prawn to make a shallow cut and carefully remove the thin black intestinal vein and discard. You might like to leave a few of the prawns unpeeled, setting them aside to use later as a garnish for the finished dish.

2 Put the dried red chillies, coconut, mustard seeds and onion in a wok, karahi or large pan and dry-fry over medium heat for 5–6 minutes, or until the mixture begins to brown. Stir to ensure even browning and to avoid burning the coconut. Transfer to a food processor or blender and process to a coarse paste.

3 Heat the vegetable oil in the pan and fry the bay leaves for about 1 minute. Add the chopped ginger and the garlic, and fry for 2–3 minutes, stirring frequently.

4 Add the ground coriander, chilli powder, salt and the paste and fry for about 5 minutes.

5 Stir in the tomatoes and about 175ml/6fl oz/¾ cup water and simmer for 5–6 minutes or until thickened.

6 Add the prawns and cook for about 4–5 minutes, or until they turn pink. Grill (broil) the reserved whole prawns, if using, until pink. Serve the curry in a ring of plain boiled rice and garnish with the whole prawns, if using.

Prawns with Okra

This spicy prawn curry has a lovely sweet taste with a strong chilli flavour. The dish should be cooked fast to prevent the okra pods from breaking up in the pan and releasing their distinctive, sticky juice. Serve with plain rice or Indian breads.

Serves 4–6

60–90ml/4–6 tbsp vegetable oil
225g/8oz okra, washed, dried and left whole
4 cloves garlic, crushed
5cm/2in piece fresh root ginger, crushed
4–6 fresh green chillies, cut diagonally
2.5ml/½ tsp turmeric
4–6 curry leaves
5ml/1 tsp cumin seeds
450g/1lb fresh king prawns (jumbo shrimp), peeled and deveined
10ml/2 tsp soft light brown sugar
juice of 2 lemons
salt

1 Heat the oil in a frying pan and fry the okra pods over a fairly high heat until they are slightly crisp and browned on all sides. Remove the okra pods from the oil and put to one side on a piece of kitchen paper to absorb a little of the oil.

2 In the same oil, gently fry the garlic, ginger, chillies, turmeric, curry leaves and cumin seeds for 2–3 minutes. Add the prawns and mix well. Cook until the prawns are tender.

3 Add the sugar, lemon juice and fried okra, and salt to taste. Increase the heat and quickly fry for a further 5 minutes, stirring gently to prevent the okra from breaking. Adjust the seasoning, if necessary. Serve immediately.

Cook's Tip
Okra, sometimes known as 'lady's fingers', is a small, long seed pod that exudes a sticky liquid when the pod is cut. This liquid is useful for dishes that require a thick sauce, but for other dishes, such as this one, the pod must be left whole to keep in the liquid. Remove the stalk using a sharp knife but do not cut into the pod itself.

Bengali Prawn Curry Energy 237kcal/996kJ; Protein 34.9g; Carbohydrate 10g, of which sugars 6.3g; Fat 6.8g, of which saturates 3.8g; Cholesterol 338mg; Calcium 166mg; Fibre 2.6g; Sodium 344mg.
Prawns with Okra Energy 143kcal/597kJ; Protein 14.5g; Carbohydrate 3.1g, of which sugars 2.4g; Fat 8.2g, of which saturates 1.1g; Cholesterol 146mg; Calcium 121mg; Fibre 1.6g; Sodium 146mg.

Curried Prawns in Coconut Milk

This is a mildly spiced dish where the prawns are cooked in a tangy coconut gravy along with cherry tomatoes. It is a simple but flavoursome dish that is quick to prepare.

Serves 4–6
600ml/1 pint/2½ cups coconut milk
30ml/2 tbsp yellow curry paste
2.5ml/½ tsp salt
5ml/1 tsp sugar
450g/1lb king prawns (jumbo shrimp), peeled, tails left intact, deveined
225g/8oz cherry tomatoes
fresh red chilli strips and coriander (cilantro) leaves, to garnish
juice of ½ lime, to serve

1 Pour half the coconut milk into a large heavy pan or wok and bring slowly to the boil.

2 Add the curry paste to the coconut milk in the pan, stir until it disperses, then simmer for about 10 minutes.

3 Add the salt, sugar and remaining coconut milk to the pan. Simmer for another 5 minutes.

4 Add the prawns and cherry tomatoes to the pan. Simmer very gently over a low heat for about 5 minutes until the prawns are pink and tender.

5 Serve the prawns garnished with chilli strips and fresh coriander and have the lime juice on hand for sprinkling over.

Cook's Tip
Curry paste is a useful standby, but if you prefer a more authentic flavour you can make your own curry powder and mix 30ml/2 tbsp of it with a little water to form a paste. Dry roast 75g/3oz/1 cup coriander seeds, 15ml/1 tbsp cumin seeds, 8 dried red chillies, 12 cardamom pods and 12 cloves gently for 10 minutes. Cool and add 5ml/1 tsp turmeric and 15ml/1 tbsp ground cinnamon. Grind to a fine powder then store in an airtight jar for up to 6 months.

Goan Prawn Curry

Goan dishes use generous amounts of chilli, mellowed by coconut milk and palm vinegar. In this delicious coconut-enriched prawn curry, cider vinegar makes an equally good alternative to palm vinegar.

Serves 4
500g/1¼lb peeled king or tiger prawns (jumbo shrimp)
2.5ml/½ tsp salt, plus extra to taste
30ml/2 tbsp palm or cider vinegar
60ml/4 tbsp sunflower or olive oil
1 large onion, finely chopped
10ml/2 tsp crushed fresh root ginger
10ml/2 tsp crushed garlic
2.5ml/½ tsp ground cumin
5ml/1 tsp ground coriander
2.5ml/½ tsp ground turmeric
2.5ml/½ tsp chilli powder
2.5ml/½ tsp ground black pepper
75g/3oz/1 cup creamed coconut, chopped, or 250ml/8floz/1 cup coconut cream
4 green chillies
30ml/2 tbsp chopped fresh coriander (cilantro) leaves
plain boiled rice, to serve

1 Put the prawns in a non-metallic bowl and add the measured salt and vinegar. Mix and set aside for 10–15 minutes.

2 Heat the sunflower or olive oil in a medium pan and add the onion. Fry over medium heat until the onion is translucent.

3 Add the ginger and garlic and continue to fry for about 2 minutes over a low heat, until lightly browned.

4 Mix the cumin, coriander, turmeric, chilli powder and pepper in a bowl and add 30ml/2 tbsp water to make a pouring consistency. Add to the onion and cook, stirring, for 4–5 minutes until the mixture is dry and the oil separates from the spice mix.

5 Next, pour in 200ml/7fl oz/¾ cup warm water, the creamed coconut and salt to taste. Stir until the coconut has dissolved.

6 Add the prawns along with all the juices in the bowl, bring the pan to the boil, reduce the heat and cook for another 5–7 minutes. When the prawns curl up, they are cooked.

7 Add the whole chillies and simmer for 2–3 minutes. Stir in the chopped coriander. Serve with plain boiled rice.

Curried Prawns Energy 118kcal/500kJ; Protein 14.1g; Carbohydrate 11g, of which sugars 11g; Fat 2.3g, of which saturates 0.6g; Cholesterol 146mg; Calcium 116mg; Fibre 0.4g; Sodium 466mg.
Goan Prawn Curry Energy 171kcal/723kJ; Protein 21.9g; Carbohydrate 10g, of which sugars 7.4g; Fat 5.3g, of which saturates 2.5g; Cholesterol 227mg; Calcium 136mg; Fibre 1g; Sodium 344mg.

Coconut Prawn Curry

This delicious dish features chayote, also known as christophene, alligator pear or custard marrow, which belongs to the squash family. Widely used in South-east Asia and some parts of India, it is pear-shaped, and generally pale yellow or yellow-green in colour.

Serves 4

1–2 chayotes or 2–3 courgettes (zucchini)
2 fresh red chillies, seeded
1 onion, quartered
5mm/¼in piece fresh galangal or 1cm/½in piece fresh root ginger, sliced
1 lemon grass stalk, lower 5cm/2in sliced, top bruised
2.5cm/1in piece fresh turmeric or 5ml/1tsp ground turmeric
200ml/7fl oz/scant 1 cup water
lemon juice, to taste
400g/14oz can coconut milk
450g/1lb cooked, peeled prawns (shrimp)
salt
fresh red chilli shreds, to garnish
plain boiled rice or noodles, to serve

1 Peel the chayotes, remove the seeds and cut into strips. If using courgettes, cut into 5cm/2in strips.

2 Grind the fresh red chillies, onion, sliced galangal or root ginger, sliced lemon grass and the turmeric to a paste in a food processor or with a pestle and mortar. Add the water to the paste mixture, with a squeeze of lemon juice and salt to taste.

3 Pour into a pan. Add the top of the lemon grass stalk. Bring to the boil and cook for 1–2 minutes. Add the chayote or courgette pieces and then cook for 2 minutes. Stir in the coconut milk. Taste and adjust the seasoning.

4 Add the prawns and cook gently for 2–3 minutes. Remove the lemon grass stalk. Garnish with the chilli shreds. Serve with plain boiled rice or noodles.

> **Variation**
> *Larger supermarkets or Asian stores usually sell chayote, but you can use courgettes (zucchini) instead.*

Paneer Balti with Prawns

Paneer is a protein-rich food and makes an excellent substitute for red meat. Here it is combined with king prawns to make a delicious dish with a truly unforgettable flavour.

Serves 4

12 cooked king prawns (jumbo shrimp)
175g/6oz paneer
30ml/2 tbsp tomato purée (paste)
60ml/4 tbsp Greek (US strained plain) yogurt
7.5ml/1½ tsp garam masala
5ml/1 tsp chilli powder
5ml/1 tsp crushed garlic
5ml/1 tsp salt
10ml/2 tsp mango powder (amchur)
5ml/1 tsp ground coriander
115g/4oz/½ cup butter
15ml/1 tbsp vegetable oil or sunflower oil
3 fresh green chillies, seeded and chopped
45ml/3 tbsp chopped fresh coriander (cilantro)
150ml/¼ pint/⅔ cup single (light) cream

1 Peel the king prawns. Using a sharp knife, remove the black intestinal vein from down the back of each prawn and discard. Cut the paneer into small cubes.

2 Put the tomato purée, yogurt, garam masala, chilli powder, garlic, salt, mango powder and ground coriander in a mixing bowl. Mix to a paste and set aside.

3 Melt the butter with the oil in a karahi, wok or deep pan. Lower the heat slightly and quickly fry the paneer and prawns for about 2 minutes. Remove the paneer and prawns with a slotted spoon and drain on kitchen paper.

4 Pour the spice paste into the fat left in the pan and cook for about 1 minute, stirring constantly.

5 Add the paneer and prawns, and cook for 7–10 minutes, stirring occasionally, until the prawns are heated through.

6 Add the fresh chillies and most of the coriander, and pour in the cream. Heat through for about 2 minutes, garnish with the remaining coriander and serve.

Coconut Prawn Curry Energy 255kcal/1066kJ; Protein 38.9g; Carbohydrate 2.4g, of which sugars 2.3g; Fat 9.9g, of which saturates 1.5g; Cholesterol 163mg; Calcium 78mg; Fibre 0.4g; Sodium 235mg.
Paneer Balti Energy 414kcal/1712kJ; Protein 15.2g; Carbohydrate 4g, of which sugars 3g; Fat 37.6g, of which saturates 21.7g; Cholesterol 162mg; Calcium 195mg; Fibre 1.5g; Sodium 419mg.

Curried Noodles with Prawns

Any vegetable from the same family as courgette or squash can be used in this spicy Indonesian curry. Other noodles can also be used instead of cellophane.

Serves 4–6
450g/1lb courgettes (zucchini)
1 onion, finely sliced
1 garlic clove, finely chopped
30ml/2 tbsp vegetable oil
2.5ml/½ tsp ground turmeric
2 tomatoes, chopped
45ml/3 tbsp water
115g/4oz peeled, cooked prawns (shrimp)
25g/1oz cellophane noodles
salt

1 Use a potato or vegetable peeler to pare away thin strips from the outside of each courgette.

2 Cut the courgettes into neat slices, then set aside. Fry the onion and garlic in hot oil in a pan for 5 minutes until beginning to soften but do not allow to brown.

3 Add the turmeric, courgette slices, chopped tomatoes, water and the cooked prawns to the pan.

4 Put the noodles in a large pan and pour over enough boiling water to cover. Leave the noodles to soak for a minute.

5 Drain the noodles thoroughly and then cut them into 5cm/2in lengths. Add them to the vegetables in the pan and stir well to combine the ingredients.

6 Cover the pan with a tight-fitting lid and allow everything to cook in its own steam for 2–3 minutes. Toss well together.

7 Season the noodles with salt to taste, and transfer to a warmed serving bowl. Serve immediately.

Cook's Tip
Keep a careful eye on the time when cooking the cellophane noodles as they will soften very quickly.

Prawn and Vegetable Balti

This fresh-tasting balti makes a delicious light lunch or supper, and is quick and simple to make.

Serves 4
175g/6oz frozen cooked peeled prawns (shrimp)
30ml/2 tbsp vegetable oil
1.5ml/¼ tsp onion seeds
4–6 curry leaves
115g/4oz/1 cup frozen peas
115g/4oz/⅔ cup frozen corn
1 large courgette (zucchini), thickly sliced
1 medium red (bell) pepper, seeded and roughly diced
5ml/1 tsp finely crushed coriander seeds
5ml/1 tsp crushed dried red chillies
1.5ml/½ tsp salt
15ml/1 tbsp lemon juice
15ml/1 tbsp fresh coriander (cilantro) leaves, to garnish
basmati rice, to serve

1 Thaw the frozen prawns and place in a sieve (strainer) to drain them of any excess liquid.

2 Heat the oil with the onion seeds and curry leaves in a karahi, wok or heavy frying pan.

3 Add the prawns to the spicy mixture in the wok and cook, stirring constantly, until the liquid has evaporated.

4 Next, add the peas, corn, courgette and red pepper. Continue to stir for 3–5 minutes.

5 Finally, add the crushed coriander seeds and dried chillies to the pan, with salt to taste and the lemon juice.

6 Serve the curry immediately, sprinkled with a few fresh coriander leaves to garnish. Accompany the balti with plain boiled basmati rice.

Cook's Tip
Freshly crushed spices have a strong and vibrant flavour. The best way to crush whole seeds is to use an electric spice grinder or a small marble pestle and mortar.

Curried Noodles Energy 330kcal/1386kJ; Protein 13.4g; Carbohydrate 44.6g, of which sugars 4.5g; Fat 12.1g, of which saturates 2.2g; Cholesterol 73mg; Calcium 71mg; Fibre 3.3g; Sodium 337mg.
Prawn and Vegetable Balti Energy 165kcal/688kJ; Protein 11.9g; Carbohydrate 14.6g, of which sugars 7g; Fat 6.9g, of which saturates 0.9g; Cholesterol 85mg; Calcium 58mg; Fibre 2.9g; Sodium 163mg.

Karahi-style Prawns and Vegetables

Here, tender prawns, crunchy vegetables and a thick curry sauce combine to produce a dish rich in flavour and texture.

Serves 4

45ml/3 tbsp corn oil
5ml/1 tsp mixed fenugreek, mustard and onion seeds
2 curry leaves
½ medium cauliflower, cut into small florets (flowerets)
8 baby carrots, halved lengthways
6 new potatoes, thickly sliced
50g/2oz/½ cup frozen peas
2 medium onions, sliced
30ml/2 tbsp tomato purée (paste)
7.5ml/1½ tsp chilli powder
5ml/1 tsp ground coriander
5ml/1 tsp crushed fresh root ginger
5ml/1 tsp crushed garlic
5ml/1 tsp salt
30ml/2 tbsp lemon juice
450g/1lb cooked prawns (shrimp)
30ml/2 tbsp chopped fresh coriander (cilantro)
1 fresh red chilli, seeded and sliced
120ml/4fl oz/½ cup single (light) cream

1 Heat the oil in a deep frying pan or a large karahi. Lower the heat slightly and add the fenugreek, mustard and onion seeds and the curry leaves.

2 Turn up the heat and add the cauliflower, carrots, potatoes and peas. Stir-fry quickly until browned, then remove from the pan with a slotted spoon and drain on kitchen paper.

3 Add the onions to the oil left in the karahi and fry over a medium heat until golden brown.

4 While the onions are cooking, mix together the tomato purée, chilli powder, ground coriander, ginger, garlic, salt and lemon juice and pour the paste on to the onions.

5 Add the prawns to the pan and stir-fry over a low heat for about 5 minutes or until they are heated through.

6 Add the fried vegetables to the pan and mix together well.

7 Add the fresh coriander and red chilli and pour over the cream. Bring to the boil and serve immediately.

Seafood Balti with Vegetables

Spicy seafood and vegetables give this curry a delicious combination of flavours.

Serves 4

For the seafood

225g/8oz cod, or firm white fish
225g/8oz cooked prawns (shrimp)
6 crab sticks, halved lengthways
15ml/1 tbsp lemon juice
5ml/1 tsp ground coriander
5ml/1 tsp chilli powder
5ml/1 tsp salt
5ml/1 tsp ground cumin
60ml/4 tbsp cornflour (cornstarch)
150ml/¼ pint/⅔ cup corn oil

For the vegetables

150ml/¼ pint/⅔ cup corn oil
2 medium onions, chopped
5ml/1 tsp onion seeds
½ cauliflower, cut into florets
115g/4oz green beans, cut into 2.5cm/1in lengths
175g/6oz/1 cup corn
5ml/1 tsp chopped fresh root ginger
5ml/1 tsp chilli powder
5ml/1 tsp salt
4 fresh green chillies, sliced
30ml/2 tbsp chopped fresh coriander (cilantro)
lime slices

1 Remove the skin from the cod or other white fish and discard. Cut the flesh into small cubes. Place into a medium mixing bowl with the prawns and crab sticks, and set aside.

2 In a separate bowl, mix together the lemon juice, ground coriander, chilli powder, salt and ground cumin. Pour this over the seafood and mix together thoroughly using your hands. Sprinkle on the cornflour and mix again. Chill for 1 hour.

3 For the vegetables, heat the oil in a deep frying pan or a karahi. Stir-fry the onions and the onion seeds until browned. Add the cauliflower, green beans, corn, ginger, chilli powder, salt, green chillies and fresh coriander. Stir-fry for 7–10 minutes over a medium heat, making sure that the florets retain their shape.

4 Spoon the fried vegetables around the edge of a shallow dish, leaving a space in the middle for the seafood, and keep warm.

5 Wash and dry the pan, then heat the oil. Fry the seafood in 2–3 batches, until they turn a golden brown, then drain. Arrange in the middle of the vegetables and keep warm while you fry the remaining seafood. Garnish with lime slices and serve.

Karahi-style Prawns Energy 151kcal/629kJ; Protein 8.5g; Carbohydrate 10.1g, of which sugars 6.6g; Fat 8.7g, of which saturates 1.7g; Cholesterol 41mg; Calcium 72mg; Fibre 1.8g; Sodium 445mg.
Seafood Balti Energy 454kcal/1894kJ; Protein 24.5g; Carbohydrate 31g, of which sugars 9.1g; Fat 26.7g, of which saturates 3.2g; Cholesterol 141mg; Calcium 84mg; Fibre 2.3g; Sodium 373mg.

Mussels with Cinnamon Pilaff

Serves 4

16 large fresh mussels, cleaned
45–60ml/3–4 tbsp olive oil
2–3 shallots, finely chopped
30ml/2 tbsp pine nuts
30ml/2 tbsp currants, soaked
10ml/2 tsp ground cinnamon
5ml/1 tsp ground allspice
5–10ml/1–2 tsp sugar
5–10ml/1–2 tsp tomato
   purée (paste)
115g/4oz/generous ½ cup short
   grain or pudding rice
1 small bunch each of fresh
   parsley, mint and dill, chopped
salt and ground black pepper
lemon wedges and fresh flat leaf
   parsley sprigs, to serve

1 Heat the oil in a pan, stir in the shallots and cook until soft. Add the pine nuts and currants, stir for 1–2 minutes, then stir in the cinnamon, allspice, sugar and tomato purée. Now add the rice, and stir until it is well coated.

2 Pour in enough water to just cover the rice. Season to taste and bring to the boil. Lower the heat, partially cover the pan and simmer for 10–12 minutes. Transfer the rice on to a plate, leave to cool, then toss in the herbs.

3 Prise open each mussel, stuff a spoonful of rice into each shell, then close the shells and pack tightly into a steamer filled with water. Cover with a sheet of baking parchment, put a plate on top and weigh it down. Place the lid on the steamer and bring to the boil. Steam the mussels for 15–20 minutes. Serve immediately on a bed of fresh parsley, with lemon wedges.

Mussels and Clams with Coconut

Serves 6

1.75kg/4–4½lb mussels
450g/1lb baby clams
120ml/4fl oz/½ cup dry white wine
1 bunch spring onions (scallions),
   finely chopped
2 lemon grass stalks, chopped
6 kaffir lime leaves, chopped
10ml/2 tsp Thai green curry paste
200ml/7fl oz/scant 1 cup
   coconut cream
30ml/2 tbsp chopped fresh
   coriander (cilantro)
salt and ground black pepper
garlic chives, to garnish

1 Clean the mussels by pulling off the beards, scrubbing the shells and removing any barnacles. Discard any mussels that are broken or do not close when tapped sharply. Wash the clams.

2 Put the dry white wine in a large pan with the spring onions, lemon grass, lime leaves and curry paste. Simmer gently until the wine has almost evaporated.

3 Add the mussels and clams to the pan, cover tightly and steam the shellfish over a high heat for 5–6 minutes, until they open.

4 Transfer the mussels and clams to a heated serving bowl. Discard any shellfish that remain closed. Strain the cooking liquid into a pan and simmer to reduce to about 250ml/8fl oz/1 cup.

5 Stir in the coconut cream and coriander, with salt and pepper to taste. Heat through. Pour the sauce over the mussels and clams and serve, garnished with garlic chives.

Curried Seafood with Coconut Milk

The pale green colour of this curry is the result of the use of green chillies and fresh herbs. You can reduce the amount of chillies if you prefer a milder curry.

Serves 4

225g/8oz raw tiger prawns
   (jumbo shrimp)
400ml/14fl oz/1⅔ cups
   coconut milk
2 kaffir lime leaves, finely shredded
30ml/2 tbsp Thai fish sauce
225g/8oz small, prepared squid,
   cut into rings, tentacles halved
450g/1lb firm white fish, skinned,
   boned and cut into chunks
2 fresh green chillies, seeded and
   finely chopped
30ml/2 tbsp torn fresh basil or
   coriander (cilantro) leaves
squeeze of fresh lime juice
cooked jasmine rice, to serve

For the curry paste

6 spring onions (scallions),
   coarsely chopped
4 fresh coriander (cilantro) stems,
   chopped, plus 45ml/3 tbsp
   chopped fresh coriander (cilantro)
4 kaffir lime leaves, shredded
8 fresh green chillies, seeded and
   coarsely chopped
1 lemon grass stalk, chopped
2.5cm/1in piece fresh root ginger,
   peeled and coarsely chopped
45ml/3 tbsp chopped fresh basil
15ml/1 tbsp vegetable oil or
   sunflower oil

1 Make the curry paste. Put all the ingredients, except the oil, in a food processor and process to a paste. Alternatively, pound together in a mortar with a pestle. Stir in the oil.

2 Heat a wok until hot, add the prawns and stir-fry, without oil, for 4 minutes, until they turn pink. Remove from the wok.

3 Leave the prawns to cool slightly, then peel the shells, saving a few with shells on for the garnish. Remove the black vein.

4 In the wok, bring the coconut milk to the boil over a medium heat. Add 30ml/2 tbsp of curry paste, the lime leaves and fish sauce. Reduce the heat and simmer gently for 10 minutes.

5 Add the squid, prawns and fish and cook for 2 minutes, until the seafood is tender. Stir in the chillies and basil or coriander. Taste and adjust the flavour with lime juice. Garnish with prawns in their shells, and serve with jasmine rice.

Mussels with Pilaff Energy 319kcal/1328kJ; Protein 13.3g; Carbohydrate 32.7g, of which sugars 7.5g; Fat 15g, of which saturates 1.9g; Cholesterol 33mg; Calcium 49mg; Fibre 0.5g; Sodium 237mg.
Mussels and Clams Energy 177kcal/745kJ; Protein 21.8g; Carbohydrate 1.9g, of which sugars 1.2g; Fat 7.8g, of which saturates 5.3g; Cholesterol 58mg; Calcium 212mg; Fibre 0.3g; Sodium 594mg.
Curried Seafood Energy 238kcal/1005kJ; Protein 40.6g; Carbohydrate 7g, of which sugars 6.2g; Fat 5.5g, of which saturates 0.9g; Cholesterol 288mg; Calcium 145mg; Fibre 1.4g; Sodium 622mg.

Spicy Seafood Stew

Serves 6
675g/1½lb small clams, scrubbed
2 × 400ml/14fl oz cans coconut
  milk, made up to 1.2litres/2
  pints/5 cups with water
50g/2oz ikan bilis (dried anchovies)
900ml/1½ pints/3¾ cups water
115g/4oz shallots, finely chopped
4 garlic cloves, chopped
6 macadamia nuts or blanched
  almonds, chopped
3 lemon grass stalks, root trimmed
90ml/6 tbsp sunflower oil
1cm/½in cube shrimp paste

25g/1oz/¼ cup mild curry powder
a few curry leaves
2–3 aubergines (eggplants), total
  weight about 675g/1½lb
675g/1½lb raw prawns (shrimp)
10ml/2 tsp sugar
1 head Chinese leaves (Chinese
  cabbage), thinly sliced
115g/4oz/2 cups beansprouts
2 spring onions (scallions), chopped
50g/2oz crispy fried onions
115g/4oz fried tofu
675g/1½lb mixed noodles
prawn crackers, to serve

1 To make the ikan bilis stock, put the ikan bilis in a pan and add the water. Bring to the boil and simmer for 20 minutes. Steam the clams for 3–4 minutes until they open. Drain.

2 Put the shallots, garlic and nuts into a mortar with the chopped lower half of two lemon grass stalks, and pound to a paste.

3 Heat the oil in a pan, add the paste and fry for 3 minutes. Add the remaining lemon grass and fry for 1 minute. Add the shrimp paste, curry, milk and curry leaves and leave to simmer.

4 Strain the ikan bilis stock into a pan. Add the aubergines; cook for 10 minutes. Peel, cut into thick strips and arrange on a dish. Sprinkle the prawns with sugar, add to the ikan bilis stock and cook for 2–4 minutes. Add the prawns, clams, Chinese leaves, beansprouts, spring onions and crispy fried onions to the dish.

5 Stir the remaining ikan bilis stock into the pan of stew and bring to the boil. Rinse the fried tofu in boiling water, cool slightly and squeeze to remove excess oil. Cut each piece in half and add to the soup. Lower the heat to a gentle simmer.

6 Cook the noodles according to the instructions, drain and pile in a dish. Serve the dish with a bowl of prawn crackers.

Indonesian Squid in Clove Sauce

Serves 3–4
675g/1½lb squid
45ml/3 tbsp groundnut (peanut) oil
1 onion, finely chopped
2 garlic cloves, crushed
1 beefsteak tomato, skinned
  and chopped
15ml/1 tbsp dark soy sauce

2.5ml/½ tsp freshly grated nutmeg
6 whole cloves
150ml/¼ pint/⅔ cup water
juice of ½ lemon
salt and ground black pepper
plain boiled rice, to serve
  spring onions (scallions) and fresh
  coriander (cilantro), to garnish

1 Wash and clean the squid and pat dry on kitchen paper. Use a sharp kitchen knife to cut the squid into long, thin ribbons. Carefully remove the 'bone' from each tentacle, and discard.

2 Heat a wok, toss in the squid and stir constantly for 2–3 minutes. Lift out and set aside in a warm place.

3 Heat the oil in a clean pan and fry the onion and garlic, until soft. Add the tomato, soy sauce, nutmeg, cloves, water and lemon juice. Bring to the boil, add the squid, and season to taste.

4 Simmer the squid in the sauce for 3–5 minutes, uncovered, over a gentle heat. Serve hot or warm, with plain rice. Garnish with shredded spring onions and fresh coriander.

Squid in Hot Yellow Sauce

Serves 4
500g/1¼lb fresh squid
juice of 2 limes
5ml/1 tsp salt
4 shallots, chopped
4 garlic cloves, chopped
25g/1oz galangal, chopped
25g/1oz fresh turmeric, chopped

6 red chillies, seeded and chopped
30ml/2 tbsp vegetable oil
7.5ml/1½ tsp palm sugar (jaggery)
2 lemon grass stalks, crushed
4 lime leaves
400ml/14fl oz/1⅔ cups
  coconut milk
salt and ground black pepper

1 First prepare the squid. Hold the body sac in one hand and pull off the head with the other. Sever the tentacles just above the eyes, and discard the rest of the head and innards. Clean the body sac and remove the skin. Pat the squid dry, cut it into thick slices and put them in a bowl, with the tentacles. Rub with the lime juice with the salt. Set aside for 30 minutes.

2 Meanwhile, using a mortar and pestle, food processor or blender, grind the shallots, garlic, galangal, turmeric and chillies until they form a coarse paste.

3 Heat the oil in a wok or heavy pan, and stir in the coarse paste. Cook the paste until fragrant, then stir in the palm sugar, lemon grass and lime leaves. Drain the squid of any juice and toss it around the wok, coating it in the flavourings.

4 Pour the coconut milk into the pan and bring it to the boil. Reduce the heat to low and simmer for 5–10 minutes, until the squid is tender. Take care not to overcook the squid or it will become rubbery. Season to taste with salt and ground black pepper and serve the curry immediately.

Spicy Seafood Stew Energy 335kcal/1405kJ; Protein 32g; Carbohydrate 22.7g, of which sugars 5.4g; Fat 10.6g, of which saturates 1.2g; Cholesterol 325mg; Calcium 161mg; Fibre 1.7g; Sodium 385mg.
Squid in Yellow Sauce Energy 185kcal/780kJ; Protein 19.8g; Carbohydrate 9.4g, of which sugars 7.6g; Fat 8g, of which saturates 1.4g; Cholesterol 281mg; Calcium 50mg; Fibre 0.2g; Sodium 739mg.
Indonesian Squid Energy 154kcal/647kJ; Protein 19.8g; Carbohydrate 5.8g, of which sugars 4.3g; Fat 5.9g, of which saturates 1g; Cholesterol 281mg; Calcium 54mg; Fibre 1g; Sodium 144mg.

Fiery Octopus

Here octopus is stir-fried to give it a rich meaty texture, then smothered in a fiery chilli sauce. The dish combines the charred octopus flavour with Korean spiciness and the zing of chillies. Serve with steamed rice and a bowl of soup.

Serves 2

2 small octopuses, cleaned
    and gutted
15ml/1 tbsp vegetable oil
½ onion, sliced 5mm/¼in thick
¼ carrot, thinly sliced
½ leek, thinly sliced
75g/3oz jalapeño chillies, trimmed
2 garlic cloves, crushed
10ml/2 tsp Korean chilli powder
5ml/1 tsp dark soy sauce
45ml/3 tbsp gochujang chilli paste
30ml/2 tbsp mirin or rice wine
15ml/1 tbsp maple syrup
sesame oil and sesame seeds,
    to garnish

1 First blanch the octopuses in boiling water to soften slightly. Drain well, and cut into pieces approximately 5cm/2in long.

2 Heat the oil in a frying pan over a medium-high heat and add the onion, carrot, leek and chillies. Stir-fry for 3 minutes.

3 Add the octopus and garlic, and sprinkle over the chilli powder. Stir-fry for 3–4 minutes, or until the octopus is tender. Add the soy sauce, gochujang paste, mirin or rice wine, and maple syrup. Mix well and stir-fry for 1 minute more.

4 Transfer to a serving platter, and garnish with a drizzle of sesame oil and a sprinkling of sesame seeds.

Variation
If the taste is too fiery, mix some softened vermicelli noodles in with the stir-fry to dilute the chilli paste.

Cook's Tip
To make the octopus more tender, knead it with a handful of plain (all-purpose) flour and rinse in salted water.

Fish Head Curry

There are numerous versions of this unusual yet delectable curry throughout India and South-east Asia. Fish heads are highly prized for the succulent meat in the cheeks. Various fish can be used but this version uses red snapper.

Serves 2

30ml/2 tbsp ghee or
    vegetable oil
10ml/2 tsp brown mustard seeds
5ml/1 tsp fenugreek seeds
5ml/1 tsp cumin seeds
a handful of curry leaves
15ml/1 tbsp palm sugar (jaggery)
30ml/2 tbsp tamarind pulp,
    soaked in 150ml/¼ pint/⅔ cup
    water and strained for juice
600ml/1 pint/2½ cups coconut milk

1 large fresh fish head,
    such as red snapper (about
    900g/2lb), cleaned
5 okra, halved diagonally
2 large tomatoes, skinned, seeded
    and quartered
salt and ground black pepper
steamed plain rice and pickles,
    to serve

For the spice paste

8 shallots, chopped
6 garlic cloves, chopped
4 red chillies, seeded and
    roughly chopped
50g/2oz fresh root ginger, peeled
    and chopped
25g/1oz fresh turmeric, chopped
1 lemon grass stalk, trimmed
    and chopped
30ml/2 tbsp fish curry powder

1 To make the spice paste, grind all the ingredients together using a mortar and pestle or food processor.

2 Heat the ghee or oil in a wok or heavy pan. Stir in the mustard seeds, fenugreek and cumin seeds along with the curry leaves. Fry until the mustard seeds begin to pop.

3 Add the spice paste to the pan. Fry until fragrant, about 2–3 minutes, then stir in the palm sugar, followed by the tamarind juice and coconut milk.

4 Bring the mixture to the boil, reduce the heat and add the fish head. Simmer gently for 10 minutes, then add the okra and tomatoes. Simmer for another 10 minutes or until the fish head is cooked and tender. Season the sauce with salt and pepper and serve with steamed rice and pickles.

Fiery Octopus Energy 235kcal/988kJ; Protein 28.6g; Carbohydrate 13.2g, of which sugars 11.9g; Fat 8g, of which saturates 1.2g; Cholesterol 72mg; Calcium 76mg; Fibre 2.4g; Sodium 204mg.
Fish Head Curry Energy 417kcal/1760kJ; Protein 42.2g; Carbohydrate 30.4g, of which sugars 29.1g; Fat 15.2g, of which saturates 2.7g; Cholesterol 74mg; Calcium 231mg; Fibre 2.7g; Sodium 497mg.

Monkfish and Okra Curry

An interesting combination of flavours and textures is used to make this delicious fish dish.

Serves 4

450g/1lb monkfish
5ml/1 tsp ground turmeric
2.5ml/½ tsp chilli powder
2.5ml/½ tsp salt
5ml/1 tsp cumin seeds
2.5ml/½ tsp fennel seeds

2 dried red chillies
45ml/3 tbsp vegetable oil
1 onion, finely chopped
2 garlic cloves, crushed
4 firm tomatoes, skinned and
   finely chopped
150ml/¼ pint/ ⅔ cup water
225g/8oz okra, trimmed and cut
   into 2.5cm/1in lengths
5ml/1 tsp garam masala
tomato rice or plain boiled rice,
   to serve

1 Remove the membrane and bones from the monkfish, cut into 2.5cm/1in cubes and place in a dish. Mix together the turmeric, chilli powder and 1.5ml/¼ tsp of the salt and rub the mixture all over the fish. Marinate for 15 minutes.

2 Put the cumin seeds, fennel seeds and chillies in a wok or a large frying pan and dry-roast for about 3–4 minutes until a fragrant aroma is released. Put the spices into a blender, or use a mortar and pestle, and grind to a coarse powder.

3 Heat 30ml/2 tbsp of the oil in the frying pan and and fry the fish for about 4–5 minutes, turning occasionally. Remove with a slotted spoon and drain on kitchen paper.

4 Add the remaining oil to the pan and gently fry the onion and garlic for about 5 minutes, until the onion is soft and translucent. Add the spice powder and the remaining salt to the pan and fry for a further 2–3 minutes.

5 Stir the chopped tomatoes and the water into the pan. Simmer the mixture gently for 5 minutes, stirring occasionally.

6 Add the prepared okra and cook for about 5–7 minutes. Return the fish to the pan with the garam masala. Cover and simmer for 5–6 minutes or until the fish is tender. Serve immediately with tomato rice or plain boiled rice.

Sea Bass Steamed in Coconut Milk

Serves 4

200ml/7fl oz coconut milk
10ml/2 tsp raw cane sugar
about 15ml/1 tbsp sesame oil
2 garlic cloves, finely chopped
1 red chilli, seeded and chopped

4cm/1½in fresh root ginger, peeled
750g/1lb 10oz sea bass fillet
1 star anise, ground
1 bunch of fresh basil
30ml/2 tbsp cashew nuts
salt and ground black pepper

1 Heat the coconut milk with the sugar in a pan, stirring until the sugar dissolves, then remove from the heat. Add the oil to a pan and stir in the garlic, chilli and ginger. Cook until they begin to brown, then add to the coconut milk and mix well.

2 Place the fish, skin side down, on a wide piece of foil and tuck up the sides to form a boat-shaped container. Cut several diagonal slashes on the top and rub with the star anise. Season with salt and pepper and spoon the coconut milk over the top.

3 Sprinkle half the basil leaves over the fish and pull the sides of the foil over the top, so that it is almost enclosed. Lay it in a steamer, cover, bring to the boil, then simmer for 20–25 minutes.

4 Roast the cashew nuts in the frying pan, adding a little extra oil if necessary. Drain on kitchen paper, then grind to crumbs.

5 When the fish is cooked, lift it out of the foil and transfer to a serving dish. Spoon the juices over, sprinkle with cashew nut crumbs and garnish with the remaining basil. Serve immediately.

Tilapia in Mango and Tomato Sauce

Serves 4

4 tilapia
juice of ½ lemon
2 garlic cloves, crushed
2.5ml/½ tsp dried thyme
30ml/2 tbsp chopped spring
   onion (scallion)
vegetable oil, for shallow-frying
plain (all-purpose) flour, for dusting
30ml/2 tbsp groundnut (peanut) oil
15g/½oz/1 tbsp butter

1 onion, finely chopped
3 tomatoes, skinned and chopped
5ml/1 tsp ground turmeric
60ml/4 tbsp white wine
1 fresh green chilli, seeded and
   finely chopped
600ml/1 pint/2½ cups fish stock
5ml/1 tsp sugar
225g/8oz mango, diced
15ml/1 tbsp chopped fresh parsley
salt and ground black pepper

1 Place the fish in a bowl, drizzle with lemon juice, rub in the garlic and thyme and season to taste. Place some of the spring onion in the cavity of each fish, cover loosely with clear film (plastic wrap) and leave to marinate for a few hours..

2 Heat a little oil in a frying pan, coat the fish with flour, and fry on both sides, until golden brown. Remove the fish to a plate.

3 Heat the oil and butter in a pan and fry the onion for 4–5 minutes. Stir in the tomatoes and cook for a few minutes. Add the turmeric, wine, chilli, stock and sugar. Simmer gently, covered, for 10 minutes. Add the fish and cook for 15–20 minutes. Add the mango, and cook for 1–2 minutes. Arrange the fish on a warmed plate with the sauce. Garnish with parsley and serve.

Monkfish Curry Energy 203kcal/851kJ; Protein 20.9g; Carbohydrate 7.7g, of which sugars 5.4g; Fat 10.2g, of which saturates 1.5g; Cholesterol 16mg; Calcium 119mg; Fibre 3.5g; Sodium 36mg.
Sea Bass Energy 235kcal/983kJ; Protein 26g; Carbohydrate 8g, of which sugars 6g; Fat 11g, of which saturates 2g; Cholesterol 100mg; Calcium 217mg; Fibre 0.3g; Sodium 0.3g.
Tilapia in Sauce Energy 238kcal/998kJ; Protein 23.4g; Carbohydrate 10.1g, of which sugars 9.6g; Fat 10.8g, of which saturates 3.1g; Cholesterol 8mg; Calcium 168mg; Fibre 2g; Sodium 97mg.

John Dory with Light Curry Sauce

This excellent combination of flavours also works well with other flat fish like turbot, halibut and brill. The curry taste of this dish should be subtle otherwise it will mask the delicate flavours, so use a very mild curry powder.

Serves 4
4 John Dory fillets, each about
    175g/6oz, skinned
15ml/1 tbsp sunflower oil
25g/1oz/2 tbsp butter
salt and ground black pepper
15ml/1 tbsp fresh coriander
    (cilantro) leaves and 1 mango,
    peeled and diced, to garnish

For the curry sauce
30ml/2 tbsp sunflower oil
1 carrot, chopped
1 onion, chopped
1 celery stick, chopped
white of 1 leek, chopped
2 garlic cloves, crushed
50g/2oz creamed coconut,
    crumbled or 120ml/4fl oz/½ cup
    coconut cream
2 tomatoes, peeled, seeded
    and diced
2.5cm/1in piece fresh root
    ginger, grated
15ml/1 tbsp tomato purée (paste)
5–10ml/1–2 tsp mild curry powder
500ml/17fl oz/generous 2 cups
    chicken or fish stock

1 Make the sauce. Heat the oil in a pan; add the vegetables and garlic. Cook gently until soft but not brown.

2 Add the coconut, tomatoes and ginger. Cook for 1–2 minutes, stir in the tomato purée and curry powder to taste. Add the stock, stir and season. Bring to the boil, then lower the heat, cover the pan and simmer over the lowest heat for 50 minutes.

3 Allow the sauce to cool, then pour into a food processor or blender and process until smooth. Return to a clean pan and reheat very gently, adding a little water if too thick.

4 Season the fish fillets. Heat the oil in a large frying pan, add the butter and heat until sizzling. Put in the fish and cook for about 2–3 minutes on each side, until pale golden and cooked through. Drain on kitchen paper.

5 Arrange the fillets on plates, pour the sauce around the fish and sprinkle on the mango and coriander leaves and serve.

Fillet of Fish Basted with Spices and Lemon Juice

The great thing about fish is that it can be grilled without sacrificing any flavour. For this recipe, there is only a minimum amount of oil used to baste the fish.

Serves 4
4 medium flatfish fillets, such as
    plaice, sole or flounder, about
    115g/4oz each

5ml/1 tsp crushed garlic
5ml/1 tsp garam masala
5ml/1 tsp chilli powder
1.5ml/¼ tsp turmeric
2.5ml/½ tsp salt
15ml/1 tbsp finely chopped fresh
    coriander (cilantro)
15ml/1 tbsp vegetable oil or
    sunflower oil
30ml/2 tbsp lemon juice

1 Line a flameproof dish or grill (broiler) tray with foil. Rinse and pat dry the flatfish fillets and place them, slightly spaced, on the foil-lined dish or tray.

2 In a small bowl, mix together the crushed garlic, garam masala, chilli powder, turmeric, salt, chopped fresh coriander, vegetable oil and lemon juice.

3 Using a pastry brush, baste the fish fillets evenly all over with the spice and lemon juice mixture.

4 Preheat the grill to very hot, then lower the heat to medium. Grill (broil) the fillets for about 10 minutes, basting occasionally, until they are cooked right through.

5 Serve immediately with an attractive garnish, such as grated carrot, tomato quarters and lime slices, if you wish.

Variation
This recipe can also be used to cook other firm white fish fillets such as cod and haddock. Check that the fish is cooked by testing with a fork – the flesh should flake easily when it is cooked through; and be careful not to overcook.

John Dory Energy 333kcal/1391kJ; Protein 34.9g; Carbohydrate 12.5g, of which sugars 11.5g; Fat 16.3g, of which saturates 4.9g; Cholesterol 13mg; Calcium 102mg; Fibre 2.6g; Sodium 291mg.
Fillet of Fish Energy 218kcal/917kJ; Protein 22.8g; Carbohydrate 11.4g, of which sugars 4.3g; Fat 9.5g, of which saturates 1.2g; Cholesterol 41mg; Calcium 36mg; Fibre 0.2g; Sodium 344mg.

Jamaican Fish Curry

This recipe uses some of the most common spices used in Caribbean cuisine. The taste in that region is for strong, pungent flavours rather than fiery heat.

Serves 4
2 halibut steaks, total weight about 500–675g/1¼–1½lb
30ml/2 tbsp groundnut (peanut) oil
2 cardamom pods
1 cinnamon stick
6 allspice berries
4 cloves
1 large onion, chopped
3 garlic cloves, crushed

10–15ml/2–3 tsp grated fresh root ginger
10ml/2 tsp ground cumin
5ml/1 tsp ground coriander
2.5ml/½ tsp cayenne pepper
4 tomatoes, peeled, seeded and chopped
1 sweet potato, about 225g/8oz, cut into 2cm/¾in cubes
475ml/16fl oz/2 cups fish stock or water
115g/4oz piece of creamed coconut or 120ml/4fl oz/½ cup coconut cream
1 bay leaf
225g/8oz/generous 1 cup white long grain rice
salt

1 Rub the halibut steaks well with salt and set aside.

2 Heat the oil in a heavy pan and stir-fry the cardamom pods, cinnamon stick, allspice berries and cloves for about 3 minutes.

3 Add the onion, garlic and ginger. Continue cooking for about 4–5 minutes over low heat until the onion is soft.

4 Add the cumin, coriander and cayenne pepper and cook briefly, stirring all the time. Stir in the tomatoes, sweet potato, fish stock or water, coconut and bay leaf. Season with salt. Bring to the boil, then lower the heat, cover and cook for 15 minutes.

5 Cook the rice according to your preferred method. Meanwhile, add the halibut to the pan of sauce and spoon the sauce over to cover them. Cover the pan and simmer gently for 10 minutes until the fish is tender and flakes easily.

6 Spoon the rice into a warmed serving dish, spoon over the curry sauce and arrange the halibut steaks on top and serve.

Spicy Fish Curry with Tamarind

The addition of tamarind to this curry gives a slightly sour note to the spicy coconut sauce.

Serves 4
7.5ml/1½ tsp ground turmeric
5ml/1 tsp salt
450g/1lb monkfish fillet, cut into eight pieces
15ml/1 tbsp lemon juice
5ml/1 tsp cumin seeds
5ml/1 tsp coriander seeds
5ml/1 tsp black peppercorns
1 garlic clove, chopped

5cm/2in piece fresh root ginger, finely chopped
25g/1oz tamarind paste
150ml/¼ pint/⅔ cup hot water
30ml/2 tbsp vegetable oil
2 onions, halved and sliced lengthways
400ml/14fl oz/1⅔ cups coconut milk
4 mild green chillies, seeded and cut into thin strips
16 large prawns (shrimp), peeled
30ml/2 tbsp chopped fresh coriander (cilantro) leaves, to garnish

1 Mix together the ground turmeric and salt in a bowl. Place the fish in a shallow dish and sprinkle over the lemon juice, then rub the turmeric mixture over the fish. Cover and chill.

2 Put the cumin and coriander seeds and peppercorns in a blender or food processor and blend to a powder. Add the garlic and ginger and process for a few seconds more.

3 Preheat the oven to 200°C/400°F/Gas 6. Mix the tamarind paste and hot water and set aside. Heat the oil in a frying pan, add the onions and cook for 5–6 minutes, until softened and golden. Transfer the onions to a shallow ovenproof dish. Add the fish to the pan, and fry over a high heat, turning to seal on all sides. Remove from the pan and place on top of the onions.

4 Fry the ground spice mixture in the pan, stirring constantly, for 1–2 minutes. Stir in the tamarind liquid, coconut milk and chilli strips then bring to the boil. Pour over the fish.

5 Cover the dish and cook in the oven for 10 minutes. Add the prawns, and cook for a further 5 minutes, or until the prawns are pink. Do not overcook them or they will toughen. Check the seasoning, sprinkle with coriander leaves and serve.

Jamaican Curry Energy 639kcal/2669kJ; Protein 34.2g; Carbohydrate 62g, of which sugars 8.3g; Fat 28.4g, of which saturates 18.7g; Cholesterol 44mg; Calcium 74mg; Fibre 2.4g; Sodium 115mg.
Spicy Fish Curry Energy 220kcal/926kJ; Protein 28g; Carbohydrate 12.8g, of which sugars 10.5g; Fat 6.8g, of which saturates 1g; Cholesterol 113mg; Calcium 103mg; Fibre 1.4g; Sodium 720mg.

Spiced Halibut Curry with a Rich Tomato Sauce

The chunky cubes of white fish contrast beautifully with the rich red spicy tomato sauce and taste just as good as they look.

Serves 4
60ml/4 tbsp lemon juice
60ml/4 tbsp rice wine vinegar
30ml/2 tbsp cumin seeds
5ml/1 tsp turmeric
5ml/1 tsp chilli powder
5ml/1 tsp salt
750g/1lb 11oz thick halibut
   fillets, skinned and cubed
60ml/4 tbsp sunflower oil
1 onion, finely chopped
3 garlic cloves, finely chopped
30ml/2 tbsp finely grated
   fresh root ginger
10ml/2 tsp black mustard seeds
2 x 400g/14oz cans
   chopped tomatoes
5ml/1 tsp sugar
chopped coriander (cilantro) leaves
   and sliced green chilli, to garnish
basmati rice, pickles and
   poppadums, to serve
natural (plain) yogurt,
   to drizzle (optional)

1 Mix together the lemon juice, vinegar, cumin, turmeric, chilli powder and salt in a shallow non-metallic bowl. Add the cubed fish and turn to coat evenly. Cover and put in the refrigerator to marinate for 25–30 minutes.

2 Meanwhile, heat a wok or large frying pan over high heat and add the oil. When hot, add the onion, garlic, ginger and mustard seeds. Reduce the heat to low and cook very gently for about 10 minutes, stirring occasionally.

3 Add the tomatoes and sugar to the pan, bring to the boil, reduce the heat, cover the pan and cook gently for about 15–20 minutes, stirring occasionally.

4 Add the fish and its marinade to the pan, stir gently to mix, then cover and simmer gently for 15–20 minutes, or until the fish is cooked through and the flesh flakes easily with a fork.

5 Serve the curry ladled into shallow bowls with basmati rice, pickles and poppadums. Garnish with fresh coriander and green chillies, and drizzle over some natural yogurt, if you like.

Curried Halibut Steaks with Lemon, Red Chilli and Coriander

Succulent fish steaks are first marinated in herbs and spices then cooked in a tasty stock with chillies and coriander, and served with a red onion topping.

Serves 4
4 halibut or cod steaks, about
   175g/6oz each
juice of 1 lemon
5ml/1 tsp garlic granules
5ml/1 tsp paprika
5ml/1 tsp ground cumin
5ml/1 tsp dried tarragon
about 60ml/4 tbsp olive oil
flour, for dusting
300ml/½ pint/1¼ cups fish stock
2 red chillies, seeded and
   finely chopped
30ml/2 tbsp chopped fresh
   coriander (cilantro)
1 red onion, cut into rings
salt and ground black pepper

1 Place the fish in a shallow bowl. Mix together the lemon juice, garlic, paprika, cumin, tarragon and a little salt and pepper.

2 Spoon the lemon mixture over the fish, cover loosely with clear film (plastic wrap) and set aside to marinate for a few hours or overnight in the refrigerator.

3 Gently heat 45ml/3 tbsp olive oil in a large non-stick frying pan, dust the fish with flour and then fry the fish for a few minutes each side, until golden brown all over.

4 Pour the fish stock around the fish, and then simmer gently, covered, for about 5 minutes, stirring occasionally until the fish is thoroughly cooked through.

5 Add the chopped red chillies and 15ml/1 tbsp of the coriander to the pan. Simmer for 5 minutes.

6 Carefully transfer the fish steaks to a serving plate. Spoon the sauce over the fish and keep warm.

7 Wipe the pan, heat 15ml/1 tbsp olive oil and stir-fry the onion rings for 1–2 minutes. Sprinkle over the fish with the remaining chopped coriander and serve immediately.

Halibut Curry Energy 335kcal/1409kJ; Protein 41.9g; Carbohydrate 8.4g, of which sugars 8.1g; Fat 15.2g, of which saturates 2.1g; Cholesterol 66mg; Calcium 73mg; Fibre 2.2g; Sodium 622mg.
Halibut Steaks Energy 265kcal/1106kJ; Protein 33g; Carbohydrate 5.4g, of which sugars 1.2g; Fat 12.5g, of which saturates 1.8g; Cholesterol 81mg; Calcium 47mg; Fibre 0.9g; Sodium 109mg.

Monkfish with Tomatoes and Spices

This spicy fish stew makes a really delicious lunch or light supper dish.

Serves 4
8 tomatoes
675g/1½lb monkfish
30ml/2 tbsp plain (all-purpose) flour
5ml/1 tsp ground coriander
2.5ml/½ tsp ground turmeric
25g/1oz/2 tbsp butter
2 garlic cloves, finely chopped
15–30ml/1–2 tbsp olive oil
40g/1½oz/4 tbsp pine nuts, toasted
1 preserved lemon, cut into pieces
12 black olives, pitted
salt and ground black pepper
whole slices of preserved lemon and chopped fresh parsley, to garnish

1 Peel the tomatoes by placing them briefly in boiling water, then cold water. Quarter the tomatoes, remove the cores and seeds and discard. Chop the tomato flesh roughly.

2 Cut the fish into bitesize chunks. Blend together the flour, coriander and turmeric, and season with salt and pepper to taste. Dust the fish with the seasoned flour and set aside.

3 Melt the butter in a non-stick frying pan and fry the tomatoes and garlic over low heat for 6–8 minutes, until the tomato mixture is very thick and most of the liquid has evaporated.

4 Push the tomatoes to the edge of the frying pan, moisten the pan with a little olive oil and fry the monkfish pieces in a single layer over medium heat for 3–5 minutes, turning frequently. You may have to do this in batches, so as the first batch cooks, place them on top of the tomatoes and fry the remaining fish, adding a little more oil to the pan, if necessary.

5 When all the fish is cooked, add the pine nuts and stir, scraping the bottom of the pan to remove the glazed tomatoes. The sauce should be thick and slightly charred in places.

6 Rinse the preserved lemon in cold water, discard the pulp and cut the peel into strips. Stir into the sauce with the olives, adjust the seasoning and serve garnished with whole slices of preserved lemon and parsley.

Tagine of Monkfish

The fish is marinated in chermoula, a lemony garlic and coriander paste. Monkfish is robust enough to handle the spices and the result is a very tasty dish.

Serves 4
900g/2lb monkfish, cut into chunks
15–20 small new potatoes
45–60ml/3–4 tbsp olive oil
4–5 garlic cloves, thinly sliced
15–20 cherry tomatoes
2 green (bell) peppers, grilled (broiled) until black, skinned, seeded and cut into strips
large handful of fleshy black olives, pits in
100ml/3½fl oz/scant ½ cup water
salt and ground black pepper
fresh bread, to serve

For the chermoula
2 garlic cloves
5ml/1 tsp coarse salt
10ml/2 tsp ground cumin
5ml/1 tsp paprika
small bunch of fresh coriander (cilantro), roughly chopped
juice of 1 lemon
15ml/1 tbsp olive oil

1 For the chermoula: pound the garlic and salt to a paste in a mortar and pestle. Add the cumin, paprika, coriander and lemon juice, and mix in the oil, reserving a little oil for cooking. Rub the chermoula over the monkfish. Cover and set aside for 1 hour.

2 Par-boil the potatoes for 10 minutes. Drain, then cut them in half lengthways. Heat the oil in a heavy pan and cook the garlic for 2–3 minutes. Add the tomatoes and cook until just softened.

3 Add the peppers to the tomatoes and garlic, together with the remaining chermoula, and season to taste.

4 Spread the potatoes over the base of a tagine or a deep frying pan. Spoon three-quarters of the tomato mixture over and place the marinated fish chunks on top, with the chermoula.

5 Spoon the rest of the tomato mixture on top of the fish and add the olives. Drizzle a little oil over the dish and add the water.

6 Heat until simmering, cover and cook over a medium heat for about 15 minutes, until the fish is cooked through. Serve with fresh, warm crusty bread to mop up the delicious juices.

Monkfish with Tomatoes Energy 306kcal/1283kJ; Protein 29g; Carbohydrate 5.1g, of which sugars 5.1g; Fat 19.1g, of which saturates 5g; Cholesterol 38mg; Calcium 29mg; Fibre 1.8g; Sodium 203mg.
Tagine of Monkfish Energy 406kcal/1710kJ; Protein 39.6g; Carbohydrate 25.2g, of which sugars 6.5g; Fat 17.1g, of which saturates 2.7g; Cholesterol 32mg; Calcium 98mg; Fibre 5.4g; Sodium 915mg.

Burmese Fish Stew

This tasty seafood curry originated in Burma but has also proved enticingly popular farther afield.

Serves 8

675g/1½lb huss, cod or mackerel,
   cleaned but left on the bone
3 lemon grass stalks
2.5cm/1in piece fresh root ginger
30ml/2 tbsp fish sauce
3 onions, roughly chopped
4 garlic cloves, roughly chopped
2–3 fresh red chillies, seeded
   and chopped
5ml/1 tsp ground turmeric
75ml/5 tbsp groundnut (peanut)
   oil, for frying
400g/14oz can coconut milk
25g/1oz/¼ cup rice flour
25g/1oz/¼ cup gram flour
540g/1lb 5oz canned bamboo
   shoots, rinsed, drained and sliced
salt and ground black pepper
wedges of hard-boiled egg, thinly
   sliced red onions, chopped
   spring onions (scallions),
   deep-fried prawns (shrimp)
   and fried chillies, to garnish
rice noodles, to serve

1 Place the fish in a large pan and pour in cold water to cover. Bruise two lemon grass stalks and half the ginger and add to the pan. Bring to the boil, add the fish sauce and cook for 10 minutes. Lift out the fish with a slotted spoon, and allow to cool. Meanwhile, strain the stock into a bowl. Discard any skin and bones from the fish and break the flesh into small pieces.

2 Cut off the lower 5cm/2in of the remaining lemon grass stalk and discard; roughly chop the remaining lemon grass. Place in a food processor or blender, along with the remaining ginger, the onions, garlic, chillies and turmeric. Process to a paste. Heat the oil in a wok or large pan, and fry the paste for 2 minutes. Remove the pan from the heat and add the fish pieces.

3 Stir the coconut milk into the reserved stock and pour into a large pan. Add water to make up to 2.5 litres/4 pints/10 cups. In a jug (pitcher), mix the rice flour and gram flour to a thin cream with some stock. Stir into the mixture. Bring to the boil, stirring.

4 Add the bamboo shoots to the pan and cook for 10 minutes. Stir in the fish mixture, season to taste, and cook until heated through. Guests pour the soup over the noodles, and add the egg, onions, spring onions, prawns and chillies as a garnish.

Fish Moolie

This is a very popular South-east Asian fish curry in a coconut sauce, which is truly delicious. Choose a firm-textured fish so that the pieces stay intact during the brief cooking process. Monkfish, halibut or cod work well in this dish.

Serves 4

500g/1¼lb monkfish or other
   firm-textured fish fillets, skinned
   and cut into 2.5cm/1in cubes
2.5ml/½ tsp salt
50g/2oz/⅔ cup desiccated (dry
   unsweetened shredded) coconut
6 shallots, chopped
6 blanched almonds
2–3 garlic cloves, roughly chopped
2.5cm/1in piece fresh root
   ginger, peeled and sliced
2 lemon grass stalks, trimmed
10ml/2 tsp ground turmeric
45ml/3 tbsp vegetable oil
2 × 400ml/14fl oz cans
   coconut milk
1–3 fresh red chillies, seeded
   and sliced into rings
salt and ground black pepper
fresh chives, to garnish
plain boiled or steamed basmati
   rice, to serve

1 Put the fish cubes in a shallow dish and sprinkle with the salt. Dry fry the coconut in a wok, turning all the time until it is crisp and golden, then transfer into a food processor and process to an oily paste. Scrape into a bowl and reserve.

2 Add the shallots, almonds, garlic and ginger to the food processor. Chop the bulbous part of each lemon grass stalk and add to the processor with the turmeric. Process the mixture to a paste. Bruise the remaining lemon grass stalks.

3 Heat the oil in a wok. Cook the shallot and spice mixture for about 2–3 minutes. Stir in the coconut milk and bring to the boil, stirring. Add the fish, most of the chilli and the lemon grass stalks. Cook for 3–4 minutes.

4 Stir in the coconut paste and cook for a further 2–3 minutes only. Adjust the seasoning.

5 Remove the lemon grass. Transfer the moolie to a hot serving dish and sprinkle with the remaining slices of chilli. Garnish with chopped and whole chives and serve with rice.

Burmese Fish Stew Energy 344kcal/1436kJ; Protein 23.3g; Carbohydrate 18.5g, of which sugars 4g; Fat 18.3g, of which saturates 10.8g; Cholesterol 135mg; Calcium 87mg; Fibre 2.5g; Sodium 146mg.
Fish Moolie Energy 319kcal/1335kJ; Protein 22.4g; Carbohydrate 16.7g, of which sugars 14.9g; Fat 18.6g, of which saturates 8.3g; Cholesterol 18mg; Calcium 96mg; Fibre 3g; Sodium 249mg.

Green Fish Curry

A delicious paste of fresh coriander, tamarind, root ginger, shallots and chilli is used to marinate the fish in this recipe, creating a refreshing taste.

Serves 4
675g/1½lb fillet of cod, haddock
   or other white fish
2 shallots, roughly chopped
25g/1oz/2 tbsp fresh root ginger,
   roughly chopped
2–4 fresh green chillies, roughly
   chopped and seeded
15g/½oz/¼ cup coriander
   (cilantro) leaves and stalks,
   roughly chopped
5ml/1 tsp tamarind mixed with
   10ml/2 tsp water and strained
   or 30ml/2 tbsp lemon juice
5ml/1 tsp salt, or to taste
75g/3oz/⅔ cup gram flour, sifted
vegetable oil or sunflower oil,
   for deep-frying
plain boiled rice, to serve

1 Wash the fish gently under running water and pat dry with absorbent kitchen paper. Cut into 5cm/2in pieces. Place the fish pieces in a large mixing bowl.

2 Process the shallots, ginger, chillies, coriander, tamarind or lemon juice and salt in a food processor or blender. Add the blended ingredients to the fish, and using a metal spoon, mix gently, but thoroughly. Set aside for about 30 minutes.

3 Add the sifted gram flour and 30–45ml/2–3 tbsp water, if necessary, and mix thoroughly until the fish is coated with the paste. You can add a little more water if the paste is not wet enough, to ensure the fish is coated thoroughly.

4 Heat the oil in a wok or other suitable pan for deep-frying over medium to high heat, then fry the fish in batches for about 2½ minutes on each side until it is a golden brown colour. Drain the fried fish on absorbent kitchen paper and serve with any vegetable or lentil dish, accompanied by plain boiled rice.

Variation
Serve these spicy fish pieces with chunky chips (French fries) for a meal of 'fish and chips', Indian style.

Cod in a Spicy Mushroom Sauce

Serves 4
4 cod fillets, skinned and boned
15ml/1 tbsp lemon juice
15ml/1 tbsp vegetable oil
1 medium onion, chopped
1 bay leaf
4 black peppercorns, crushed
115g/4oz/1 cup mushrooms
175ml/6fl oz/¾ cup yogurt
5ml/1 tsp grated fresh root ginger
5ml/1 tsp crushed garlic
2.5ml/½ tsp garam masala
2.5ml/½ tsp chilli powder
5ml/1 tsp salt
15ml/1 tbsp fresh coriander
   (cilantro) leaves, to garnish
cooked green beans, to serve

1 Preheat the grill (broiler). Sprinkle the cod fillets with lemon juice, then par-cook under the grill for 5 minutes on each side. Remove the fillets from the heat and set aside.

2 Heat the oil in a karahi or wok and fry the onion with the bay leaf and peppercorns for 2–3 minutes. Lower the heat, add the whole mushrooms and stir-fry for a further 4–5 minutes.

3 In a bowl mix the yogurt, ginger, garlic, garam masala, chilli and salt. Pour over the onions and mushrooms and stir-fry for 3 minutes.

4 Add the cod to the sauce and cook for 2 minutes. Serve garnished with coriander and accompanied by green beans.

Curried Cod in a Tomato Sauce

Serves 4
30ml/2 tbsp cornflour (cornstarch)
5ml/1 tsp salt
5ml/1 tsp garlic powder
5ml/1 tsp chilli powder
5ml/1 tsp ground ginger
5ml/1 tsp ground fennel seeds
5ml/1 tsp ground coriander
2 medium cod fillets, cut in half
15ml/1 tbsp vegetable oil

For the sauce
30ml/2 tbsp tomato purée (paste)
5ml/1 tsp garam masala
5ml/1 tsp chilli powder
5ml/1 tsp crushed garlic
5ml/1 tsp grated fresh root ginger
2.5ml/½ tsp salt
175ml/6fl oz/¾ cup water
15ml/1 tbsp vegetable oil
1 bay leaf
3 or 4 black peppercorns
1cm/½in piece cinnamon stick
15ml/1 tbsp chopped fresh
   coriander (cilantro)
15ml/1 tbsp chopped fresh
   mint leaves
mashed potatoes, to serve

1 Mix the cornflour, salt, garlic, chilli, ginger, fennel and coriander. Use to coat the four cod pieces. Preheat the grill (broiler) to very hot, then reduce the heat slightly and place the cod under the heat. After 5 minutes spoon the oil over the cod. Turn the cod over. Cook for 5 minutes, check that the fish is cooked through and set aside.

2 Make the sauce by mixing together the tomato purée, garam masala, chilli powder, garlic, ginger, salt and water. Set aside.

3 Heat the oil in a wok and add the bay leaf, peppercorns and cinnamon. Add the sauce and reduce the heat to low. Bring slowly to the boil, stirring, then simmer for about 5 minutes. Add the pieces of fish and cook for a further 2 minutes. Add the coriander and mint and serve with mashed potatoes.

Green Fish Curry Energy 357kcal/1490kJ; Protein 35g; Carbohydrate 13.6g, of which sugars 1.6g; Fat 18.3g, of which saturates 2.2g; Cholesterol 81mg; Calcium 55.8mg; Fibre 2.6g; Sodium 116mg.
Cod in Mushroom Sauce Energy 202kcal/847kJ; Protein 31.7g; Carbohydrate 6.9g, of which sugars 3.4g; Fat 5.7g, of which saturates 0.9g; Cholesterol 70mg; Calcium 116mg; Fibre 0.3g; Sodium 131mg.
Curried Cod Energy 294kcal/1229kJ; Protein 41.8g; Carbohydrate 2.7g, of which sugars 2.7g; Fat 12.8g, of which saturates 1.9g; Cholesterol 104mg; Calcium 26mg; Fibre 0.9g; Sodium 143mg.

Tanzanian Fish Curry

With lakes on its western and northern borders, and the sea to the east, Tanzania has a rich inspiration for its fish dishes.

Serves 2–3

1 large snapper or red bream
1 lemon
45ml/3 tbsp vegetable oil
1 onion, finely chopped
2 garlic cloves, crushed
45ml/3 tbsp curry powder
400g/14oz can chopped tomatoes
20ml/1 heaped tbsp smooth peanut butter, preferably unsalted
½ green (bell) pepper, seeded and chopped
2 slices fresh root ginger, chopped
1 fresh green chilli, seeded and finely chopped
about 600ml/1 pint/2½ cups fish stock
15ml/1 tbsp finely chopped fresh coriander (cilantro)
salt and ground black pepper

1 Season the fish with salt and pepper and squeeze half a lemon over it. Cover, and leave in a cool place for 2 hours.

2 Heat the oil in a pan and fry the onion and garlic for about 5–6 minutes. Reduce the heat and stir in the curry powder.

3 Stir in the tomatoes and then the peanut butter, mixing well, then add the green pepper, ginger, chilli and stock. Stir well and simmer gently for 10 minutes.

4 Cut the fish into pieces and gently lower into the sauce. Simmer for a further 20 minutes or until the fish is cooked, then using a slotted spoon, transfer the fish pieces to a plate.

5 Stir the coriander into the sauce and adjust the seasoning. If the sauce is very thick, add a little stock or water. Return the fish to the sauce, heat through and then serve immediately.

> **Cook's Tip**
> The fish can be fried before adding to the sauce, if preferred. Dip in seasoned flour and fry in oil in a pan or a wok for a few minutes before adding to the sauce.

Fish Jalfrezi

In parts of India, fish curry and rice are eaten together on a daily basis. This dish, using canned tuna cooked in the style of jalfrezi, is packed into pitta bread instead.

Serves 4

45ml/3 tbsp vegetable oil
1.5ml/¼ tsp cumin seeds
2.5ml/½ tsp ground cumin
2.5ml/½ tsp ground coriander
2.5ml/½ tsp chilli powder
1.5ml/¼ tsp salt
2 garlic cloves, crushed
1 onion, sliced
1 red (bell) pepper, sliced
1 green (bell) pepper, sliced
400g/14oz can tuna, drained
1 fresh green chilli, finely chopped
2.5cm/1in piece fresh root ginger, grated
1.5ml/¼ tsp garam masala
5ml/1 tsp lemon juice
30ml/2 tbsp chopped fresh coriander (cilantro)
fresh coriander (cilantro) sprig, to garnish
pitta bread and cucumber raita, to serve

1 Heat the oil in a wok, karahi or large pan over medium heat and fry the cumin seeds for about 30–40 seconds until they begin to splutter and release their fragrance.

2 Add the ground cumin and coriander, chilli powder and salt to the pan. Cook for 2 minutes.

3 Add the garlic, onion and peppers and increase the heat a little. Stir-fry the vegetables for about 5–7 minutes until the onions have browned and softened.

4 Stir the tuna, fresh chilli and grated ginger into the pan and cook for 5 minutes more.

5 Add the garam masala, lemon juice and fresh coriander and continue to cook for a further 3–4 minutes. Serve in warmed pitta bread with the raita, garnished with fresh coriander.

> **Cook's Tip**
> Place the pitta bread on a grill (broiler) rack and cook until it puffs up. It will then be easy to split with a sharp knife.

Tanzanian Curry Energy 483kcal/2020kJ; Protein 44.5g; Carbohydrate 12.8g, of which sugars 10.9g; Fat 28.7g, of which saturates 3.7g; Cholesterol 86mg; Calcium 129mg; Fibre 3.2g; Sodium 364mg.
Fish Jalfrezi Energy 144kcal/598kJ; Protein 3g; Carbohydrate 11.4g, of which sugars 7g; Fat 10.1g, of which saturates 1.1g; Cholesterol 0mg; Calcium 56mg; Fibre 2.4g; Sodium 12mg.

Balti Fried Fish

Pieces of succulent white fish are coated in a spicy marinade before being pan-fried. This dish is delicious served with pungent chutneys and Indian breads.

Serves 4–6

675g/1½lb cod, or any other firm, white fish
1 medium onion, sliced
15ml/1 tbsp lemon juice
5ml/1 tsp salt
5ml/1 tsp garlic pulp
5ml/1 tsp crushed dried red chillies
7.5ml/1½ tsp garam masala
30ml/2 tbsp chopped fresh coriander (cilantro)
2 medium tomatoes
30ml/2 tbsp cornflour (cornstarch)
150ml/¼ pint/⅔ cup corn oil

1 Skin the fish and cut the flesh into small cubes. Put the fish pieces into the refrigerator to chill.

2 Put the onion into a bowl and add the lemon juice, salt, garlic, crushed red chillies, garam masala and fresh coriander. Mix together well and set to one side.

3 Skin the tomatoes by dropping them into boiling water for a few seconds. Remove with a slotted spoon and gently peel off the skins. Chop the tomatoes roughly and add to the onion mixture in the bowl. Place the contents of the bowl into a food processor or blender and process for about 30 seconds.

4 Remove the fish from the refrigerator. Pour the contents of the food processor or blender over the fish and mix together well to coat the fish evenly. Add the cornflour and mix again until the fish pieces are well coated.

5 Heat the oil in a karahi or deep frying pan. Lower the heat slightly and add the fish pieces, a few at a time. Turn them gently with a slotted spoon as they will break easily. Cook for about 5 minutes until the fish is lightly browned.

6 Remove the fish pieces from the pan and drain on kitchen paper to absorb any excess oil. Keep warm and continue frying the remaining fish. Serve the fish immediately with a selection of Indian chutneys and breads.

Masala-stuffed Fish

Serves 4

2 large pomfrets
10ml/2 tsp salt
juice of 1 lemon

For the masala

115g/4oz/1⅓ cups desiccated (dry unsweetened shredded) coconut
115g/4oz/4 cups fresh coriander (cilantro), including the stalks
8 fresh green chillies, or to taste
5ml/1 tsp cumin seeds
6 garlic cloves
10ml/2 tsp sugar
10ml/2 tsp lemon juice

1 Scale the fish and cut off the fins. Gut the fish and remove the heads, if you wish. Using a sharp knife, make two diagonal gashes on each side, then pat dry with kitchen paper.

2 Rub the fish inside and out with salt and lemon juice. Cover and leave to stand in a cool place for about 1 hour. Pat dry.

3 For the masala, grind all the ingredients together using a pestle and mortar or food processor.

4 Stuff the fish with most of the masala mixture. Rub the rest into the gashes and all over the fish on both sides.

5 Place each fish on a separate piece of greased foil. Tightly wrap the foil over each fish. Place in a steamer and steam for 20 minutes, or bake in a preheated oven for 30 minutes at 200°C/400°F/Gas 6 or until cooked. Remove the fish from the foil and serve immediately.

Pan-fried Spicy Fish with Cumin and Chilli

Serves 4–6

1 small onion, coarsely chopped
4 garlic cloves, crushed
5cm/2in piece fresh root ginger, chopped
5ml/1 tsp ground turmeric
10ml/2 tsp chilli powder
4 red mullets or snappers
vegetable oil, for shallow-frying
5ml/1 tsp cumin seeds
3 fresh green chillies, seeded and finely sliced
salt
lemon or lime wedges, to serve

1 In a food processor or blender, grind the first five ingredients with a pinch of salt to a smooth paste.

2 Make several slashes on both sides of the fish and rub them with the paste. Leave to rest for 1 hour. Pat the fish dry with kitchen paper without removing the paste.

3 Heat the oil in a large frying pan and fry the cumin seeds and sliced chillies for 1 minute, stirring constantly, until the seeds begin to release their fragrant aroma.

4 Add the fish to the pan, in a couple of batches if necessary, and fry on one side. When the first side is sealed, turn them over very gently with a fish slice or metal spatula to ensure they do not break. Fry until golden brown on both sides, drain and serve immediately, with lemon or lime wedges.

Balti Fried Fish 369kcal/1539kJ; Protein 36.2g; Carbohydrate 6.7g, of which sugars 3.2g; Fat 22.2g, of which saturates 3.7g; Cholesterol 94mg; Calcium 46mg; Fibre 1.4g; Sodium 370mg.
Masala-stuffed Fish Energy 305kcal/1267kJ; Protein 25.1g; Carbohydrate 5.2g, of which sugars 5.1g; Fat 20.5g, of which saturates 15.4g; Cholesterol 63mg; Calcium 102mg; Fibre 5.4g; Sodium 143mg.
Pan-fried Spicy Fish Energy 122kcal/509kJ; Protein 10.7g; Carbohydrate 1.3g, of which sugars 1.1g; Fat 8.3g, of which saturates 0.7g; Cholesterol 0mg; Calcium 42mg; Fibre 0.3g; Sodium 55mg.

Curried Fish with Pine Nuts

For this delicious dish, a whole fish is cooked in a mildly spiced tomato sauce with peppers and chillies and finished with a handful of toasted pine nuts.

Serves 6–8

1–1.5kg/2¼–3¼lb fish, such as snapper, cleaned, with head and tail left on (optional)
2.5ml/½ tsp salt
juice of 2 lemons
45–60ml/3–4 tbsp extra virgin olive oil
2 onions, sliced
5 garlic cloves, chopped
1 green (bell) pepper, seeded and chopped
1–2 fresh green chillies, seeded and finely chopped
2.5ml/½ tsp ground turmeric
2.5ml/½ tsp curry powder
2.5ml/½ tsp ground cumin
120ml/4fl oz/½ cup passata (bottled strained tomatoes)
5–6 fresh or canned tomatoes, chopped
45–60ml/3–4 tbsp chopped fresh coriander (cilantro) leaves and/or parsley
65g/2½oz pine nuts, toasted
few sprigs of fresh parsley, to garnish

1 Prick the fish all over with a fork and rub with the salt. Place the fish in a roasting pan or dish and pour over the lemon juice. Leave to stand for 2 hours.

2 Preheat the oven to 180°C/350°F/Gas 4. Heat the oil in a heavy pan, add the onions and half the garlic and fry for about 5 minutes, or until they have softened.

3 Add the pepper, chillies, turmeric, curry powder and cumin to the pan and cook gently for a further 2–3 minutes. Stir in the passata, tomatoes and herbs.

4 Sprinkle half of the pine nuts over the base of an ovenproof dish, top with half of the sauce, then add the fish and marinade.

5 Sprinkle the remaining garlic over the fish, then add the remaining sauce and the remaining pine nuts.

6 Cover the dish tightly with a lid or foil and bake in the oven for 30 minutes, or until the fish is tender. Garnish with the sprigs of parsley and serve immediately.

Spicy Fish Tagine

This aromatic one-pot dish proves how good fish can be. Serve with couscous, which can be steamed over the cooking pot.

Serves 8

1.3kg/3lb firm fish fillets, skinned and cut into 5cm/2in chunks
60ml/4 tbsp olive oil
1 large aubergine (eggplant), cut into 1cm/½in cubes
2 courgettes (zucchini), cut into 1cm/½in cubes
4 onions, chopped
400g/14oz can chopped tomatoes
400ml/14fl oz/1⅔ cups passata (bottled strained tomatoes)
200ml/7fl oz/scant 1 cup fish stock
1 preserved lemon, chopped
90g/3½oz/scant 1 cup olives
60ml/4 tbsp chopped fresh coriander (cilantro), plus extra whole leaves to garnish
salt and ground black pepper

For the harissa

3 large fresh red chillies, seeded and chopped
3 garlic cloves, peeled
15ml/1 tbsp ground coriander
30ml/2 tbsp ground cumin
5ml/1 tsp ground cinnamon
grated rind of 1 lemon
30ml/2 tbsp sunflower oil or vegetable oil

1 Make the harissa. Blend everything in a food processor to a smooth paste. Put the fish in a wide bowl and add 30ml/2 tbsp of the harissa. Toss to coat, cover and chill for at least 1 hour.

2 Heat half the oil in a heavy pan. Add the aubergine cubes and fry for 10 minutes, or until they are golden brown. Add the courgettes and fry for 2 minutes. Remove the vegetables from the pan using a slotted spoon and set aside.

3 Add the remaining oil to the pan, add the onions and cook gently for about 10 minutes until golden brown. Stir in the remaining harissa and cook for 5 minutes, stirring occasionally.

4 Add the vegetables to the pan, then stir in the tomatoes, the passata and stock. Bring to the boil, then simmer for 20 minutes.

5 Stir the fish chunks and preserved lemon into the pan. Add the olives. Cover and simmer over low heat for 15–20 minutes. Season to taste with salt and pepper. Stir in the coriander. Serve with couscous, if you like, and garnish with coriander leaves.

Curried Fish Energy 195kcal/815kJ; Protein 14.3g; Carbohydrate 6.7g, of which sugars 5.8g; Fat 12.6g, of which saturates 1g; Cholesterol 0mg; Calcium 62mg; Fibre 1.6g; Sodium 104mg.
Spicy Fish Tagine Energy 263kcal/1099kJ; Protein 32.3g; Carbohydrate 8.3g, of which sugars 7g; Fat 11.3g, of which saturates 1.7g; Cholesterol 75mg; Calcium 57mg; Fibre 3.2g; Sodium 360mg.

Chunky Fish Balti with Peppers

Try to find peppers in different colours to make this wonderful dish as colourful as possible.

Serves 2–4
450g/1lb cod, or any other firm
   white fish, such as haddock
7.5ml/1½ tsp ground cumin
10ml/2 tsp mango powder
   (amchur)
5ml/1 tsp ground coriander
2.5ml/½ tsp chilli powder
5ml/1 tsp salt
5ml/1 tsp grated fresh
   root ginger
45ml/3 tbsp cornflour
   (cornstarch)
150ml/¼ pint/⅔ cup corn oil
1 each green, orange and red
   (bell) peppers, seeded
   and chopped
8–10 cherry tomatoes

1 Skin the fish and cut it into small cubes. Put the cubes in a large mixing bowl and add the ground cumin, mango powder, ground coriander, chilli powder, salt, grated ginger and cornflour. Mix together thoroughly until the fish is well coated with the spice mix.

2 Heat the oil in a karahi, wok or large, deep pan. Lower the heat slightly and add the fish pieces, three or four at a time. Fry for about 3 minutes, turning constantly.

3 Drain the cooked fish pieces on kitchen paper and transfer to a serving dish. Keep the cooked fish warm in a low oven while you fry the remaining fish pieces.

4 Fry the chopped peppers in the oil remaining in the pan for about 4–5 minutes. The pieces of pepper should still be slightly crisp. Drain well on kitchen paper.

5 Add the cooked peppers to the fish and garnish with the cherry tomatoes. Serve immediately.

Cook's Tip
Amchur is an Indian seasoning made by grinding dried unripe mangoes into a powder and is used to add sourness.

Vietnamese Fried Fish with Dill

In this classic dish from Vietnam, the dill is just as important as the fish, and they complement each other beautifully. A simple accompaniment of plain rice or noodles is all that is needed to make an impressive meal.

Serves 4
75g/3oz/⅔ cup rice flour
7.5ml/1½ tsp ground turmeric
500g/1¼lb white fish fillets, such
   as cod, skinned and cut into
   bitesize chunks
vegetable oil, for deep-frying
1 large bunch fresh dill
15ml/1 tbsp groundnut
   (peanut) oil
30ml/2 tbsp roasted peanuts
4 spring onions (scallions), cut
   into bitesize pieces
1 small bunch of fresh basil,
   stalks removed, leaves
   finely chopped
1 small bunch of fresh coriander
   (cilantro), stalks removed
1 lime, cut into quarters, and
   nuoc cham (Vietnamese fish
   sauce), to serve

1 Mix the flour with the turmeric and toss the fish chunks in it until well coated. Heat the oil in a wok or heavy pan and cook the fish in batches until crisp and golden. Drain the cooked fish well on kitchen paper.

2 Sprinkle some of the dill fronds on a serving dish, arrange the fish on top and keep warm. Chop some of the remaining dill fronds and set aside for the garnish.

3 Heat the groundnut oil in a small pan or wok. Stir in the peanuts and cook for 1 minute, then add the spring onions, the remaining dill fronds, basil and coriander. Stir-fry for no more than 30 seconds, then spoon the herbs and peanuts over the fish. Garnish with the chopped dill and serve with lime wedges and nuoc cham to drizzle over the top.

Cook's Tip
Nuoc cham is a popular Vietnamese condiment and dipping sauce made from dried red chillies, garlic and sugar, mixed with water, fish sauce and lime juice.

Chunky Fish Balti Energy 296kcal/1236kJ; Protein 22.9g; Carbohydrate 22.9g, of which sugars 11.1g; Fat 13g, of which saturates 1.6g; Cholesterol 52mg; Calcium 51mg; Fibre 3.8g; Sodium 98mg
Vietnamese Fried Fish Energy 350kcal/1458kJ; Protein 27g; Carbohydrate 17g, of which sugars 1g; Fat 19g, of which saturates 3g; Cholesterol 85mg; Calcium 112mg; Fibre 1.2g; Sodium 0.2g.

Fish Fillets with a Chilli Sauce

Serves 4

4 flat-fish fillets, about 115g/4oz each
30ml/2 tbsp lemon juice
15ml/1 tbsp finely chopped fresh
   coriander (cilantro)
15ml/1 tbsp oil
lime wedges and a fresh
   coriander sprig, to garnish
yellow basmati rice, to serve

For the sauce

5ml/1 tsp grated fresh root ginger
30ml/2 tbsp tomato purée (paste)
5ml/1 tsp sugar
5ml/1 tsp salt
15ml/1 tbsp chilli sauce
15ml/1 tbsp malt vinegar
300ml/½ pint/1¼ cups water

1 Rinse and pat dry the fish fillets and place in a medium bowl. Add the lemon juice, coriander and oil and rub into the fish. Leave to marinate for at least 1 hour.

2 Make the sauce. Mix the grated ginger, tomato purée, sugar, salt and chilli sauce in a bowl. Stir in the vinegar and water. Pour into a small pan and simmer gently over a low heat for about 6 minutes, stirring occasionally.

3 Meanwhile, preheat the grill (broiler) to medium. Lift the fish out of the marinade and place in a grill pan. Grill (broil) for 5–7 minutes. When the fish is cooked, arrange it on a serving dish.

4 The chilli sauce should now be fairly thick – about the consistency of a thick chicken soup. Spoon the sauce over the fish fillets, garnish with the lime wedges and coriander sprig and serve immediately with yellow basmati rice.

Sour Carp with Tamarind and Basil

Serves 4

500g/1¼lb carp fillets, cut
   into 3 or 4 pieces
30ml/2 tbsp sesame oil
10ml/2 tsp ground turmeric
1 small bunch each fresh coriander
   (cilantro) and basil, stalks removed
20 lettuce leaves or rice
   paper wrappers
nuoc cham (Vietnamese fish sauce)
   or other dipping sauce, to serve

For the marinade

30ml/2 tbsp tamarind paste
15ml/1 tbsp soy sauce
juice of 1 lime
1 green or red Thai chilli, chopped
2.5cm/1in galangal root, peeled
   and grated
a few sprigs of fresh coriander
   (cilantro) leaves, finely chopped

1 Mix together all the marinade ingredients in a bowl. Toss the fish pieces in the marinade, cover with clear film (plastic wrap) and chill in the refrigerator for at least 6 hours, or overnight.

2 Lift the pieces of fish out of the marinade and lay them on a plate. Heat a wok, add the oil and stir in the turmeric. Working quickly, stir-fry the fish pieces, for 2–3 minutes. Add any remaining marinade to the pan and cook for a further 2–3 minutes.

3 To serve, divide the fish among four plates, sprinkle with the coriander and basil, and add some lettuce leaves or rice paper wrappers and a small bowl of dipping sauce to each serving. To eat, tear off a bitesize piece of fish, place it on a wrapper with a few herb leaves, fold it up into a roll, then dip it into the sauce.

Catfish with Spicy Coconut Sauce

In this popular dish, catfish is simply fried and served with a fragrant and spicy sauce. Serve with rice and pickled vegetables or a salad, with green mango or papaya.

Serves 4

200ml/7fl oz/scant 1 cup
   coconut milk
30–45ml/2–3 tbsp coconut cream
30–45ml/2–3 tbsp rice flour,
   tapioca flour or cornflour
   (cornstarch)
5–10ml/1–2 tsp ground coriander
8 fresh catfish fillets
30–45ml/2–3 tbsp coconut, palm,
   groundnut (peanut) or corn oil

salt and ground black pepper
1 lime, quartered, to serve

For the spice paste

2 shallots, chopped
2 garlic cloves, chopped
2–3 red chillies, seeded
   and chopped
25g/1oz galangal, chopped
15g/½oz fresh turmeric, chopped,
   or 2.5ml/½ tsp ground turmeric
2–3 lemon grass stalks, chopped
15–30ml/1–2 tbsp palm oil
   or groundnut (peanut) oil
5ml/1 tsp shrimp paste
15ml/1 tbsp tamarind paste
5ml/1 tsp palm sugar (jaggery)

1 First make the spice paste. Using a mortar and pestle or food processor, grind the shallots, garlic, chillies, galangal, turmeric and lemon grass to a coarse paste.

2 Heat the oil in a wok or heavy pan, stir in the paste and fry until it becomes fragrant. Add the shrimp paste, tamarind paste and sugar and continue to stir until the paste darkens.

3 Stir the coconut milk and coconut cream into the spice paste and boil the mixture for about 10 minutes, until the coconut milk and cream separate, leaving behind an oily fragrant paste. Season the sauce with salt and pepper to taste.

4 Meanwhile, on a large plate, mix the flours with the coriander and seasoning. Toss the fillets in the flour to coat.

5 Heat the oil in a heavy frying pan and quickly fry the fillets for about 2 minutes on each side, until golden brown. Transfer the fish to a warmed serving dish and serve with the spicy coconut sauce and wedges of lime to squeeze over the fish.

Fish Fillets Energy 162kcal/684kJ; Protein 26.8g; Carbohydrate 3.8g, of which sugars 3.7g; Fat 4.5g, of which saturates 1g; Cholesterol 75mg; Calcium 37mg; Fibre 0.8g; Sodium 708mg.
Sour Carp with Tamarind Energy 298kcal/1246kJ; Protein 24g; Carbohydrate 19g, of which sugars 5g; Fat 14g, of which saturates 2g; Cholesterol 121mg; Calcium 120mg; Fibre 0g; Sodium 300mg.
Catfish Energy 338kcal/1412kJ; Protein 38.1g; Carbohydrate 11.9g, of which sugars 4.9g; Fat 15.3g, of which saturates 5.7g; Cholesterol 92mg; Calcium 56mg; Fibre 0.9g; Sodium 190mg.

Indian Fish Stew

Cooking fish with vegetables is very much a tradition in eastern regions. This hearty dish with potatoes, peppers and tomatoes is perfect served with breads such as chapatis or parathas.

Serves 4
30ml/2 tbsp vegetable oil
5ml/1 tsp cumin seeds
1 onion, chopped
1 red (bell) pepper,
    thinly sliced
1 garlic clove, crushed
2 fresh red chillies, seeded and
    finely chopped
2 bay leaves
2.5ml/½ tsp salt
5ml/1 tsp ground cumin
5ml/1 tsp ground coriander
5ml/1 tsp chilli powder
400g/14oz can chopped
    tomatoes
2 large potatoes, cut into
    2.5cm/1in chunks
300ml/½ pint/1¼ cups fish
    stock
4 cod fillets
chapatis or parathas, to serve

1 Heat the oil in a wok, karahi or large pan over a medium heat and fry the cumin seeds for 30–40 seconds until they begin to splutter. Add the onion, red pepper, garlic, chillies and bay leaves and fry for 5–7 minutes more until the onions have browned.

2 Add the salt, ground cumin, ground coriander and chilli powder and cook for 1–2 minutes.

3 Stir the tomatoes, potatoes and fish stock into the pan. Bring the mixture to the boil and simmer for a further 10 minutes, or until the potatoes are almost tender.

4 Add the fish fillets, then cover the pan and allow to simmer for 5–6 minutes until the fish is just cooked. Serve immediately with warm chapatis or parathas.

> **Cook's Tip**
> *Avoid reheating this dish. Serve it as soon as it is cooked because cod flesh flakes very easily. If preparing in advance, follow the recipe up to the end of step 3, then cover the sauce and store in the refrigerator. Complete step 4 before serving.*

Red-hot Fish Curry

The island of Bali has wonderful fish, surrounded as it is by sparkling blue sea. This simple fish curry is packed with many of the characteristic flavours associated with Indonesia.

Serves 4–6
675g/1½lb cod or haddock fillet
1cm/½in cube shrimp paste
2 red or white onions
2.5cm/1in fresh root ginger,
    peeled and sliced
1cm/½in fresh galangal, peeled
    and sliced
2 garlic cloves
1–2 fresh red chillies, seeded,
    or 10ml/2 tsp chilli sambal, or
    5–10ml/1–2 tsp chilli powder
90ml/6 tbsp sunflower oil
15ml/1 tbsp dark soy sauce
5ml/1 tsp tamarind pulp, soaked
    in 30ml/2 tbsp warm water
250ml/8fl oz/1 cup water
celery leaves or chopped fresh
    chilli, to garnish
boiled rice, to serve

1 Skin the fish fillets, remove any bones and then cut the flesh into bitesize pieces. Pat the fish dry with kitchen paper and set aside in a cool place until needed.

2 Grind the shrimp paste, onions, ginger, fresh galangal, garlic and fresh chillies, if using, to a paste in a food processor or blender or with a mortar and pestle. Stir in the chilli sambal or the chilli powder, if using.

3 Heat 30ml/2 tbsp of the oil and fry the spice mixture, stirring, until it gives off a rich aroma.

4 Add the soy sauce to the pan. Strain the soaked tamarind pulp, discarding the seeds and pulp, and add the juice and water to the pan, mixing well. Cook gently for 2–3 minutes.

5 In a separate pan, fry the fish fillets in the remaining oil for 2–3 minutes. Turn the fish once only so that the pieces stay whole and don't break apart. Lift out with a slotted spoon and place them in the pan with the sauce.

6 Simmer the fish in the sauce for a further 3 minutes and serve with boiled rice. Garnish with feathery celery leaves or a little chopped fresh chilli, if you like.

Indian Fish Stew Energy 332kcal/1396kJ; Protein 36.9g; Carbohydrate 27.6g, of which sugars 7.9g; Fat 9.2g, of which saturates 1.3g; Cholesterol 81mg; Calcium 59mg; Fibre 2.9g; Sodium 132mg.
Red-hot Fish Curry Energy 322kcal/1342kJ; Protein 33g; Carbohydrate 8g, of which sugars 5g; Fat 18g, of which saturates 2g; Cholesterol 84mg; Calcium 53mg; Fibre 1.1g; Sodium 200mg.

Goan Vinegar Fish

Fish cooked in a spicy mixture that includes chillies, ginger and vinegar is delicious. The method lends itself particularly well to strong-flavoured oily fish, such as the mackerel that are regularly caught off the coast of Goa.

Serves 2–3
2 or 3 mackerel, filleted
2 or 3 fresh red chillies, seeded and roughly chopped
4 macadamia nuts or 8 almonds
1 red onion, quartered
2 garlic cloves, crushed
1cm/½in piece fresh root ginger, sliced
5ml/1 tsp ground turmeric
45ml/3 tbsp coconut oil or vegetable oil
45ml/3 tbsp wine vinegar
150ml/¼ pint/⅔ cup water
salt
deep-fried onions and finely chopped fresh chilli, to garnish
rice, to serve (optional)

1 Rinse the mackerel fillets under cold running water and dry well on kitchen paper. Set aside.

2 Put the chillies, macadamia nuts or almonds, onion, garlic, ginger, turmeric and 15ml/1 tbsp of the oil in a food processor and process to form a paste. Alternatively, pound them together in a mortar with a pestle.

3 Heat the remaining oil in a karahi, wok or large pan. Add the spice and nut paste to the pan and cook over medium heat for about 1–2 minutes without browning. Stir in the wine vinegar and water, and season with salt to taste. Bring the sauce to the boil, then lower the heat.

4 Add the mackerel fillets to the sauce and simmer for 6–8 minutes, or until the fish is tender and cooked.

5 Transfer the cooked mackerel to a warm serving platter. Bring the spicy sauce in the pan to the boil and cook for about 2–3 minutes, or until it has reduced slightly.

6 Pour the sauce over the fish, garnish with the deep-fried onions and chopped chilli and serve with rice, if you like.

Mackerel in Tamarind

Coconut cream makes a heavenly sauce when flavoured with fresh ginger, chillies, coriander and turmeric in this delicious dish, which originated from western India. Mackerel has a superbly rich flesh and yet it is a surprisingly inexpensive fish.

Serves 6–8
1kg/2¼lb fresh mackerel fillets, skinned
30ml/2 tbsp tamarind pulp, soaked in 200ml/7fl oz/scant 1 cup water
1 onion
1cm/½in piece fresh root ginger
2 garlic cloves
1 or 2 fresh red chillies, seeded, or 5ml/1 tsp chilli powder
5ml/1 tsp ground coriander
5ml/1 tsp ground turmeric
2.5ml/½ tsp finely ground fennel seeds
15ml/1 tbsp soft dark brown sugar
90–105ml/6–7 tbsp vegetable oil
200ml/7fl oz/scant 1 cup coconut cream
salt
1 fresh green chilli, seeded and finely sliced, to garnish

1 Rinse the fish fillets in cold water and dry them well on kitchen paper. Put into a shallow dish and sprinkle with a little salt. Strain the tamarind and pour the juice over the fish fillets. Set aside to marinate for 30 minutes.

2 Quarter the onion, peel and slice the ginger and peel the garlic. Grind the onion, ginger, garlic and chillies or chilli powder to a paste in a food processor, blender or with a mortar and pestle. Add the ground coriander, turmeric, fennel seeds and sugar to the paste and mix well.

3 Heat half the oil in a frying pan. Drain the fish fillets and fry for 5 minutes, or until cooked. Set aside.

4 Wipe out the pan with kitchen paper and heat the remaining oil. Fry the spice paste, stirring all the time, until it gives off a spicy aroma. Do not let it brown.

5 Add the coconut cream and simmer gently for a few minutes. Add the fish fillets and gently heat through. Taste for seasoning and serve sprinkled with sliced chilli.

Goan Vinegar Fish Energy 624kcal/2589kJ; Protein 40.4g; Carbohydrate 1.4g, of which sugars 0.6g; Fat 50.8g, of which saturates 8.5g; Cholesterol 108mg; Calcium 65mg; Fibre 1.4g; Sodium 135mg.
Mackerel in Tamarind Energy 578kcal/2420kJ; Protein 43.5g; Carbohydrate 35.2g, of which sugars 1.5g; Fat 30.2g, of which saturates 5.7g; Cholesterol 80mg; Calcium 48mg; Fibre 3.1g; Sodium 110mg.

Fish Curry with Chillies, Shallots and Lemon Grass

This is a thin, soupy curry with wonderfully strong Thai flavourings of lemon grass, garlic, chillies and the classic fish sauce.

Serves 4
450g/1lb salmon fillet
500ml/17fl oz/2¼ cups
  vegetable stock

4 shallots, finely chopped
2 garlic cloves, finely chopped
2.5cm/1in piece fresh galangal,
  finely chopped
1 lemon grass stalk,
  finely chopped
2.5ml/½ tsp dried chilli flakes
15ml/1 tbsp Thai fish sauce
5ml/1 tsp palm sugar (jaggery) or
  light muscovado (brown) sugar

1 Place the salmon fillet in the freezer for 30–40 minutes to firm up the flesh slightly, ready for slicing.

2 Remove and discard the skin on the salmon, then use a sharp knife to cut the fish into bitesize pieces, about 2.5cm/1in cubes, removing any stray bones with your fingers or with tweezers as you do so.

3 Pour the vegetable stock into a large, heavy pan and bring it to the boil over medium heat.

4 Add the shallots, garlic, galangal, lemon grass, chilli flakes, fish sauce and sugar. Bring back to the boil, stir well, then reduce the heat and simmer gently for 15 minutes.

5 Add the fish to the pan, bring the mixture back to the boil, then turn off the heat.

6 Leave the curry to stand for 10–15 minutes until the fish is cooked through, then serve in warmed bowls.

> **Cook's Tip**
> A bowl of this curry will make a perfect appetizer, or serve with lots of sticky rice for a more substantial lunch or main course.

Jungle Fish Cooked with Fresh Turmeric in Banana Leaves

Steaming fish in banana leaves over hot charcoal is a great way of locking in the flavour. Here, the fish is cooked in six layers of leaves, allowing for the outer ones to burn. For this simple yet extremely tasty dish you could use trout, any of the catfish or carp family, or even talapia.

Serves 4
350g/12oz freshwater fish fillets,
  such as trout, cut into
  bitesize chunks
6 banana leaves

vegetable oil, for brushing
sticky rice, noodles or salad, to serve

For the marinade
2 shallots
5cm/2in turmeric root, peeled
  and grated
2 spring onions (scallions),
  finely sliced
2 garlic cloves, crushed
1–2 green Thai chillies, seeded
  and finely chopped
15ml/1 tbsp nuoc cham
  (Vietnamese fish sauce)
2.5ml/½ tsp raw cane sugar
salt and ground black pepper

1 To make the marinade, grate the shallots into a bowl, then combine with the other marinade ingredients, seasoning with salt and ground black pepper.

2 Toss the chunks of fish in the marinade, making sure they are well coated, then cover and chill for at least 6 hours, or overnight.

3 Prepare a barbecue. Place one of the banana leaves on a flat surface and brush it with oil. Transfer the marinated fish on to the banana leaf, spreading it out evenly, then fold over the sides to form an envelope. Place this envelope, fold side down, on top of another leaf and fold that one in the same manner. Repeat with the remaining leaves until they are used up. Secure the last layer of banana leaves with a piece of bendy wire.

4 Place the banana leaf packet on the barbecue. Cook for about 20 minutes, turning it over from time to time to make sure it is cooked on both sides – the outer leaves will burn. Carefully untie the wire (it will be hot) and unravel the banana leaf packet, then serve the fish with sticky rice, noodles or salad.

Fish Curry Energy 212kcal/882kJ; Protein 23.1g; Carbohydrate 1.7g, of which sugars 1.6g; Fat 12.5g, of which saturates 2.2g; Cholesterol 56mg; Calcium 28mg; Fibre 0.2g; Sodium 267mg.
Jungle Fish Energy 155kcal/648kJ; Protein 18g; Carbohydrate 4g, of which sugars 2g; Fat 8g, of which saturates 1g; Cholesterol 59mg; Calcium 36mg; Fibre 0.7g; Sodium 0.2g.

Salmon Parcels with Spices

In this Indian dish, the fish is cooked in a banana leaf parcel. The salmon really works well with the gutsy flavours of the spices.

Serves 6

50g/2oz fresh coconut, skinned and finely grated, or 65g/2½oz/scant 1 cup desiccated (dry unsweetened shredded) coconut, soaked in 30ml/2 tbsp water

1 large lemon, skin, pith and seeds removed, chopped

4 large garlic cloves, crushed

3 large fresh mild green chillies, seeded and chopped

50g/2oz fresh coriander (cilantro), roughly chopped

25g/1oz fresh mint leaves, roughly chopped

5ml/1 tsp ground cumin

5ml/1 tsp sugar

2.5ml/½ tsp fenugreek seeds, finely ground

5ml/1 tsp salt

2 large, whole banana leaves

6 salmon fillets, total weight about 1.2kg/2½lb, skinned

1 Place all the ingredients except the banana leaves and salmon in a food processor. Pulse to a fine paste. Scrape the mixture into a bowl, cover and chill for 30 minutes.

2 To make the parcels, cut each banana leaf widthways into three and cut off the hard outer edges of each piece. Put the pieces of leaf and the edge strips in a bowl of hot water. Soak for 10 minutes. Drain, rinse, and pour over boiling water to soften. Drain, then place the leaves, smooth side up, on a board.

3 Smear the top and bottom of each with the coconut paste. Place one fillet on each banana leaf. Bring the trimmed edge of the leaf over the salmon, then fold in the sides. Bring up the remaining edge to cover the salmon and make a neat parcel. Tie each parcel securely with a leaf strip.

4 Lay each parcel on a sheet of foil, bring up the edges and scrunch together to seal. Position a lightly oiled grill rack over a moderately hot barbecue. Place the salmon parcels on the grill rack and cook for about 10 minutes, turning over once.

5 Place on individual plates and leave to stand for 2–3 minutes. Remove the foil, then unwrap and eat the fish out of the parcel.

Curried Coconut Salmon

Salmon is a robust fish, and is delicious cooked with a blend of spices, garlic and chilli in this curry, which is made in a slow cooker.

Serves 4

15ml/1 tbsp vegetable oil

1 onion, finely chopped

2 fresh green chillies, seeded and chopped

2 garlic cloves, crushed

2.5cm/1in piece fresh root ginger, grated

175ml/6fl oz/¾ cup coconut milk

10ml/2 tsp ground cumin

5ml/1 tsp ground coriander

4 salmon steaks, each about 175g/6oz

10ml/2 tsp chilli powder

2.5ml/½ tsp ground turmeric

15ml/1 tbsp white or red wine vinegar

1.5ml/¼ tsp salt

fresh coriander (cilantro) sprigs, to garnish

rice tossed with spring onions (scallions), to serve

1 Heat the oil in a pan, add the onion, chillies, garlic and ginger and fry for about 5–6 minutes, until fairly soft. Place in a food processor or blender with 120ml/4fl oz/½ cup of the coconut milk and blend until smooth.

2 Transfer the paste into the ceramic cooking pot. Stir in 5ml/ 1 tsp of the cumin, the ground coriander and the rest of the coconut milk. Cover and cook on high for 1½ hours.

3 About 20 minutes before the end of cooking time, arrange the salmon steaks in a single layer in a shallow glass dish. Combine the remaining 5ml/1 tsp cumin, the chilli powder, turmeric, vinegar and salt in a bowl to make a paste. Rub the mixture over the salmon steaks and leave to marinate at room temperature while the sauce finishes cooking.

4 Add the salmon steaks to the sauce, arranging them in a single layer, and spoon some of the coconut sauce over the top to keep the fish moist while it cooks. Cover with the lid, reduce the temperature to low and cook for 45 minutes–1 hour, or until the salmon is opaque and tender.

5 Transfer the fish to a serving dish, spoon over the sauce and garnish with fresh coriander. Serve with the rice.

Salmon Parcels Energy 567kcal/2349kJ; Protein 34.9g; Carbohydrate 1g, of which sugars 0.8g; Fat 47.1g, of which saturates 7.5g; Cholesterol 113mg; Calcium 64mg; Fibre 0.6g; Sodium 1723mg.
Coconut Salmon Energy 363kcal/1512kJ; Protein 35.9g; Carbohydrate 5.1g, of which sugars 4.2g; Fat 22.2g, of which saturates 3.8g; Cholesterol 88mg; Calcium 59mg; Fibre 0.5g; Sodium 275mg.

Sour Fish, Star Fruit and Chilli Stew

Somewhere between a stew and a soup, this refreshing dish is just one of many variations on the theme of sour fish stew found throughout South-east Asia. The star fruit are added towards the end of cooking so that they retain a bite.

Serves 4–6
30ml/2 tbsp coconut or palm oil
900ml/1½ pints/3¾ cups water
2 lemon grass stalks, bruised
25g/1oz fresh root ginger, finely sliced
about 675g/1½lb freshwater or saltwater fish, such as trout or sea bream, cut into thin steaks
2 firm star fruit (carambola), thinly sliced
juice of 1–2 limes

For the spice paste
4 shallots, chopped
4 fresh red chillies, seeded and chopped
2 garlic cloves, chopped
25g/1oz galangal, chopped
25g/1oz fresh turmeric, chopped
3–4 candlenuts or macadamia nuts, chopped

To serve
1 bunch fresh basil leaves
1 lime, cut into wedges
plain steamed or boiled basmati rice

1 Using a mortar and pestle or food processor, grind all the spice paste ingredients together to form a coarse paste.

2 Heat the oil in a wok or wide, heavy pan, stir in the spice paste and fry until fragrant. Pour in the water and add the lemon grass and ginger. Bring to the boil, stirring all the time, then reduce the heat and simmer for 10 minutes.

3 Slip the fish steaks into the pan, making sure there is enough cooking liquid to cover the fish and adding more water if necessary. Simmer gently for 3–4 minutes, then add the star fruit and lime juice to the pan. Simmer for about 2–3 minutes more, until the fish is cooked through.

4 Divide the fish and star fruit between four to six warmed serving bowls and add a little of the cooking liquid. Garnish with basil leaves and a wedge of lime to squeeze over it. Serve the stew with bowls of steamed rice, which is moistened by spoonfuls of the remaining cooking liquid.

Fish Curry in a Rich Tomato Sauce

In many regions of India, coconut is used extensively to add a mellow and creamy taste to fish dishes.

Serves 4
675g/1½lb steaks of firm-textured fish such as tuna or monkfish, skinned
30ml/2 tbsp lemon juice
5ml/1 tsp salt
5ml/1 tsp ground turmeric
vegetable oil, for shallow-frying
40g/1½oz/½ cup plain (all-purpose) flour
1.5ml/¼ tsp ground black pepper
60ml/4 tbsp vegetable oil
10ml/2 tsp sugar
1 large onion, finely chopped
15ml/1 tbsp grated fresh root ginger
15ml/1 tbsp crushed garlic
5ml/1 tsp ground coriander
2.5–5ml/½–1 tsp hot chilli powder
175g/6oz canned chopped tomatoes, including the juice
300ml/½ pint/1¼ cups warm water
30ml/2 tbsp chopped fresh coriander (cilantro) leaves, to garnish
plain boiled rice, to serve

1 Cut the fish into 7.5cm/3in pieces and put into a bowl. Add the lemon juice and sprinkle with half the salt and half the turmeric. Mix gently and set aside for 15 minutes.

2 Pour some oil into a 23cm/9in frying pan to cover the base to a depth of 1cm/½in and heat to medium. Mix the flour and pepper and dust the fish in the seasoned flour. Add to the oil and fry until browned on both sides. Drain on kitchen paper.

3 In a wok, karahi or large pan, heat 60ml/4 tbsp oil. When the oil is hot, but not smoking, add the sugar and let it caramelize. As soon as the sugar is brown, add the onion, ginger and garlic and fry for 7–8 minutes, until beginning to colour. Stir regularly.

4 Add the ground coriander, chilli powder and the remaining turmeric. Stir-fry for 30 seconds and add the tomatoes. Cook until the tomatoes are soft and the oil separates from the paste.

5 Pour the warm water and remaining salt into the pan, and bring to the boil. Add the fish, reduce the heat to low and simmer, uncovered, for 5–6 minutes. Garnish with the coriander leaves and serve with plain boiled rice.

Sour Fish Stew Energy 240kcal/1001kJ; Protein 25.9g; Carbohydrate 7.3g, of which sugars 4.7g; Fat 12.1g, of which saturates 1.2g; Cholesterol 0mg; Calcium 27mg; Fibre 1.7g; Sodium 67mg.
Fish Curry in Sauce Energy 242kcal/1010kJ; Protein 22.2g; Carbohydrate 6.4g, of which sugars 5.5g; Fat 14.3g, of which saturates 1.9g; Cholesterol 43mg; Calcium 65mg; Fibre 1.6g; Sodium 182mg.

Korean Mackerel with White Radish

Oily fish such as mackerel is a perfect match for the clean, dry taste of sake. Garlic and chilli mute the strong flavour of the fish, while the diced radish absorbs all the flavours of the cooking liquid for a unique and delicious taste.

Serves 2–3
1 large mackerel, filleted
300g/11oz Chinese white
  radish, peeled

120ml/4fl oz/½ cup light
  soy sauce
30ml/2 tbsp sake or rice wine
30ml/2 tbsp maple syrup
3 garlic cloves, crushed
10ml/2 tsp Korean
  chilli powder
½ onion, chopped
1 fresh red chilli, seeded and
  finely sliced
1 fresh green chilli, seeded
  and finely sliced

1 Slice the mackerel fillets into medium pieces. Cut the white radish into 2.5cm/1in cubes, and then arrange evenly across the base of a large pan. Cover with a layer of mackerel.

2 Pour the soy sauce over the fish in the pan and slowly pour in about 200ml/7fl oz/scant 1 cup water, the sake or rice wine, followed by the maple syrup.

3 Sprinkle the crushed garlic and chilli powder into the pan, and gently stir the liquid, trying not to disturb the fish and radish. Add the onion and sliced chillies, and cover the pan.

4 Place over high heat and bring the liquid to the boil. Reduce the heat and simmer for 8–10 minutes, or until the fish is tender, spooning the soy liquid over the fish as it cooks. Ladle into bowls and serve immediately.

Variation
If Chinese white radish is not available then potatoes make a good alternative. They will give a sweeter, more delicate flavour to the fish, while a pinch of coriander (cilantro) leaves will add more of a Thai flavour to the recipe.

Sardines with Coconut and Herbs

This dish is particularly fiery but the heat is tempered by the inclusion of coconut milk and herbs such as fresh mint, basil and flat leaf parsley, which help to cut the spice and calm the heat.

Serves 4
6–8 red chillies, according to
  taste, seeded and chopped
4 shallots, chopped
4 garlic cloves, chopped
1 lemon grass stalk, chopped
25g/1oz galangal, chopped
30ml/2 tbsp coconut or palm oil
10ml/2 tsp coriander seeds
5ml/1 tsp cumin seeds

5ml/1 tsp fennel seeds
1 small bunch fresh mint leaves,
  finely chopped
1 small bunch fresh flat leaf
  parsley, finely chopped
15ml/1 tbsp palm sugar (jaggery)
15ml/1 tbsp tamarind paste
4 sardines or small mackerel,
  gutted, kept whole
300ml/½ pint/1¼ cups
  coconut milk
salt and ground black pepper

To serve
steamed rice or sago
1 large bunch fresh flat
  leaf parsley
fresh basil leaves

1 Using a mortar and pestle, pound the chillies, shallots, garlic, lemon grass and galangal to a paste.

2 Heat the oil in a wok or wide, heavy pan, stir in the coriander, cumin and fennel seeds and fry for 3–4 minutes, stirring frequently, until they give off a nutty aroma.

3 Add the paste and stir until it becomes fragrant and golden in colour. Add the chopped mint and parsley and stir for 1 minute then add the sugar and tamarind paste.

4 Carefully toss the fish into the pan, coating it in the paste, and pour in the coconut milk. Bring to the boil, then reduce the heat and cook gently for 10–15 minutes, until the fish is tender. Season the sauce with salt and pepper to taste.

5 Cover the bottom of a warmed serving dish with parsley and place the fish on top, then spoon the sauce over the top. Serve with a bowl of steamed rice or sago and stalks of fresh parsley and basil leaves to cut the spice.

Sardines Energy 287kcal/1199kJ; Protein 22.8g; Carbohydrate 11g, of which sugars 10.2g; Fat 17.2g, of which saturates 3.7g; Cholesterol 0mg; Calcium 167mg; Fibre 2.1g; Sodium 213mg.
Korean Mackerel Energy 207kcal/861kJ; Protein 13.4g; Carbohydrate 11.4g, of which sugars 10.9g; Fat 11g, of which saturates 2.3g; Cholesterol 36mg; Calcium 33mg; Fibre 1.2g; Sodium 81mg.

Fragrant Chicken Curry

This dish is perfect for a party as the chicken and sauce can be prepared in advance and combined and heated at the last minute.

Serves 4

45ml/3 tbsp vegetable oil
1 onion, coarsely chopped
2 garlic cloves, crushed
15ml/1 tbsp Thai red curry paste
115g/4oz creamed coconut dissolved in 900ml/1½ pints/3¾ cups boiling water, or 1 litre/1¾ pints/4 cups coconut milk

2 lemon grass stalks, coarsely chopped
6 kaffir lime leaves, chopped
150ml/¼ pint/⅔ cup Greek (US strained plain) yogurt
30ml/2 tbsp apricot jam
1 cooked chicken, about 1.5kg/3–3½lb
30ml/2 tbsp chopped fresh coriander (cilantro)
salt and ground black pepper
kaffir lime leaves, shredded, toasted shredded coconut and fresh coriander (cilantro), to garnish
plain boiled rice, to serve

1 Heat the oil in a large pan. Add the onion and garlic and cook over low heat for 5–10 minutes until soft.

2 Stir in the red curry paste. Cook, stirring constantly, for 2–3 minutes. Stir in the diluted creamed coconut or coconut milk, then add the lemon grass, lime leaves, yogurt and apricot jam. Stir well. Cover and simmer for 30 minutes.

3 Remove from the heat and cool slightly. Transfer the sauce to a food processor or blender and process to a purée, then strain it back into the rinsed-out pan, pressing as much of the puréed mixture as possible through the sieve (strainer) with the back of a wooden spoon. Set aside while you prepare the chicken.

4 Remove the skin from the chicken and discard, slice the meat off the bones and cut it into bitesize pieces. Add to the sauce.

5 Bring the curry sauce back to simmering point. Stir in the chopped fresh coriander and season with salt and black pepper. Garnish with extra lime leaves, toasted shredded coconut and coriander. Serve immediately with rice, sprinkled with coriander leaves and black pepper.

Coronation Chicken

Devised for Elizabeth II's coronation in 1953, this salad has been popular ever since.

Serves 8

½ lemon
2.25kg/5lb chicken
1 onion, quartered
1 carrot, quartered
1 large bouquet garni
8 black peppercorns, crushed
salt
watercress sprigs, to garnish

For the sauce

1 small onion, chopped
15g/½oz/1 tbsp butter
15ml/1 tbsp curry paste
15ml/1 tbsp tomato purée (paste)
125ml/4fl oz/½ cup red wine
1 bay leaf
juice of ½ lemon, or to taste
10–15ml/2–3 tsp apricot jam
300ml/½ pint/1¼ cups mayonnaise
125ml/4fl oz/½ cup whipping cream
salt and ground black pepper

1 Put the lemon half inside the chicken cavity, then place it in a close-fitting pan. Add the vegetables, bouquet garni, peppercorns and a little salt to the pan. Add water to come two-thirds of the way up the chicken, bring just to the boil, cover and cook very gently for 1½ hours, until the chicken juices run clear. Leave to cool.

2 When the chicken is cool enough to handle, remove all the skin and bones, and chop the flesh into bitesize pieces.

3 To make the sauce, cook the onion in the butter until soft. Add the curry paste, tomato purée, wine, bay leaf and lemon juice, then cook gently for 10 minutes. Stir in the jam, press through a sieve (strainer) and cool.

4 Beat the sauce into the mayonnaise. Whip the cream and fold it in. Add seasoning and lemon juice, then stir in the chicken. Garnish and serve immediately.

Malaysian Fried Chicken

Serves 4

2 shallots, chopped
4 garlic cloves, chopped
50g/2oz fresh root ginger or galangal, peeled and chopped
25g/1oz fresh turmeric, chopped

2 lemon grass stalks, chopped
12 chicken thighs or drumsticks
30ml/2 tbsp kecap manis
salt and ground black pepper
vegetable oil, for deep-frying
fragrant rice and a green salad, to serve

1 Using a mortar and pestle or food processor, grind the shallots, garlic, ginger or galangal, turmeric and lemon grass to a paste. Place the chicken pieces in a heavy pan or flameproof earthenware pot and smear with the spice paste. Add the kecap manis and about 150ml/¼ pint/⅔ cup water.

2 Bring to the boil, reduce the heat and cook the chicken for about 25 minutes, turning it from time to time, until the liquid has evaporated. The chicken should be dry, with the spices sticking to it. Season with salt and pepper.

3 Heat enough oil for deep-frying in a wok. Fry the chicken pieces in batches until golden brown and crisp. Drain them on kitchen paper and serve hot with rice and a green salad.

Fragrant Chicken Energy 837kcal/3472kJ; Protein 50.2g; Carbohydrate 14.2g, of which sugars 13.7g; Fat 64.6g, of which saturates 29.2g; Cholesterol 253mg; Calcium 85mg; Fibre 0.3g; Sodium 240mg.
Coronation Chicken Energy 587kcal/2429kJ; Protein 10.1g; Carbohydrate 17.1g, of which sugars 4.7g; Fat 51.6g, of which saturates 8.8g; Cholesterol 228mg; Calcium 97mg; Fibre 1.1g; Sodium 401mg.
Malaysian Chicken Energy 396kcal/1639kJ; Protein 27g; Carbohydrate 1.5g, of which sugars 1.1g; Fat 31.3g, of which saturates 6.8g; Cholesterol 150mg; Calcium 38mg; Fibre 0.2g; Sodium 358mg.

Chicken and Coconut Milk Curry

This is a mild coconut curry flavoured with turmeric, coriander and cumin seeds. Serve with noodles or rice.

Serves 4

60ml/4 tbsp vegetable oil
1 large garlic clove, crushed
1 chicken, weighing about 1.5kg/
    3–3½lb, chopped into
    12 large pieces
400ml/14fl oz/1⅔ cups
    coconut cream
250ml/8fl oz/1 cup
    chicken stock
30ml/2 tbsp fish sauce
30ml/2 tbsp sugar
juice of 2 limes

To garnish
2 small fresh red chillies, seeded
    and finely chopped
1 bunch spring onions (scallions),
    thinly sliced

For the curry paste
5ml/1 tsp dried chilli flakes or
    chopped fresh red chilli
2.5ml/½ tsp salt
5cm/2in piece fresh turmeric
    or 5ml/1 tsp ground
    turmeric
2.5ml/½ tsp coriander seeds
2.5ml/½ tsp cumin seeds
5ml/1 tsp dried shrimp paste

1 First make the curry paste. Blend all the ingredients into a smooth paste using a pestle and mortar, food processor or spice grinder.

2 Heat the oil in a wok or large frying pan and cook the garlic until golden. Add the chicken pieces and brown on all sides. Remove the chicken and set aside.

3 Reheat the oil in the pan and add the curry paste and then half the coconut cream. Cook for a few minutes, stirring occasionally, until fragrant.

4 Return the chicken to the wok or pan, add the stock, mixing well, then add the remaining coconut cream, the fish sauce, sugar and lime juice. Stir well and bring to the boil, then lower the heat and simmer for 15 minutes.

5 Spoon the curry into four warm serving bowls, garnish with the chopped fresh chillies and spring onions. Serve immediately accompanied by noodles or rice, if you like.

Thai Chicken Curry

This is a flavourful and fragrant Thai curry with a lovely creamy taste thanks to the coconut milk. It is quite easy to make so will be ideal for a quick midweek meal for the whole family.

Serves 6

400ml/14oz can coconut milk
6 skinless chicken breast fillets,
    finely sliced
225g/8oz can bamboo shoots,
    drained and sliced
30ml/2 tbsp Thai fish sauce
15ml/1 tbsp soft light
    brown sugar
cooked jasmine rice, to serve

For the green curry paste
4 fresh green chillies, seeded
1 lemon grass stalk, sliced
1 small onion, sliced
3 garlic cloves
1cm/½in piece galangal or
    fresh root ginger, peeled
grated rind of ½ lime
5ml/1 tsp coriander seeds
5ml/1 tsp cumin seeds
2.5ml/½ tsp Thai fish sauce

To garnish
1 fresh red chilli, seeded and
    cut into fine strips
finely pared rind of ½ lime,
    finely shredded
fresh Thai purple basil or
    coriander (cilantro), chopped

1 First make the green curry paste: put all the ingredients in a food processor or blender and process to a thick paste. Set aside while you prepare the rest of the dish.

2 Bring half the coconut milk to the boil in a wok or large frying pan, then reduce the heat and simmer gently for about 5 minutes, or until reduced by half. Stir in the green curry paste and simmer for a further 5 minutes.

3 Add the finely sliced chicken breast fillets to the pan with the remaining coconut milk, bamboo shoots, fish sauce and sugar. Stir well to combine all the ingredients and bring the curry
back to simmering point, then simmer gently for about 10 minutes, or until the chicken slices are cooked through. The mixture will look grainy or curdled during cooking but this is quite normal and is nothing to worry about.

4 Spoon the curry and rice into warmed bowls, garnish with

Chicken Curry Energy 706kcal/2935kJ; Protein 48.1g; Carbohydrate 15.8g, of which sugars 15.6g; Fat 50.4g, of which saturates 12.8g; Cholesterol 240mg; Calcium 91mg; Fibre 1.5g; Sodium 305mg.
Thai Chicken Energy 236kcal/991kJ; Protein 33.8g; Carbohydrate 7.2g, of which sugars 5.9g; Fat 8.3g, of which saturates 1.6g; Cholesterol 165mg; Calcium 149mg; Fibre 3.1g; Sodium 253mg.

Green Chicken Curry

Use more or fewer chillies in this delectable dish, depending on how hot you like your curry.

Serves 3–4

4 spring onions (scallions), trimmed and coarsely chopped
1–2 fresh green chillies, seeded and coarsely chopped
2cm/¾in piece fresh root ginger, peeled
2 garlic cloves
5ml/1 tsp fish sauce
large bunch fresh coriander (cilantro), roughly chopped
small handful of fresh parsley, roughly chopped
30–45ml/2–3 tbsp water
30ml/2 tbsp sunflower oil
4 skinless chicken breast fillets, diced
1 green (bell) pepper, seeded and thinly sliced
600ml/1 pint/2½ cups coconut milk
salt and ground black pepper
coconut rice, to serve

1 Put the spring onions, chillies, ginger, garlic, fish sauce and herbs in a food processor or blender. Pour in about 30ml/2 tbsp of the water and process to a smooth paste, adding more water if the mixture is a little dry.

2 Heat half the oil in a large frying pan. Cook the diced chicken until evenly browned. Transfer to a plate. Heat the remaining oil in the pan. Add the green pepper and stir-fry for 3–4 minutes,

3 Add the chilli and ginger paste to the pan. Stir-fry for a further 3–4 minutes, until the mixture becomes fairly thick.

4 Return the chicken to the pan and add the coconut milk. Season with salt and pepper and bring to the boil, then reduce the heat, half cover the pan and simmer for 8–10 minutes.

5 When the chicken is cooked, transfer it, with the green pepper, to a plate. Boil the cooking liquid remaining in the pan for 10–12 minutes, until it is well reduced and fairly thick.

6 Return the chicken and pepper to the green curry sauce, stir well and cook gently for 2–3 minutes to heat through. Spoon the curry over the coconut rice, and serve immediately.

Fruity Chicken and Vegetable Curry

Coconut milk creates a rich sauce for this dish that is sweet with fruit and fragrant with fresh herbs and spices.

Serves 4

4 garlic cloves, chopped
15ml/1 tbsp chopped fresh root ginger
2–3 chillies, chopped
½ bunch fresh coriander (cilantro) leaves, roughly chopped
1 onion, chopped
juice of 1 lemon
pinch of cayenne pepper
2.5ml/½ tsp curry powder
2.5ml/½ tsp ground cumin
2–3 pinches of ground cloves
large pinch of ground coriander
3 skinless chicken breast fillets or thighs, cut into bitesize pieces
30ml/2 tbsp vegetable oil
2 cinnamon sticks
250ml/8fl oz/1 cup chicken stock
250ml/8fl oz/1 cup coconut milk
15–30ml/1–2 tbsp sugar
1–2 bananas
¼ pineapple, peeled and chopped
small handful of sultanas (golden raisins)
handful of raisins or currants
2–3 sprigs of mint, thinly sliced
juice of ¼–½ lemon
salt
flat bread, to serve

1 Purée the garlic, ginger, chillies, fresh coriander, onion, lemon juice, cayenne pepper, curry powder, cumin, cloves, ground coriander and salt in a food processor or blender.

2 Toss together the chicken pieces with about 15–30ml/1–2 tbsp of the spice mixture and set aside.

3 Heat the oil in a wok or frying pan, then add the remaining spice mixture and cook over medium heat, stirring, for 10 minutes, or until the paste is lightly browned.

4 Stir the cinnamon sticks, stock, coconut milk and sugar into the pan, bring to the boil, then simmer for 10 minutes.

5 Stir the chicken into the sauce and cook for 3–4 minutes, or until the chicken is nearly cooked through.

6 Meanwhile, thickly slice the bananas. Stir the fruit into the pan and cook for 1–2 minutes. Add the mint and lemon juice. Remove the cinnamon sticks and serve immediately, with flat bread.

Green Chicken Curry Energy 208kcal/877kJ; Protein 28g; Carbohydrate 8g, of which sugars 7.9g; Fat 7.4g, of which saturates 1.3g; Cholesterol 79mg; Calcium 76mg; Fibre 0.7g; Sodium 237mg.
Fruity Curry Energy 383kcal/1622kJ; Protein 29.5g; Carbohydrate 11.9g, of which sugars 11.7g; Fat 10.4g, of which saturates 2g; Cholesterol 140mg; Calcium 78mg; Fibre 1.1g; Sodium 462mg.

Hot Chicken Curry

The heat of the chillies in this curry is balanced by sweet onion, yogurt and coconut.

Serves 4

1.1kg/2½lb skinless chicken joints
115g/4oz/½ cup natural
    (plain) yogurt
10ml/2 tsp gram flour
5ml/1 tsp ground turmeric
5ml/1 tsp salt or to taste
25g/1oz/⅓ cup desiccated (dry
    unsweetened shredded) coconut
1 large onion, roughly chopped
2.5cm/1in piece of fresh root
    ginger, chopped
5 large garlic cloves, chopped

60ml/4 tbsp sunflower or olive oil
5cm/2in piece of cinnamon
    stick, halved
6 green cardamom pods, bruised
6 cloves
5–10ml/1–2 tsp chilli powder
2.5ml/½ tsp ground black pepper
115g/4oz chopped canned
    tomatoes, with their juice
2.5ml/½ tsp garam masala
15ml/1 tbsp chopped fresh
    coriander (cilantro) leaves
1 small tomato, seeded and cut
    into julienne strips, to garnish
1–2 green chillies, seeded and cut
    into julienne strips, to garnish
plain boiled rice, to serve

1 Cut each chicken joint into two pieces by separating the leg from the thigh and cutting each breast joint in half. In a large mixing bowl, whisk the yogurt with the gram flour, then add the turmeric and salt. Mix in the chicken and set aside for 1 hour.

2 In a heavy pan, dry-roast the coconut over a medium heat until lightly browned. Leave to cool and grind in a blender.

3 Purée the onion, ginger and garlic in a food processor until smooth. Heat the oil and add the cinnamon, cardamom and cloves. Stir-fry for 2–3 minutes, then add the onion, ginger and garlic paste. Cook until the mixture is beginning to brown. Add the chilli powder and black pepper, and cook for 2–3 minutes.

4 Add the chicken and stir-fry for 3–4 minutes. Add the tomatoes and 200ml/7fl oz/¾ cup warm water. Bring to the boil, reduce the heat, cover and cook until the chicken is tender.

5 Stir in the coconut and cook for 4–5 minutes. Stir in the garam masala and coriander. Remove from the heat. Transfer to a dish, garnish with tomato and chilli, and serve with rice.

Chicken and Lemon Grass Curry

This tasty curry, with a tang of lemon grass, is quick and simple to prepare.

Serves 4

45ml/3 tbsp vegetable oil
2 garlic cloves, crushed
500g/1¼lb skinless, boneless
    chicken thighs, diced
45ml/3 tbsp fish sauce
120ml/4fl oz/½ cup
    chicken stock
5ml/1 tsp sugar
1 lemon grass stalk, chopped into
    4 sticks and lightly crushed
5 kaffir lime leaves, rolled
    into cylinders and thinly
    sliced across, plus extra
    to garnish

For the curry paste
1 lemon grass stalk,
    coarsely chopped
2.5cm/1in piece fresh galangal,
    peeled and coarsely chopped
2 kaffir lime leaves, chopped
3 shallots, coarsely chopped
6 coriander (cilantro) roots,
    coarsely chopped
2 garlic cloves
2 fresh green chillies, seeded
    and coarsely chopped
5ml/1 tsp shrimp paste
5ml/1 tsp ground turmeric
chopped roasted peanuts
    and chopped fresh coriander
    (cilantro), to garnish

1 First make the curry paste. Place all the ingredients in a large mortar or food processor and pound with a pestle or process to a smooth paste.

2 Heat the vegetable oil in a wok, add the garlic and cook over low heat, stirring frequently, until golden brown. Be careful not to let the garlic burn or it will taste bitter.

3 Add the curry paste to the pan and cook for a further 30 seconds, stirring constantly.

4 Add the chicken pieces to the pan and stir until they are thoroughly coated with the curry paste. Stir in the fish sauce and chicken stock, then add the sugar, and cook, stirring constantly, for 2 minutes more.

5 Add the lemon grass and lime leaves, reduce the heat and simmer for 10 minutes. Spoon the curry into four warmed dishes, garnish and serve immediately.

Hot Curry Energy 605kcal/2508kJ; Protein 37.8g; Carbohydrate 13.8g, of which sugars 8.9g; Fat 44.7g, of which saturates 13.2g; Cholesterol 176.2mg; Calcium 107.8mg; Fibre 2.5g; Sodium 170mg.
Chicken and Lemon Grass Energy 122kcal/512kJ; Protein 17.4g; Carbohydrate 3.7g, of which sugars 3g; Fat 4.3g, of which saturates 0.8g; Cholesterol 85mg; Calcium 77mg; Fibre 1.6g; Sodium 131mg.

Curried Madura Chicken with Aromatic Spices

With the inclusion of nutmeg, ginger and cloves, this dish combines both taste and aroma.

Serves 4

1.3–1.6kg/3–3½lb chicken, cut into quarters, or
  4 chicken quarters
5ml/1 tsp sugar
30ml/2 tbsp coriander seeds
10ml/2 tsp cumin seeds
6 whole cloves
2.5ml/½ tsp grated nutmeg
2.5ml/½ tsp ground turmeric
1 small onion
2.5cm/1in piece fresh root ginger, thinly sliced
300ml/½ pint/1¼ cups chicken stock or water
salt and ground black pepper
deep-fried onions, to garnish
plain boiled basmati rice, to serve

1 Cut each chicken quarter in half to make eight pieces. Place the pieces in a flameproof casserole, sprinkle with the sugar and season to taste with salt and pepper. Toss the chicken pieces and seasoning together. Use the chicken backbone and any remaining carcass, if using, to make a fresh chicken stock for use later in the recipe, if you like.

2 In a preheated wok or large pan, dry-fry the coriander and cumin seeds and the whole cloves until the spices give off a good aroma. Add the nutmeg and turmeric and heat briefly. Remove and cool. Grind in a spice grinder or food processor or with a mortar and pestle.

3 In a food processor, process the onion and ginger until finely chopped. Otherwise, finely chop the onion and ginger and pound to a paste with a mortar and pestle. Add the spices and stock or water and mix well.

4 Pour the spice mixture over the chicken in the flameproof casserole, and stir well. Cover the casserole and cook over a low heat for 45–50 minutes until the chicken pieces are tender.

5 Serve the chicken with the sauce on plain boiled basmati rice, sprinkled with crisp deep-fried onions.

Chicken Coconut Stew

Serves 4

675g/1½lb chicken leg or breast joints on the bone
60ml/4 tbsp sunflower oil
2.5cm/1in piece of cinnamon stick
6 cardamom pods, bruised
4 cloves
12–15 curry leaves
1 large onion, finely chopped
10ml/2 tsp ginger purée
10ml/2 tsp garlic purée
2 green chillies, sliced at an angle
2.5ml/½ tsp ground turmeric
400g/14fl oz/1½ cups canned coconut milk
5ml/1 tsp salt, or to taste
500g/1¼lb medium potatoes
175g/6oz/1½ cups frozen garden peas
plain boiled basmati rice, to serve

1 Skin the chicken joints, and cut each one into two pieces.

2 Heat the oil in a pan over a low heat and add the cinnamon, cardamom pods, cloves and curry leaves. Sauté for 25–30 seconds and add the onion. Increase the heat to medium and fry until the onion is soft, about 5–6 minutes, then add the ginger, garlic and chillies and cook for 2–3 minutes. Stir in the turmeric.

3 Add the chicken. Increase the heat to high and brown the chicken. Pour in the coconut milk, add the salt, stir well. Reduce the heat to low, cover and simmer for 15–20 minutes.

4 Halve the potatoes, add to the stew and pour in 250ml/8fl oz/1 cup warm water. Bring to the boil, reduce the heat to low, then cover and cook for 20 minutes, until the potatoes are tender. Add the peas, cook for 5 minutes longer and remove from the heat. Serve with plain boiled basmati rice.

Chicken in a Spicy Marinade

Serves 4

1.5kg/3–3½lb chicken
4 garlic cloves, crushed
2 lemon grass stems, lower 5cm/2in sliced
1cm/½in fresh root ginger, peeled and sliced
5ml/1 tsp ground turmeric
475ml/16fl oz/2 cups water
3–4 bay leaves
45ml/3 tbsp each dark and light soy sauce
50g/2oz butter
salt
celery leaves, to garnish
plain boiled rice or noodles, to serve

1 Cut the chicken into four or eight portions. Slash the fleshy part of each portion twice. Grind the garlic, lemon grass, root ginger, turmeric and salt into a paste in a food processor. Rub the paste into the chicken pieces and leave for 30 minutes.

2 Transfer the chicken to a wok and add the water and bay leaves and bring to the boil. Cover and cook gently for 30 minutes, adding a little more water if necessary. Stir from time to time. Add the soy sauces and butter to the pan. Stir well to combine.

3 Cook until the chicken is well-coated and the sauce has almost been absorbed. Transfer the chicken to a preheated grill (broiler), or an oven preheated to 200°C/400°F/Gas 6, to finish cooking. Cook for 10–15 minutes, turning the pieces often so they become golden brown all over. Baste with the remaining sauce while cooking. Garnish with celery leaves. Serve with rice.

Chicken with Spices Energy 604kcal/2514kJ; Protein 55.7g; Carbohydrate 4.1g, of which sugars 2.2g; Fat 40.6g, of which saturates 10.8g; Cholesterol 330mg; Calcium 66mg; Fibre 1.7g; Sodium 269mg.
Chicken Coconut Stew Energy 552kcal/2309kJ; Protein 40g; Carbohydrate 43.6g, of which sugars 16g; Fat 25.5g, of which saturates 6.9g; Cholesterol 192.5mg; Calcium 104.5mg; Fibre 5.4g; Sodium 271mg.
Chicken in a Marinade Energy 634kcal/2642kJ; Protein 65g; Carbohydrate 8.3g, of which sugars 3.6g; Fat 38.3g, of which saturates 5.8g; Cholesterol 302mg; Calcium 210mg; Fibre 4.4g; Sodium 320mg.

Curried Chicken with Shallots

This richly spiced dish makes a delectable main course for a light summer dinner.

Serves 4

675g/1½lb skinned chicken thigh or breast fillets, cut into 5cm/2in cubes
juice of ½ lemon
5ml/1 tsp salt or to taste
60ml/4 tbsp sunflower oil
2 medium onions, finely chopped
15ml/1 tbsp ginger purée
15ml/1 tbsp garlic purée
7.5ml/1½ tsp ground coriander
5ml/1 tsp ground cumin
5ml/1 tsp ground turmeric
2.5–5ml/½–1 tsp chilli powder
225g/8oz canned chopped tomatoes, with their juice
15ml/1 tbsp ghee
8–10 small whole shallots
2.5–5ml/½–1 tsp garam masala
15ml/1 tbsp chopped fresh mint or 5ml/1 tsp dried mint
4–5 whole green chillies
10ml/2 tbsp chopped fresh coriander (cilantro) leaves
naan bread and a vegetable side dish, to serve

1 Put the chicken in a bowl and add the lemon juice and salt. Mix thoroughly, cover and set aside in a cool place for 30 minutes.

2 In a medium-sized pan, preferably non-stick, heat the oil and sauté the onions, ginger and garlic over a medium heat for 7–8 minutes. Add the coriander, cumin, turmeric and chilli powder and cook gently for about one minute, then add the tomatoes. Cook, stirring regularly, until the tomatoes reach a paste-like consistency and the oil separates from the paste.

3 Increase the heat to high and add the chicken. Cook, stirring constantly, for 4–5 minutes. Pour in 250ml/8fl oz/1 cup warm water, bring it to the boil and reduce the heat to low. Cover and cook for 15–20 minutes, stirring occasionally for even flavour.

4 In a separate pan, heat the ghee over a medium heat. Add the shallots and stir-fry until lightly browned, then stir in the garam masala. Add this mixture to the chicken and stir over a medium heat until the sauce has thickened.

5 Add the mint, chillies and chopped coriander. Stir them in and cook for 1–2 minutes longer. Serve with naan bread and a vegetable side dish.

Spicy Chicken and Pork Cooked with Vinegar and Ginger

This dish can be made with chicken, with pork or with both, as in this recipe. It can also be prepared with fish, shellfish and vegetables.

Serves 4–6

30ml/2 tbsp coconut or groundnut (peanut) oil
6–8 garlic cloves, crushed whole
50g/2oz fresh root ginger, sliced into matchsticks
6 spring onions (scallions), cut into 2.5cm/1in pieces
5–10ml/1–2 tsp whole black peppercorns, crushed
30ml/2 tbsp palm (jaggery) or muscovado (molasses) sugar
8–10 chicken thighs, or thighs and drumsticks
350g/12oz pork tenderloin (fillet), cut into chunks
150ml/¼ pint/⅔ cup coconut or white wine vinegar
150ml/¼ pint/⅔ cup dark soy sauce
300ml/½ pint/1¼ cups chicken stock
2–3 bay leaves
salt

To serve
stir-fried greens
cooked rice

1 Heat the oil in a wok with a lid or a flameproof casserole, stir in the garlic and ginger and fry until they become fragrant and begin to colour. Add the spring onions and black pepper to the pan and stir in the sugar.

2 Add the chicken and pork to the wok or casserole and fry until they begin to colour. Pour in the vinegar, soy sauce and chicken stock and add the bay leaves. Bring to the boil, reduce the heat, cover and simmer gently for about 1 hour, until the meat is tender and the liquid has reduced.

3 Season the stew with salt to taste and serve immediately with stir-fried greens and plain boiled rice, over which the cooking liquid is spooned.

Cook's Tip
For the best flavour, make this dish the day before eating. Leave to cool, put in the refrigerator, then reheat the next day.

Curried Chicken Energy 401kcal/1678kJ; Protein 42.6g; Carbohydrate 18.2g, of which sugars 10.6g; Fat 18.3g, of which saturates 3.3g; Cholesterol 75mg; Calcium 99mg; Fibre 3.7g; Sodium 143mg.
Spicy Chicken Energy 270kcal/1135kJ; Protein 42.2g; Carbohydrate 9g, of which sugars 7.6g; Fat 7.4g, of which saturates 1.6g; Cholesterol 118mg; Calcium 24mg; Fibre 0.6g; Sodium 1892mg.

Chicken and Sweet Potato Curry

Lemon grass, garlic and sweet potatoes give this South-east Asian curry a wonderful aromatic flavour.

Serves 4
1 chicken, about 1.3–1.6kg/
    3–3½lb
225g/8oz sweet potatoes
60ml/4 tbsp vegetable oil
1 onion, finely sliced
3 garlic cloves, crushed
30–45ml/2–3 tbsp Thai
    curry powder
5ml/1 tsp sugar
10ml/2 tsp Thai fish sauce

600ml/1 pint/2½ cups
    coconut milk
1 lemon grass stalk, cut in half
350g/12oz rice vermicelli, soaked
    in hot water until soft
salt
1 lemon, cut into wedges,
    to serve

For the garnish
115g/4oz beansprouts
2 spring onions (scallions), finely
    sliced diagonally
2 red chillies, seeded and
    finely sliced
8–10 mint leaves

1 Skin the chicken. Cut the flesh into small pieces and set aside. Peel the sweet potatoes and cut them into large chunks, about the same size as the chicken pieces.

2 Heat half the oil in a large heavy pan. Add the onion and garlic and fry until the onion softens.

3 Add the chicken pieces to the pan and stir-fry until they change colour. Stir in the curry powder. Season with salt and sugar and mix thoroughly, then stir in the fish sauce. Pour in the coconut milk and add the lemon grass. Stir well and cook over low heat for about 15 minutes.

4 Meanwhile, heat the remaining oil in a large frying pan. Fry the sweet potatoes until lightly golden. Using a slotted spoon, add them to the chicken. Cook for 10–15 minutes more, or until both the chicken and sweet potatoes are tender.

5 Drain the rice vermicelli and cook it in a pan of boiling water for 3–5 minutes. Drain well. Place in shallow bowls, with the chicken curry. Garnish with beansprouts, spring onions, chillies and mint leaves and serve with lemon wedges.

Curried Chicken Noodles

Chicken or pork can be used to provide the protein in this tasty dish. It is so quick and easy to prepare and cook, it makes the perfect snack for busy people who find themselves with little spare time.

Serves 2
30ml/2 tbsp vegetable oil
10ml/2 tsp magic paste
1 lemon grass stalk,
    finely chopped
5ml/1 tsp Thai red
    curry paste

90g/3½oz skinless chicken breast
    fillet or pork fillet (tenderloin),
    sliced into slivers
30ml/2 tbsp light soy sauce
400ml/14fl oz/1⅔ cups
    coconut milk
2 kaffir lime leaves, rolled into
    cylinders and thinly sliced
250g/9oz medium egg noodles
90g/3½oz Chinese leaves
    (Chinese cabbage), shredded
90g/3½oz spinach or watercress
    (leaves), shredded
juice of 1 lime
small bunch fresh coriander
    (cilantro), chopped

1 Heat the oil in a wok or large, heavy frying pan. Add the magic paste and lemon grass and stir-fry over low to medium heat for 4–5 seconds, until they give off their aroma.

2 Stir in the curry paste, then add the chicken or pork. Stir-fry over a medium to high heat for 2 minutes, until the chicken or pork is coated in the paste and seared on all sides.

3 Add the soy sauce, coconut milk and sliced lime leaves. Bring to a simmer, then add the noodles. Simmer for 4 minutes.

4 Add the Chinese leaves and spinach or watercress to the pan. Stir, then add the lime juice. Spoon the noodles into a bowl and sprinkle with the chopped coriander before serving.

Cook's Tip
Magic paste is a mixture of crushed garlic, coriander (cilantro) root and white pepper. It is extensively used in Thai cooking, and is available in jars from larger supermarkets and Asian speciality stores and markets.

Chicken Curry Energy 763kcal/3199kJ; Protein 51.6g; Carbohydrate 92g, of which sugars 11.6g; Fat 21.3g, of which saturates 4.1g; Cholesterol 109mg; Calcium 170mg; Fibre 4g; Sodium 545mg.
Curried Chicken Energy 702kcal/2965kJ; Protein 28.7g; Carbohydrate 101.6g, of which sugars 14.2g; Fat 23g, of which saturates 4.9g; Cholesterol 69mg; Calcium 187mg; Fibre 4.7g; Sodium 1564mg.

Chicken with Spices and Soy Sauce

This simple but delicious curry is an example of Nonya cuisine – the food of the Chinese Malaysians.

Serves 4

1.3–1.6kg/3–3½lb chicken, jointed and cut into 16 pieces
3 onions, sliced
about 1 litre/1¾ pints/4 cups water
3 garlic cloves, crushed
3–4 fresh chillies, seeded and sliced, or 15ml/1 tbsp chilli powder

45ml/3 tbsp vegetable oil
2.5ml/½ tsp grated nutmeg
6 cloves
5ml/1 tsp tamarind pulp, soaked in 45ml/3 tbsp warm water
30–45ml/2–3 tbsp dark or light soy sauce
salt
fresh green and red chillies, shredded, to garnish
plain boiled or steamed basmati rice, to serve

1 Place the chicken pieces in a large pan with one of the sliced onions. Pour over enough water to just cover. Bring to the boil and then reduce the heat and simmer gently for 20 minutes.

2 Grind the remaining onions, with the garlic and chillies or chilli powder, to a fine paste in a food processor or with a mortar and pestle. Heat a little of the oil in a wok or frying pan and cook the paste to bring out the flavour. Stir frequently so that the paste does not brown.

3 When the chicken has cooked for 20 minutes, lift it out of the stock and into the spicy mixture. Toss everything together over a fairly high heat so that the spices permeate the chicken pieces. Reserve 300ml/½ pint/1¼ cups of the chicken stock to add to the pan later.

4 Stir in the nutmeg and cloves. Strain the tamarind, discarding the pulp, and add the tamarind juice and soy sauce to the chicken. Cook for a further 2–3 minutes, then add the reserved stock.

5 Taste and adjust the seasoning and cook, uncovered, for a further 25–35 minutes, or until the chicken pieces are tender.

6 Transfer the chicken to a bowl, top with shredded green and red chillies, and serve with rice.

Spicy Chicken in Cashew Nut Sauce

This mildly spiced, slow-cooker dish has a rich yet delicately flavoured sauce.

Serves 4

1 large onion, roughly chopped
1 garlic clove, crushed
15ml/1 tbsp tomato purée (paste)
50g/2oz/½ cup cashew nuts
7.5ml/1½ tsp garam masala
5ml/1 tsp chilli powder
1.5ml/¼ tsp ground turmeric
5ml/1 tsp salt
15ml/1 tbsp lemon juice

15ml/1 tbsp natural (plain) yogurt
30ml/2 tbsp vegetable oil
450g/1lb chicken breast fillets, skinned and cubed
175g/6oz/2¼ cups button (white) mushrooms
15ml/1 tbsp sultanas (golden raisins)
300ml/½ pint/1¼ cups chicken or vegetable stock
30ml/2 tbsp chopped fresh coriander (cilantro), plus extra to garnish
rice and fruit chutney, to serve

1 Put the onion, garlic, tomato purée, cashew nuts, garam masala, chilli powder, turmeric, salt, lemon juice and yogurt in a food processor and process to a paste.

2 Heat the oil in a large frying pan or wok and fry the cubes of chicken for a few minutes, or until just beginning to brown. Using a slotted spoon, transfer the chicken to the ceramic cooking pot, leaving the oil in the pan.

3 Add the spice paste and mushrooms to the pan, lower the heat and fry gently, stirring frequently, for 3–4 minutes. Transfer the mixture to the ceramic pot.

4 Add the sultanas to the pot and stir in the chicken or vegetable stock. Cover with the lid and switch the slow cooker to high. Cook for 3–4 hours, stirring halfway through the cooking time. The chicken should be cooked through and very tender, and the sauce fairly thick.

5 Stir the chopped coriander into the sauce, then taste and add a little more salt and pepper, if necessary. Serve the curry from the ceramic cooking pot or transfer to a warmed serving dish and garnish with a sprinkling of chopped fresh coriander. Serve with rice and a fruit chutney, such as mango.

Chicken with Spices Energy 630kcal/2615kJ; Protein 48.8g; Carbohydrate 13.8g, of which sugars 10.7g; Fat 42.5g, of which saturates 10.6g; Cholesterol 248mg; Calcium 52mg; Fibre 2.6g; Sodium 798mg.
Chicken in Cashew Sauce Energy 239kcal/1006kJ; Protein 31.6g; Carbohydrate 10.7g, of which sugars 7.6g; Fat 8.1g, of which saturates 1.7g; Cholesterol 78.9mg; Calcium 39mg; Fibre 1.9g; Sodium 696mg.

Indian Stuffed Chicken

At one time this dish was cooked only in royal palaces and the ingredients varied according to individual chefs. The saffron and the rich stuffing make it a truly royal dish.

Serves 4–6

1 sachet saffron powder
2.5ml/½ tsp grated nutmeg
15ml/1 tbsp warm milk
1.3kg/3lb whole chicken
75g/3oz/6 tbsp ghee
75ml/5 tbsp hot water

For the stuffing

3 medium onions, finely chopped
2 fresh green chillies, chopped
50g/2oz/⅓ cup sultanas
   (golden raisins)
50g/2oz/½ cup ground almonds
50g/2oz ready-to-eat dried
   apricots, soaked until soft
3 hard-boiled eggs, peeled and
   coarsely chopped
salt

For the masala

4 spring onions (scallions),
   finely chopped
2 garlic cloves, crushed
5ml/1 tsp Chinese
   five-spice powder
4–6 green cardamom pods
2.5ml/½ tsp turmeric
5ml/1 tsp ground black pepper
30ml/2 tbsp natural
   (plain) yogurt
50g/2oz/1 cup desiccated (dry
   unsweetened shredded)
   coconut, toasted

1 Mix together the saffron, nutmeg and milk. Use to brush the inside of the chicken and over the skin. Heat 50g/2oz/4 tbsp of the ghee in a large frying pan and fry the chicken on all sides to seal it. Remove and keep warm.

2 To make the stuffing, in the same ghee, fry the onions, chillies and sultanas for 2–3 minutes. Allow to cool and add the ground almonds, apricots, chopped eggs and salt. Use to stuff the chicken.

3 Heat the remaining ghee in a large, heavy pan and gently fry all the masala ingredients except the coconut for 2–3 minutes. Add the water. Place the chicken on the bed of masala, cover the pan and cook until the chicken is tender.

4 Remove the chicken from the pan. Cook the liquid to reduce excess fluids in the masala. When the mixture thickens, pour over the chicken. Sprinkle with toasted coconut and serve hot.

Thai Roast Chicken with Turmeric

In Thailand, this chicken would be spit-roasted, as ovens are seldom used. However, it works very well as a conventional roast.

Serves 4

4 garlic cloves, 2 finely chopped
   and 2 bruised but left whole
small bunch coriander (cilantro),
   with roots, coarsely chopped
5ml/1 tsp ground turmeric
5cm/2in piece fresh turmeric
1 roasting chicken, about
   1.5kg/3¼lb
1 lime, cut in half
4 medium/large sweet potatoes,
   peeled and cut into wedges
300ml/½ pint/1¼ cups chicken
   or vegetable stock
30ml/2 tbsp soy sauce
salt and ground black pepper

1 Preheat the oven to 190°C/375°F/Gas 5. Calculate the cooking time for the chicken, allowing 20 minutes per 500g/1¼lb, plus 20 minutes. With a mortar and pestle, grind the chopped garlic, coriander, 10ml/2 tsp salt and turmeric.

2 Place the chicken in a roasting pan and smear it with the paste. Squeeze the lime juice over and place the lime halves and garlic cloves inside. Cover with foil and roast in the oven.

3 Meanwhile, bring a pan of water to the boil and par-boil the sweet potatoes for 10–15 minutes, until just tender. Drain well and place them around the chicken in the roasting pan. Baste with the cooking juices and sprinkle with salt and pepper. Replace the foil and return the chicken to the oven.

4 About 20 minutes before the end of cooking, remove the foil and baste the chicken. Turn the sweet potatoes over. At the end of the calculated roasting time, check that the chicken is cooked. Lift it out of the roasting pan, place on a carving board, and cover with foil to rest before carving. Transfer the sweet potatoes to a dish and keep warm while you make the gravy.

5 Pour off the oil from the pan but keep the juices. Place the pan on top of the stove and heat until bubbling. Pour in the stock. Bring to the boil, scraping to incorporate the residue. Stir in the soy sauce then pour into a jug (pitcher). Carve the chicken and serve with the sweet potatoes and gravy.

Indian Stuffed Chicken Energy 658kcal/2727kJ; Protein 34.1g; Carbohydrate 17.9g, of which sugars 14.9g; Fat 50.5g, of which saturates 19.2g; Cholesterol 234mg; Calcium 95mg; Fibre 3.7g; Sodium 158mg.
Thai Roast Chicken Energy 620kcal/2581kJ; Protein 47g; Carbohydrate 21.3g, of which sugars 5.7g; Fat 38.9g, of which saturates 11.4g; Cholesterol 240mg; Calcium 43mg; Fibre 2.4g; Sodium 228mg.

Curried Apricot and Chicken Casserole

Serves 4

15ml/1 tbsp vegetable oil
8 large chicken thighs, skinned
   and boned
1 onion, finely chopped
5ml/1 tsp medium curry powder
30ml/2 tbsp plain (all-purpose) flour
450ml/¾ pint/scant 2 cups
   hot chicken stock

juice of 1 large orange
8 ready-to-eat dried apricots, halved
15ml/1 tbsp sultanas (golden raisins)
salt and ground black pepper

For the almond rice
225g/8oz/1 cup cooked rice
15g/½oz/1 tbsp butter
50g/2oz/½ cup toasted almonds

1 Preheat the oven to 190°C/375°F/Gas 5. Heat the oil in a large frying pan. Cut the chicken into cubes and brown quickly all over in the oil. Add the onion to the pan and cook gently until soft and lightly browned.

2 Transfer to a flameproof casserole, add the curry powder and cook again for a few minutes. Add the flour, and blend in the stock and orange juice. Bring to the boil and season to taste.

3 Add the apricots and sultanas to the pan, cover and cook in the oven for 1 hour, or until tender. Adjust the seasoning to taste.

4 To make the almond rice, reheat the pre-cooked rice thoroughly with the butter and season to taste. Stir in the toasted almonds. Serve immediately alongside the chicken.

Persian Slow-cooked Chicken Stew

Serves 4–6

50g/2oz/¼ cup green split peas
45–60ml/3–4 tbsp olive oil
1 large onion, finely chopped
500g/1¼lb chicken thighs,
   bones removed
500ml/17fl oz/2¼ cups
   chicken stock
5ml/1 tsp ground turmeric

2.5ml/½ tsp ground cinnamon
1.5ml/¼ tsp grated nutmeg
2 aubergines (eggplants), diced
8–10 ripe tomatoes, diced
2 garlic cloves, crushed
30ml/2 tbsp dried mint
salt and ground black pepper
fresh mint, to garnish
rice, to serve

1 Put the split peas in a bowl, pour over cold water to cover, then leave to soak for about 4 hours. Drain well.

2 Heat a little of the oil in a pan, add two-thirds of the onions and cook for about 5 minutes. Add the chicken and cook until golden brown on all sides.

3 Add the soaked split peas to the chicken mixture, then the stock, turmeric, cinnamon and nutmeg. Cook over medium-low heat for about 40 minutes, until the split peas are tender.

4 Heat the remaining oil in a pan, add the aubergines and remaining onions and cook until lightly browned and tender. Add the tomatoes, garlic and mint. Season with salt and pepper.

5 Just before serving, stir the aubergine mixture into the chicken and split pea stew. Garnish with fresh mint leaves and serve with rice.

Malay Chicken with Chilli Relish

This chicken curry reflects the varied population of the region through its use of Chinese, Malay, Portuguese and Indian spices and flavourings in dishes.

Serves 4
For the rempah spice paste
6–8 dried red chillies, soaked in
   warm water, seeded and
   squeezed dry
6–8 shallots, chopped
4–6 garlic cloves, chopped
25g/1oz fresh root ginger, grated
5ml/1 tsp shrimp paste
10ml/2 tsp ground turmeric
10ml/2 tsp Chinese five-spice
   powder

For the curry
15–30ml/1–2 tbsp tamarind pulp
1 fresh coconut, grated
30–45ml/2–3 tbsp vegetable oil
1–2 cinnamon sticks
12 chicken thighs, boned and cut
   lengthways into bitesize strips
600ml/1 pint/2½ cups
   coconut milk
15ml/1 tbsp palm sugar (jaggery)
salt and ground black pepper

For the relish
1 green chilli, seeded and sliced
1 red chilli, seeded and sliced
fresh coriander (cilantro) leaves,
   finely chopped
2 limes
steamed rice, to serve

1 First make the rempah. Using a mortar and pestle or food processor, grind the chillies, shallots, garlic and ginger to a paste. Beat in the shrimp paste and stir in the dried spices.

2 Soak the tamarind pulp in 150ml/¼ pint/⅔ cup warm water until soft. Squeeze the pulp to soften it, then strain to extract the juice and discard the pulp. In a heavy pan, roast half the grated coconut until it is brown and smells nutty. Using a mortar and pestle or food processor, grind the roasted coconut until it resembles sugar grains.

3 Heat the oil in a wok or flameproof pot, and stir in the rempah and cinnamon sticks until fragrant. Add the chicken strips. Pour in the coconut milk and tamarind water, and stir in the sugar. Reduce the heat and cook gently for 10 minutes. Stir in half the ground roasted coconut to thicken the sauce and season. In a bowl, mix the remaining grated coconut with the chillies, coriander and juice of one lime to serve as a relish. Serve the chicken with rice, relish and lime wedges.

Chicken Casserole Energy 500kcal/2105kJ; Protein 54.1g; Carbohydrate 37g, of which sugars 13.2g; Fat 16g, of which saturates 3.6g; Cholesterol 148mg; Calcium 86mg; Fibre 3.1g; Sodium 150mg.
Persian Chicken Stew Energy 208kcal/875kJ; Protein 19.8g; Carbohydrate 14.2g, of which sugars 8.5g; Fat 8.5g, of which saturates 1.6g; Cholesterol 79mg; Calcium 38mg; Fibre 3.8g; Sodium 85mg.
Malay Chicken Energy 487kcal/2024kJ; Protein 29.2g; Carbohydrate 11.3g, of which sugars 10.6g; Fat 36.4g, of which saturates 19.2g; Cholesterol 150mg; Calcium 114mg; Fibre 4.4g; Sodium 267mg.

Ethiopian Curried Chicken

The long-simmered stews eaten in Ethiopia are known as wats. This delectable curry is made in a slow cooker to replicate the traditional techniques used in making wats.

Serves 4

30ml/2 tbsp vegetable oil
2 large onions, chopped
3 garlic cloves, chopped
2.5cm/1in piece peeled and finely chopped fresh root ginger
175ml/6fl oz/¾ cup chicken or vegetable stock
250ml/8fl oz/1 cup passata (bottled strained tomatoes)
or 400g/14oz can chopped tomatoes
seeds from 5 cardamom pods
2.5ml/½ tsp ground turmeric
large pinch of ground cinnamon
large pinch of ground cloves
large pinch of grated nutmeg
1.3kg/3lb chicken, cut into 8–12 portions
4 hard-boiled eggs
cayenne pepper or hot paprika, to taste
salt and ground black pepper
roughly chopped fresh coriander (cilantro) and onion rings, to garnish
flatbread or rice, to serve

1 Heat the oil in a large pan, add the onions and cook for 10 minutes until softened. Add the garlic and ginger to the pan and cook for about 1–2 minutes.

2 Add the stock and the passata or chopped tomatoes to the pan. Bring to the boil and cook, stirring frequently, for about 10 minutes, or until the mixture has thickened, then season.

3 Transfer the mixture to the ceramic cooking pot and stir in the cardamom, turmeric, cinnamon, cloves and nutmeg. Add the chicken in a single layer, pushing the pieces well down so that they are covered by the sauce. Cover the slow cooker with the lid and cook on high for 3 hours.

4 Remove the shells from the eggs, then prick the eggs a few times with a fork or very fine skewer. Add to the sauce and cook for 30–45 minutes, or until the chicken is cooked through and tender. Season to taste with cayenne pepper or hot paprika. Garnish with the fresh coriander and onion rings and serve immediately with flatbread or rice.

Yellow Chicken and Papaya

Serves 4

300ml/½ pint/1¼ cups chicken stock
30ml/2 tbsp thick tamarind juice, made by mixing tamarind paste with warm water
15ml/1 tbsp sugar
200ml/7fl oz/scant 1 cup coconut milk
1 green papaya, peeled, seeded and thinly sliced
250g/9oz skinless chicken breast fillets, diced
juice of 1 lime
lime slices, to garnish

For the curry paste

1 fresh red chilli, seeded and coarsely chopped
4 garlic cloves, coarsely chopped
3 shallots, coarsely chopped
2 lemon grass stalks, sliced
5cm/2in piece fresh turmeric, coarsely chopped, or 5ml/1 tsp ground turmeric
5ml/1 tsp shrimp paste
5ml/1 tsp salt

1 Make the paste. Put the red chilli, garlic, shallots, lemon grass and turmeric in a mortar or food processor. Add the shrimp paste and salt. Pound or process to a paste.

2 Pour the stock into a wok and bring it to the boil. Stir in the curry paste. Bring back to the boil and add the tamarind juice, sugar and coconut milk. Add the papaya and chicken to the pan and cook over medium to high heat for about 10–15 minutes, stirring frequently, until the chicken is cooked through.

3 Stir in the lime juice, transfer to a warm dish and serve immediately, garnished with lime slices.

Red Chicken Curry

Serves 4–6

1 litre/1¾ pints/4 cups coconut milk
30ml/2 tbsp red curry paste
450g/1lb skinless chicken breast fillets, cut into bitesize pieces
30ml/2 tbsp fish sauce
15ml/1 tbsp sugar
225g/8oz drained canned bamboo shoots, rinsed and sliced
5 kaffir lime leaves, torn
salt and ground black pepper
chopped fresh red chillies, seeded, and kaffir lime leaves, to garnish

1 Pour half of the coconut milk into a wok or large heavy pan. Bring to the boil, stirring constantly until it has separated.

2 Stir in the red curry paste and cook the mixture for about 2–3 minutes, stirring constantly.

3 Add the chicken pieces, fish sauce and sugar to the wok or pan. Stir well, then cook for 5–6 minutes until the chicken changes colour and is cooked through, stirring constantly to prevent the mixture from sticking to the bottom of the pan.

4 Pour the remaining coconut milk into the pan, then add the sliced bamboo shoots and torn kaffir lime leaves. Bring back to the boil over a medium heat, stirring constantly to prevent the mixture sticking, then taste and season if necessary.

5 To serve, spoon the curry into a warmed serving dish and garnish with chopped chillies and kaffir lime leaves.

Ethiopian Chicken Energy 388kcal/1629kJ; Protein 54.6g; Carbohydrate 13g, of which sugars 9.6g; Fat 13.4g, of which saturates 2.8g; Cholesterol 13mg; Calcium 81mg; Fibre 2.5g; Sodium 311mg.
Chicken and Papaya Energy 125kcal/533kJ; Protein 15.7g; Carbohydrate 52.8g, of which sugars 51.5g; Fat 7.5g, of which saturates 1.2g; Cholesterol 79mg; Calcium 92mg; Fibre 2.6g; Sodium 150mg.
Red Chicken Curry Energy 261kcal/1105kJ; Protein 29.6g; Carbohydrate 19.6g, of which sugars 18.3g; Fat 7.8g, of which saturates 1.5g; Cholesterol 79mg; Calcium 95mg; Fibre 1.1g; Sodium 837mg.

Malay Clay-pot Chicken

This dish is cooked in a low oven where the gentle heat is evenly distributed and retained by a clay pot, resulting in very tender meat.

Serves 4–6
1 × 1.3–1.6kg/3–3½lb chicken, oven-ready
45ml/3 tbsp grated fresh coconut
30ml/2 tbsp vegetable oil
2 shallots or 1 small onion, finely chopped
2 garlic cloves, crushed
5cm/2in piece lemon grass
2.5cm/1in piece fresh galangal or fresh root ginger, thinly sliced
2 fresh green chillies, seeded and chopped
12mm/½in cube shrimp paste
400g/14oz can coconut milk
300ml/½ pint/1¼ cups hot chicken stock
2 kaffir lime leaves (optional)
15ml/1 tbsp sugar
15ml/1 tbsp rice or wine vinegar
2 ripe tomatoes
30ml/2 tbsp chopped fresh coriander (cilantro) leaves, to garnish

1 To joint the chicken, remove the legs and wings with a sharp knife. Skin the pieces, divide the drumsticks from the thighs and, using kitchen scissors, remove the lower part of the chicken, leaving only the breast piece. Remove as many of the bones as you can. Cut the breast into four or six pieces and set aside.

2 Dry-fry the coconut in a large wok until evenly browned. Add the oil, shallots or onion, garlic, lemon grass, galangal or ginger, chillies and shrimp paste. Fry for 2–4 minutes to release the flavours. Preheat the oven to 180°C/350°F/Gas 4. Add the chicken to the wok and brown with the spices for 2–3 minutes.

3 Strain the coconut milk, and add the thin part with the chicken stock, lime leaves, if using, sugar and vinegar. Transfer to a glazed clay pot, cover and bake in the centre of the oven for 50 minutes, or until the chicken is tender. Stir in the thick part of the coconut milk and return to the oven for 5–10 minutes.

4 Place the tomatoes in a bowl and cover with boiling water to loosen and remove the skins. Halve the tomatoes, then remove the seeds and chop into large dice. Add the tomatoes to the finished dish, sprinkle with the chopped coriander and serve. Plain rice would make a good accompaniment.

Spiced Cambodian Chicken Curry

Many recipes for Cambodian chicken or seafood curries exist, but they all use Indian curry powder and coconut milk in their sauces.

Serves 4
45ml/3 tbsp Indian curry powder or garam masala
15ml/1 tbsp ground turmeric
500g/1¼lb skinless chicken thighs or chicken portions
25ml/1½ tbsp raw cane sugar
30ml/2 tbsp sesame oil
2 shallots, chopped
2 garlic cloves, chopped
4cm/1½in galangal, peeled and chopped
2 lemon grass stalks, chopped
10ml/2 tsp chilli paste or dried chilli flakes
2 medium sweet potatoes, peeled and cubed
45ml/3 tbsp nuoc cham (Vietnamese fish sauce)
600ml/1 pint/2½ cups coconut milk
1 small bunch each fresh basil and coriander (cilantro), stalks removed
salt and ground black pepper

1 In a small bowl, mix together the curry powder or garam masala and the turmeric. Put the chicken in a bowl and coat with half of the spice. Set aside.

2 To make the caramel sauce, heat the sugar in a small pan with 7.5ml/1½ tsp water, until the sugar dissolves and the syrup turns golden. Remove from the heat and set aside.

3 Heat a wok or heavy pan and add the oil. Stir-fry the shallots, garlic, galangal and lemon grass.

4 Stir in the rest of the turmeric and curry powder or garam masala with the chilli paste or flakes, followed by the chicken, and cook for 2–3 minutes, stirring frequently.

5 Add the sweet potatoes, then the nuoc mam, caramel sauce, coconut milk and 150ml/¼ pint/⅔ cup water, mixing thoroughly to combine the flavours. Bring to the boil, reduce the heat and cook for about 15 minutes until the chicken is cooked through.

6 Season and stir in half the basil and coriander. Garnish with the remaining herbs and serve immediately.

Malay Clay-pot Chicken Energy 372kcal/1560kJ; Protein 36.2g; Carbohydrate 46.8g, of which sugars 1g; Fat 4g, of which saturates 1.2g; Cholesterol 93mg; Calcium 54mg; Fibre 0.7g; Sodium 721mg.
Cambodian Curry Energy 387kcal/1632kJ; Protein 31g; Carbohydrate 38g, of which sugars 19g; Fat 14g, of which saturates 3g; Cholesterol 131mg; Calcium 1.8mg; Fibre 1g; Sodium 1000mg.

Creamy Chicken Korma

This chicken korma recipe calls for creamy coconut milk and chilli. Subtle flavours are added with a little nutmeg and mace.

Serves 4

50g/2oz/½ cup raw cashew nuts
200g/7oz/¾ cup thick set natural (plain) yogurt
10ml/2 tsp gram flour
10ml/2 tsp crushed fresh root ginger
10ml/2 tsp crushed garlic
2.5ml/½ tsp ground turmeric
2.5–5ml/½–1 tsp chilli powder
5ml/1 tsp salt, or to taste

675g/1½lb skinless chicken breast fillets, cut into 5cm/2in cubes
75g/3oz/6 tbsp ghee or unsalted butter
2.5cm/1in piece of cinnamon stick
6 green cardamom pods, bruised
6 cloves
2 bay leaves
1 large onion, finely chopped
15ml/1 tbsp sesame seeds, finely ground
200ml/7fl oz/¾ cup canned coconut milk
1.5ml/¼ tsp freshly grated nutmeg
1.5ml/¼ tsp ground mace
Indian bread or boiled basmati rice, to serve

1 Soak the cashew nuts in 150ml/¼ pint/⅔ cup boiling water for 20 minutes. Whisk the yogurt and gram flour together until smooth. Add the ginger, garlic, turmeric, chilli powder and salt. Mix well and stir into the chicken. Set aside for 30–35 minutes.

2 Reserve 5ml/1 tsp of ghee or butter and melt the remainder in a medium pan over a low heat. Add the cinnamon, cardamom, cloves and bay leaves. Stir-fry for 3–4 minutes.

3 Increase the heat and fry the onion until translucent. Stir in the ground sesame seeds and the chicken. Cook for 5 minutes. Add the coconut milk and 150ml/¼ pint/⅔ cup warm water. Bring to the boil, reduce the heat, cover and simmer for 20 minutes.

4 Meanwhile, purée the cashews with the water in which they were soaked and add to the chicken. Simmer, uncovered, for 5–6 minutes until the sauce thickens.

5 Melt the reserved ghee or butter in a pan over low heat. Add the nutmeg and mace, then cook gently for 30 seconds. Stir the spiced butter into the chicken. Serve with rice or bread.

Savoury Chicken Korma

There are many types of korma, and contrary to popular belief, a korma is not an actual dish, but a technique that is used in Indian cooking.

Serves 4

675g/1½lb boned chicken thighs or breast fillets, skinned and cut into 5cm/2in pieces
75g/3oz/⅓ cup whole milk natural (plain) yogurt
10ml/2 tsp gram flour
5ml/1 tsp salt
10ml/2 tsp crushed fresh root ginger

10ml/2 tsp crushed garlic
60ml/4 tbsp ghee or unsalted butter
2.5cm/1in piece of cinnamon stick
1 large onion, finely sliced
2.5ml/½ tsp ground turmeric
15ml/1 tbsp ground coriander
2.5ml/½ tsp chilli powder, or to taste
50g/2oz/½ cup raw unsalted cashew nuts, soaked in boiling water for about 15 minutes
150ml/¼ pint/⅔ cup double (heavy) cream
2.5ml/½ tsp ground cardamom
2.5ml/½ tsp ground mace

1 Put the chicken in a large mixing bowl. Beat the yogurt and the gram flour together and add to the chicken. Add the salt, ginger and garlic, and mix thoroughly. Cover and leave in the dish to marinate for about an hour or so.

2 Heat the ghee or butter in a heavy pan over medium heat and add the cinnamon, followed by the onion. Stir-fry for 5–6 minutes until the onion is soft and translucent.

3 Add the turmeric, coriander and chilli powder, stir-fry for 1 minute, then place the marinated chicken into the pan.

4 Increase the heat slightly and stir-fry the ingredients for about 3–4 minutes until the chicken changes colour. Pour in 300ml/½ pint/1¼ cups warm water, bring it to the boil, reduce the heat to low, cover and simmer for 15 minutes.

5 Drain the cashew nuts and purée them in a food processor or blender with the cream. Add to the chicken and simmer for 2–3 minutes. Stir in the ground cardamom and mace, remove from the heat and serve.

Creamy Korma Energy 398kcal/1671kJ; Protein 46.4g; Carbohydrate 19.1g, of which sugars 12.5g; Fat 16g, of which saturates 3.8g; Cholesterol 76mg; Calcium 195mg; Fibre 2.1g; Sodium 265mg.
Savoury Korma Energy 343kcal/1450kJ; Protein 54g; Carbohydrate 18g, of which sugars 10.7g; Fat 6.8g, of which saturates 2.6g; Cholesterol 151mg; Calcium 66mg; Fibre 1.8g; Sodium 197mg.

Chicken in Golden Saffron Sauce

Saffron is said to be worth its weight in gold, and its characteristic bouquet adds a unique aroma and flavour to this succulent dish.

Serves 4

50g/2oz blanched almonds
675g/1½lb skinless, boneless chicken thighs or breast fillets, cut into 5cm/2in cubes
10ml/2 tsp crushed garlic
10ml/2 tsp crushed fresh root ginger
5ml/1 tsp ground cumin
7.5ml/1½ tsp ground coriander
2.5–5ml/½–1 tsp crushed dried chillies
1 large onion, finely chopped

75g/3oz/⅓ cup natural (plain) yogurt
10ml/2 tsp gram flour
4 cloves
4 green cardamom pods, split at the top of each pod
2.5cm/1in piece of cinnamon stick
25g/1oz ghee or unsalted butter
300ml/½ pint/1¼ cups full cream (whole) milk
2.5ml/½ tsp saffron strands, pounded and soaked in 15ml/1 tbsp hot milk
2.5ml/½ tsp garam masala
1–2 fresh green chillies, seeded and cut into julienne strips, to garnish
naan bread, to serve

1 Soak the almonds in 150ml/¼ pint/⅔ cup boiling water for 20 minutes. Put the chicken, garlic, ginger, cumin, coriander, crushed chillies and onion in a heavy pan. Beat the yogurt and gram flour together and add to the pan. Add the cloves, cardamom pods and cinnamon, and place the pan over medium heat. Stir until the contents sizzle. Reduce the heat to low, cover the pan with a lid and cook for 20–25 minutes.

2 Remove the lid and increase the heat to high. Cook until the liquid is reduced to a thick batter-like consistency, stirring frequently. Add the ghee or butter and stir-fry the chicken for another 3–4 minutes until the fat rises to the surface.

3 Purée the almonds with the soaking water and add to the pan. Stir in the milk, the saffron and the soaking milk. Bring it to the boil. Reduce the heat and simmer for 5–6 minutes.

4 Stir in the garam masala. Transfer to a serving dish and garnish with the green chilli. Serve immediately with naan bread.

Classic Chicken Curry

This recipe uses plenty of curry powder to give it a real bite. It is best served with plain boiled rice to moderate the spicy flavours.

Serves 4

675g/1½lb chicken leg or breast joint pieces on the bone
2.5ml/½ tsp ground turmeric
15ml/1 tbsp plain (all-purpose) flour
5ml/1 tsp salt, or to taste
1 large onion, roughly chopped

2.5cm/1in piece of fresh root ginger, roughly chopped
4–5 garlic cloves, roughly chopped
60ml/4 tbsp sunflower oil or olive oil
25ml/1½ tbsp curry powder
2.5ml/½ tsp chilli powder (optional)
175g/6oz fresh tomatoes, peeled and chopped
30ml/2 tbsp chopped fresh coriander (cilantro)
plain boiled or steamed basmati rice, to serve

1 Skin the chicken and separate the legs from the thighs. If you are using breast meat, cut each one into three pieces. Mix the turmeric, flour and salt together and rub this mixture into the chicken. Set aside the chicken in a cool place to marinate while you prepare the other flavourings.

2 Put the onion, ginger and garlic in a food processor to make a purée; alternatively, you can pound them together into a paste using a mortar and pestle.

3 Heat the sunflower or olive oil in a medium pan and add the puréed ingredients. Cook over medium heat for about 8–10 minutes, stirring regularly so that the paste does not burn.

4 Add the curry powder and chilli powder, if using, and cook for 2–3 minutes. Add about 30ml/2 tbsp water and continue to cook for a further 2–3 minutes.

5 Add the chicken, increase the heat to medium-high and stir until the chicken begins to brown. Add 425ml/15fl oz/1¾ cups warm water, bring it to the boil, cover and reduce the heat to low. Cook for another 35–40 minutes and add the tomatoes. Cook for 2–3 minutes longer, stir in the chopped coriander and remove from the heat. Serve with rice.

Chicken in Saffron Energy 554kcal/2321kJ; Protein 75.6g; Carbohydrate 5.1g, of which sugars 4.7g; Fat 25.9g, of which saturates 12.2g; Cholesterol 255mg; Calcium 146mg; Fibre 0.8g; Sodium 792mg.
Classic Curry Energy 392kcal/1632kJ; Protein 24.3g; Carbohydrate 12.5g, of which sugars 7.3g; Fat 27.6g, of which saturates 5.8g; Cholesterol 135mg; Calcium 67mg; Fibre 2.6g; Sodium 108mg.

Chicken with Golden Turmeric

Fresh turmeric is a root like ginger. It has a completely different taste to dried turmeric and produces a luxurious golden colour in a dish. Dried and ground turmeric can be used instead and will produce an acceptable colour, although the flavour will be somewhat different.

Serves 4
1.3–1.6kg/3–3½lb chicken, cut
 into 8 pieces, or 4 chicken
 quarters, halved
15ml/1 tbsp soft light brown sugar
3 macadamia nuts or 6 almonds
2 garlic cloves, crushed
1 large onion, quartered
2.5cm/1in piece fresh galangal
 or 1cm/½in piece fresh root
 ginger, sliced, or 5ml/1 tsp
 galangal powder
1–2 lemon grass stalks, lower
 5cm/2in sliced, top bruised
1cm/½in cube shrimp paste
4cm/1½in piece fresh turmeric,
 sliced, or 10ml/2 tsp
 ground turmeric
15ml/1 tbsp tamarind pulp,
 soaked in 150ml/¼ pint/⅔ cup
 warm water
60–90ml/4–6 tbsp vegetable oil
400g/14oz can coconut milk
salt and ground black pepper
deep-fried onions,
 to garnish (optional)

1 Rub each of the chicken joints all over with a little of the light brown sugar and set them aside.

2 Grind the nuts and garlic in a food processor with the onion, galangal or ginger, sliced lemon grass, shrimp paste and turmeric. Alternatively, pound the ingredients to a paste with a mortar and pestle. Strain the tamarind pulp and reserve the juice.

3 Heat the oil in a wok or large pan, and cook the paste, without browning, until it gives off a spicy aroma. Add the pieces of chicken and toss well in the spices. Add the strained tamarind juice. Spoon the coconut cream off the top of the milk and set it to one side.

4 Add the coconut milk to the pan. Cover and cook for 45 minutes, or until the chicken is tender.

5 Before serving, stir in the coconut cream. Season to taste and serve, garnished with deep-fried onions, if using.

Tandoori Chicken

Serves 4
30ml/2 tbsp vegetable oil
2 small onions, cut into wedges
2 garlic cloves, sliced
4 skinless chicken breast fillets,
 cut into cubes
100ml/3½fl oz/⅓ cup water
300g/11oz jar tandoori sauce
salt and ground black pepper
fresh coriander (cilantro) sprigs,
 to garnish

To serve
5ml/1 tsp ground turmeric
350g/12oz/1⅔ cups basmati rice

1 Heat the oil in a flameproof casserole. Add the onions and garlic, and cook for about 3 minutes, or until the onion is beginning to soften, stirring frequently.

2 Add the cubes of chicken to the casserole and cook for 6 minutes. Stir the water into the tandoori sauce and pour it over the chicken. Bring to the boil, then reduce the heat and simmer for 10 minutes, or until the chicken pieces are cooked through and the sauce is slightly reduced and thickened.

3 Meanwhile, bring a large pan of lightly salted water to the boil, add the turmeric and rice and bring back to the boil. Stir once, reduce the heat to prevent the water from boiling over and simmer the rice for 12 minutes, or according to the time suggested on the packet, until tender.

4 Drain the rice well and serve immediately alongside the tandoori chicken on warmed individual serving plates, garnished with the sprigs of fresh coriander.

Chicken with Orange and Pepper

Serves 4
225g/8oz low-fat cream cheese
50ml/2fl oz/¼ cup yogurt
120ml/4fl oz/½ cup orange juice
7.5ml/1½ tsp crushed fresh
 root ginger
5ml/1 tsp crushed garlic
5ml/1 tsp ground black pepper
5ml/1 tsp salt
5ml/1 tsp ground coriander
1 baby chicken, about 675g/1½lb,
 skinned and cut into 8 pieces
15ml/1 tbsp corn oil
1 bay leaf
1 large onion, chopped
15ml/1 tbsp fresh mint leaves
1 green chilli, seeded and chopped

1 In a large mixing bowl, whisk together the cream cheese, yogurt, orange juice, ginger, garlic, pepper, salt and coriander.

2 Add the chicken pieces to the bowl, ensuring it is well coated, and set aside for 3–4 hours to marinate.

3 Heat the oil with the bay leaf in a wok or large frying pan and fry the onion until soft and translucent.

4 Pour the chicken mixture into the pan and cook for 3–5 minutes over medium heat. Lower the heat, cover and cook for 10–12 minutes, adding a little water if the sauce is too thick.

5 When the chicken is cooked through, add the fresh mint and chilli and cook for 1–2 minutes. Serve immediately.

Chicken with Turmeric Energy 706kcal/2935kJ; Protein 48.1g; Carbohydrate 15.8g, of which sugars 15.6g; Fat 50.4g, of which saturates 12.8g; Cholesterol 240mg; Calcium 91mg; Fibre 1.5g; Sodium 305mg.
Tandoori Chicken Energy 592kcal/2479kJ; Protein 44g; Carbohydrate 77.5g, of which sugars 4.5g; Fat 11.4g, of which saturates 1.1g; Cholesterol 105mg; Calcium 54mg; Fibre 0.4g; Sodium 826mg.
Chicken with Orange Energy 268kcal/1129kJ; Protein 34.9g; Carbohydrate 14.8g, of which sugars 11.9g; Fat 8.3g, of which saturates 2.8g; Cholesterol 99mg; Calcium 96mg; Fibre 0.3g; Sodium 111mg.

Balti Butter Chicken

Kashmiri Chicken Curry

Butter chicken is one of the most popular balti chicken dishes. Cooked in butter, with a subtle blend of aromatic spices, cream and almonds, this mild dish will be enjoyed by everyone.

Serves 4–6

150ml/¼ pint/⅔ cup natural
  (plain) yogurt
50g/2oz/½ cup ground almonds
7.5ml/1½ tsp chilli powder
1.5ml/¼ tsp crushed bay leaves
1.5ml/¼ tsp ground cloves
1.5ml/¼ tsp ground cinnamon
5ml/1 tsp garam masala
4 green cardamom pods
2.5cm/1in piece fresh root
  ginger, grated
1 garlic clove, crushed
400g/14oz/2 cups canned
  chopped tomatoes
6.5ml/1¼ tsp salt
1kg/2¼lb/6½ cups skinless
  chicken breast fillets, cubed
75g/3oz/6 tbsp butter
15ml/1 tbsp corn oil
2 medium onions, sliced
30ml/2 tbsp chopped fresh
  coriander (cilantro)
60ml/4 tbsp single (light) cream
coriander (cilantro) sprigs,
  to garnish

1 Put the yogurt, ground almonds, all the dry spices, ginger, garlic, tomatoes and salt into a mixing bowl and blend together thoroughly. Put the chicken into a large mixing bowl and pour over the yogurt mixture. Set aside.

2 Melt the butter and oil together in a medium wok or deep frying pan. When the oil is hot, add the onions and fry for about 3 minutes, stirring frequently.

3 Add the chicken mixture and stir-fry for 7–10 minutes. Stir in about half of the coriander and mix well.

4 Pour the cream over the chicken mixture and stir in well. Bring to the boil. Serve immediately garnished with the remaining chopped coriander and a few extra coriander sprigs.

> **Variation**
> *Replace the natural (plain) yogurt with Greek (US strained plain) yogurt for an even richer and creamier flavour.*

Surrounded by the snow-capped Himalayas, Kashmir is popularly known as the 'Switzerland of the East'. The state is also renowned for its rich culinary heritage, and this aromatic dish is one of the simplest among the region's repertoire.

Serves 4–6

20ml/4 tsp Kashmiri masala paste
60ml/4 tbsp tomato ketchup
5ml/1 tsp Worcestershire sauce
5ml/1 tsp Chinese
  five-spice powder
5ml/1 tsp sugar
8 chicken joints, skinned
5cm/2in piece fresh
  root ginger
45ml/3 tbsp vegetable oil
4 garlic cloves, crushed
juice of 1 lemon
15ml/1 tbsp coriander (cilantro)
  leaves, finely chopped
salt
plain boiled rice, to serve (optional)

1 To make the marinade, mix the masala paste, tomato ketchup, Worcestershire sauce and five-spice powder with the sugar and a little salt. Leave the mixture to rest in a warm place until the sugar has dissolved.

2 Rub the chicken pieces all over with the marinade and set aside in a cool place for at least 2 hours, or preferably in the refrigerator overnight. Bring the chicken back to room temperature before cooking.

3 Thinly peel the ginger, using a sharp knife or vegetable peeler. Grate the peeled root finely.

4 Heat the oil in a karahi, wok or large pan and fry half the ginger and all the garlic until golden.

5 Add the chicken to the pan and fry until both sides are sealed. Cover and cook until the chicken is tender, and the oil has separated from the sauce.

6 Sprinkle the chicken with the lemon juice, remaining grated ginger and chopped coriander leaves, and mix in well. Serve the chicken piping hot. Plain boiled rice would make a good accompaniment to this curry.

Butter Chicken Energy 606kcal/2540kJ; Protein 84g; Carbohydrate 6.8g, of which sugars 3.4g; Fat 27.3g, of which saturates 3.8g; Cholesterol 239mg; Calcium 57mg; Fibre 1.3g; Sodium 214mg.
Kashmiri Chicken Energy 256kcal/1066kJ; Protein 16.9g; Carbohydrate 12.3g, of which sugars 10.2g; Fat 15.8g, of which saturates 3.5g; Cholesterol 75mg; Calcium 93mg; Fibre 2.4g; Sodium 411mg.

Chicken Murgh

This is a marvellous way to re-heat tandoori chicken.

Serves 4

For the chicken tikka

juice of ½ lemon

5ml/1 tsp salt or to taste

675g/1½lb skinless chicken breast fillets, cut into 5cm/2in cubes

120ml/4floz/½ cup Greek (US strained plain) yogurt

15ml/1 tbsp crushed garlic

15ml/1 tbsp crushed fresh ginger

2.5ml/½ tsp ground turmeric

5ml/1 tsp garam masala

2.5ml/½ tsp chilli powder

10ml/2 tsp cornflour (cornstarch)

5ml/1 tsp sugar

45ml/3 tbsp sunflower oil

50g/2oz/4 tbsp butter, melted

For the sauce

150g/5oz/10 tbsp unsalted butter

5cm/2in cinnamon stick, broken up

3 cardamom pods, bruised

4 cloves

2 green chillies, roughly chopped

15ml/1 tbsp crushed fresh ginger

15ml/1 tbsp crushed garlic

5–10ml/1–2 tsp chilli powder

400g/14oz canned chopped tomatoes

30ml/2 tbsp tomato purée (paste)

10ml/2 tsp sugar

10ml/2 tsp salt

200ml/7fl oz/¾ cup warm water

10ml/2 tsp dried fenugreek leaves

150ml/¼ pint/½ cup double (heavy) cream

1 Rub the lemon juice and salt into the chicken. Whisk the yogurt and stir in the remaining tikka ingredients, except the melted butter. Stir into the chicken, cover and chill overnight.

2 Pre-heat the grill (broiler) to high and brush the skewers with oil. Thread the chicken on to skewers and place on the grill pan. Cook for 5 minutes. Mix the marinade with melted butter. Brush over the chicken and cook for 3–4 minutes. Turn over and baste. Cook for 2–3 minutes. Remove from the heat.

3 For the sauce, melt half the butter. Add the spices, chillies, ginger, garlic and chilli powder. Cook for 2–3 minutes. Add the remaining ingredients except the cream. Simmer for 20 minutes. Cool. Purée until smooth with a hand blender or sieve (strainer).

4 Return the pan to the heat, and add the remaining butter and cream. Let the mixture come to a simmer, then add the chicken. Simmer for 5–6 minutes, and serve with boiled rice.

Baby Chicken Curry with Spiced Apples

This mild yet aromatic dish is pleasantly flavoured with a warming combination of spices and chilli. Yogurt and almonds make a creamy sauce, which is given an additional lift by the use of sliced apples.

Serves 4

10ml/2 tsp vegetable oil

2 medium onions, diced

1 bay leaf

2 cloves

2.5cm/1in piece cinnamon stick

4 black peppercorns

1 baby chicken, about 675g/1½lb, skinned and cut into 8 pieces

5ml/1 tsp garam masala

5ml/1 tsp grated fresh root ginger

5ml/1 tsp crushed garlic

5ml/1 tsp salt

5ml/1 tsp chilli powder

15ml/1 tbsp ground almonds

150ml/¼ pint/⅔ cup natural (plain) low-fat yogurt

2 green eating apples, peeled, cored and roughly sliced

15ml/1 tbsp chopped fresh coriander (cilantro)

15g/½oz flaked (sliced) almonds, lightly toasted, and fresh coriander leaves, to garnish

1 Heat the oil in a karahi, wok or heavy pan and fry the onions with the bay leaf, cloves, cinnamon and peppercorns for about 3–5 minutes until the onions are beginning to soften and turn translucent but have not yet begun to brown.

2 Add the chicken pieces to the onions in the pan and continue to stir-fry for at least another 3 minutes.

3 Lower the heat and add the garam masala, ginger, garlic, salt, chilli powder and ground almonds to the pan and cook, stirring constantly, for about 2–3 minutes.

4 Pour the yogurt into the pan and stir for a couple more minutes. Add the apples and chopped coriander, cover and cook for about 10–15 minutes.

5 Check that the chicken is cooked through and serve the curry immediately, garnished with the flaked almonds and the whole coriander leaves.

Chicken Murgh Energy 793kcal/3293kJ; Protein 45.8g; Carbohydrate 14.2g, of which sugars 9g; Fat 64.4g, of which saturates 37.1g; Cholesterol 227mg; Calcium 102mg; Fibre 1.2g; Sodium 1491mg.
Chicken Curry Energy 349kcal/1450kJ; Protein 25g; Carbohydrate 14.2g, of which sugars 11.8g; Fat 21.8g, of which saturates 5.6g; Cholesterol 108mg; Calcium 140mg; Fibre 2.8g; Sodium 124mg.

Baby Chicken in a Chilli Tamarind Sauce

The tamarind in this recipe gives the dish a tasty sweet-and-sour flavour.

Serves 4–6

60ml/4 tbsp tomato ketchup
15ml/1 tbsp tamarind paste
60ml/4 tbsp water
7.5ml/1½ tsp chilli powder
7.5ml/1½ tsp salt
15ml/1 tbsp sugar
7.5ml/1½ tsp crushed fresh root ginger
7.5ml/1½ tsp crushed garlic
30ml/2 tbsp desiccated (dry unsweetened shredded) coconut
30ml/2 tbsp sesame seeds
5ml/1 tsp poppy seeds
5ml/1 tsp ground cumin
7.5ml/1½ tsp ground coriander
2 X 450g/1lb baby chickens, skinned and cut into 6–8 pieces each
75ml/5 tbsp corn oil
about 20 curry leaves
2.5ml/½ tsp onion seeds
3 large dried red chillies
2.5ml/½ tsp fenugreek seeds
10–12 cherry tomatoes
45ml/3 tbsp chopped fresh coriander (cilantro)
2 fresh green chillies, chopped

1 Put the tomato ketchup, tamarind paste and water into a large mixing bowl and use a fork to blend everything together.

2 Add the chilli powder, salt, sugar, ginger, garlic, coconut, sesame and poppy seeds, ground cumin and ground coriander to the mixture. Stir well until combined.

3 Add the chicken pieces and stir until they are well coated with the spice mixture. Set to one side.

4 Heat the oil in a deep frying pan or a large karahi. Add the curry leaves, onion seeds, dried red chillies and fenugreek seeds and fry for about 1 minute.

5 Add the chicken pieces to the pan, along with their spice paste, mixing as you go. Simmer gently for about 12–15 minutes, or until the chicken is thoroughly cooked.

6 Stir in the tomatoes, fresh coriander and green chillies for a minute to heat through, and serve immediately.

Chicken with Green Mango

Green or unripe mango is meant only for cooking purposes. These fruits are smaller than eating mangoes, and they have a sharper taste. They can be bought from Indian stores but if not available, cooking apples make an easy alternative.

Serves 4

1 green (unripe) mango or cooking apple
450g/1lb chicken breast fillets, skinned and cubed
1.5ml/¼ tsp onion seeds
5ml/1 tsp grated fresh root ginger
2.5ml/½ tsp crushed garlic
5ml/1 tsp chilli powder
1.5ml/¼ tsp ground turmeric
5ml/1 tsp salt
5ml/1 tsp ground coriander
30ml/2 tbsp vegetable oil
2 onions, sliced
4 curry leaves
300ml/½ pint/1¼ cups water
2 tomatoes, quartered
2 fresh green chillies, chopped
30ml/2 tbsp chopped fresh coriander (cilantro)

1 To prepare the mango, peel the skin and slice the flesh thickly. Discard the stone (pit) from the middle. Place the mango slices in a bowl, cover and set aside. If using apple, coat the slices with lemon juice to prevent discoloration.

2 Put the cubed chicken into a large mixing bowl and add the onion seeds, ginger, garlic, chilli powder, turmeric, salt and ground coriander. Mix the spices with the chicken, then stir in half the mango or apple slices.

3 Heat the oil in a wok, karahi or large pan over medium heat, and fry the sliced onions until golden brown. Add the curry leaves to the pan, and stir very gently to release their flavour.

4 Gradually add the chicken to the pan, stirring all the time. Stir-fry briskly over medium heat until the chicken is opaque.

5 Add the water, lower the heat and simmer for about 12–15 minutes, stirring, until the chicken is cooked and the water has completely evaporated.

6 Add the remaining mango or apple slices, the tomatoes, green chillies and fresh coriander. Serve immediately.

Baby Chicken Energy 268kcal/1120kJ; Protein 26g; Carbohydrate 4.1g, of which sugars 4g; Fat 16.6g, of which saturates 4.5g; Cholesterol 70mg; Calcium 60mg; Fibre 2.2g; Sodium 152mg.
Chicken with Mango Energy 264kcal/1107kJ; Protein 26.6g; Carbohydrate 18.1g, of which sugars 13.1g; Fat 10.1g, of which saturates 1.8g; Cholesterol 118mg; Calcium 56mg; Fibre 3.1g; Sodium 114mg.

Balti Chicken with Paneer and Peas

This is rather an unusual combination, but it really works well. Serve with plain boiled rice.

Serves 4

1 small chicken, about
   675g/1½lb
30ml/2 tbsp tomato
   purée (paste)
45ml/3 tbsp natural (plain)
   low-fat yogurt
7.5ml/1½ tsp garam masala
5ml/1 tsp crushed garlic
5ml/1 tsp grated fresh
   root ginger
pinch of ground cardamom
15ml/1 tbsp chilli powder

1.5ml/¼ tsp ground turmeric
5ml/1 tsp salt
5ml/1 tsp sugar
10ml/2 tsp sunflower or
   vegetable oil
2.5cm/1in cinnamon stick
2 black peppercorns
300ml/½ pint/1¼ cups water
115g/4oz paneer, cubed
30ml/2 tbsp fresh coriander
   (cilantro) leaves, roughly torn
   into pieces
2 fresh green chillies, seeded
   and chopped
50g/2fl oz/¼ cup low-fat fromage
   frais or ricotta cheese
75g/3oz/¾ cup frozen
   peas, thawed

1 Skin the chicken and cut it into six to eight equal pieces.

2 Mix the tomato purée, yogurt, garam masala, garlic, ginger, cardamom, chilli powder, turmeric, salt and sugar in a bowl.

3 Heat the oil with the whole spices in a karahi, wok or heavy pan, then pour the yogurt mixture into the oil. Lower the heat and cook gently for about 3 minutes, then pour in the water and bring to a simmer.

4 Add the chicken pieces to the pan. Cook for 2 minutes, stirring frequently, then cover the pan and cook over a medium heat for about 10 minutes.

5 Add the paneer cubes to the pan, followed by half the coriander leaves and half the green chillies. Mix well and cook for a further 5–7 minutes.

6 Stir in the fromage frais or ricotta and peas, heat through and serve with the reserved coriander and chillies.

Balti Chilli Chicken

Serves 4–6

75ml/5 tbsp corn oil
8 large fresh green chillies, slit
2.5ml/½ tsp mixed onion seeds
   and cumin seeds
4 curry leaves
5ml/1 tsp grated fresh root ginger
5ml/1 tsp chilli powder
5ml/1 tsp ground coriander
5ml/1 tsp crushed garlic

5ml/1 tsp salt
2 medium onions, chopped
675g/1½lb skinless chicken
   fillets, cubed
15ml/1 tbsp lemon juice
15ml/1 tbsp roughly chopped
   fresh mint
15ml/1 tbsp roughly chopped
   fresh coriander (cilantro)
8–10 cherry tomatoes

1 Heat the oil in a karahi, wok or deep frying pan. Lower the heat slightly and add the slit green chillies. Cook, stirring frequently, until the skin starts to change colour.

2 Add the onion seeds and cumin seeds, curry leaves, ginger, chilli powder, ground coriander, garlic, salt and onions, and fry for a minute, stirring constantly.

3 Add the chicken pieces to the pan. Stir-fry over a medium heat for about 7–10 minutes, or until the chicken is cooked right through. Take care not to overcook the chicken or it will become dry in texture.

4 Sprinkle on the lemon juice and add the roughly chopped fresh mint and coriander. Dot with the cherry tomatoes and serve immediately from the pan.

Balti Chicken with Vegetables

Serves 4–6

60ml/4 tbsp corn oil
2 medium onions, sliced
4 garlic cloves, thickly sliced
450g/1lb skinless chicken breast
   fillets, cut into strips
5ml/1 tsp salt
30ml/2 tbsp lime juice
3 fresh green chillies, seeded
   and chopped
2 medium carrots, cut into batons

2 medium potatoes, peeled and
   cut into 1cm/½in strips
1 medium courgette (zucchini),
   cut into batons

For the garnish
3 lime slices
15ml/1 tbsp chopped fresh
   coriander (cilantro)
2 fresh green chillies, seeded and
   cut into thin strips (optional)

1 Heat the oil in a wok. Lower the heat slightly and add the onions. Fry until the onions are lightly browned and softened.

2 Add half the garlic slices and fry for a few seconds before adding the chicken strips and salt. Cook, stirring frequently, until all the moisture has evaporated and the chicken is lightly browned.

3 Add the lime juice, green chillies and all the vegetables to the pan. Increase the heat and add the rest of the garlic. Stir-fry for 7–10 minutes, or until the chicken is cooked through and the vegetables are just tender.

4 Transfer the curry to a warmed serving dish and garnish with lime slices, coriander and green chilli strips. Serve immediately.

Chicken with Paneer Energy 313kcal/1303kJ; Protein 27.7g; Carbohydrate 7.3g, of which sugars 5.6g; Fat 19.3g, of which saturates 5.9g; Cholesterol 117mg; Calcium 87mg; Fibre 1.3g; Sodium 75mg.
Balti Chilli Chicken Energy 244kcal/1016kJ; Protein 21g; Carbohydrate 1.6g, of which sugars 0.5g; Fat 17.2g, of which saturates 2.2g; Cholesterol 56mg; Calcium 47mg; Fibre 0.7g; Sodium 56mg.
Chicken with Vegetables Energy 248kcal/1039kJ; Protein 21.2g; Carbohydrate 22.1g, of which sugars 10g; Fat 8.9g, of which saturates 1.2g; Cholesterol 53mg; Calcium 63mg; Fibre 3.7g; Sodium 70mg.

Balti Chicken in Saffron Sauce

This is a beautifully aromatic chicken dish that is partly cooked in the oven.

Serves 4
50g/2oz/¼ cup butter
30ml/2 tbsp corn oil
1.2–1.3kg/2½–3lb chicken, skinned and cut into 8 pieces
1 medium onion, chopped
5ml/1 tsp crushed garlic
2.5ml/½ tsp crushed black peppercorns
2.5ml/½ tsp crushed cardamom pods
2.5ml/¼ tsp ground cinnamon
7.5ml/1½ tsp chilli powder
150ml/¼ pint/⅔ cup natural (plain) yogurt
50g/2oz/½ cup ground almonds
15ml/1 tbsp lemon juice
5ml/1 tsp salt
5ml/1 tsp saffron strands
150ml/¼ pint/⅔ cup water
150ml/¼ pint/⅔ cup single (light) cream
30ml/2 tbsp chopped fresh coriander (cilantro)
fruity pilau or boiled rice, to serve

1 Preheat the oven to 180°C/350°F/Gas 4. Melt the butter with the corn oil in a karahi, wok or deep frying pan. Add the chicken pieces and fry until lightly browned, about 5–7 minutes. Remove the chicken from the pan using a slotted spoon, leaving behind the fat.

2 Add the onion to the same pan, and fry over a medium heat. Meanwhile, mix together the next 10 ingredients in a bowl. When the onions are lightly browned, pour the spice mixture into the pan and stir-fry for about 1 minute.

3 Add the chicken pieces, and continue to fry for a further 2 minutes stirring constantly. Pour in the water and bring to a simmer. Transfer the contents of the pan to a flameproof casserole and cover with a lid, or, if using a karahi with heatproof handles, cover with foil. Transfer to the preheated oven and cook for about 30–35 minutes.

4 Once you are sure that the chicken is cooked right through, remove it from the oven. Transfer the mixture to a frying pan or place the karahi on the stove and stir in the cream.

5 Reheat gently for about 2 minutes. Garnish with fresh coriander and serve with a fruity pilau or boiled rice.

Balti Chicken Pasanda

Yogurt and cream give this tasty dish its characteristic richness. Serve it with garlic and coriander naan to complement the almonds.

Serves 4
60ml/4 tbsp Greek (US strained plain) yogurt
2.5ml/½ tsp black cumin seeds
4 cardamom pods
6 whole black peppercorns
10ml/2 tsp garam masala
2.5cm/1in cinnamon stick
15ml/1 tbsp ground almonds
5ml/1 tsp crushed garlic
5ml/1 tsp grated fresh root ginger
5ml/1 tsp chilli powder
5ml/1 tsp salt
675g/1½lb skinless, boneless chicken, cut into bitesize cubes
75ml/5 tbsp corn oil
2 medium onions, diced
3 fresh green chillies, seeded and finely chopped
30ml/2 tbsp chopped fresh coriander (cilantro), plus extra to garnish
120ml/4fl oz/½ cup single (light) cream

1 Mix the Greek yogurt, black cumin seeds, cardamom pods, whole black peppercorns, garam masala and cinnamon stick together in a medium mixing bowl. Add the ground almonds, crushed garlic, grated ginger, chilli powder and salt and mix together well to combine.

2 Add the chicken cubes, stir to coat, and leave in the spice mixture to marinate for about 2 hours.

3 Heat the corn oil in a large karahi, wok or deep frying pan. Add the onions and fry for 2–3 minutes.

4 Add the chicken pieces mixture to the pan and stir until they are well blended with the onions.

5 Cook for 12–15 minutes over a medium heat until the sauce thickens and the chicken is cooked through.

6 Add the chopped green chillies and fresh coriander to the chicken in the wok, and pour in the single cream. Bring to the boil, stirring constantly, and serve the dish garnished with more fresh coriander, if you like.

Balti Chicken Pasanda Energy 434kcal/1812kJ; Protein 44.9g; Carbohydrate 13.2g, of which sugars 7.4g; Fat 23g, of which saturates 6g; Cholesterol 135mg; Calcium 107mg; Fibre 1.4g; Sodium 129mg.
Balti Chicken Energy 554kcal/2321kJ; Protein 75.6g; Carbohydrate 5.1g, of which sugars 4.7g; Fat 25.9g, of which saturates 12.2g; Cholesterol 255mg; Calcium 146mg; Fibre 0.8g; Sodium 792mg.

Chicken and Tomato Balti

If you like tomatoes, you will love this tangy chicken curry. It makes a delicious semi-dry balti and is also excellent served with a spicy lentil dish and plain boiled rice.

Serves 4

60ml/4 tbsp corn oil
6 curry leaves
2.5ml/½ tsp mixed onion and mustard seeds
8 medium tomatoes, sliced
5ml/1 tsp ground coriander
5ml/1 tsp chilli powder
5ml/1 tsp salt
5ml/1 tsp ground cumin
5ml/1 tsp crushed garlic
675g/1½lb skinless, boneless chicken, cubed
150ml/¼ pint/⅔ cup water
15ml/1 tbsp sesame seeds, roasted
15ml/1 tbsp chopped fresh coriander (cilantro)

1 Heat the oil in a karahi, wok or deep frying pan. Add the curry leaves and mixed onion and mustard seeds.

2 Toss the seeds over the heat for 1–2 minutes so that they become fragrant. Do not let the seeds burn.

3 Lower the heat slightly and add the tomatoes.

4 While the tomatoes are gently cooking, mix together the ground coriander, chilli powder, salt, ground cumin and crushed garlic in a mixing bowl.

5 Add the spices to the tomatoes in the wok or pan and stir well to combine the ingredients thoroughly.

6 Add the chicken pieces to the pan and stir well. Cook for about 5 minutes more, stirring frequently.

7 Pour the water into the pan and continue cooking, stirring occasionally, until the sauce reduces and thickens and the chicken is fully cooked and tender.

8 Sprinkle the roasted sesame seeds and chopped fresh coriander over the chicken and tomato balti. Serve immediately, from the pan with plain boiled rice, if you like.

Balti Chicken in Hara Masala Sauce

This creamy chicken curry, made with yogurt and fromage frais or ricotta cheese, can be served as an accompaniment to any of the rice dishes in this book.

Serves 4

1 crisp green eating apple, peeled, cored and cut into small cubes
60ml/4 tbsp fresh coriander (cilantro) leaves
30ml/2 tbsp fresh mint leaves
120ml/4fl oz/½ cup natural (plain) low-fat yogurt
45ml/3 tbsp low-fat fromage frais or ricotta cheese
2 fresh green chillies, seeded and chopped
1 bunch spring onions (scallions), chopped
5ml/1 tsp salt
5ml/1 tsp sugar
5ml/1 tsp crushed garlic
5ml/1 tsp grated fresh root ginger
15ml/1 tbsp vegetable oil
225g/8oz skinless chicken breast fillets, cubed
25g/1oz/2 tbsp sultanas (golden raisins)

1 Place the apple, 45ml/3 tbsp of the coriander leaves, the mint leaves, yogurt, fromage frais or ricotta, green chillies, spring onions, salt, sugar, garlic and fresh root ginger in a food processor and pulse for 1 minute.

2 Heat the oil in a karahi, wok or heavy frying pan.

3 Pour in the yogurt mixture and cook over low heat for about 2 minutes, stirring frequently.

4 Next, add the chicken pieces and blend everything together. Cook over medium to low heat for 12–15 minutes or until the chicken is fully cooked and tender.

5 Stir in the sultanas and the remaining 15ml/1 tbsp fresh coriander leaves and serve immediately.

> **Cook's Tip**
> *This dish makes an attractive centrepiece for a dinner party served with rice and a selection of Indian breads.*

Chicken and Tomato Energy 347kcal/1457kJ; Protein 43.4g; Carbohydrate 7.3g, of which sugars 4.7g; Fat 16.5g, of which saturates 2.4g; Cholesterol 118mg; Calcium 58mg; Fibre 1.8g; Sodium 118mg.
Balti Chicken Energy 299kcal/1254kJ; Protein 41.5g; Carbohydrate 3.4g, of which sugars 1.7g; Fat 13.5g, of which saturates 1.9g; Cholesterol 118mg; Calcium 28mg; Fibre 0.6g; Sodium 106mg.

Balti Chicken

Serves 4–6

1–1.3kg/2¼–3lb chicken, skinned and cut into 8 pieces
45ml/3 tbsp corn oil
3 medium onions, sliced
3 medium tomatoes, sliced
2.5cm/1in cinnamon stick
2 large black cardamom pods
4 black peppercorns
2.5ml/½ tsp black cumin seeds

5ml/1 tsp crushed fresh root ginger
5ml/1 tsp crushed garlic
5ml/1 tsp garam masala
5ml/1 tsp chilli powder
5ml/1 tsp salt
30ml/2 tbsp natural (plain) yogurt
60ml/4 tbsp lemon juice
30ml/2 tbsp chopped fresh coriander (cilantro)
2 fresh green chillies, chopped

1 Heat the oil in a large wok. Add the onions and fry until they are golden brown. Add the tomatoes, cinnamon, cardamoms, peppercorns, black cumin seeds, ginger, garlic, garam masala, chilli and salt. Lower the heat and stir-fry for 3–5 minutes.

2 Add the chicken pieces two at a time, and stir-fry for at least 7 minutes until the spice mixture has penetrated the chicken. Add the yogurt to the pan and mix well.

3 Lower the heat and cover the pan with a piece of foil. Cook gently for about 15 minutes, checking to make sure the sauce is not sticking. Finally, stir in the lemon juice, fresh coriander and green chillies, and serve immediately.

Khara Masala Balti Chicken

Serves 4

3 curry leaves
1.5ml/¼ tsp mustard seeds
1.5ml/¼ tsp fennel seeds
1.5ml/¼ tsp onion seeds
2.5ml/½ tsp white cumin seeds
1.5ml/¼ tsp fenugreek seeds
2.5ml/½ tsp pomegranate seeds
2.5ml/½ tsp dried red chillies
5ml/1 tsp salt

5ml/1 tsp grated fresh root ginger
3 garlic cloves, sliced
60ml/4 tbsp corn oil
4 fresh green chillies, slit
1 large onion, sliced
1 medium tomato, sliced
675g/1½lb skinless, boneless chicken, cubed
15ml/1 tbsp chopped fresh coriander (cilantro)

1 In a large mixing bowl, combine the curry leaves, mustard, fennel, onion, cumin and fenugreek seeds, chillies, pomegranate seeds and salt. Mix well to combine all the ingredients.

2 Add the grated ginger and garlic cloves to the spice mixture in the bowl and stir well to combine.

3 Heat the oil in a medium karahi, wok or deep pan. Add the spice mixture, then the green chillies. Spoon the sliced onion into the pan and fry over medium heat for about 5–7 minutes, stirring constantly to coat and flavour the onion with the spices.

4 Add the tomato and chicken pieces, and cook over medium heat for about 10–12 minutes, stirring frequently. The chicken should be cooked through and the sauce reduced.

5 Serve immediately from the pan, garnished with chopped fresh coriander.

Goan Chicken Curry

Coconut in all its forms is widely used to enrich Goan cuisine.

Serves 4

75g/3oz/1 cup desiccated (dry unsweetened shredded) coconut
30ml/2 tbsp vegetable oil
2.5ml/½ tsp cumin seeds

4 black peppercorns
15ml/1 tbsp fennel seeds
15ml/1 tbsp coriander seeds
2 onions, finely chopped
2.5ml/½ tsp salt
8 small chicken pieces, such as thighs and drumsticks, skinned
fresh coriander (cilantro) sprigs and lemon wedges, to garnish

1 Put the desiccated coconut in a bowl with 45ml/3 tbsp water. Leave to soak for 15 minutes.

2 Heat 15ml/1 tbsp of the oil in a karahi, wok or large pan and fry the cumin seeds, peppercorns, fennel and coriander seeds over a low heat for 3–4 minutes until they begin to splutter and release their fragrant aromas.

3 Add the finely chopped onions and fry for about 5 minutes without browning, stirring occasionally, until the onion has softened and turned translucent.

4 Stir in the coconut, along with the soaking water and salt, and continue to fry for a further 5 minutes, stirring occasionally to prevent the mixture from sticking to the pan.

5 Put the coconut mixture into a food processor or blender and process to form a coarse paste. Spoon into a bowl and set aside until required.

6 Heat the remaining oil and fry the chicken for 10 minutes. Add the coconut paste and cook over low heat for 15–20 minutes, or until the coconut mixture is golden brown and the chicken is cooked through and tender.

7 Transfer the curry to a warmed serving plate, and garnish with sprigs of fresh coriander and the lemon wedges. Chutney, rice or lentils make good accompaniments.

Balti Chicken Energy 231kcal/971kJ; Protein 29.6g; Carbohydrate 11.1g, of which sugars 6.2g; Fat 8.1g, of which saturates 1.3g; Cholesterol 79mg; Calcium 45mg; Fibre 1.7g; Sodium 77mg.
Khara Masala Energy 299kcal/1254kJ; Protein 41.5g; Carbohydrate 3.4g, of which sugars 1.7g; Fat 13.5g, of which saturates 1.9g; Cholesterol 118mg; Calcium 28mg; Fibre 0.6g; Sodium 106mg.
Goan Chicken Curry Energy 353kcal/1472kJ; Protein 33.3g; Carbohydrate 7.1g, of which sugars 5.4g; Fat 21.5g, of which saturates 11.9g; Cholesterol 158mg; Calcium 34mg; Fibre 3.6g; Sodium 143mg.

Creamy Mughlai-style Chicken

This recipe, with the heady and unmistakable aroma of saffron and the captivating flavour of a silky almond sauce, is perfect for a special occasion or family feast. This curry is inspired by the cuisine of the Mughal dynasty in India.

Serves 4–6
1 large onion
2 eggs
4 skinless chicken breast fillets
15–30ml/1–2 tbsp garam masala
90ml/6 tbsp ghee or vegetable oil
5cm/2in piece fresh root ginger, finely crushed
4 garlic cloves, finely crushed
4 cloves
4 green cardamom pods
5cm/2in piece cinnamon stick
2 bay leaves
15–20 saffron threads
150ml/¼ pint/⅔ cup natural (plain) yogurt, beaten with 5ml/1 tsp cornflour (cornstarch)
75ml/2½fl oz/⅓ cup double (heavy) cream
50g/2oz/½ cup ground almonds
salt and ground black pepper

1 Chop the onion finely. Break the eggs into a mixing bowl and beat with salt and black pepper.

2 Rub the chicken breast fillets all over with the garam masala, then brush with the beaten egg.

3 In a karahi, wok, or large pan, heat the ghee or vegetable oil and fry the prepared chicken pieces until browned on both sides. Remove the chicken from the pan with a slotted spoon and keep warm.

4 In the same pan, fry the chopped onion, ginger, garlic, cloves, cardamom pods, cinnamon and bay leaves. When the onion turns golden, remove the pan from the heat, allow the contents to cool a little and add the saffron and yogurt mixture to the pan. Stir well to prevent the yogurt from curdling.

5 Return the chicken to the pan, along with any juices, and gently cook until the chicken is cooked through and tender. Adjust the seasoning. Just before serving, pour in the cream. Fold it in then repeat the process with the ground almonds. Serve immediately.

Chicken with Mixed Chillies

Minced chicken is seldom cooked in Indian or Pakistani homes. However, it works very well in this dish.

Serves 4
275g/10oz skinless chicken breast fillets
2 thick red chillies
3 thick green chillies
45ml/3 tbsp corn oil
6 curry leaves
3 medium onions, sliced
7.5ml/1½ tsp crushed garlic
7.5ml/1½ tsp ground coriander
7.5ml/1½ tsp crushed fresh root ginger
5ml/1 tsp chilli powder
5ml/1 tsp salt
15ml/1 tbsp lemon juice
30ml/2 tbsp chopped fresh coriander (cilantro) leaves
chapatis and lemon wedges, to serve

1 Cut the chicken breast fillets into medium pieces. Add to a pan of boiling water and boil gently for about 10–12 minutes until soft and cooked through. Drain well.

2 Place the chicken in a food processor to mince (grind), or use a meat mincer if available.

3 Cut the chillies in half lengthways and remove the seeds, if you like. If you want a more fiery dish, you can retain the seeds and add them to the pan with the rest of the chillies. Cut the chilli flesh into thin strips.

4 Heat the oil in a non-stick wok or large frying pan and fry the curry leaves and onions until the onions are a soft golden brown, stirring frequently.

5 Lower the heat and stir the crushed garlic, ground coriander, crushed ginger, chilli powder and salt into the onions.

6 Add the minced chicken to the pan and stir-fry for about 3–5 minutes until it is beginning to brown.

7 Add the lemon juice, the chilli strips and most of the fresh coriander leaves. Stir-fry for a further 3–5 minutes, then serve, garnished with the remaining coriander leaves and accompanied by chapatis and lemon wedges.

Mughlai-style Chicken Energy 350kcal/1453kJ; Protein 25.8g; Carbohydrate 4.3g, of which sugars 3g; Fat 25.7g, of which saturates 6.8g; Cholesterol 139mg; Calcium 94mg; Fibre 0.8g; Sodium 99mg.
Chicken with Chillies Energy 196kcal/819kJ; Protein 18.4g; Carbohydrate 10.2g, of which sugars 7.3g; Fat 9.4g, of which saturates 1.2g; Cholesterol 48mg; Calcium 60mg; Fibre 2.4g; Sodium 49mg.

Hot Chilli Chicken

Not for the faint-hearted, this delicious fiery, hot curry is made with a spicy chilli masala paste.

Serves 4

30ml/2 tbsp tomato
   purée (paste)
2 garlic cloves, roughly chopped
2 green chillies, roughly chopped
5 dried red chillies
2.5ml/½ tsp salt
1.5ml/¼ tsp sugar
5ml/1 tsp chilli powder
2.5ml/½ tsp paprika
15ml/1 tbsp curry paste
30ml/2 tbsp vegetable oil
2.5ml/½ tsp cumin seeds
1 onion, finely chopped
2 bay leaves
5ml/1 tsp ground coriander
5ml/1 tsp ground cumin
1.5ml/¼ tsp ground turmeric
400g/14oz can
   chopped tomatoes
150ml/¼ pint/⅔ cup water
8 chicken thighs, skinned
5ml/1 tsp garam masala
fresh green chillies, seeded and
   sliced, to garnish
chapatis and natural (plain)
   yogurt, to serve

1 Put the tomato purée, garlic, green and dried red chillies, salt, sugar, chilli powder, paprika and curry paste into a food processor or blender and process to a smooth paste. Alternatively, grind all the ingredients together to a paste using a mortar and pestle.

2 Heat the oil in a large heavy pan or wok and fry the cumin seeds for about 2 minutes. Add the onion and bay leaves to the pan and fry for a further 5 minutes.

3 Add the spice paste to the pan and fry for 2–3 minutes until it releases a fragrant aroma. Add the remaining ground spices and cook, stirring constantly, for 2 minutes.

4 Add the chopped tomatoes and the measured water to the pan. Bring the mixture to the boil, reduce the heat and simmer for 5 minutes until the sauce thickens.

5 Add the chicken and garam masala to the sauce. Cover the pan with a lid and simmer for about 25–30 minutes until the chicken is tender. Serve with chapatis and natural yogurt, garnished with sliced green chillies.

Karahi Chicken with Fresh Fenugreek

Fresh fenugreek is a flavour that many people are unfamiliar with, and this recipe is a good introduction to this delicious herb. The chicken is boiled before being quickly stir-fried, to make sure that it is cooked all the way through.

Serves 4

115g/4oz boneless chicken thigh
   meat, skinned and cut
   into strips
115g/4oz chicken breast fillet,
   skinned and cut into strips
2.5ml/½ tsp crushed garlic
5ml/1 tsp chilli powder
2.5ml/½ tsp salt
10ml/2 tsp tomato purée (paste)
30ml/2 tbsp vegetable oil
1 bunch fresh fenugreek leaves
15ml/1 tbsp chopped fresh
   coriander (cilantro)
300ml/½ pint/1¼ cups water
pilau rice and wholemeal
   (whole-wheat) chapatis,
   to serve (optional)

1 Bring a pan of water to the boil, add the chicken strips and cook for about 5–7 minutes. Drain the chicken strips well and set aside while you prepare the rest of the dish.

2 In a mixing bowl, combine the crushed garlic, chilli powder and salt with the tomato purée.

3 Heat the oil in a large, heavy pan. Lower the heat and stir in the tomato purée and spice mixture.

4 Add the chicken pieces to the spices and stir-fry for about 5–7 minutes, then lower the heat further.

5 Add the fenugreek leaves and chopped fresh coriander to the pan. Continue to cook for 5–7 minutes, stirring frequently, until all the ingredients are well mixed.

6 Pour in the water, cover the pan and bring to the boil. Reduce the heat to medium and simmer for about 5 minutes, stirring several times during the cooking.

7 Place the chicken in a serving dish and serve with pilau rice and warm wholemeal chapatis, if you like.

Hot Chilli Chicken Energy 269kcal/1128kJ; Protein 27g; Carbohydrate 9g, of which sugars 7g; Fat 15g,0 of which saturates 3g; Cholesterol 120mg; Calcium 68mg; Fibre 1.5g; Sodium 400g.
Karahi Chicken Energy 127kcal/529kJ; Protein 13g; Carbohydrate 1.7g, of which sugars 0.7g; Fat 7.7g, of which saturates 1.2g; Cholesterol 60mg; Calcium 42mg; Fibre 0.9g; Sodium 64mg.

Sweet-and-sour Balti Chicken

This dish combines a tangy sweet-and-sour flavour with a deliciously creamy texture. It is excellent served with pilau or plain basmati rice or Indian breads, such as naan or paratha.

Serves 4

45ml/3 tbsp tomato
   purée (paste)
30ml/2 tbsp Greek (US strained
   plain) yogurt
7.5ml/1½ tsp garam masala
5ml/1 tsp chilli powder
5ml/1 tsp crushed garlic
30ml/2 tbsp mango chutney
5ml/1 tsp salt
2.5ml/½ tsp sugar
60ml/4 tbsp corn oil
675g/1½lb skinless, boneless
   chicken, cubed
150ml/¼ pint/⅔ cup water
2 fresh green chillies, seeded
   and chopped
30ml/2 tbsp chopped fresh
   coriander (cilantro)
30ml/2 tbsp single (light) cream

1 Mix the tomato purée, Greek yogurt, garam masala, chilli powder, crushed garlic, mango chutney, salt and sugar in a medium mixing bowl. Stir well.

2 Heat the oil in a karahi, wok or deep pan. Lower the heat slightly and pour in the spice mixture. Bring to the boil and cook for about 2 minutes, stirring occasionally.

3 Add the chicken pieces and stir until they are well coated.

4 Stir the water into the pan to thin the sauce slightly. Continue cooking for about 5–7 minutes, or until the chicken is fully cooked and tender.

5 Finally, add the fresh chillies, coriander and cream, cook for a further 2 minutes over low heat, then serve.

> **Variation**
> *If you like, you could lightly fry 1 sliced green (bell) pepper and 115g/4oz/1½ cups whole small button (white) mushrooms in 15ml/1 tbsp oil and add them to the spice mixture along with the chicken pieces in step 3.*

Balti Chicken with Spicy Potatoes

The baby potatoes in this dish are first tossed in spices and then baked separately in the oven before being added to the balti chicken, making an unusual yet delectable curry.

Serves 4

150ml/¼ pint/⅔ cup natural
   (plain) low-fat yogurt
25g/1oz/¼ cup ground almonds
7.5ml/1½ tsp ground coriander
2.5ml/½ tsp chilli powder
5ml/1 tsp garam masala
15ml/1 tbsp coconut milk
5ml/1 tsp crushed garlic
5ml/1 tsp grated fresh root ginger
30ml/2 tbsp chopped fresh
   coriander (cilantro)
1 fresh red chilli, seeded
   and chopped
225g/8oz skinless chicken
   breast fillets, cubed
15ml/1 tbsp vegetable oil
2 medium onions, sliced
3 green cardamom pods
2.5cm/1in cinnamon stick
2 cloves

For the potatoes

15ml/1 tbsp vegetable oil
8 baby potatoes, thickly sliced
1.5ml/¼ tsp cumin seeds
15ml/1 tbsp finely chopped
   fresh coriander (cilantro)

1 In a large bowl, mix together the first eight ingredients with half the fresh coriander and half the red chilli. Place the chicken pieces in the mixture, mix well, then cover and leave to marinate for about 2 hours.

2 Meanwhile, start to prepare the spicy potatoes. Heat the oil in a karahi, wok or heavy pan. Add the sliced potatoes, cumin seeds and fresh coriander and quickly stir-fry for 2–3 minutes.

3 Preheat the oven to 180°C/350°F/Gas 4. Spoon the potatoes into a baking dish, cover and bake in the oven for about 30 minutes or until they are cooked through.

4 Halfway through the potatoes' cooking time, heat the oil and fry the onions, cardamoms, cinnamon and cloves for 2 minutes.

5 Add the chicken mixture to the fried onions and stir-fry for 5–7 minutes. Lower the heat, cover and cook for 5–7 minutes until cooked through. Top the balti with the potatoes and garnish with the fresh coriander and red chilli before serving.

Sweet-and-sour Chicken Energy 355kcal/1486kJ; Protein 43.8g; Carbohydrate 10.1g, of which sugars 6.5g; Fat 15.9g, of which saturates 3g; Cholesterol 122mg; Calcium 85mg; Fibre 1.1g; Sodium 160mg.
Balti Chicken Energy 169kcal/711kJ; Protein 16.8g; Carbohydrate 16.2g, of which sugars 5.9g; Fat 4.6g, of which saturates 0.6g; Cholesterol 39mg; Calcium 128mg; Fibre 4.4g; Sodium 75mg.

Balti Chicken in a Lentil Sauce

Traditionally, this curry is made with lamb, but it is just as delicious when made with chicken breast meat.

Serves 4

30ml/2 tbsp chana dhal (yellow lentils)
50g/2oz/¼ cup masoor dhal or red split peas
15ml/1 tbsp vegetable oil
2 medium onions, chopped
5ml/1 tsp crushed garlic
5ml/1 tsp grated fresh root ginger
2.5ml/½ tsp ground turmeric
7.5ml/1½ tsp chilli powder
5ml/1 tsp garam masala
2.5ml/½ tsp ground coriander

7.5ml/1½ tsp salt
175g/6oz skinless chicken breast fillets, cubed
45ml/3 tbsp fresh coriander (cilantro) leaves
1 or 2 fresh green chillies, seeded and chopped
30–45ml/2–3 tbsp lemon juice
300ml/½ pint/1¼ cups water
2 tomatoes, peeled and halved

For the tarka

5ml/1 tsp vegetable oil
2.5ml/½ tsp cumin seeds
2 garlic cloves
2 dried red chillies
4 curry leaves

1 Put the dhal or peas in a pan with water and bring to the boil. Cook for 30–45 minutes until soft and mushy. Drain and set aside. Heat the oil in a karahi, wok or heavy frying pan and fry the onions until soft and golden brown. Add the garlic, ginger, turmeric, chilli powder, garam masala, ground coriander and salt to the pan and stir well.

2 Next, add the chicken pieces to the pan and fry for about 5–7 minutes, stirring constantly over a medium heat to seal in the juices and lightly brown the meat.

3 Add half the fresh coriander, the green chillies, lemon juice and water and cook for 3–5 minutes. Stir in the cooked lentils, then add the tomatoes. Sprinkle over the remaining coriander leaves. Take the pan off the heat and set aside.

4 To make the tarka, heat the oil and add the cumin seeds, whole garlic cloves, dried red chillies and curry leaves. Heat for about 30 seconds then spread over the top of the chicken and lentils. Serve the dish immediately.

Balti Chicken with Chillied Lentils

This is rather an unusual combination of flavours, but highly recommended. The mango powder gives a delicious tangy flavour to this spicy dish.

Serves 4–6

75g/3oz/½ cup chana dhal (yellow lentils)
60ml/4 tbsp corn oil
2 medium leeks, chopped

6 large dried red chillies
4 curry leaves
5ml/1 tsp mustard seeds
10ml/2 tsp mango powder
2 medium tomatoes, chopped
2.5ml/½ tsp chilli powder
5ml/1 tsp ground coriander
5ml/1 tsp salt
450g/1lb chicken, skinned, boned and cubed
15ml/1 tbsp chopped fresh coriander (cilantro)

1 Wash the yellow lentils and and carefully pick through to remove any stones or bits of grit.

2 Put the lentils into a pan with enough water to cover, and boil for about 10 minutes until they are soft but not mushy. Drain and set aside in a bowl.

3 Heat the oil in a medium karahi or large frying pan. Lower the heat slightly and add the leeks, dried red chillies, curry leaves and mustard seeds to the pan. Stir-fry gently for a few minutes until the leeks soften and the spices are fragrant.

4 Add the mango powder, tomatoes, chilli powder, ground coriander, salt and chicken, and stir-fry for 8–10 minutes.

5 Mix in the cooked lentils and fry for a further 2 minutes, or until you are sure that the chicken is cooked right through. Garnish with the fresh coriander and serve immediately accompanied by naan or paratha bread.

> **Cook's Tip**
> *Chana dhal, a yellow split lentil, is available from Asian stores and larger supermarkets. However, yellow split peas are a good substitute if you cannot find them.*

Balti Chicken Energy 196kcal/823kJ; Protein 20.3g; Carbohydrate 9.8g, of which sugars 2.6g; Fat 8.7g, of which saturates 1.2g; Cholesterol 47mg; Calcium 41mg; Fibre 2.5g; Sodium 51mg.
Balti Chicken Energy 196kcal/822kJ; Protein 20.3g; Carbohydrate 9.8g, of which sugars 2.6g; Fat 8.7g, of which saturates 1.2g; Cholesterol 47mg; Calcium 41mg; Fibre 2.5g; Sodium 51mg.

Chicken Saag

This mildly spiced curry uses a popular Indian combination of spinach and chicken. This dish is best made using fresh spinach.

Serves 4

225g/8oz fresh spinach leaves, washed but not dried
2.5cm/1in piece fresh root ginger, grated
2 garlic cloves, crushed
1 fresh green chilli, seeded and roughly chopped
200ml/7fl oz/scant 1 cup water
15ml/1 tbsp vegetable oil
2 bay leaves
1.5ml/¼ tsp black peppercorns
1 onion, finely chopped
4 tomatoes, peeled and finely chopped
10ml/2 tsp curry powder
5ml/1 tsp salt
5ml/1 tsp chilli powder
45ml/3 tbsp natural (plain) low-fat yogurt
8 chicken thighs, skinned
naan bread, to serve
natural low-fat yogurt and chilli powder, to garnish

1 Cook the spinach leaves, without extra water, in a tightly covered pan for 5 minutes. Put the cooked spinach, ginger, garlic and chilli with 50ml/2fl oz/¼ cup of the measured water into a food processor or blender and process to a thick purée. Set aside while you prepare the other ingredients.

2 Heat the oil in a large, heavy pan, add the bay leaves and black peppercorns and fry for 2 minutes. Stir in the onion and fry for a further 6–8 minutes until the onion has browned.

3 Add the tomatoes to the pan, lower the heat and simmer gently for about 5–8 minutes.

4 Stir in the curry powder, salt and chilli powder. Cook for 2 minutes over medium heat, stirring once or twice. Stir in the spinach purée and the remaining measured water, then simmer for 5 minutes. Add the yogurt, 15ml/1 tbsp at a time, and simmer for 5 minutes.

5 Add the chicken thighs and stir to coat them in the sauce. Cover and cook for 25–30 minutes until the chicken is tender. Serve on naan bread, drizzle over some natural yogurt and dust with chilli powder.

Chicken Dhansak with Chillies

Dhansak curries originate from the Parsee community and are traditionally made with lentils and meat.

Serves 4

75g/3oz/½ cup green lentils
475ml/16fl oz/2 cups chicken stock
45ml/3 tbsp vegetable oil
5ml/1 tsp cumin seeds
2 curry leaves
1 onion, finely chopped
2.5cm/1in piece fresh root ginger, chopped
1 green chilli, seeded and finely chopped
5ml/1 tsp ground cumin
5ml/1 tsp ground coriander
1.5ml/¼ tsp salt
1.5ml/¼ tsp chilli powder
400g/14oz can chopped tomatoes
8 chicken pieces, skinned
60ml/4 tbsp chopped fresh coriander (cilantro)
5ml/1 tsp garam masala
fresh coriander (cilantro) sprigs, to garnish
plain and yellow rice, to serve

1 Rinse the lentils under cold running water, and carefully pick through to remove any stones. Put the lentils into a large heavy pan with the chicken stock. Bring to the boil, cover the pan and simmer for about 15–20 minutes. Remove the pan from the heat and set aside.

2 Heat the oil in a karahi or large heavy pan. Fry the cumin seeds and curry leaves for 2 minutes until the fragrant aromas are released and the cumin seeds begin to splutter.

3 Add the onion, ginger and chilli to the pan. Cook for about 5 minutes, until the onion begins to soften and turn translucent. Stir in the ground cumin, ground coriander, salt and chilli powder with 30ml/2 tbsp water.

4 Add the chopped tomatoes and the chicken pieces. Cover the pan and simmer for 10–15 minutes.

5 Add the lentils with the chicken stock, chopped fresh coriander and garam masala and cook for 10 minutes, or until the chicken is cooked through and tender when pierced with a knife. Transfer the chicken to a bowl. Garnish with coriander sprigs and serve with plain and yellow rice.

Chicken Saag Energy 238kcal/998kJ; Protein 34.7g; Carbohydrate 6.8g, of which sugars 5.6g; Fat 8.2g, of which saturates 1.7g; Cholesterol 158mg; Calcium 155mg; Fibre 3g; Sodium 735mg.
Chicken Dhansak Energy 392kcal/1653kJ; Protein 54.9g; Carbohydrate 16.7g, of which sugars 4g; Fat 12.4g, of which saturates 1.9g; Cholesterol 140mg; Calcium 52mg; Fibre 2.9g; Sodium 135mg.

Chicken and Pasta Balti

This is not a traditional balti dish, as pasta is not eaten widely in India or Pakistan, however, it is a delicious fusion curry. Pomegranate seeds give this curry an unusual and delicious tangy flavour. Use vari-coloured pasta shells for a most attractive appearance.

Serves 4–6
75g/3oz/¾ cup small pasta shells
75ml/5 tbsp corn oil
4 curry leaves
4 whole dried red chillies
1 large onion, sliced
5ml/1 tsp crushed garlic
5ml/1 tsp chilli powder
5ml/1 tsp grated fresh root ginger
5ml/1 tsp crushed pomegranate seeds
5ml/1 tsp salt
2 medium tomatoes, chopped
175g/6oz/1⅓ cups chicken, skinned, boned and cubed
225g/8oz/1½ cups canned chickpeas, drained
115g/4oz/⅔ cup corn
50g/2oz mangetouts (snow peas), diagonally sliced
15ml/1 tbsp chopped fresh coriander (cilantro) (optional)
chutneys and pickles, to serve

1 Cook the pasta in boiling water, following the directions on the packet. Add 15ml/1 tbsp of the oil to the water to stop the pasta from sticking together. When it is cooked, drain well and set to one side while you prepare the other ingredients.

2 Heat the remaining oil in a deep, heavy frying pan or a large karahi, and add the curry leaves, whole dried chillies and the onion. Fry for about 5 minutes.

3 Add the garlic, chilli powder, ginger, pomegranate seeds, salt and tomatoes. Stir-fry for about 3 minutes.

4 Next add the chicken, chickpeas, corn and mangetouts to the onion mixture in the pan. Cook over a medium heat for about 5–7 minutes, stirring frequently.

5 Add in the pasta and stir well. Cook for a further 7–10 minutes until the chicken is cooked through.

6 Serve this curry garnished with the fresh coriander, if you like, and accompanied by Indian chutneys and pickles.

Chicken Tikka Masala

This classic Indian curry features tender pieces of chicken cooked in a creamy tomato sauce with ginger and chillies, and served on naan bread.

Serves 4
675g/1½lb skinless chicken breast fillets
90ml/6 tbsp tikka paste
60ml/4 tbsp natural (plain) yogurt
30ml/2 tbsp vegetable oil
1 onion, chopped
1 garlic clove, crushed
1 green chilli, seeded and chopped
2.5cm/1in piece fresh root ginger, grated
15ml/1 tbsp tomato purée (paste)
15ml/1 tbsp ground almonds
250ml/8fl oz/1 cup water
45ml/3 tbsp butter, melted
50ml/2fl oz/¼ cup double (heavy) cream
15ml/1 tbsp lemon juice
fresh coriander (cilantro) sprigs, natural (plain) yogurt and toasted cumin seeds, to garnish
naan bread, to serve

1 Cut the chicken into 2.5cm/1in pieces. Put 45ml/3 tbsp of the tikka paste and all of the yogurt into a bowl. Add the chicken, coat thoroughly and leave to marinate for 20 minutes. Soak some wooden skewers in water for 30 minutes.

2 For the tikka sauce, heat the oil and fry the onion, garlic, chilli and ginger for 5 minutes. Add the remaining tikka paste and fry for 2 minutes. Stir in the tomato purée, almonds and water. Simmer gently for about 15 minutes.

3 Thread the chicken on to the soaked wooden skewers. Preheat the grill (broiler) to medium. Brush the chicken with the butter and grill (broil) under a medium heat for 15 minutes, turning occasionally.

4 Pour the tikka sauce into a food processor or blender and process until smooth. Return the sauce to the pan.

5 Add the cream and lemon juice, remove the chicken from the skewers, add to the pan and simmer for 5 minutes. Garnish with coriander, yogurt and toasted cumin seeds and serve with naan bread.

Chicken Balti Energy 350kcal/1468kJ; Protein 20.6g; Carbohydrate 29.4g, of which sugars 5.9g; Fat 17.6g, of which saturates 2.7g; Cholesterol 36mg; Calcium 51mg; Fibre 4.2g; Sodium 157mg.
Chicken Tikka Energy 416kcal/1730kJ; Protein 46g; Carbohydrate 2.1g, of which sugars 0.2g; Fat 24.8g, of which saturates 8.5g; Cholesterol 203mg; Calcium 21mg; Fibre 0.5g; Sodium 172mg.

Chicken Dopiaza

Dopiaza translates literally as 'two onions' and describes this chicken curry in which two types of onion – medium and small – are used at different stages.

Serves 4

30ml/2 tbsp vegetable oil
8 small onions, halved
2 bay leaves
8 green cardamom pods
4 cloves
3 dried red chillies
8 black peppercorns
2 medium onions, finely chopped
2 garlic cloves, crushed
2.5cm/1in piece fresh root ginger, finely chopped
5ml/1 tsp ground coriander
5ml/1 tsp ground cumin
2.5ml/½ tsp ground turmeric
5ml/1 tsp chilli powder
2.5ml/½ tsp salt
4 tomatoes, peeled and finely chopped
120ml/4fl oz/½ cup water
8 chicken pieces, such as thighs and drumsticks, skinned
plain boiled rice, to serve

1 Heat half the oil in a wok or large heavy pan and fry the small onions over medium heat for about 8–10 minutes, or until golden brown. Remove and set aside.

2 Add the remaining oil and fry the bay leaves, cardamoms, cloves, chillies and peppercorns for 2 minutes.

3 Add the medium onions, garlic and ginger and fry for 5 minutes. Add the ground spices and salt and cook for 2 minutes.

4 Add the tomatoes and water and simmer for 5 minutes until the sauce thickens. Add the chicken and cook for 15 minutes.

5 Add the reserved small onions, then cover and cook for a further 10 minutes, or until the chicken is cooked through. Spoon the mixture on to a serving dish or individual plates. Serve immediately with plain boiled rice.

> **Cook's Tip**
> Soak the small onions in boiling water for about 2–3 minutes to make them easier to peel.

Red Hot Chicken Curry

Serves 4

30ml/2 tbsp vegetable oil
1.5ml/¼ tsp fenugreek seeds
1.5ml/¼ tsp onion seeds
2.5ml/½ tsp crushed garlic
2.5ml/½ tsp grated fresh root ginger
5ml/1 tsp ground coriander
5ml/1 tsp chilli powder
5ml/1 tsp salt
400g/14oz can tomatoes
30ml/2 tbsp lemon juice
350g/12oz chicken, skinned and cubed
30ml/2 tbsp chopped fresh coriander (cilantro)
3 fresh green chillies, chopped
2 medium onions, diced
½ red (bell) pepper, seeded and cut into chunks
½ green (bell) pepper
fresh coriander (cilantro), to garnish

1 In a medium pan, heat the oil and stir-fry the fenugreek and onion seeds. Add the chopped onions, crushed garlic and fresh ginger. Fry for about 5 minutes until the onions turn soft and golden brown. Reduce the heat to very low.

2 In a bowl, mix together the ground coriander, chilli powder, salt, canned tomatoes and lemon juice. Stir well.

3 Pour this mixture into the pan and increase the heat to medium. Stir-fry for 3 minutes. Add the chicken and stir-fry for 5–7 minutes. Add the coriander, chillies and pepper to the pan and stir well.

4 Lower the heat, cover the pan and allow to simmer for about 10 minutes, until the chicken cubes are cooked. Serve the curry hot, garnished with fresh coriander.

Spicy Chicken Jalfrezi

Serves 4

675g/1½lb skinless chicken breast fillets, cut into 2.5cm/1in pieces
30ml/2 tbsp vegetable oil
5ml/1 tsp cumin seeds
1 onion, finely chopped
1 green (bell) pepper, finely chopped
1 red (bell) pepper, finely chopped
2cm/¾in piece fresh root ginger, finely chopped
1 garlic clove, crushed
15ml/1 tbsp curry paste
1.5ml/¼ tsp chilli powder
5ml/1 tsp ground coriander
5ml/1 tsp ground cumin
2.5ml/½ tsp salt
400g/14oz can chopped tomatoes
30ml/2 tbsp chopped fresh coriander (cilantro), plus leaves, to garnish
plain boiled rice, to serve

1 Heat the oil in a wok and fry the cumin seeds for 2–3 minutes until they begin to splutter. Add the onion, green and red peppers, ginger and garlic to the pan and fry for 6–8 minutes. Add the curry paste to the pan and fry for about 2 minutes, stirring constantly.

2 Stir the chilli powder, ground coriander, cumin and salt into the pan and stir in about 15ml/1 tbsp cold water. Cook, stirring constantly, for a further 2–4 minutes. Add the chicken to the pan and cook for about 5 minutes, stirring occasionally. Add the tomatoes and the fresh coriander to the pan and stir well.

3 Cover the pan with a lid and simmer over low heat for about 15–20 minutes, or until the chicken is cooked through and tender. Garnish with the coriander and serve immediately with plain boiled rice, if you like.

Chicken Dopiaza Energy 331kcal/1391kJ; Protein 44.7g; Carbohydrate 9.8g, of which sugars 4.8g; Fat 13.1g, of which saturates 2.6g; Cholesterol 210mg; Calcium 51mg; Fibre 1.4g; Sodium 194mg.
Hot Chicken Energy 177kcal/747kJ; Protein 24.2g; Carbohydrate 15.8g, of which sugars 11.2g; Fat 2.5g, of which saturates 0.5g; Cholesterol 61mg; Calcium 51mg; Fibre 3.1g; Sodium 560mg.
Spicy Jalfrezi Energy 338kcal/1422kJ; Protein 44.8g; Carbohydrate 20.1g, of which sugars 14g; Fat 9.5g, of which saturates 1.5g; Cholesterol 118mg; Calcium 66mg; Fibre 3.8g; Sodium 120mg.

Balti Chicken Madras

This is a fairly hot chicken curry, which is excellent served with either plain boiled rice, pilau rice or naan bread. Reduce the number of chillies if you prefer a milder curry.

Serves 4

275g/10oz skinless chicken
   breast fillets
45ml/3 tbsp tomato purée (paste)
large pinch of ground fenugreek
1.5ml/¼ tsp ground fennel seeds
5ml/1 tsp grated fresh root ginger
7.5ml/1½ tsp ground coriander
5ml/1 tsp crushed garlic
5ml/1 tsp chilli powder
1.5ml/¼ tsp ground turmeric
30ml/2 tbsp lemon juice
5ml/1 tsp salt
300ml/½ pint/1¼ cups water
15ml/1 tbsp vegetable oil
2 medium onions, diced
2–4 curry leaves
2 fresh green chillies, seeded
   and chopped
15ml/1 tbsp fresh coriander
   (cilantro) leaves
naan bread or boiled rice, to serve

1 Remove any visible fat from the chicken breast fillets and cut the meat into bitesize pieces.

2 Place the tomato purée in a bowl and mix in the fenugreek, fennel seeds, ginger, coriander, garlic, chilli powder, turmeric, lemon juice, salt and measured water.

3 Heat the oil in a karahi, wok or heavy pan and fry the diced onions together with the curry leaves until the onions are golden brown and softened.

4 Add the chicken pieces to the onions and stir over the heat for about 1 minute to seal the meat.

5 Next, pour in the prepared spice mixture and continue to stir the chicken for about 2 minutes.

6 Lower the heat and cook for about 8–10 minutes, stirring frequently to prevent any of the mixture from catching and burning on the bottom of the pan.

7 Seed and chop the chillies. Add the chillies and coriander leaves and serve immediately with naan bread or rice.

Jungle Curry of Guinea Fowl

This traditional Thai wild food curry is an unusual and delectable dish. It can be made using any game, fish or chicken.

Serves 4

1 guinea fowl or similar
   game bird
15ml/1 tbsp vegetable oil
10ml/2 tsp green curry paste
15ml/1 tbsp Thai fish sauce
2.5cm/1in piece fresh galangal,
   peeled and finely chopped
15ml/1 tbsp fresh
   green peppercorns
3 kaffir lime leaves, torn
15ml/1 tbsp whisky
300ml/½ pint/1¼ cups
   chicken stock
50g/2oz yard-long beans, cut into
   7.5cm/3in lengths
   (about ½ cup)
225g/8oz/3¼ cups chestnut
   mushrooms, sliced
1 piece drained canned
   bamboo shoot, about
   50g/2oz, shredded

1 Cut up the guinea fowl, remove and discard the skin, then take all the meat off the bones. Chop the meat into bitesize pieces and set aside on a plate.

2 Heat the oil in a wok or frying pan and add the curry paste. Cook over a medium heat, stirring constantly, for 30 seconds, until the paste gives off its aroma.

3 Add the fish sauce and the guinea fowl meat and stir-fry until the meat is browned all over. Add the galangal, peppercorns, lime leaves and whisky to the pan, then pour in the stock.

4 Bring to the boil. Add the vegetables to the pan, return to a simmer and cook gently for 2–3 minutes, until they are just cooked. Spoon into a dish, and serve immediately.

Cook's Tip
Fresh green peppercorns are simply unripe berries. They are sold on the stem and look rather like miniature Brussels sprout stalks. Look for them at Thai supermarkets. If unavailable, substitute bottled green peppercorns, but rinse well and drain them before adding them to the curry.

Chicken Madras Energy 159kcal/667kJ; Protein 19.3g; Carbohydrate 11.5g, of which sugars 7.8g; Fat 4.4g, of which saturates 0.6g; Cholesterol 48mg; Calcium 65mg; Fibre 2.4g; Sodium 573mg.
Jungle Curry Energy 321kcal/1345kJ; Protein 42.2g; Carbohydrate 1.1g, of which sugars 0.7g; Fat 15g, of which saturates 4.4g; Cholesterol 0mg; Calcium 72mg; Fibre 1.1g; Sodium 136mg.

Red Duck Curry with Pea Aubergines

The rich flavour of duck is perfectly suited to this red hot curry.

Serves 4

4 skinless duck breast fillets
400ml/14fl oz can coconut milk
200ml/7fl oz/scant 1 cup
   chicken stock
30ml/2 tbsp red Thai curry paste
8 spring onions (scallions),
   finely sliced
10ml/2 tsp grated fresh
   root ginger
30ml/2 tbsp Chinese rice wine
15ml/1 tbsp fish sauce
15ml/1 tbsp soy sauce
2 lemon grass stalks,
   halved lengthways
3–4 kaffir lime leaves
300g/11oz pea aubergines
   (eggplants)
10ml/2 tsp sugar
salt and ground black pepper
10–12 fresh basil and mint
   leaves, to garnish
steamed or boiled jasmine rice,
   to serve

1 Using a sharp knife, trim any fat from the duck breast fillets and cut the meat into even, bitesize pieces.

2 Place a wok or large frying pan over a low heat and add the coconut milk, chicken stock, curry paste, spring onions, ginger, rice wine, fish and soy sauces, lemon grass and lime leaves. Slowly bring the mixture to the boil.

3 Add the duck, aubergines and sugar to the pan and gently simmer for 25–30 minutes, stirring occasionally.

4 Remove the wok from the heat and leave to stand, covered with a lid, for about 15 minutes.

5 Season to taste with salt and black pepper. Serve the curry ladled into shallow bowls with jasmine rice, garnished with fresh mint and basil leaves.

> **Cook's Tip**
> Tiny pea aubergines (eggplants) are available in Asian markets and stores, but if you have difficulty finding them, use larger aubergines cut into bitesize chunks.

Duck and Orange Curry

Robust spices, coconut milk and chillies combined with orange make this a very tasty curry. The duck is best marinated for as long as possible, although it tastes good even if you only have time to marinate it briefly.

Serves 4

4 duck breast portions, skinned
   and boned
30ml/2 tbsp Chinese
   five-spice powder
30ml/2 tbsp sesame oil
grated rind and juice of 1 orange
1 medium butternut squash,
   peeled and cubed
10ml/2 tsp Thai red curry paste
30ml/2 tbsp Thai fish sauce
15ml/1 tbsp palm sugar (jaggery)
   or light muscovado
   (brown) sugar
300ml/½ pint/1¼ cups
   coconut milk
2 fresh red chillies, seeded
4 kaffir lime leaves, torn
small bunch coriander (cilantro),
   chopped, to garnish
egg noodles, to serve

1 Cut the duck meat into bitesize pieces and place in a bowl with the five-spice powder, sesame oil and grated orange rind and juice. Stir well to mix all the ingredients and coat the duck pieces in the marinade.

2 Cover the bowl with a piece of clear film (plastic wrap) and set aside in a cool place to marinate for at least 15 minutes but preferably overnight in the refrigerator.

3 Meanwhile, bring a pan of water to the boil. Add the squash and cook for 10–15 minutes, until tender. Drain and set aside.

4 Pour the marinade from the duck into a wok and heat until boiling. Stir in the curry paste and cook for 2–3 minutes, until well blended and fragrant. Add the duck and cook for 3–4 minutes, stirring constantly, until browned on all sides.

5 Add the fish sauce and palm sugar and cook for 2 minutes more. Stir in the coconut milk until the mixture is smooth, then add the cooked squash, with the chillies and lime leaves.

6 Simmer gently, stirring frequently, for 5 minutes, then spoon into a dish, sprinkle with coriander and serve with noodles.

Red Duck Curry Energy 241kcal/1017kJ; Protein 31.1g; Carbohydrate 10.2g, of which sugars 10g; Fat 10.5g, of which saturates 2.3g; Cholesterol 165mg; Calcium 65mg; Fibre 1.8g; Sodium 546mg.
Duck and Orange Curry Energy 280kcal/1181kJ; Protein 30.8g; Carbohydrate 23.8g, of which sugars 23.8g; Fat 10g, of which saturates 2g; Cholesterol 165mg; Calcium 48mg; Fibre 0.4g; Sodium 195mg.

Duck and Sesame Stir-fry

For a special family meal that is a guaranteed success, this is ideal. It tastes fantastic and cooks fast.

Serves 4
250g/9oz boneless
 duck meat
15ml/1 tbsp sesame oil
15ml/1 tbsp vegetable oil
4 garlic cloves, finely sliced
2.5ml/½ tsp dried chilli flakes
15ml/1 tbsp Thai fish sauce
15ml/1 tbsp light soy sauce
120ml/4fl oz/½ cup water
1 head broccoli, cut into
 small florets
coriander (cilantro) and 15ml/
 1 tbsp toasted sesame seeds,
 to garnish

1 Cut all the duck meat into bitesize pieces. Heat the oils in a wok or large, heavy frying pan and stir-fry the garlic over medium heat until it is golden brown – do not let it burn otherwise it will give the food a bitter taste.

2 Add the duck to the pan and stir-fry for a further 2 minutes, until the meat begins to brown.

3 Stir in the chilli flakes, fish sauce, soy sauce and water. Add the broccoli and continue to stir-fry for about 2 minutes, until the duck is just cooked through.

4 Serve on warmed plates, garnished with coriander and the toasted sesame seeds.

Cook's Tip
Broccoli has excited interest recently since it is claimed that eating this dark green vegetable regularly can help to reduce the risk of some cancers. Broccoli is a source of protein, calcium, iron and magnesium, as well as vitamins A and C.

Variation
Pak choi (bok choy) or Chinese flowering cabbage can be used instead of broccoli.

Balinese Spiced Duck

This delicious duck dish is popular in Bali and across the neighbouring islands.

Serves 4
8 skinless duck breast fillets,
 fat trimmed
50g/2oz desiccated (dry
 unsweetened shredded) coconut
175ml/6fl oz/¾ cup coconut milk
salt and ground black pepper
deep-fried onions, to garnish
salad leaves or herb sprigs, to serve

For the spice paste
1 small onion or 4–6 shallots,
 finely sliced
2 garlic cloves, sliced
2.5cm/½ in fresh root ginger,
 peeled and sliced
1cm/½in fresh lengkuas, peeled
 and sliced
2.5cm/1 in fresh turmeric or
 2.5ml/½ tsp ground turmeric
1–2 red chillies, seeded and sliced
4 macadamia nuts or 8 almonds
5ml/1 tsp coriander seeds, dry-fried

1 Place the duck fat trimmings in a heated frying pan, without oil, and allow the fat to render. Reserve the fat.

2 Dry-fry the desiccated coconut in a preheated pan until crisp and brown in colour.

3 To make the spice paste, blend the onion or shallots, garlic, ginger, lengkuas, fresh or ground turmeric, chillies, nuts and coriander seeds to a paste in a food processor.

4 Spread the spice paste over the duck portions and leave to marinate in a cool place for 3–4 hours. Preheat the oven to 160°C/325°F/Gas 3. Shake off the spice paste and transfer the duck fillets to an oiled roasting pan. Cover with a double layer of foil and cook the duck in the oven for 2 hours.

5 Turn the oven temperature up to 190°C/375°F/Gas 5. Heat the reserved fat in a pan, add the paste and fry for 2 minutes. Stir in the coconut milk and simmer for 2 minutes. Discard the duck juices then cover the duck with the spice mix and sprinkle with the toasted coconut. Cook in the oven for 20–30 minutes.

6 Arrange the duck on a warm serving platter and sprinkle with the deep-fried onions. Season to taste and serve with the salad leaves or fresh herb sprigs of your choice.

Duck and Sesame Stir-fry Energy 165kcal/686kJ; Protein 17.4g; Carbohydrate 2.3g, of which sugars 2g; Fat 10.6g, of which saturates 1.8g; Cholesterol 69mg; Calcium 72mg; Fibre 2.9g; Sodium 345mg.
Balinese Spiced Duck Energy 305kcal/1270kJ; Protein 18.7g; Carbohydrate 9.2g, of which sugars 4.2g; Fat 22g, of which saturates 9.3g; Cholesterol 63mg; Calcium 79mg; Fibre 2.8g; Sodium 108mg.

Sweet-and-Sour Pork with Coconut

There are many variations of this recipe in South-east Asia, and this version includes papaya, because the enzymes in the unripe fruit are excellent for helping to tenderize meat.

Serves 4–6

675g/1¹/₂lb lean pork, diced
1 garlic clove, crushed
5ml/1 tsp paprika
5ml/1 tsp crushed black
   peppercorns
15ml/1 tbsp sugar
175ml/6fl oz/³/₄ cup palm or
   cider vinegar

2 small bay leaves
425ml/15fl oz/1³/₄ cups
   chicken stock
50g/2oz creamed coconut
   (see Cook's Tip)
150ml/¹/₄ pint/³/₄ cup vegetable
   oil or sunflower oil, for
   shallow-frying
1 under-ripe papaya, peeled,
   seeded and chopped
salt
¹/₂ cucumber, peeled and cut
   into batons, 2 firm tomatoes,
   skinned, seeded and
   chopped, and 1 small
   bunch chives, chopped,
   to garnish

1 Mix the pork with the garlic, paprika, black pepper, sugar, vinegar and bay leaves in a large bowl. Cover and leave in a cool place for 2 hours or overnight in the refrigerator to marinate. Add the chicken stock and coconut and mix well.

2 Transfer the mixture to a wok or large pan and simmer gently over low heat for about 30–35 minutes, then remove the pork pieces with a slotted spoon and drain.

3 In a heavy frying pan, heat the vegetable or sunflower oil and brown the pork pieces. Remove and drain well.

4 Return the pork to the sauce with the papaya, season with salt and simmer for 15–20 minutes, until tender. Garnish with the cucumber batons, chopped tomatoes and chives and serve.

Cook's Tip
If creamed coconut is not available, you can substitute it with 50ml/2fl oz/10 tsp coconut cream.

Pork and Pineapple Coconut Curry

The spicy heat of this curry helps to balance out the sweetness of the pineapple to make a delicious dish.

Serves 4

400ml/14fl oz coconut milk
¹/₂ medium pineapple
10ml/2 tsp Thai red curry paste
400g/14oz pork loin steaks,
   trimmed and thinly sliced
15ml/1 tbsp Thai fish sauce
5ml/1 tsp palm sugar (jaggery)
   or light muscovado
   (brown) sugar
15ml/1 tbsp tamarind juice, made
   by mixing tamarind paste with
   warm water
2 kaffir lime leaves, torn
1 fresh red chilli, seeded and
   finely chopped
lime rind, to garnish

1 Pour the coconut milk into a bowl and let it settle, so that the cream rises to the surface. Scoop the cream into a measuring jug (cup). You should have about 250ml/8fl oz/1 cup. If necessary, add a little of the coconut milk.

2 Pour the coconut cream into a large pan and bring it to the boil over high heat, stirring once or twice.

3 Cook the coconut cream for about 8 minutes, until the cream separates, stirring frequently to prevent it from sticking to the base of the pan. Peel and chop the pineapple.

4 Ladle a little of the coconut cream into a bowl and stir in the red curry paste. Return the mixture to the pan and stir until well mixed. Cook, stirring occasionally, for about 3 minutes, until the paste releases its fragrant aromas.

5 Add the sliced pork and stir in the fish sauce, sugar and tamarind juice. Cook, stirring constantly, for 2–3 minutes, until the sugar has dissolved and the pork is no longer pink.

6 Add the remaining coconut milk and the lime leaves to the pan. Bring to the boil, then stir in the pineapple pieces. Reduce the heat and simmer gently for about 3 minutes, or until the pork is fully cooked. Spoon into a large heated serving bowl or four individual bowls and sprinkle the chilli and strips of lime rind over. Serve immediately.

Sweet and Sour Pork Energy 727kcal/3035kJ; Protein 32.7g; Carbohydrate 76.5g, of which sugars 39.4g; Fat 32.8g, of which saturates 5.8g; Cholesterol 272mg; Calcium 85mg; Fibre 2.7g; Sodium 1048mg.
Pork Curry Energy 187kcal/790kJ; Protein 22.2g; Carbohydrate 15.3g, of which sugars 15.3g; Fat 4.5g, of which saturates 1.6g; Cholesterol 63mg; Calcium 55mg; Fibre 1.2g; Sodium 449mg.

Pork and Butternut Curry

This curry can be made with butternut squash, pumpkin or winter melon. It is delicious served with rice and a fruit-based salad, or even just with chunks of fresh crusty bread to mop up the tasty sauce.

Serves 4–6
30ml/2 tbsp groundnut (peanut) oil
25g/1oz galangal, finely sliced
2 fresh red chillies, peeled, seeded and finely sliced
3 shallots, halved and finely sliced
30ml/2 tbsp kroeung or curry paste
10ml/2 tsp ground turmeric
5ml/1 tsp ground fenugreek
10ml/2 tsp palm sugar (jaggery)
450g/1lb pork loin, cut into bitesize chunks
30ml/2 tbsp fish sauce
900ml/1½ pints/3¾ cups coconut milk
1 butternut squash, peeled, seeded and cut into bitesize chunks
4 kaffir lime leaves
salt and ground black pepper
1 small bunch fresh coriander (cilantro), coarsely chopped, and 1 small bunch fresh mint, stalks removed, to garnish
rice or noodles and salad, to serve

1 Heat the oil in a large wok or heavy pan. Stir in the galangal, chillies and shallots and stir-fry until fragrant. Add the kroeung or curry paste and stir-fry until it begins to colour. Add the turmeric, fenugreek and sugar and stir to combine.

2 Stir the chunks of pork loin into the pan and cook, stirring occasionally, until golden brown on all sides. Stir in the fish sauce and pour in the coconut milk.

3 Bring to the boil, add the squash and the lime leaves, and reduce the heat. Cook gently, uncovered, for 15–20 minutes, until the squash and pork are tender and the sauce has reduced. Season to taste. Garnish the curry with the coriander and mint, and serve with rice or noodles and salad.

Cook's Tip
Increase the number of chillies if you want a really hot curry.

Curried Pork with Pickled Garlic

This very rich Thai-style curry is best accompanied by lots of plain boiled rice and perhaps a light vegetable side dish. It could serve four with a vegetable curry on the side, and perhaps some steamed greens, such as pak choi or curly kale.

Serves 2
130g/4½oz lean pork steaks
30ml/2 tbsp vegetable oil
1 garlic clove, crushed
15ml/1 tbsp red curry paste
130ml/4½fl oz/generous ½ cup coconut cream
2.5cm/1in piece fresh root ginger, finely chopped
30ml/2 tbsp vegetable or chicken stock
30ml/2 tbsp Thai fish sauce
5ml/1 tsp sugar
2.5ml/½ tsp ground turmeric
10ml/2 tsp lemon juice
4 pickled garlic cloves, finely chopped
strips of lemon and lime rind, to garnish

1 Place the pork steaks in the freezer for 30–40 minutes, until firm, then, using a sharp knife, cut the meat into fine slivers, trimming off any excess fat.

2 Heat the oil in a wok or large, heavy frying pan and cook the garlic over low to medium heat until golden brown. Do not let it burn otherwise it will create a bitter taste. Add the curry paste and stir it in well.

3 Add the coconut cream and stir until the liquid begins to reduce and thicken. Stir in the pork. Cook for 2 minutes more, until the pork is cooked through.

4 Add the ginger, stock, fish sauce, sugar and turmeric to the pan, stirring constantly, then add the lemon juice and pickled garlic and heat through. Serve immediately in warmed bowls, garnished with strips of lemon and lime rind.

Cook's Tip
Asian stores sell pickled garlic. It is well worth buying, because the taste is sweet and delicious.

Pork and Butternut Energy 149kcal/628kJ; Protein 17g; Carbohydrate 10.6g, of which sugars 10.2g; Fat 4.6g, of which saturates 1.5g; Cholesterol 47mg; Calcium 71mg; Fibre 0.7g; Sodium 221mg.
Curried Pork Energy 227kcal/947kJ; Protein 16.3g; Carbohydrate 9.8g, of which sugars 6.1g; Fat 14g, of which saturates 2.4g; Cholesterol 41mg; Calcium 30mg; Fibre 1g; Sodium 474mg.

Cambodian Braised Pork with Ginger

This Cambodian curry is quick, tasty and beautifully warming thanks to the ginger and black pepper in the sauce. It is sure to be a popular choice for a family meal.

Serves 4–6
1 litre/1¾ pints/4 cups pork stock or water
45ml/3 tbsp tuk trey
30ml/2 tbsp soy sauce
15ml/1 tbsp sugar
4 garlic cloves, crushed
40g/1½oz fresh root ginger, peeled and finely shredded
15ml/1 tbsp ground black pepper
675g/1½lb pork shoulder or rump, fat trimmed, cut into bitesize cubes
steamed jasmine rice, crunchy salad and pickles or stir-fried greens, such as water spinach or yard-long beans, to serve

1 In a large heavy pan, bring the pork stock or water, tuk trey and soy sauce to the boil.

2 Reduce the heat and add the sugar, garlic, ginger, black pepper and pork into the pan. Stir well.

3 Cover the pan and simmer for about 1½ hours, until the pork is very tender and the liquid has reduced.

4 Serve the pork with steamed jasmine rice, drizzling the braising juices from the pan over it, and accompany the dish with a fresh crunchy salad, pickled vegetables or stir-fried greens, such as the delicious stir-fried water spinach with nuoc cham, or yard-long beans.

Cook's Tips
• Tuk trey is a Khmer marinade, consisting of nuoc mam (Vietnamese fish sauce), vinegar, lime juice, sugar and garlic. It is indispensable in Cambodian cookery.
• Yard-long beans, also known as snake or asparagus beans, are much used in stir-fries in South-east Asian cooking. They are at their best when young and tender. If they are not available, ordinary green beans are a good substitute.

Goan Pork with Hot Spices

Pork and beef dishes are not very common in India, but Goa, on the west coast of the country, has a cuisine influenced by Hinduism, Islam and Christianity.

Serves 4
60ml/4 tbsp vegetable oil
15ml/1 tbsp grated fresh root ginger
15ml/1 tbsp crushed garlic
2.5cm/1in piece cinnamon stick, broken up
2–4 dried red chillies, chopped or torn
4 cloves
10ml/2 tsp cumin seeds
10 black peppercorns
675g/1½lb cubed leg of pork, crackling and fat removed
5ml/1 tsp ground turmeric
200ml/7fl oz/scant 1 cup warm water
25ml/1½ tbsp tomato purée (paste)
2.5ml/½ tsp chilli powder (optional)
1 large onion, finely sliced
5ml/1 tsp salt
5ml/1 tsp sugar
10ml/2 tbsp cider vinegar
1 green chilli, split, to garnish

1 Heat 30ml/2 tbsp of the oil in a wok, karahi or large pan, and add the ginger and garlic. Fry for 30 seconds.

2 Grind the next five ingredients to a fine powder, using a spice or coffee grinder. Add the spice mix to the pan and fry for a further 30 seconds, stirring.

3 Add the pork and turmeric to the pan and increase the heat slightly. Fry for about 5–6 minutes or until the meat starts to release its juices, stirring regularly.

4 Add the water, tomato purée and chilli powder, if using, to the pan and bring to the boil. Cover the pan with a lid and simmer gently for 35–40 minutes.

5 Heat the remaining oil and fry the onion for 8–9 minutes until browned, stirring regularly.

6 Add the onion to the pork with the salt, sugar and vinegar. Stir, cover and simmer for 30–35 minutes or until the pork is tender. Remove from the heat, garnish with the split green chilli and serve.

Cambodian Pork Energy 147Kcal/619kJ; Protein 24g; Carbohydrate 2.7g, of which sugars 2.7g; Fat 4g, of which saturates 2g; Cholesterol 71mg; Calcium 11mg; Fibre 0.1g; Sodium 81mg.
Goan Pork Energy 543kcal/2260kJ; Protein 38.9g; Carbohydrate 6.6g, of which sugars 6.4g; Fat 40.4g, of which saturates 14.6g; Cholesterol 142mg; Calcium 19mg; Fibre 0g; Sodium 1475mg.

Black-eyed Bean Stew with Sausage

Bean stews made with spicy cured sausage, or cured, dried beef fillet, are the ideal one-pot meal for the whole family. A wide variety of spicy cured sausages will work well in this recipe. Meaty black-eyed beans are used in this curry, but any dried beans or chickpeas can be used instead.

Serves 4–6

175g/6oz/scant 1 cup dried black-eyed beans (peas), soaked in cold water overnight
30ml/2 tbsp ghee or 15ml/1 tbsp each olive oil and butter
1 large onion, cut in half lengthways and sliced along the grain
2–3 garlic cloves, roughly chopped and bruised with the flat side of a knife
5ml/1 tsp cumin seeds
5–10ml/1–2 tsp coriander seeds
5ml/1 tsp fennel seeds
5–10ml/1–2 tsp sugar or clear honey
1 spicy cured sausage, about 25cm/10in long, sliced
150ml/¼ pint/⅔ cup white wine
400g/14oz can tomatoes
1 bunch of fresh flat leaf parsley, roughly chopped
salt and ground black pepper

1 Drain the beans, transfer them into a pan and fill the pan with plenty of cold water. Bring to the boil and boil for 1 minute, then lower the heat and partially cover the pan. Simmer the beans for about 25 minutes, or until they are *al dente*. Drain, rinse well under cold running water and remove any loose skins by rubbing the beans between your fingers.

2 Preheat the oven to 180°C/350°F/Gas 4. Melt the ghee or oil and butter in a flameproof casserole. Stir in the onion, garlic and spices and fry until the onion begins to colour.

3 Stir the sugar or honey into the casserole, toss in the spicy sausage and cook until it begins to brown.

4 Add the beans, followed by the wine. Bubble up the wine, then lower the heat and add the tomatoes. Stir in half the parsley and season with salt and pepper.

5 Cover and bake for about 40 minutes. Before serving, taste for seasoning and sprinkle with the remaining parsley.

Chilli Pork with Curry Leaves

Curry leaves and chillies are two of the hallmark ingredients used in the southern states of India. This recipe is from the state of Andhra Pradesh, where the hottest chillies, known as guntur after the region where they are produced, are grown in abundance.

Serves 4–6

30ml/2 tbsp vegetable oil
1 large onion, finely sliced
5cm/2in piece fresh root ginger, finely grated
4 garlic cloves, crushed
12 curry leaves
45ml/3 tbsp extra-hot curry paste, or 60ml/4 tbsp hot curry powder
15ml/1 tbsp chilli powder
5ml/1 tsp Chinese five-spice powder
5ml/1 tsp ground turmeric
900g/2lb pork, cubed
175ml/6fl oz/¾ cup thick coconut milk
salt
red onion, finely sliced, to garnish
Indian bread and fruit raita, to serve

1 Heat the oil in a karahi, wok or large pan, and fry the onion, ginger, garlic and curry leaves until the onion is soft.

2 Add the curry paste or powder, chilli and five-spice powder, turmeric and salt to the pan. Stir well.

3 Add the pork to the pan and stir well over a medium heat to seal and evenly brown the meat pieces. Keep stirring until the oil separates from the paste. Cover the pan with the lid and cook for about 20–25 minutes.

4 Stir in the coconut milk and simmer, still covered, for about 10 minutes or until the meat is cooked. Toward the end of cooking, uncover the pan to allow the excess liquid to reduce and the sauce to thicken slightly. Garnish with red onion and serve with Indian bread, and with fruit raita, for a cooling effect.

Cook's Tip
For extra flavour, reserve half the curry leaves and add them with the coconut milk in step 3.

Black-eyed Bean Stew Energy 382kcal/1594kJ; Protein 18g; Carbohydrate 20g, of which sugars 6.7g; Fat 24.4g, of which saturates 10g; Cholesterol 52mg; Calcium 55mg; Fibre 6g; Sodium 944mg.
Chilli Pork Energy 283kcal/1182kJ; Protein 34.8g; Carbohydrate 11.1g, of which sugars 5.2g; Fat 11.5g, of which saturates 2.8g; Cholesterol 95mg; Calcium 58mg; Fibre 0.9g; Sodium 143mg.

Spiced Lamb in a Yogurt Sauce

The lamb is first marinated and then cooked slowly in a hot yogurt sauce. It is served with dried apricots that have been lightly sautéed with spices.

Serves 4

15ml/1 tbsp tomato
  purée (paste)
175ml/6fl oz/²/₃ cup natural
  (plain) low-fat yogurt
5ml/1 tsp garam masala
1.5ml/¼ tsp cumin seeds
5ml/1 tsp salt

5ml/1 tsp crushed garlic
5ml/1 tsp crushed fresh
  root ginger
5ml/1 tsp chilli powder
225g/8oz lean spring lamb, cut
  into strips
15ml/3 tsp corn oil
2 medium onions, finely sliced
25g/1oz low-fat spread
2.5cm/1in cinnamon stick
2 green cardamom pods
5 ready-to-eat dried
  apricots, quartered
15ml/1 tbsp fresh coriander
  (cilantro) leaves

1 In a bowl, blend together the tomato purée, yogurt, garam masala, cumin seeds, salt, garlic, ginger and chilli powder. Place the lamb in the sauce and leave to marinate for about 1 hour.

2 Heat 10ml/2 tsp of the oil in a non-stick wok or frying pan and fry the onions until crisp and golden brown.

3 Remove the onions using a slotted spoon, allow to cool and then grind down by processing briefly in a food processor or with a pestle in a mortar. Reheat the oil remaining in the wok and return the onions to the wok or frying pan.

4 Add the lamb and stir-fry for about 2 minutes. Cover, lower the heat and cook for 15 minutes, or until the meat is cooked through. If required, add about 150ml/¼ pint/²/₃ cup water during the cooking. Remove from the heat and set aside.

5 Heat the low-fat spread with the remaining oil in a pan and drop in the cinnamon stick and cardamoms.

6 Add the dried apricots to the pan and stir over low heat for about 2 minutes to heat through. Pour this over the lamb. Serve immediately garnished with the coriander.

Creamy Lamb Korma

Serves 4–6

15ml/1 tbsp white sesame seeds
15ml/1 tbsp white poppy seeds
50g/2oz almonds, blanched
2 green chillies, seeded
5cm/2in piece fresh root ginger, sliced
6 garlic cloves, sliced
1 onion, finely chopped
45ml/3 tbsp ghee or vegetable oil
6 green cardamoms

5cm/2in piece cinnamon stick
4 cloves
900g/2lb lean lamb, cubed
5ml/1 tsp ground cumin
5ml/1 tsp ground coriander
salt
300ml/½ pint/1¼ cups double (heavy)
  cream mixed with 2.5ml/½ tsp
  cornflour (cornstarch)
roasted sesame seeds, to garnish

1 Heat a heavy frying pan and dry-roast the sesame and poppy seeds, almonds, chillies, ginger, garlic and onion for about 3–5 minutes until the aromatic fragrances of the spices are released. Leave the mixture to cool and grind to a fine paste using a food processor.

2 Heat the ghee or oil in a wok. Add the cardamoms, cinnamon and cloves and stir-fry until the cloves begin to swell. Add the lamb, ground cumin and coriander, and the prepared paste to the pan. Season with salt, to taste. Cover the pan and cook over a low heat until the lamb is almost done, about 30–40 minutes.

3 Remove the pan from the heat, leave it to cool a little and then gradually fold in the double cream, reserving about 15ml/1 tsp to use as a garnish.

4 To serve, gently reheat the lamb uncovered and serve hot, garnished with the sesame seeds and the remaining cream.

Lamb Korma with Mint

Serves 4

2 fresh green chillies
120ml/4fl oz/½ cup natural
  (plain) low-fat yogurt
50ml/2fl oz/¼ cup coconut milk
15ml/1 tbsp ground almonds
5ml/1 tsp salt
5ml/1 tsp crushed garlic
5ml/1 tsp grated fresh root ginger
5ml/1 tsp garam masala

1.5ml/¼ tsp ground cardamom
large pinch of ground cinnamon
15ml/1 tbsp chopped fresh mint
15ml/1 tbsp vegetable oil
2 medium onions, diced
1 bay leaf
4 black peppercorns
225g/8oz lean lamb, cut into strips
150ml/¼ pint/²/₃ cup water
fresh mint leaves, torn, to garnish

1 Finely chop the chillies. Whisk the yogurt with the chillies, coconut milk, ground almonds, salt, garlic, ginger, garam masala, cardamom, cinnamon and mint.

2 Heat the oil in a wok and fry the onions with the bay leaf and peppercorns for about 5 minutes. When the onions are soft and golden brown, add the lamb and stir-fry for about 2 minutes.

3 Pour in the yogurt and coconut mixture and the water, lower the heat, cover and cook for about 15 minutes or until the lamb is cooked through, stirring occasionally. Uncover and stir the mixture over the heat for a further 2 minutes to reduce the sauce. Serve garnished with fresh mint leaves.

Spiced Lamb Energy 302kcal/1259kJ; Protein 16.4g; Carbohydrate 19.6g, of which sugars 15.4g; Fat 18.3g, of which saturates 4.9g; Cholesterol 44mg; Calcium 139mg; Fibre 2.7g; Sodium 141mg.
Creamy Lamb Korma Energy 220kcal/916kJ; Protein 14.2g; Carbohydrate 14.5g, of which sugars 11.1g; Fat 12.2g, of which saturates 3.8g; Cholesterol 42mg; Calcium 101mg; Fibre 2.1g; Sodium 90mg.
Lamb Korma with Mint Energy 197kcal/823kJ; Protein 14.5g; Carbohydrate 13.6g, of which sugars 9.9g; Fat 10g, of which saturates 3.5g; Cholesterol 43mg; Calcium 101mg; Fibre 1.8g; Sodium 583mg.

Malay Lamb Korma with Coconut Milk

Adapted from the traditional Indian korma, the creamy Malay version is flavoured with coconut milk. This tasty curry is often accompanied by a fragrant rice or flatbread and a salad or sambal.

Serves 4–6
25g/1oz fresh root ginger, peeled and chopped
4 garlic cloves, chopped
2 red chillies, seeded and chopped
10ml/2 tsp garam masala
10ml/2 tsp ground coriander
5ml/1 tsp ground cumin
5ml/1 tsp ground turmeric
675g/1½lb lamb shoulder, cut into bitesize cubes
45ml/3 tbsp ghee, or 30ml/2 tbsp vegetable oil and 15g/½ oz/ 1 tbsp butter
2 onions, halved lengthways and sliced along the grain
2.5ml/½ tsp sugar
4–6 cardamom pods, bruised
1 cinnamon stick
400ml/14fl oz/1⅔ cups coconut milk
salt and ground black pepper
30ml/2 tbsp roasted peanuts, crushed, and fresh coriander (cilantro) and mint leaves, coarsely chopped, to garnish

1 Using a mortar and pestle or food processor, grind the ginger, garlic and chillies to a paste. Stir in the garam masala, ground coriander, cumin and turmeric. Put the lamb into a shallow dish and rub the paste into it. Cover and leave to marinate for 1 hour.

2 Heat the ghee or oil and butter in a heavy pan or flameproof pot. Add the onions and sugar, and cook until brown and almost caramelized. Stir in the cardamom pods and cinnamon stick and add the lamb with all the marinade. Mix well and cook until the meat is browned all over.

3 Pour in the coconut milk, stir well and bring to the boil. Reduce the heat, cover the pan and cook the meat gently for 30–40 minutes until tender. Make sure the meat doesn't become dry and stir in a little extra coconut milk, or water, if necessary.

4 Season to taste with salt and pepper. Sprinkle the peanuts over and garnish with the coriander and mint. Serve immediately.

Spicy Lamb with Mint Peas

A simple curry for a family meal, this is easy to prepare and very versatile. It is equally delicious whether served with plain boiled rice or bread. Another excellent use for the lamb mixture is for filling samosas.

Serves 4
15ml/1 tbsp vegetable oil
1 medium onion, chopped
2.5ml/½ tsp crushed garlic
2.5ml/½ tsp grated fresh root ginger
2.5ml/½ tsp chilli powder
1.5ml/¼ tsp ground turmeric
5ml/1 tsp ground coriander
5ml/1 tsp salt
2 medium tomatoes, sliced
275g/10oz lean leg of lamb, minced (ground)
1 large carrot, sliced or cut into batons
75g/3oz/½ cup petits pois (baby peas)
15ml/1 tbsp chopped fresh mint
15ml/1 tbsp chopped fresh coriander (cilantro)
1 fresh green chilli, chopped
fresh coriander (cilantro) sprigs, to garnish

1 In a deep, heavy frying pan, heat the oil and fry the chopped onion over a medium heat for 5 minutes until golden.

2 Meanwhile, in a small mixing bowl, mix the garlic, ginger, chilli powder, turmeric, ground coriander and salt. Stir well.

3 Add the sliced tomatoes and the spice mixture to the cooked onion in the frying pan and fry for about 2–3 minutes, stirring constantly.

4 Add the minced lamb to the mixture and cook for about 7–10 minutes, stirring frequently, to seal.

5 Break up any lumps of meat which may form in the pan, using a potato masher, if necessary.

6 Finally add the carrot, petits pois, chopped fresh mint and coriander and the chopped green chilli and mix well.

7 Cook, stirring for 2–3 minutes until the carrot slices or batons and the petits pois are cooked, then serve immediately, garnished with fresh coriander sprigs.

Malay Lamb Korma Energy 267kcal/1117kJ; Protein 24.3g; Carbohydrate 8.5g, of which sugars 6.8g; Fat 15.4g, of which saturates 6.4g; Cholesterol 86mg; Calcium 46mg; Fibre 1.2g; Sodium 211mg.
Spicy Lamb with Peas Energy 192kcal/802kJ; Protein 15.8g; Carbohydrate 7.6g, of which sugars 5.7g; Fat 11.2g, of which saturates 4.1g; Cholesterol 52mg; Calcium 49mg; Fibre 2.9g; Sodium 77mg.

Balti Mini Lamb Kebabs

In this unusual balti dish the meat patties are cooked on skewers before being added to the karahi along with the other vegetables. This makes a great meal on its own or serve with Indian breads.

Serves 6
450g/1lb lean minced
  (ground) lamb
1 medium onion, finely chopped
5ml/1 tsp garam masala
5ml/1 tsp crushed garlic
2 medium fresh green chillies,
  finely chopped
30ml/2 tbsp chopped fresh
  coriander (cilantro), plus extra
  to garnish
5ml/1 tsp salt
15ml/1 tbsp plain
  (all-purpose) flour
60ml/4 tbsp corn oil
12 baby (pearl) onions
4 fresh green chillies, sliced
12 cherry tomatoes

1 Mix the lamb, onion, garam masala, garlic, green chillies, fresh coriander, salt and flour in a medium bowl, using your hands. Transfer the mixture to a food processor or blender and process for about 1–2 minutes, until the mixture has turned even finer in texture.

2 Put the mixture back into the bowl. Break off small pieces and wrap them around skewers to form small sausage shapes. Put about two of these shapes on each skewer.

3 Continue making up the sausage shapes until you have used up all the mixture. Preheat the grill (broiler) to its maximum setting. Baste the meat with 15ml/1 tbsp of the oil and grill (broil) the kebabs for 12–15 minutes, turning and basting occasionally, until the meat is evenly browned.

4 Heat the remaining 45ml/3 tbsp of the oil in a karahi, wok or deep pan. Lower the heat slightly and add the whole baby onions. As soon as the onions start to darken, add the fresh chillies and tomatoes to the pan.

5 Slide the lamb patties off their skewers and add them to the onion and tomato mixture. Stir gently for about 3 minutes until they are heated through. Transfer to a warmed serving dish and garnish with fresh coriander.

Indian Lamb and Chickpea Burgers

Serves 4–6
50g/2oz/1/3 cup chickpeas,
  soaked overnight in water
2 onions, finely chopped
250g/9oz lean lamb, cubed
5ml/1 tsp cumin seeds
5ml/1 tsp garam masala
4–6 fresh green chillies, chopped
5cm/2in piece fresh root ginger
175ml/6fl oz/3/4 cup water
a few fresh coriander (cilantro)
  and mint leaves, chopped
juice of 1 lemon
15ml/1 tbsp gram flour
2 eggs, beaten
vegetable oil, for shallow-frying
salt
1/2 lime, to garnish

1 Drain the chickpeas and cook them in a pan of boiling water for 1 hour. Drain again, return to the pan and add the onions, lamb, cumin seeds, garam masala, chillies, crushed ginger and water, and salt to taste. Bring to the boil. Simmer, covered, for about 2 hours until the meat and chickpeas are cooked.

2 Remove the lid and continue to cook uncovered to reduce the excess liquid. Leave to cool, and then grind to a paste in a food processor, blender or with a mortar and pestle.

3 Scrape the mixture into a mixing bowl and add the fresh coriander and mint, lemon juice and flour. Knead well. Divide the mixture into 10–12 portions and roll each into a ball, then flatten slightly. Chill in the refrigerator for 1 hour.

4 Dip the burgers in the beaten egg and shallow-fry each side until golden brown. Serve immediately, with the lime.

Keema Lamb with Curry Leaves

Serves 4
10ml/2 tsp corn oil
2 medium onions, chopped
10 curry leaves
6 green chillies
350g/12oz lean minced
  (ground) lamb
5ml/1 tsp crushed fresh
  root ginger
5ml/1 tsp crushed garlic
5ml/1 tsp chilli powder
1.5ml/1/4 tsp ground turmeric
5ml/1 tsp salt
2 tomatoes, skinned
  and quartered
15ml/1 tbsp chopped fresh
  coriander (cilantro)

1 Heat the oil in a non-stick wok or frying pan. Stir-fry the onions together with the curry leaves and three of the whole green chillies for 3–4 minutes, until the onions begin to soften and turn translucent but not browned.

2 Put the lamb into a large mixing bowl and add the ginger and garlic, chilli powder, turmeric and salt. Mix well to blend everything together thoroughly.

3 Add the lamb mixture to the pan with the onions and cook for about 7–10 minutes, stirring frequently and lowering the heat to medium if necessary.

4 Add the tomatoes and coriander to the pan. Stir in the remaining whole green chillies. Continue to stir-fry for a further 2 minutes before serving.

Balti Mini Lamb Kebabs Energy 253kcal/1053kJ; Protein 15.8g; Carbohydrate 8.1g, of which sugars 3.9g; Fat 17.8g, of which saturates 5.8g; Cholesterol 58mg; Calcium 37mg; Fibre 1.1g; Sodium 56mg.
Indian Lamb Burgers Energy 245kcal/1019kJ; Protein 14g; Carbohydrate 14.4g, of which sugars 4.9g; Fat 15.1g, of which saturates 3.7g; Cholesterol 95mg; Calcium 60mg; Fibre 2.1g; Sodium 67mg.
Keema Lamb Energy 239kcal/998kJ; Protein 19.7g; Carbohydrate 13.5g, of which sugars 9.3g; Fat 12.3g, of which saturates 4.9g; Cholesterol 67mg; Calcium 50mg; Fibre 2.5g; Sodium 578mg.

Balti Lamb Koftas with Vegetables

These koftas look attractive served on their bed of vegetables, especially if you make them quite small.

Serves 4
For the koftas
450g/1lb lean minced (ground) lamb
5ml/1 tsp garam masala
5ml/1 tsp ground cumin
5ml/1 tsp ground coriander
5ml/1 tsp crushed garlic
5ml/1 tsp chilli powder
5ml/1 tsp salt
15ml/1 tbsp chopped fresh coriander (cilantro)
1 small onion, finely diced
150ml/¼ pint/⅔ cup corn oil

For the vegetables
45ml/3 tbsp corn oil
1 bunch spring onions (scallions), roughly chopped
½ large red (bell) pepper, seeded and chopped
½ large green (bell) pepper, seeded and chopped
175g/6oz/1 cup corn
225g/8oz/1½ cups canned butter (lima) beans, drained
½ cauliflower, cut into florets
4 fresh green chillies, chopped
5ml/1 tsp chopped fresh mint
15ml/1 tbsp chopped fresh coriander (cilantro)
15ml/1 tbsp grated fresh root ginger
lime slices
15ml/1 tbsp lemon juice

1 Put the lamb into a food processor or blender and process for 1 minute. Transfer the lamb into a bowl. Add the garam masala, ground cumin, ground coriander, garlic, chilli powder, salt, fresh coriander and onion, and mix everything thoroughly. Cover the bowl and set aside in the refrigerator.

2 Heat the oil for the vegetables in a deep frying pan or a medium karahi. Add the spring onions and stir-fry for 2 minutes. Add the peppers, corn, butter beans, cauliflower and chillies, and stir-fry over a high heat for about 2 minutes. Set to one side.

3 Roll small pieces of the kofta mixture into walnut-sized portions. Heat the oil for the koftas in a frying pan. Cook the koftas in batches, turning until they are evenly browned.

4 Put the vegetables back over a medium heat, and add the koftas. Stir gently for about 5 minutes, or until everything is heated through. Garnish with the mint, coriander, ginger and lime slices. Just before serving, sprinkle over the lemon juice.

Koftas in Spicy Sauce

Little meatballs are called koftas in Indian cooking and are usually served in a spicy curry sauce. This curry is popular in most Indian homes.

Serves 4
225g/8oz/1 cup lean minced (ground) lamb
10ml/2 tsp poppy seeds
1 medium onion, chopped
5ml/1 tsp grated fresh root ginger
5ml/1 tsp crushed garlic
5ml/1 tsp salt
5ml/1 tsp chilli powder
7.5ml/1½ tsp ground coriander

30ml/2 tbsp fresh coriander (cilantro) leaves
1 small egg, (US medium) beaten

For the sauce
75ml/2½fl oz/⅓ cup natural (plain) low-fat yogurt
30ml/2 tbsp tomato purée (paste)
5ml/1 tsp chilli powder
5ml/1 tsp salt
5ml/1 tsp crushed garlic
5ml/1 tsp crushed fresh root ginger
5ml/1 tsp garam masala
10ml/2 tsp vegetable oil
1 cinnamon stick
400ml/14fl oz/1⅔ cups water

1 Place the lamb in a food processor and mince it further for about 1 minute. Scrape the meat into a bowl, sprinkle the poppy seeds on top and set aside.

2 Place the onion in the food processor with the next five ingredients and half the fresh coriander. Blend for about 30 seconds, then add it to the lamb. Add the egg and mix well. Leave to stand for about 1 hour.

3 To make the sauce, whisk together the yogurt, tomato purée, chilli powder, salt, crushed garlic, ginger and garam masala. Heat the oil with the cinnamon stick in a pan for about 1 minute, then pour in the sauce. Lower the heat and cook for 1 minute. Remove from the heat and set aside.

4 Roll small balls of the meat mixture using your hands. Return the sauce to the heat and stir in the water. Drop in the koftas one by one. Add the remaining coriander to the pan, cover with a lid and cook for about 7–10 minutes, stirring occasionally. Serve immediately.

Balti Lamb Koftas Energy 634kcal/2639kJ; Protein 31.2g; Carbohydrate 28.3g, of which sugars 10.1g; Fat 45g, of which saturates 10.7g; Cholesterol 87mg; Calcium 76mg; Fibre 5.6g; Sodium 446mg.
Koftas in Spicy Sauce Energy 208kcal/868kJ; Protein 14.7g; Carbohydrate 11.8g, of which sugars 1.2g; Fat 11.6g, of which saturates 4.7g; Cholesterol 57mg; Calcium 24mg; Fibre 1g; Sodium 63mg

Curried Moroccan Lamb

This sweet and spicy dish is eaten by Moroccan Jews at Rosh Hashanah, the Jewish New Year. Ras al hanout is a mixture of spices that may include cardamom, clove, cinnamon, paprika, cumin, nutmeg and turmeric.

Serves 6
130g/4¹/₂oz/generous ¹/₂ cup pitted prunes
350ml/12fl oz/1¹/₂ cups hot tea
1kg/2¹/₄lb stewing or braising lamb, cut into chunky portions
1 onion, chopped
75–90ml/5–6 tbsp chopped fresh parsley
2.5ml/¹/₂ tsp ground ginger
2.5ml/¹/₂ tsp curry powder or ras al hanout
pinch of freshly grated nutmeg
10ml/2 tsp ground cinnamon
1.5ml/¹/₄ tsp saffron threads
30ml/2 tbsp hot water
75–120ml/5–9 tbsp honey, to taste
250ml/8fl oz/1 cup beef or lamb stock
115g/4oz/1 cup blanched almonds, toasted
30ml/2 tbsp chopped fresh coriander (cilantro) leaves
3 hard-boiled eggs, cut into wedges
salt and ground black pepper

1 Preheat the oven to 180°C/350°F/Gas 4. Put the prunes in a bowl, pour over the tea and cover. Leave to soak and plump up.

2 Meanwhile, put the lamb, chopped onion, parsley, ginger, curry powder or ras al hanout, nutmeg, cinnamon, salt and pepper in a roasting pan. Mix together well. Cover and cook in the oven for about 2 hours, or until the meat is tender.

3 Drain the pitted prunes; add their liquid to the lamb. Combine the saffron and hot water in a small bowl and add to the pan with the honey and stock.

4 Place in the preheated oven and bake, uncovered, for about 30 minutes, turning the lamb occasionally.

5 Add the prunes to the pan and stir gently to mix.

6 Serve the dish sprinkled with the toasted almonds and the chopped coriander, and topped with the wedges of hard-boiled egg.

Chilli Lamb Chops

Serves 4
1 large red chilli, seeded
30ml/2 tbsp chopped fresh coriander (cilantro)
15ml/1 tbsp chopped fresh mint
5ml/1 tsp salt
5ml/1 tsp soft light brown sugar
5ml/1 tsp garam masala
5ml/1 tsp crushed garlic
5ml/1 tsp crushed fresh root ginger
175ml/6fl oz/³/₄ cup natural (plain) low-fat yogurt
8 small lean spring lamb chops
10ml/2 tsp corn oil

1 Finely chop the chilli, then mix with the coriander, mint, salt, brown sugar, garam masala, garlic and ginger. Pour the yogurt into the herb mixture and mix thoroughly with a fork.

2 Place the chops in a large bowl. Pour the yogurt mixture over the top of the chops and turn to make sure they are completely covered. Leave to marinate overnight in the refrigerator.

3 Heat the oil in a wok or large frying pan and add the chops. Lower the heat to medium. After 5 minutes, turn them over, then continue frying until they are cooked through, turning again if needed. When the lamb is cooked, place on to warmed plates.

Moghul-style Spicy Roast Lamb

Serves 4–6
4 large onions, chopped
4 garlic cloves
5cm/2in piece fresh root ginger, chopped
45ml/3 tbsp ground almonds
10ml/2 tsp ground cumin
10ml/2 tsp ground coriander
10ml/2 tsp ground turmeric
10ml/2 tsp garam masala
4–6 green chillies
juice of 1 lemon
salt, to taste
300ml/¹/₂ pint/1¹/₄ cups natural (plain) yogurt, beaten
1.8kg/4lb leg of lamb
8–10 cloves
4 firm tomatoes, halved and grilled, to serve
15ml/1 tbsp flaked (sliced) almonds, to garnish

1 Place the onions, garlic, ginger, almonds, cumin, coriander, turmeric, garam masala, chillies, lemon and salt to taste in a food processor and blend to a smooth paste. Gradually add the yogurt and blend. Grease a large roasting pan and preheat the oven to 190°C/375°F/Gas Mark 5.

2 Remove most of the fat and skin from the lamb. Using a sharp knife, make deep pockets above the bone at each side of the thick end. Make deep diagonal gashes on both sides.

3 Push the cloves into the leg of lamb and stuff some of the spice mixture into the pockets and gashes on the lamb. Spread the remainder evenly all over the meat.

4 Place the lamb on the roasting pan and cover with a piece of foil. Roast in the oven for about 2–2¹/₂ hours, or until the lamb is cooked, removing the foil for the last 10 minutes of cooking.

5 Remove the pan from the oven and allow the meat to rest for 10 minutes before carving. Serve with grilled tomatoes and garnish the joint with flaked almonds.

Moroccan Lamb Energy 618kcal/2564kJ; Protein 42.7g; Carbohydrate 0.8g, of which sugars 0.1g; Fat 49.3g, of which saturates 21.2g; Cholesterol 183mg; Calcium 16mg; Fibre 0.2g; Sodium 150mg.
Chilli Lamb Energy 183kcal/764kJ; Protein 15.5g; Carbohydrate 14.1g, of which sugars 9.1g; Fat 7.8g, of which saturates 3.2g; Cholesterol 43mg; Calcium 102mg; Fibre 1.8g; Sodium 77mg.
Spicy Roast Lamb Energy 517kcal/2154kJ; Protein 43.5g; Carbohydrate 20.4g, of which sugars 13.1g; Fat 29.9g, of which saturates 9.7g; Cholesterol 146mg; Calcium 162mg; Fibre 2.3g; Sodium 160mg.

Spicy Spring Roast Lamb

Coating a leg of lamb with a spicy, fruity rub gives it a wonderful flavour.

Serves 6

1.6kg/3½lb lean leg of
  spring lamb
5ml/1 tsp chilli powder
5ml/1 tsp crushed garlic
5ml/1 tsp ground coriander
5ml/1 tsp ground cumin
5ml/1 tsp salt
15ml/1 tbsp dried breadcrumbs

45ml/3 tbsp natural (plain)
  low-fat yogurt
30ml/2 tbsp lemon juice
30ml/2 tbsp sultanas
  (golden raisins)
15ml/1 tbsp vegetable oil

For the garnish
mixed salad leaves
fresh coriander (cilantro)
2 tomatoes, quartered
1 large carrot, shredded
lemon wedges

1 Preheat the oven to 180°C/350°F/Gas 4. Trim any excess fat from the lamb. Rinse the joint, pat it dry and set aside on a sheet of foil large enough to enclose it completely.

2 In a medium bowl, mix together the chilli powder, garlic, ground coriander, ground cumin and salt.

3 Mix together the breadcrumbs, yogurt, lemon juice and sultanas in a food processor or blender.

4 Add the contents of the food processor to the spice mixture together with the oil and mix together well. Pour this on to the leg of lamb and rub all over the meat.

5 Enclose the meat in the foil and place in an ovenproof dish. Cook in the oven for about 1½ hours.

6 Remove the lamb from the oven, open up the foil wrapping and, using the back of a spoon, spread the mixture evenly over the top of the meat. Return the lamb, uncovered this time, to the oven for another 45–50 minutes or until the meat is cooked right through and tender.

7 Slice the meat and serve with the mixed salad leaves, fresh coriander, tomatoes, carrot and lemon wedges.

Apricot Lamb Curry

This recipe comes from the wonderful fruit-laden valley of Kashmir. The curries of Kashmir are renowned for the imaginative use of all the exotic fruits and nuts that grow abundantly in that state. Serve this curry with an apricot chutney to complement the fruit in the recipe.

Serves 4–6
900g/2lb stewing lamb

30ml/2 tbsp vegetable oil
2.5cm/1in piece cinnamon stick
4 green cardamom pods
1 onion, chopped
15ml/1 tbsp curry paste
5ml/1 tsp ground cumin
5ml/1 tsp ground coriander
1.5ml/¼ tsp salt
175g/6oz/¾ cup ready-to-eat
  dried apricots
350ml/12fl oz/1½ cups
  lamb stock
fresh coriander (cilantro),
  to garnish

1 Cut away and discard any visible fat from the lamb, then cut the meat into 2.5cm/1in cubes.

2 Heat the oil in a wok, karahi or large pan and fry the cinnamon stick and cardamoms for 2 minutes. Add the onion and fry for 6–8 minutes until soft.

3 Add the curry paste and fry for about 2 minutes. Stir in the cumin, coriander and salt and fry for 2–3 minutes.

4 Add the cubed lamb, dried apricots and the lamb stock to the pan. Cover the pan with a tight-fitting lid and cook over a medium heat for 1–1½ hours, until the lamb is tender.

5 Transfer to a serving dish and garnish with the fresh coriander. Pilau rice and apricot chutney would make good accompaniments to this dish.

Cook's Tip
Choose whichever curry paste you prefer for this dish. Look for a hot variety if you prefer your curries with plenty of kick. A milder paste will also work well.

Spring Roast Lamb Energy 478kcal/1987kJ; Protein 39.1g; Carbohydrate 3.5g, of which sugars 0.6g; Fat 34.4g, of which saturates 10.1g; Cholesterol 145mg; Calcium 37mg; Fibre 0g; Sodium 119mg.
Apricot Lamb Curry Energy 765kcal/3192kJ; Protein 58.5g; Carbohydrate 27.5g, of which sugars 23.4g; Fat 47.5g, of which saturates 14.7g; Cholesterol 218mg; Calcium 53mg; Fibre 2.5g; Sodium 181mg.

Spicy Lamb Stew with Cassava

Serves 4

500g/1¼lb boneless lamb leg steaks
90ml/6 tbsp vegetable oil
1 medium onion, finely chopped
5ml/1 tsp ground cumin
15ml/1 tbsp chilli sauce
1 bunch coriander (cilantro)

1 litre/1¾ pints/4 cups water
500g/1¼lb small potatoes, peeled
500g/1¼lb cassava, peeled and
   cut into 7.5cm/3in chunks
250g/9oz/2 cups frozen peas
salt
boiled rice and chilli sauce, to serve

1 Cut the lamb into 5cm/2in pieces. Heat the oil in a pan and fry the meat until brown. Reduce the heat, add the onion and fry until golden, then add the cumin and chilli sauce and stir well.

2 Purée the coriander in a blender with 250ml/8fl oz/1 cup of the water. Add the paste to the pan with the remaining water, the potatoes and cassava. Season. Cover the pan and leave to simmer for 30 minutes, or until tender. Add the peas ten minutes before serving. Serve immediately with boiled rice and chilli sauce.

Kashmiri-style Lamb with Chilli

Serves 4–6

60ml/4 tbsp vegetable oil
900g/2lb lean lamb, cubed
1.5ml/¼ tsp asafoetida
5cm/2in piece fresh root
   ginger, crushed
2 garlic cloves, crushed

60ml/4 tbsp rogan josh masala paste
5ml/1 tsp chilli powder
8–10 strands saffron (optional)
salt
150ml/¼ pint/⅔ cup yogurt,
   beaten, plus extra to serve
ground almonds, to garnish

1 Heat the oil in a pan and brown the lamb. Reduce the heat, cover, then cook for 10 minutes. Add the remaining ingredients and 15ml/1 tbsp boiling water, except the yogurt and almonds and mix well. Cover and cook on a low heat for a 10 minutes.

2 Remove the pan from the heat and leave to cool a little. Stir in the yogurt, 15ml/1 tbsp at a time. Cook uncovered over a low heat until the gravy becomes thick. Spoon on to a serving dish and serve with yogurt, garnished with the ground almonds.

Lamb with Spiced Spinach

This recipe is based on the Indian curry sag gosht – meat cooked with spinach. It is flavoured with whole spices, which are not intended to be eaten.

Serves 3–4

45ml/3 tbsp vegetable oil
500g/1¼lb lean boneless lamb,
   cut into 2.5cm/1in cubes
1 onion, chopped
3 garlic cloves, finely chopped
1cm/½in piece fresh root ginger,
   finely chopped
6 black peppercorns
4 cloves

1 bay leaf
3 green cardamom pods, crushed
5ml/1 tsp ground cumin
5ml/1 tsp ground coriander
generous pinch of cayenne pepper
150ml/¼ pint/⅔ cup water
2 tomatoes, peeled, seeded
   and chopped
5ml/1 tsp salt
400g/14oz fresh spinach, trimmed,
   washed and finely chopped
5ml/1 tsp garam masala
crisp-fried onions and fresh
   coriander (cilantro) sprigs,
   to garnish
naan bread or spiced basmati
   rice, to serve

1 Heat a large pan or wok until hot. Add 30ml/2 tbsp of the oil and swirl it around. When hot, stir-fry the lamb in batches until evenly browned. Remove the lamb and set aside. Heat the remaining oil in the pan, add the onion, garlic and ginger and stir-fry for about 2–3 minutes.

2 Add the peppercorns, cloves, bay leaf, cardamom pods, cumin, coriander and cayenne pepper to the pan. Cook for about 30–45 seconds, stirring constantly.

3 Return the lamb to the pan, add the water, tomatoes and salt and bring to the boil. Simmer, covered, over a very low heat for about 1 hour, stirring occasionally, until the meat is tender.

4 Increase the heat, then gradually add the spinach to the lamb, stirring to mix. Keep stirring and cooking until the spinach wilts completely and most, but not all of the liquid has evaporated and you are left with a thick green sauce.

5 Stir in the garam masala. Garnish with crisp-fried onions and coriander sprigs. Serve with naan bread or spiced basmati rice.

Spicy Lamb Energy 662kcal/2771kJ; Protein 34.2g; Carbohydrate 62.1g, of which sugars 16.1g; Fat 32.6g, of which saturates 8.7g; Cholesterol 95mg; Calcium 113mg; Fibre 9.2g; Sodium 180mg.
Kashmiri-style Lamb Energy 410kcal/1709kJ; Protein 32.2g; Carbohydrate 5.4g, of which sugars 1.9g; Fat 29.3g, of which saturates 9.4g; Cholesterol 114mg; Calcium 78mg; Fibre 0g; Sodium 153mg.
Lamb with Spinach Energy 359kcal/1494kJ; Protein 28.7g; Carbohydrate 7.1g, of which sugars 4.7g; Fat 24.1g, of which saturates 7.7g; Cholesterol 95mg; Calcium 237mg; Fibre 4.8g; Sodium 780mg.

Balti Lamb with Yogurt and Spices

This is a traditional tikka recipe, in which the lamb is marinated in a mixture of yogurt and spices. The lamb is usually cut into bitesize cubes, but the cooking time for the curry can be halved by cutting it into thinner strips instead, as is done with this recipe.

Serves 4
450g/1lb lamb, cut into strips
175ml/6fl oz/¾ cup natural (plain) yogurt
5ml/1 tsp ground cumin
5ml/1 tsp ground coriander
5ml/1 tsp chilli powder
5ml/1 tsp crushed garlic
5ml/1 tsp salt
5ml/1 tsp garam masala
30ml/2 tbsp chopped fresh coriander (cilantro)
30ml/2 tbsp lemon juice
30ml/2 tbsp corn oil
15ml/1 tbsp tomato purée (paste)
1 large green (bell) pepper, seeded and sliced
3 large fresh red chillies

1 Put the lamb strips, yogurt, ground cumin, ground coriander, chilli powder, garlic, salt, garam masala, fresh coriander and lemon juice into a large mixing bowl and stir thoroughly. Set aside for at least 1 hour to marinate.

2 Heat the corn oil in a deep, heavy frying pan or a medium karahi or wok. Lower the heat slightly and add the tomato purée to the pan.

3 Add the lamb strips to the pan, a few at a time, leaving any excess marinade behind in the bowl.

4 Cook the lamb, stirring frequently, for about 7–10 minutes or until it is well browned all over.

5 Finally, add the green pepper slices and the whole red chillies. Heat through, checking that the lamb is cooked, and serve.

Cook's Tip
Use tender cuts of lamb for this curry, such as leg or loin meat, so that it cooks quickly in the pan.

Fragrant Lamb Curry

Essentially a Muslim dish known as rezala, this curry comes from Bengal.

Serves 4
1 large onion, roughly chopped
10ml/2 tsp grated fresh root ginger
10ml/2 tsp crushed garlic
4–5 cloves
2.5ml/½ tsp black peppercorns
6 green cardamom pods
5cm/2in cinnamon stick, halved
8 lamb rib chops
60ml/4 tbsp vegetable oil
1 large onion, finely sliced
175ml/6fl oz/¾ cup natural (plain) yogurt
50g/2oz/¼ cup butter
5ml/1 tsp salt
2.5ml/½ tsp ground cumin
2.5ml/½ tsp hot chilli powder
2.5ml/½ tsp freshly grated nutmeg
2.5ml/½ tsp sugar
15ml/1 tbsp lime juice
pinch of saffron, steeped in 15ml/1 tbsp hot water for 10–15 minutes
15ml/1 tbsp rose water
rose petals or other flower petals, to garnish

1 Process the onion in a blender or food processor. Add a little water if necessary to form a purée. Put the purée in a glass bowl and add the grated ginger, crushed garlic, cloves, peppercorns, cardamom pods, and cinnamon. Mix well.

2 Put the lamb in a glass dish and add the spice mixture. Mix thoroughly, cover and leave to marinate for 3–4 hours.

3 In a wok, karahi or large pan, heat the oil over a medium-high heat and fry the sliced onion for 6–7 minutes, until golden brown. Remove the onion slices, squeezing out as much oil as possible back into the pan. Drain the onion on kitchen paper. In the remaining oil, fry the lamb chops for 5 minutes, stirring frequently. Reduce the heat, cover and simmer for 5–7 minutes.

4 Meanwhile, mix the yogurt and butter together in a pan and cook over a low heat for 5 minutes, then stir into the lamb chops along with the salt. Add the cumin and chilli powder and cover the pan. Cook for 45–50 minutes until the chops are tender.

5 Add the nutmeg and sugar, cook for 1–2 minutes and add the lime juice, saffron and rose water. Stir well and simmer for 2 minutes. Serve garnished with the fried onion and rose petals.

Balti Lamb Energy 221kcal/923kJ; Protein 15.2g; Carbohydrate 13.1g, of which sugars 9.5g; Fat 12.6g, of which saturates 6.5g; Cholesterol 57mg; Calcium 122mg; Fibre 1.5g; Sodium 136mg.
Fragrant Lamb Curry Energy 399kcal/1664kJ; Protein 22.6g; Carbohydrate 35.1g, of which sugars 7.5g; Fat 18.8g, of which saturates 7.8g; Cholesterol 74mg; Calcium 70mg; Fibre 1.4g; Sodium 131mg.

Lamb Dhansak

This piquant curry features lamb with a medley of spices.

Serves 4

45ml/3 tbsp sunflower oil
1 large onion, finely chopped
10ml/2 tsp ginger purée
10ml/2 tsp garlic purée
5ml/1 tsp coriander seeds
2.5ml/½ tsp cumin seeds
4 green cardamom pods
2.5cm/1in cinnamon stick, broken
10–12 black peppercorns
2 bay leaves
5–6 fenugreek seeds
2.5ml/½ tsp black mustard seeds
5ml/1 tsp chilli powder or to taste

675g/1½lb boned leg of lamb, cut into 5cm/2in cubes
150g/5oz canned tomatoes
5ml/1 tsp salt, or to taste

For the lentils and vegetables
75g/3oz/⅓ cup each yellow split peas and red split lentils
30ml/2 tbsp sunflower oil
1 medium onion, finely chopped
2 green chillies, chopped
5ml/1 tsp ground turmeric
1 small aubergine (eggplant), cubed
5ml/1 tsp salt or to taste
30ml/2 tbsp lime juice
15ml/1 tbsp chopped coriander (cilantro), plus extra to garnish

1 In a heavy pan, heat the oil and fry the onion until soft, then add the ginger and garlic and fry until brown. Grind the coriander, cumin, cardamom, cinnamon, peppercorns, bay leaves, fenugreek and mustard seeds finely in a food processor. Add the chilli and ground spices to the onion and cook for 2 minutes.

2 Add the meat and fry over a high heat until brown. Add the tomatoes and salt, and pour in 120ml/4fl oz/½ cup warm water. Bring the pan to the boil, cover and simmer for 35–40 minutes.

3 Wash the split peas and lentils and drain. Heat the oil in a medium pan and fry the onion and chillies until browned, about 8–9 minutes. Stir in the turmeric, lentils and aubergine.

4 Pour in 600ml/1 pint/2½ cups warm water, and simmer for 20–25 minutes, stirring. Add salt, then push the lentils through a sieve (strainer). Discard any coarse mixture left in the sieve.

5 Add the lime juice to the lentils. Pour over the lamb and simmer for 20 minutes, stirring occasionally. Stir in the coriander and remove from the heat. Serve garnished with coriander.

Ethiopian Lamb Berbere

This dish from Ethiopia is a powerful blend of chillies with herbs and spices.

Serves 4

450g/1lb lamb fillet
45ml/3 tbsp olive oil
1 red onion, sliced
2.5ml/½ tsp grated fresh root ginger
2 garlic cloves, crushed

½ fresh green chilli, seeded and finely chopped (optional)
15ml/1 tbsp clarified butter or ghee
salt and ground black pepper

For the berbere
2.5ml/½ tsp each chilli powder, paprika, ground ginger, ground cinnamon, ground cardamom seeds and dried basil
5ml/1 tsp garlic powder

1 To make the berbere, combine all the ingredients in a small bowl and transfer into an airtight container. Berbere will keep for several months if stored in a cool, dry place. Trim the lamb of any fat and then cut the meat into 2cm/¾in cubes.

2 Heat the oil in a large frying pan or wok and fry the meat and onion for about 5–6 minutes, stirring occasionally, until the meat is browned on all sides and the onion has softened.

3 Add the ginger and garlic to the pan, together with 10ml/2 tsp of the berbere, then cook over a medium-high heat, stirring frequently, for a further 5–10 minutes.

4 Add the chilli to the pan, if using, and season well with salt and black pepper. Just before serving, add the butter or ghee and stir well. Serve immediately.

> **Cook's Tip**
> Clarified butter is traditionally used for this recipe. It can be made by gently heating unsalted butter, up to boiling point, and then scooping off and discarding the milk solids that rise to the surface. You are then left with clarified butter, which is a clear yellow liquid. Ghee is an Indian version of clarified butter which is made by simmering butter until all the moisture has evaporated and the butter caramelizes.

Lamb Dhansak Energy 470kcal/1970kJ; Protein 32.7g; Carbohydrate 36.5g, of which sugars 9g; Fat 22.7g, of which saturates 7.1g; Cholesterol 85.5mg; Calcium 106mg; Fibre 4.8g; Sodium 133mg.
Ethiopian Lamb Energy 336kcal/1392kJ; Protein 22g; Carbohydrate 1.2g, of which sugars 0.9g; Fat 27g, of which saturates 10.3g; Cholesterol 92mg; Calcium 9mg; Fibre 0.2g; Sodium 92mg.

Lamb in Mango-flavoured Sauce

This recipe has a pleasant sweet-and-sour taste combined with the heady bouquet of spices.

Serves 4
675g/1½lb boned leg of lamb
60ml/4 tbsp sunflower oil
1 large onion, finely chopped
10ml/2 tsp ginger purée
10ml/2 tsp garlic purée
5ml/1 tsp ground turmeric
10ml/2 tsp ground cumin
2.5–5ml/½–1 tsp chilli powder
50g/2oz/¼ cup thick set natural (plain) yogurt
10ml/2 tsp gram flour
5ml/1 tsp salt, or to taste
2 firm, ripe tomatoes, skinned and chopped
115g/4oz dried ready-to-eat mango
2.5ml/½ tsp garam masala
25ml/1½ tbsp red wine vinegar
30ml/2 tbsp chopped coriander (cilantro) leaves
naan bread, to serve

1 Remove all visible fat from the meat, then cut into 5cm/2in cubes and set aside.

2 In a heavy pan, heat the oil over a medium heat and add the onion. Fry for 3–4 minutes, stirring constantly, then add the ginger and garlic.

3 Continue to fry the ginger and garlic for a further 3–4 minutes, then add the turmeric, cumin and chilli powder. Stir-fry for 30 seconds and add 3 tbsp water. Stir-fry until the water has evaporated and repeat this process twice more.

4 Add the meat to the pan and reduce the heat to low. Whisk the yogurt and the gram flour together, and then add this mixture to the meat. Blend thoroughly, cover the pan and cook for around 40–45 minutes.

5 Add the salt, tomatoes and mango. Simmer, uncovered, for 10–12 minutes, or until the sauce has thickened to a good 'gravy-like' consistency.

6 Stir in the garam masala, vinegar and half of the chopped coriander. Serve in bowls and garnish with the remaining chopped coriander. Naan bread of any variety makes an ideal accompaniment to this dish.

Spiced Lamb with Tomatoes

Select lean tender lamb from the leg for this lightly spiced curry with succulent peppers and wedges of onion. Serve with warm naan bread.

Serves 6
1.5kg/3¼lb lean boneless lamb, cubed
250ml/8fl oz/1 cup natural (plain) yogurt
30ml/2 tbsp sunflower oil
3 onions
2 red (bell) peppers, cut into chunks
3 garlic cloves, finely chopped
1 red chilli, seeded and chopped
2.5cm/1in piece fresh root ginger, peeled and chopped
30ml/2 tbsp mild curry paste
2 x 400g/14oz cans chopped tomatoes
large pinch of saffron strands, ground to powder
800g/1¾lb plum tomatoes, halved, seeded and cut into chunks
salt and ground black pepper
chopped fresh coriander (cilantro), to garnish

1 Mix the lamb with the yogurt in a bowl. Cover and chill for about 1 hour. Heat the oil in a wok or large pan. Drain the lamb and reserve the yogurt, then cook the lamb in batches until it is golden on all sides – this takes about 15 minutes in total. Remove from the pan and set aside.

2 Cut two of the onions into wedges and add to the oil remaining in the pan. Fry the onion wedges over a medium heat for about 10 minutes, or until they are beginning to colour. Add the peppers and cook for a further 5 minutes. Remove the vegetables from the pan and set aside.

3 Meanwhile, chop the remaining onion. Add it to the oil remaining in the pan with the garlic, chilli and ginger, and cook, stirring often, until softened. Stir in the curry paste and canned tomatoes with the reserved yogurt marinade. Replace the lamb, add seasoning to taste and stir well. Bring to the boil, reduce the heat and simmer for about 30 minutes.

4 Dissolve the ground saffron in a little boiling water. Add this liquid to the curry. Replace the onion and pepper mixture. Stir in the fresh tomatoes and bring back to simmering point, then cook for 15 minutes. Garnish with coriander to serve.

Lamb in Mango Energy 534kcal/2230kJ; Protein 38.8g; Carbohydrate 23.6g, of which sugars 17g; Fat 32.6g, of which saturates 10.8g; Cholesterol 133mg; Calcium 98mg; Fibre 3.8g; Sodium 176mg.
Spiced Lamb Energy 559kcal/2343kJ; Protein 54.4g; Carbohydrate 20.5g, of which sugars 18.8g; Fat 29.6g, of which saturates 13.5g; Cholesterol 191mg; Calcium 139mg; Fibre 4.6g; Sodium 278mg.

Lahore-style Lamb

Named after the city of Lahore in Pakistan, this hearty curry has a wonderfully aromatic flavour imparted by the winter spices such as cloves, black peppercorns and cinnamon. Serve with a hot puffy naan in true Pakistani style.

Serves 4

60ml/4 tbsp vegetable oil
1 bay leaf
2 cloves
4 black peppercorns
1 onion, sliced
450g/1lb lean lamb, boned and cubed
1.5ml/¼ tsp ground turmeric
7.5ml/1½ tsp chilli powder
5ml/1 tsp crushed coriander seeds
2.5cm/1in piece cinnamon stick
5ml/1 tsp crushed garlic
7.5ml/1½ tsp salt
1.5 litres/2½ pints/6¼ cups water
50g/2oz/⅓ cup chana dhal (yellow lentils) or yellow split peas
2 tomatoes, quartered
2 fresh green chillies, chopped
15ml/1 tbsp chopped fresh coriander (cilantro)

1 Heat the oil in a wok, karahi or large pan. Lower the heat slightly and add the bay leaf, cloves, peppercorns and onion. Fry for about 5 minutes, or until the onion is golden brown.

2 Add the cubed lamb, turmeric, chilli powder, coriander seeds, cinnamon stick, garlic and most of the salt, and stir-fry for about 5 minutes over a medium heat.

3 Pour in 900ml/1½ pints/3¾ cups of the water and cover the pan. Simmer for 35–40 minutes or until the lamb is tender.

4 Put the chana dhal or split peas into a large pan with the remaining water and a good pinch of salt. Boil for 12–15 minutes, or until the water has almost evaporated and the lentils or peas are soft. If they are too thick, add a little extra water.

5 When the lamb is tender, remove the lid or foil and stir-fry the mixture using a wooden spoon, until some free oil begins to appear on the sides of the pan.

6 Add the cooked lentils to the lamb and mix together. Stir in the tomatoes, chillies and fresh coriander and serve.

Spicy Lamb with Courgettes

For this simple curry, lamb is cooked first with yogurt, and then sliced courgettes, which have already been browned, are added to the mixture.

Serves 4

15ml/1 tbsp vegetable oil
2 medium onions, chopped
225g/8oz lean lamb steaks, cut into strips
120ml/4fl oz/½ cup natural (plain) low-fat yogurt
5ml/1 tsp garam masala
5ml/1 tsp chilli powder
5ml/1 tsp crushed garlic
5ml/1 tsp grated fresh root ginger
2.5ml/½ tsp ground coriander
2 medium courgettes (zucchini), thickly sliced
15ml/1 tbsp chopped fresh coriander (cilantro), to garnish

1 Heat the oil in a karahi, wok or heavy pan and fry the onions until golden brown (see Cook's Tip).

2 Add the lamb strips to the pan and stir-fry with the onions for about 1 minute to seal the meat.

3 Put the yogurt, garam masala, chilli powder, garlic, ginger and ground coriander into a bowl. Whisk the mixture together.

4 Pour the yogurt mixture over the lamb and cook for about 2 minutes, stirring frequently. Cover the pan and cook over a medium to low heat for about 12–15 minutes.

5 Preheat the grill (broiler) to medium-high. Place the courgettes in a flameproof dish and brown lightly under the heat for about 3 minutes, turning once.

6 Check that the lamb is cooked through and tender and that the sauce is quite thick, then add the courgettes to the curry and serve garnished with the fresh coriander.

Cook's Tip
It is best to stir the onions only occasionally so that their moisture will be retained.

Lahore-style Lamb Energy 331kcal/1379kJ; Protein 26.5g; Carbohydrate 9.7g, of which sugars 1.9g; Fat 20.6g, of which saturates 5.6g; Cholesterol 83mg; Calcium 40mg; Fibre 1.8g; Sodium 99mg.
Spicy Lamb Energy 198kcal/824kJ; Protein 15.8g; Carbohydrate 11.4g, of which sugars 8.3g; Fat 10.4g, of which saturates 3.7g; Cholesterol 43mg; Calcium 120mg; Fibre 1.7g; Sodium 84mg.

Balti Lamb Chops with Potatoes

These chops are marinated before being cooked in a delicious spicy sauce.

Serves 8
8 lamb chops
30ml/2 tbsp olive oil
150ml/¼ pint/⅔ cup lemon juice
5ml/1 tsp salt
15ml/1 tbsp chopped fresh mint
  and coriander (cilantro)
mint sprigs and lime slices,
  to garnish

For the sauce
45ml/3 tbsp corn oil
8 medium tomatoes, chopped
1 bay leaf
5ml/1 tsp garam masala
30ml/2 tbsp natural (plain) yogurt
5ml/1 tsp crushed garlic
5ml/1 tsp chilli powder
5ml/1 tsp salt
2.5ml/½ tsp black cumin seeds
3 black peppercorns
2 medium potatoes, peeled,
  roughly chopped and boiled
  until just tender

1 Put the chops into a large bowl. Mix together 15ml/1 tbsp of the olive oil, lemon juice, salt and fresh mint and coriander. Pour the oil mixture over the chops and rub it in well with your fingers. Leave to marinate for at least 3 hours.

2 To make the sauce, heat the corn oil in a deep frying pan or a karahi. Lower the heat and add the chopped tomatoes. Stir-fry for 2 minutes. Gradually add the bay leaf, garam masala, yogurt, garlic, chilli powder, salt, black cumin seeds and peppercorns, and stir-fry for a further 2–3 minutes.

3 Lower the heat again and add the cooked potatoes, mixing everything together. Remove from the heat and set aside.

4 Heat the remaining olive oil in a separate frying pan. Lower the heat slightly, add the chops and fry them on both sides until they are cooked through. This will take 10–12 minutes. Remove with a slotted spoon and drain on kitchen paper.

5 Heat the sauce in the karahi, bringing it to the boil. Add the chops and lower the heat. Simmer for 5–7 minutes.

6 Transfer the curry to a warmed serving dish and garnish with the mint sprigs and lime slices before serving.

Balti Bhoona Lamb

Bhooning is the term for a traditional Indian technique when stir-frying curries, which simply involves making semi-circular movements while the curry is cooking, scraping the bottom of the pan each time in the centre. Serve this dish of spring lamb with freshly made chapatis or naan breads.

Serves 4
225–275g/8–10oz boneless lean
  spring lamb
3 medium onions
15ml/1 tbsp vegetable oil
15ml/1 tbsp tomato
  purée (paste)
5ml/1 tsp crushed garlic
7.5ml/1½ tsp finely grated
  fresh root ginger, plus 15ml/
  1 tbsp shredded
5ml/1 tsp salt
1.5ml/¼ tsp ground turmeric
600ml/1 pint/2½ cups water
15ml/1 tbsp lemon juice
15ml/1 tbsp chopped fresh
  coriander (cilantro)
15ml/1 tbsp chopped
  fresh mint
1 fresh red chilli, seeded
  and chopped

1 Using a sharp knife, remove any excess fat from the lamb and cut the meat into small cubes.

2 Dice the onions finely. Heat the oil in a karahi, wok or heavy pan and fry the onions until soft.

3 Meanwhile, mix together the tomato purée, garlic and grated ginger, salt and turmeric. Pour the spice mixture on to the onions in the pan and stir-fry for a few seconds.

4 Add the lamb and continue to stir-fry for about 2–3 minutes. Stir in the water, lower the heat, cover the pan and cook for 15–20 minutes, stirring occasionally.

5 When the water has almost evaporated, start bhooning or stirring over a medium heat, making sure that the sauce does not catch on the bottom of the pan. Continue for 5–7 minutes.

6 Pour in the lemon juice, followed by the shredded ginger, chopped fresh coriander, mint and red chilli. Stir to mix, then serve straight from the pan.

Balti Lamb Chops Energy 276kcal/1154kJ; Protein 16.5g; Carbohydrate 11.4g, of which sugars 3.5g; Fat 18.7g, of which saturates 5.2g; Cholesterol 57mg; Calcium 30mg; Fibre 1.7g; Sodium 80mg.
Balti Bhoona Lamb Energy 188kcal/785kJ; Protein 13.7g; Carbohydrate 12.1g, of which sugars 7.8g; Fat 10g, of which saturates 3.3g; Cholesterol 43mg; Calcium 69mg; Fibre 2.5g; Sodium 67mg.

Balti Lamb Tikka

One of the best ways of tenderizing meat is to marinate it in papaya, which must be unripe or it will lend its sweetness to what should be a savoury dish.

Serves 4
675g/1½lb lean lamb, cubed
1 unripe papaya
45ml/3 tbsp natural (plain) yogurt
5ml/1 tsp crushed fresh root ginger
5ml/1 tsp chilli powder

5ml/1 tsp crushed garlic
1.5ml/¼ tsp turmeric
10ml/2 tsp ground coriander
5ml/1 tsp ground cumin
5ml/1 tsp salt
30ml/2 tbsp lemon juice
15ml/1 tbsp chopped fresh
  coriander (cilantro), plus extra
  to garnish
1.5ml/¼ tsp red food colouring
300ml/½ pint/1¼ cups corn oil
lemon wedges and onion rings,
  to garnish

1 Place the lamb in a bowl. Peel and halve the papaya, and scoop out the seeds. Cut the flesh into cubes and blend in a food processor or blender, adding a little water if necessary.

2 Pour 30ml/2 tbsp of the papaya over the lamb and rub it in well with your fingers. Set aside for at least 3 hours.

3 Mix together the yogurt, ginger, chilli powder, garlic, turmeric, ground coriander, cumin, salt, lemon juice, fresh coriander, food colouring and 30ml/2 tbsp of oil. Pour over the lamb and mix.

4 Heat the remaining oil in a deep frying pan or a karahi. Lower the heat slightly and add the lamb cubes, a few at a time. Deep-fry each batch for 5–7 minutes or until the lamb is cooked. Keep warm while the remainder is fried.

5 Transfer to a serving dish and garnish with lemon wedges, onion rings and fresh coriander. Serve with raita and naan.

Cook's Tip
A meat tenderizer, available from supermarkets, can be used in place of the papaya. However, the meat will need a longer marinating time and should be left to tenderize overnight.

Balti Lamb with Cauliflower

This tasty curry is given a final tarka, a dressing of oil, cumin seeds and curry leaves, to enhance the flavour.

Serves 4
10ml/2 tsp vegetable oil
2 medium onions, sliced
7.5ml/1½ tsp grated fresh
  root ginger
5ml/1 tsp chilli powder
5ml/1 tsp crushed garlic
1.5ml/¼ tsp ground turmeric
2.5ml/½ tsp ground coriander
30ml/2 tbsp fresh fenugreek leaves

275g/10oz boneless lean
  spring lamb, cut into strips
1 small cauliflower, cut into
  small florets
300ml/½ pint/1¼ cups water
30ml/2 tbsp fresh coriander
  (cilantro) leaves
½ red (bell) pepper, seeded
  and sliced
15ml/1 tbsp lemon juice

For the tarka
10ml/2 tsp vegetable oil
2.5ml/½ tsp cumin seeds
4–6 curry leaves

1 Heat the oil in a karahi, wok or heavy pan and fry the onions until they are golden brown. Lower the heat and then add the ginger, chilli powder, garlic, turmeric and ground coriander. Stir well, then add the fenugreek leaves and mix well to combine all the ingredients.

2 Add the lamb strips to the wok and stir-fry until the lamb is completely coated with the spices. Add half the cauliflower florets and stir the mixture well. Pour in the water, cover the wok and cook for 5–7 minutes until the cauliflower and lamb are almost cooked through.

3 Add the remaining cauliflower, half the fresh coriander, the red pepper and lemon juice and stir-fry for about 5 minutes, ensuring the sauce does not scorch on the bottom of the pan. Check that the lamb is completely cooked, then remove the pan from the heat and set it aside.

4 To make the tarka, heat the oil and fry the seeds and curry leaves for about 30 seconds. While it is still hot, pour the seasoned oil over the cauliflower and lamb and serve garnished with the remaining fresh coriander leaves.

Balti Lamb Tikka Energy 438kcal/1827kJ; Protein 34.4g; Carbohydrate 7.8g, of which sugars 7.7g; Fat 30.3g, of which saturates 10.4g; Cholesterol 128mg; Calcium 74mg; Fibre 2.3g; Sodium 162mg.
Lamb with Cauliflower Energy 277kcal/1154kJ; Protein 18.7g; Carbohydrate 14.4g, of which sugars 9g; Fat 16.7g, of which saturates 4.7g; Cholesterol 52mg; Calcium 62mg; Fibre 3.2g; Sodium 73mg.

Balti Lamb with Peas and Potatoes

Fresh mint leaves are used in this curry, but if they are unobtainable or out of season, you can use ready-minted frozen peas to bring an added freshness. Serve with plain boiled rice.

Serves 4
225g/8oz boneless lean
  spring lamb
120ml/4fl oz/½ cup natural
  (plain) low-fat yogurt
1 cinnamon stick
2 green cardamom pods
3 black peppercorns

5ml/1 tsp crushed garlic
5ml/1 tsp grated fresh
  root ginger
5ml/1 tsp chilli powder
5ml/1 tsp garam masala
5ml/1 tsp salt
30ml/2 tbsp roughly chopped
  fresh mint
15ml/1 tbsp vegetable oil
2 medium onions, sliced
300ml/½ pint/1¼
  cups water
1 large potato, diced
115g/4oz/1 cup frozen peas
1 firm tomato, peeled, seeded
  and diced

1 Using a sharp knife, trim any excess fat from the lamb and cut the meat into strips. Place it in a bowl.

2 Add the yogurt, cinnamon, cardamoms, peppercorns, garlic, ginger, chilli powder, garam masala, salt and half the mint. Stir well, cover the bowl and leave in a cool place to marinate for a minimum of 2 hours.

3 Heat the oil in a karahi, wok or heavy pan and fry the onions until golden brown. Stir in the lamb and the marinade and stir-fry for about 3 minutes.

4 Pour in the water, lower the heat and cook for 15 minutes until the meat is cooked right through and tender. Meanwhile, cook the diced potato in a pan of boiling water until just soft, but do not let it go mushy.

5 Add the peas and cooked potato to the lamb and stir gently to combine all the ingredients.

6 Finally, add the remaining mint and the tomato and cook for a further 5 minutes before serving.

Balti Lamb with Fresh Fenugreek

The combination of lamb with fresh fenugreek works very well in this dish, which is delicious accompanied by plain boiled rice and mango chutney.

Serves 4
450g/1lb lean minced
  (ground) lamb
5ml/1 tsp grated fresh root ginger
5ml/1 tsp crushed garlic
7.5ml/1½ tsp chilli powder
5ml/1 tsp salt

1.5ml/¼ tsp turmeric
45ml/3 tbsp corn oil
2 medium onions, sliced
2 medium potatoes, peeled,
  par-boiled and roughly diced
1 bunch fresh fenugreek,
  chopped
2 tomatoes, chopped
50g/2oz/½ cup frozen peas
30ml/2 tbsp chopped fresh
  coriander (cilantro)
3 fresh red chillies, seeded
  and sliced, to garnish

1 Put the minced lamb, grated ginger, garlic, chilli powder, salt and turmeric into a large bowl, and mix together thoroughly. Set aside while you prepare the other ingredients.

2 Heat the oil in a karahi, wok or deep pan. Add the onion slices and fry for about 5 minutes until golden brown.

3 Add the minced lamb to the pan and fry over a medium heat for 5–7 minutes, stirring frequently.

4 Stir the par-boiled potatoes, chopped fenugreek, tomatoes and frozen peas into the pan and cook for a further 5–7 minutes, stirring constantly.

5 Just before serving, stir in the fresh coriander. Spoon the curry into a large serving dish or on to individual plates and serve hot. Garnish with fresh red chillies.

Cook's Tip
Look for fresh fenugreek in large supermarkets and Asian stores. Only use the leaves from the plant in this curry as the stalks can taste rather bitter.

Lamb with Peas Energy 317kcal/1322kJ; Protein 18.1g; Carbohydrate 25.6g, of which sugars 10.7g; Fat 16.8g, of which saturates 4.4g; Cholesterol 43mg; Calcium 113mg; Fibre 3.8g; Sodium 89mg.
Balti Lamb with Fenugreek 418kcal/1748kJ; Protein 27.3g; Carbohydrate 28.8g, of which sugars 9.2g; Fat 22.4g, of which saturates 7.1g; Cholesterol 86mg; Calcium 93mg; Fibre 4.5g; Sodium 123mg.

Lamb and New Potato Curry

This dish makes the most of an economical cut of meat by cooking it slowly until the meat is falling from the bone. Chillies and coconut cream give it lots of flavour.

Serves 4
25g/1oz/2 tbsp butter
2 onions, sliced into rings
4 garlic cloves, crushed
2.5ml/½ tsp ground cumin
2.5ml/½ tsp ground coriander
2.5ml/½ tsp turmeric
2.5ml/½ tsp cayenne pepper
2–3 red chillies, seeded and finely chopped
300ml/½ pint/1¼ cups hot chicken stock
200ml/7fl oz/scant 1 cup coconut cream
4 lamb shanks, excess fat removed
450g/1lb new potatoes, halved
6 ripe tomatoes, quartered
salt and ground black pepper
fresh coriander (cilantro) leaves, to garnish
spicy rice, to serve

1 Preheat the oven to 160°C/325°F/Gas 3. Melt the butter in a large flameproof casserole, add the onions and cook, stirring frequently, over a low heat for 6–8 minutes, until beginning to soften. Add the garlic for 3–4 minutes. Stir in the spices and chillies, then cook for a further 2 minutes.

2 Stir in the hot chicken stock and coconut cream. Place the lamb shanks in the liquid and cover the casserole with foil. Cook in the oven for about 2 hours, turning the shanks twice in the cooking liquid, first after about 1 hour of cooking and again roughly another 30 minutes later.

3 Par-boil the potatoes for about 10 minutes or until barely tender, drain and add to the casserole with the tomatoes, then cook uncovered in the oven for a further 35 minutes. Season to taste with salt and pepper. Serve garnished with coriander leaves and accompanied by the spicy rice.

Cook's Tip
Make this dish a day in advance, if possible. Cool and chill overnight, then skim off the excess fat that has risen to the surface. Reheat thoroughly before you serve it.

Spicy Lamb and Potato Stew

Indian spices help to transform a simple lamb and potato stew into a mouthwatering curry that is fit for princes. It's a meal in itself so requires no accompaniments, although naan breads will go well if you are feeding many people.

Serves 6
675g/1½lb lean lamb fillet (tenderloin)
15ml/1 tbsp vegetable oil
1 onion, finely chopped
2 bay leaves
1 fresh green chilli, seeded and finely chopped
2 garlic cloves, finely chopped
10ml/2 tsp ground coriander
5ml/1 tsp ground cumin
2.5ml/½ tsp ground turmeric
2.5ml/½ tsp chilli powder
2.5ml/½ tsp salt
2 tomatoes, peeled and roughly chopped
600ml/1 pint/2½ cups chicken stock
2 large potatoes, cut into large chunks
chopped fresh coriander (cilantro), to garnish

1 Remove any visible fat from the lamb and cut the meat into neat 2.5cm/1in cubes.

2 Heat the oil in a large, heavy pan and fry the onion, bay leaves, chilli and garlic for 5 minutes.

3 Add the cubed meat to the pan and cook for a further 6–8 minutes until lightly browned.

4 Add the ground coriander, ground cumin, ground turmeric, chilli powder and salt and cook the spices for 3–4 minutes, stirring constantly to prevent the spices from sticking to the bottom of the pan and burning.

5 Add the tomatoes and stock and simmer for 5 minutes. Bring to the boil, cover and simmer for 1 hour.

6 Add the bitesize chunks of potato to the simmering mixture, stir in, and cook for a further 30–40 minutes, or until the meat is tender and much of the excess juices have evaporated, leaving a thick but minimal sauce. Garnish with chopped fresh coriander and serve piping hot.

Lamb and Potato Curry Energy 364kcal/1528kJ; Protein 23.5g; Carbohydrate 30.5g, of which sugars 12.1g; Fat 17.4g, of which saturates 8.8g; Cholesterol 89mg; Calcium 58mg; Fibre 3.5g; Sodium 205mg.
Spicy Lamb and Potato Stew Energy 284kcal/1192kJ; Protein 24g; Carbohydrate 14.1g, of which sugars 3.1g; Fat 15.1g, of which saturates 6.3g; Cholesterol 86mg; Calcium 23mg; Fibre 1.3g; Sodium 109mg.

Rogan Josh with Spices and Tomato

Javanese Goat Curry

This sumptuous curry uses Kashmiri chilli powder, which gives it a rich, red colour.

Serves 4
675g/1½lb boned leg of lamb, cut into 2.5cm/1in cubes
30ml/2 tbsp red wine vinegar
5ml/1 tsp salt, or to taste
50g/2oz/4 tbsp ghee or unsalted butter
30ml/2 tbsp sunflower or olive oil
2.5cm/1in piece of cinnamon stick
2 brown cardamom pods, bruised

5 cloves
1 large onion, finely chopped
10ml/2 tsp ginger purée
10ml/2 tsp garlic purée
7.5ml/1½ tsp ground coriander
10ml/2 tsp ground cumin
5ml/1 tsp ground turmeric
2.5–7.5ml/½–1½ tsp Kashmiri chilli powder
400g/14oz can tomatoes with juice
2.5ml/½ tsp ground cardamom
2.5ml/½ tsp grated nutmeg
30ml/2 tbsp chopped fresh coriander (cilantro)

1 Put the meat in a non-metallic bowl and add the vinegar and salt. Rub them well into the meat and set aside for about an hour.

2 Reserve 15ml/1 tbsp ghee or butter, then heat the remainder with the oil in a heavy pan over a low heat. Add the cinnamon, cardamom and cloves, and let them sizzle for 2 minutes.

3 Add the onion and cook for 5–6 minutes until it softens. Add the ginger and garlic purées, and continue to cook, stirring frequently, until the mixture is tinged with a light brown colour.

4 Add the ground coriander, cumin, turmeric and chilli powder and cook for 1 minute, then add half the tomatoes. Cook over medium heat until the tomato juice has evaporated and then add the remaining tomatoes. Cook until it resembles a thick paste.

5 Add the meat, and increase the heat to high, then cook until it changes colour. Add 150ml/¼ pint/⅔ cup warm water and bring the mixture to the boil. Reduce the heat to low, cover and simmer for 45–50 minutes, stirring occasionally.

6 Melt the reserved 15ml/1 tbsp ghee or butter and fry the cardamom and nutmeg briefly. Pour over the meat and add half the fresh coriander. Serve garnished with the remaining coriander.

This slow-cooked curry is from Java where goat's meat is commonly used, although lamb could be used instead.

Serves 4
30–60ml/2–4 tbsp palm, coconut or groundnut (peanut) oil
10ml/2 tsp shrimp paste
15ml/1 tbsp palm sugar (jaggery)
5ml/1 tsp coriander seeds
5ml/1 tsp cumin seeds
2.5ml/½ tsp grated nutmeg
2.5ml/½ tsp ground black pepper
2–3 lemon grass stalks, halved and bruised
700g/1lb 9oz boneless shoulder or leg of goat, or lamb, cut into bitesize pieces
400g/14oz can coconut milk

200ml/7fl oz/scant 1 cup water
12 yard-long beans
1 bunch fresh coriander (cilantro) leaves, roughly chopped

For the spice paste
2–3 shallots, chopped
2–3 garlic cloves, chopped
3–4 chillies, seeded and chopped
25g/1oz galangal, chopped
40g/1½oz fresh turmeric, chopped, or 10ml/2 tsp ground turmeric
1 lemon grass stalk, chopped
2–3 candlenuts or macadamia nuts, finely ground

To serve
cooked rice
2–3 chillies, seeded and finely chopped

1 For the spice paste, grind all the ingredients in a food processor or blender, or crush to a paste with a pestle and mortar.

2 Heat 15–30ml/1–2 tbsp of the oil in a heavy pan, stir in the spice paste and fry for 2 minutes. Add the shrimp paste and palm sugar and continue to stir-fry for 1–2 minutes.

3 Heat the remaining 15–30ml/1–2 tbsp oil in a large, flameproof casserole. Stir in the coriander seeds, cumin seeds, nutmeg and black pepper, then add the spice paste and lemon grass. Stir-fry for 2–3 minutes, until the mixture is fragrant.

4 Stir the meat, coconut milk and water into the pan. Bring to the boil, then reduce the heat, cover and simmer for 3 hours.

5 Add the beans and cook for 10–15 minutes. Toss some of the coriander leaves into the curry and season to taste. Garnish with the remaining coriander and serve with rice and chillies.

Rogan Josh Energy 557kcal/2334kJ; Protein 54.2g; Carbohydrate 20.4g, of which sugars 18.7g; Fat 29.5g, of which saturates 13.5g; Cholesterol 190mg; Calcium 139mg; Fibre 4.6g; Sodium 277mg.
Javanese Curry Energy 450kcal/1877kJ; Protein 37.9g; Carbohydrate 10.8g, of which sugars 9.1g; Fat 28.7g, of which saturates 10.3g; Cholesterol 146mg; Calcium 129mg; Fibre 2.4g; Sodium 375mg.

Beef Kofta Curry

Koftas come in various shapes and sizes. In this variation, the more commonly used lamb is replaced by beef, which works well with the hot curry sauce.

Serves 4

For the meatballs
450g/1lb minced (ground) beef
45ml/3 tbsp finely chopped onion
15ml/1 tbsp chopped fresh
    coriander (cilantro)
15ml/1 tbsp natural (plain) yogurt
about 60ml/4 tbsp plain
    (all-purpose) flour
10ml/2 tsp ground cumin
5ml/1 tsp garam masala
5ml/1 tsp ground turmeric
5ml/1 tsp ground coriander
1 fresh green chilli, seeded and
    finely chopped
2 garlic cloves, crushed
1.5ml/¼ tsp black mustard seeds
1 egg (optional)
salt and ground black pepper

For the curry sauce
30ml/2 tbsp butter
1 onion, finely chopped
2 garlic cloves, crushed
45ml/3 tbsp curry powder
4 green cardamom pods
600ml/1 pint/2½ cups hot beef
    stock or water
15ml/1 tbsp tomato purée (paste)
30ml/2 tbsp natural (plain) yogurt
15ml/1 tbsp chopped fresh
    coriander (cilantro)

1 To make the meatballs, put the beef into a large bowl, add all the remaining meatball ingredients and mix well with your hands. Roll the mixture into small balls and set aside.

2 For the curry sauce, heat the butter in a pan over a medium heat. Fry the onion and garlic for 8 minutes, until the onion is soft.

3 Reduce the heat and then add the curry powder and cardamon pods and cook for a few minutes, stirring well.

4 Slowly stir in the stock or water, the tomato purée, yogurt and chopped coriander and stir well. Simmer for 10 minutes.

5 Add the koftas to the sauce a few at a time, allow to cook briefly and then add a few more, until all of the koftas are in the pan. Simmer, uncovered, for about 20 minutes, until the koftas are cooked. The sauce will thicken slightly but add a little water if it is drying out too much. Serve immediately.

Persian Tangy Beef and Herb Koresh

In modern-day Iran, as in ancient Persia, rice is eaten at almost every meal. That the diet is never dull is thanks to the koresh. This is a delicately spiced sauce or stew that serves as a topping. This is a classic meat koresh, but there are also vegetarian versions, often with fruit and herbs.

Serves 4
45ml/3 tbsp olive oil
1 large onion, chopped
450g/1lb lean stewing beef, cut
    into bitesize cubes
15ml/1 tbsp fenugreek leaves,
    stalks discarded
10ml/2 tsp ground turmeric
2.5ml/½ tsp ground cinnamon
600ml/1 pint/2½ cups water
25g/1oz fresh parsley, chopped
25g/1oz fresh chives, chopped
400g/14oz can red kidney beans
juice of 1 lemon
salt and ground black pepper
plain boiled basmati rice,
    to serve

1 Heat 30ml/2 tbsp of the oil in a large pan or flameproof casserole and fry the onion for 4–5 minutes, until lightly golden.

2 Add the beef to the pan and fry for a further 10 minutes until browned on all sides.

3 Add the fenugreek, turmeric and cinnamon and cook for about 1 minute, then add the water and bring to the boil. Cover with a tight-fitting lid and simmer over a low heat for about 45 minutes, stirring occasionally.

4 Heat the remaining oil in a small frying pan and fry the fresh parsley and chives over a medium heat for about 2–3 minutes, stirring frequently so that they do not burn.

5 Rinse the kidney beans thoroughly and drain well. Stir them into the beef in the pan with the fried herbs and lemon juice. Season with salt and black pepper.

6 Simmer the stew for a further 30–35 minutes, until the meat is tender. Serve immediately on a bed of plain boiled rice.

Beef Kofta Curry Energy 313kcal/1301kJ; Protein 25.8g; Carbohydrate 4.9g, of which sugars 3.7g; Fat 21.3g, of which saturates 11.3g; Cholesterol 90mg; Calcium 42mg; Fibre 1g; Sodium 192mg.
Persian Tangy Beef Energy 357kcal/1491kJ; Protein 32.5g; Carbohydrate 22.9g, of which sugars 7.3g; Fat 15.5g, of which saturates 4g; Cholesterol 71mg; Calcium 117mg; Fibre 7.7g; Sodium 468mg.

Dry Beef and Peanut Butter Curry

Although this is called a dry curry, the method of cooking helps to keep the beef succulent.

Serves 4–6
400g/14oz can coconut milk
900g/2lb stewing beef, finely chopped
300ml/½ pint/1¼ cups beef stock
30–45ml/2–3 tbsp red curry paste
30ml/2 tbsp crunchy peanut butter
juice of 2 limes
lime slices, shredded coriander (cilantro) and fresh red chilli slices, to garnish

1 Strain the coconut milk into a bowl, retaining the thicker coconut milk in the sieve (strainer).

2 Pour the thin coconut milk from the bowl into a large, heavy pan or wok, then scrape in half the residue from the sieve. Reserve the remaining thick coconut milk. Add the chopped beef to the pan. Pour in the beef stock and bring the mixture to the boil. Reduce the heat, cover the pan and simmer gently for about 50 minutes.

3 Strain the beef, reserving the cooking liquid, and place a cupful of this liquid in a wok. Stir in 30–45ml/2–3 tbsp of the curry paste, according to taste. Boil rapidly until all the liquid has evaporated. Stir in the reserved thick coconut milk, the peanut butter and the beef. Simmer, uncovered, for 15–20 minutes, adding a little more cooking liquid if the mixture starts to stick to the pan, but keep the curry dry.

4 Just before serving, stir in the lime juice. Serve in warmed individual bowls, garnished with the lime slices, shredded coriander and sliced red chillies.

Variation
The curry is equally delicious made with lean leg or shoulder of lamb, or with pork fillet (tenderloin).

Beef Curry in Sweet Peanut Sauce

This curry is deliciously rich and thick. It is usually served with rice, but would also make a good filling for pitta breads.

Serves 4–6
600ml/1 pint/2½ cups coconut milk
45ml/3 tbsp red curry paste
45ml/3 tbsp fish sauce
30ml/2 tbsp light muscovado (brown) sugar
2 lemon grass stalks, bruised
450g/1lb rump (round) steak, cut into thin strips
75g/3oz/¾ cup roasted peanuts, ground
2 fresh red chillies, sliced
5 kaffir lime leaves, torn
salt and ground black pepper
2 salted eggs, cut in wedges, and 10–15 Thai basil leaves, to garnish

1 Pour half the coconut milk into a large, heavy pan or wok. Place over a medium heat and bring slowly to the boil, stirring constantly until the milk separates.

2 Stir the red curry paste into the coconut milk and cook for 2–3 minutes until the mixture is fragrant and thoroughly blended. Add the fish sauce, sugar and bruised lemon grass stalks. Mix well until combined.

3 Continue to cook until the colour deepens. Gradually add the remaining coconut milk, stirring constantly. Bring back to the boil, stirring constantly.

4 Add the beef and peanuts. Cook, stirring constantly, for 8–10 minutes, or until most of the liquid has evaporated. Add the chillies and lime leaves. Season to taste and serve, garnished with wedges of salted eggs and Thai basil leaves.

Cook's Tip
Red curry paste is a popular ingredient in Thai cuisine. It includes red chillies, shallots, garlic, galangal, lemon grass, shrimp paste and kaffir lime zest. A wide range of ready-made Thai curry pastes is available in Asian stores as well as large supermarkets.

Dry Beef Curry Energy 296kcal/1238kJ; Protein 35.2g; Carbohydrate 4.9g, of which sugars 4.5g; Fat 15.2g, of which saturates 4.8g; Cholesterol 103mg; Calcium 66mg; Fibre 0.7g; Sodium 262mg.
Beef Curry Energy 227kcal/953kJ; Protein 21g; Carbohydrate 14.3g, of which sugars 11.5g; Fat 9.9g, of which saturates 2.6g; Cholesterol 44mg; Calcium 92mg; Fibre 2.5g; Sodium 723mg.

Spicy Beef with Green Beans

Green beans slowly cooked with beef is a variation on a traditional Indian curry which uses lamb. The sliced red pepper provides a contrast to the colour of the beans and chillies, and adds extra flavour.

Serves 4

275g/10oz fine green beans,
  cut into 2.5cm/1in pieces
15ml/1 tbsp vegetable oil
1 onion, sliced
5ml/1 tsp grated fresh root ginger
5ml/1 tsp crushed garlic
5ml/1 tsp chilli powder
6.5ml/1¼ tsp salt
1.5ml/¼ tsp ground turmeric
2 tomatoes, chopped
450g/1lb lean beef, cubed
475ml/16fl oz/2 cups water
1 red (bell) pepper, seeded
  and sliced
15ml/1 tbsp chopped fresh
  coriander (cilantro)
2 fresh green chillies, chopped
warm chapatis, to serve (optional)

1 Blanch the beans in boiling water for 3–4 minutes, then rinse under cold running water, drain and set aside.

2 Heat the oil in a large, heavy pan and gently fry the onion slices, stirring frequently, until golden brown.

3 In a bowl, mix the ginger, garlic, chilli powder, salt, turmeric and chopped tomatoes. Spoon the mixture into the pan and stir-fry with the onion for 5–7 minutes.

4 Add the cubed beef and stir-fry for a further 3 minutes. Pour in the water, bring it to the boil and lower the heat. Half-cover the pan and cook for 1–1¼ hours until most of the water has evaporated and the meat is tender. If the mixture looks like it is drying out during cooking, add a little more water.

5 Add the green beans to the pan and mix everything together well. Finally, add the red pepper, chopped fresh coriander and green chillies. Cook the mixture with the lid removed, stirring occasionally, for a further 7–10 minutes, or until the green beans and pepper are tender.

6 Spoon into a large bowl or individual plates. Serve the beef hot, with warm chapatis, if you like.

Citrus Beef Curry

This superbly aromatic curry is not too hot but it is nonetheless packed with flavour. For a special family meal, it goes perfectly with fried noodles.

Serves 4

450g/1lb rump (round) steak
30ml/2 tbsp sunflower oil
30ml/2 tbsp medium curry paste
2 bay leaves
400ml/14fl oz/1⅔ cups
  coconut milk
300ml/½ pint/1¼ cups
  beef stock
30ml/2 tbsp lemon juice
45ml/3 tbsp fish sauce
15ml/1 tbsp sugar
115g/4oz baby (pearl) onions,
  peeled but left whole
225g/8oz new potatoes, scrubbed
  and halved
115g/4oz/1 cup unsalted roasted
  peanuts, roughly chopped
115g/4oz fine green
  beans, halved
1 red (bell) pepper, seeded and
  thinly sliced
unsalted roasted peanuts,
  to garnish

1 Trim any fat off the beef and use a sharp knife to cut it into 5cm/2in strips. Slicing the meat is easier if it is very cold, so place it in the freezer for 10 minutes before slicing, if time.

2 Heat the oil in a large, heavy pan, add the curry paste and cook over a medium heat for 30 seconds, stirring constantly.

3 Add the beef to the pan and cook, stirring constantly, for about 2 minutes until it is beginning to brown and is thoroughly coated with the spices.

4 Stir in the bay leaves, coconut milk, stock, lemon juice, fish sauce and sugar, and bring to the boil, stirring.

5 Add the onions and potatoes, then bring back to the boil, reduce the heat and simmer, uncovered, for 5 minutes.

6 Stir in the peanuts, beans and pepper and simmer for a further 10 minutes, or until the beef and potatoes are tender. Serve in warmed shallow bowls, with a fork and spoon, to enjoy all the rich and creamy juices. Sprinkle with extra unsalted roasted peanuts, to garnish.

Beef with Green Beans Energy 309kcal/1289kJ; Protein 29.7g; Carbohydrate 15.1g, of which sugars 10g; Fat 15g, of which saturates 4.9g; Cholesterol 65mg; Calcium 70mg; Fibre 3.8g; Sodium 83mg.
Citrus Beef Curry Energy 476kcal/1990kJ; Protein 33.8g; Carbohydrate 27.5g, of which sugars 16.3g; Fat 26.4g, of which saturates 6.6g; Cholesterol 69mg; Calcium 77mg; Fibre 4.1g; Sodium 169mg.

Beef Tagine with Peas and Saffron

Saffron is cultivated commercially in Morocco and is a favourite ingredient in dishes like this classic fresh pea and preserved lemon tagine.

Serves 6

1.2kg/2½lb chuck steak or stewing beef, trimmed and cubed
30ml/2 tbsp olive oil
1 onion, chopped
25g/1oz fresh root ginger, peeled and finely chopped
5ml/1 tsp ground ginger
pinch of cayenne pepper
pinch of saffron threads
1.2kg/2½lb shelled fresh peas
2 tomatoes, skinned and chopped
1 preserved lemon, chopped
a handful of brown kalamata olives
salt and ground black pepper
bread or couscous, to serve

1 Put the cubed beef in a tagine, flameproof casserole or large heavy pan with the olive oil, chopped onion, fresh and ground ginger, cayenne pepper and saffron and season with salt and plenty of ground black pepper.

2 Pour in enough water to cover the meat completely, stir well to combine, and then bring to the boil.

3 Reduce the heat and then cover the pan with a lid and simmer for about 1½ hours, until the meat is very tender. Cook for a little longer, if necessary.

4 Add the peas, tomatoes, preserved lemon and olives. Stir well and cook, uncovered, for about 10 minutes, or until the peas are tender and the sauce has reduced. Check the seasoning and serve with bread or plain couscous.

Cook's Tip

Saffron is the yellow-orange stigmas from a small purple crocus. It is the world's most expensive spice because each flower has only three stigmas, which are hand-picked and then dried. About 15,000 stigmas are needed to produce 25g/1oz of saffron. Store in an airtight container in a cool, dark place for up to 6 months.

Beef and Chorizo Stew

This spicy dish from the Philippines can be made with beef, chicken or pork, all of which are cooked the same way. If using pork or chicken, take care that it is cooked through.

Serves 4–6

30–45ml/2–3 tbsp groundnut (peanut) or corn oil
1 onion, chopped
2 garlic cloves, chopped
40g/1½oz fresh root ginger, chopped
2 x 175g/6oz chorizo sausages, cut diagonally into bitesize pieces
700g/1lb 9oz lean rump (round) beef, cut into bitesize pieces
4 tomatoes, skinned, seeded and quartered
900ml/1½ pints/3¾ cups beef or chicken stock
2 plantains, peeled and sliced diagonally
2 x 400g/14oz cans chickpeas, rinsed and drained
salt and ground black pepper
1 small bunch fresh coriander (cilantro) leaves, roughly chopped, to garnish

To accompany

corn oil, for deep-frying
1–2 firm bananas or 1 plantain, peeled and sliced diagonally
stir-fried greens

1 Heat the oil in a wok with a lid or a flameproof casserole, stir in the onion, garlic and ginger and fry until they begin to brown. Add the chorizo sausages and beef and fry until they begin to brown. Add the tomatoes and pour in the stock. Bring to the boil, reduce the heat, cover and simmer for 45 minutes.

2 Add the plantains and chickpeas to the stew and cook for a further 20–25 minutes, adding a little extra water if the cooking liquid reduces too much.

3 Meanwhile, heat enough oil for deep-frying in a wok or large, shallow pan. Deep-fry the bananas or plantain, in batches, for about 3 minutes, until crisp and golden brown. Remove from the pan, drain on kitchen paper and set aside.

4 Season the stew with salt and pepper to taste and sprinkle with chopped coriander leaves to garnish. Serve with the deep-fried bananas or plantain and stir-fried greens.

Beef Tagine Energy 492kcal/2049kJ; Protein 57.9g; Carbohydrate 25.6g, of which sugars 7g; Fat 18.2g, of which saturates 6g; Cholesterol 126mg; Calcium 61mg; Fibre 10.1g; Sodium 134mg.
Beef and Chorizo Stew Energy 583kcal/2441kJ; Protein 40.5g; Carbohydrate 35.8g, of which sugars 6.2g; Fat 31.9g, of which saturates 11.1g; Cholesterol 91mg; Calcium 104mg; Fibre 6.1g; Sodium 778mg.

Curried Chilli Beef with Spicy Plum Tomatoes

When served with boiled yam or rice, this delicious curry makes a hearty dish for anyone who likes spice.

Serves 4
450g/1lb stewing beef
5ml/1 tsp dried thyme
45ml/3 tbsp palm or vegetable oil
1 large onion, finely chopped
2 garlic cloves, crushed

4 canned plum tomatoes, chopped,
    plus 60ml/4 tbsp of the juice
15ml/1 tbsp tomato purée (paste)
2.5ml/½ tsp mixed (apple
    pie) spice
1 fresh red chilli, seeded
    and chopped
900ml/1½ pints/3¾ cups beef
    stock or water
1 large aubergine (eggplant)
salt and ground black pepper

1 Cut the beef into cubes and season with 2.5ml/½ tsp of the thyme and salt and black pepper.

2 Heat 15ml/1 tbsp of the oil in a large pan and fry the meat, in batches if necessary, for 8–10 minutes, stirring constantly, until evenly browned all over. Transfer to a large bowl using a slotted spoon and set aside.

3 Heat the remaining oil in the pan and fry the onion and garlic for a few minutes until the onion begins to soften.

4 Add the tomatoes and tomato juice to the pan and simmer for a further 8–10 minutes, stirring occasionally.

5 Add the tomato purée, mixed spice, chilli and remaining thyme to the pan and stir well.

6 Add the cubed beef and the chicken stock or water to the pan. Bring to the boil, reduce the heat, cover the pan and simmer gently for 30 minutes.

7 Cut the aubergine into 1cm/½in dice. Stir into the beef mixture and cook, covered, for a further 30 minutes until the beef is completely tender. Taste the sauce, adjust the seasoning if necessary, and serve immediately.

Mussaman Beef

This dish is traditionally based on beef, but chicken, lamb or tofu can be used instead. Mussaman curry paste, available from specialist Asian stores, imparts a rich, sweet and spicy flavour.

Serves 4–6
675g/1½lb stewing steak
600ml/1 pint/2½ cups
    coconut milk
250ml/8fl oz/1 cup coconut cream

45ml/3 tbsp Mussaman curry paste
30ml/2 tbsp Thai fish sauce
15ml/1 tbsp palm sugar
    (jaggery) or light muscovado
    (brown) sugar
60ml/4 tbsp tamarind juice
    (tamarind paste mixed with
    warm water)
6 green cardamom pods
1 cinnamon stick
1 large potato, about 225g/8oz,
    cut into even chunks
1 onion, cut into wedges
50g/2oz/½ cup roasted peanuts

1 Trim off any excess fat from the stewing steak, then, using a sharp knife, cut it into 2.5cm/1in chunks. Pour the coconut milk into a large, heavy pan and bring to the boil over a medium heat. Add the chunks of beef to the coconut milk, reduce the heat to low, partially cover the pan and simmer gently for about 40–45 minutes, or until tender.

2 Pour the coconut cream into a separate pan. Cook over a medium heat, stirring constantly, for about 5 minutes, or until it separates. Stir in the Mussaman curry paste and cook rapidly for 2–3 minutes, until fragrant and thoroughly blended.

3 Add the coconut cream and curry paste mixture to the pan with the beef and stir until thoroughly blended. Simmer for a further 4–5 minutes, stirring occasionally.

4 Stir the fish sauce, sugar, tamarind juice, cardamom pods, cinnamon stick, potato chunks and onion wedges into the beef curry. Continue to simmer for a further 15–20 minutes, or until the potato is cooked and tender.

5 Add most of the roasted peanuts to the pan and stir well. Cook for 5 minutes, then transfer to warmed individual bowls, garnish with the reserved peanuts and serve immediately.

Chilli Beef Curry Energy 251kcal/1050kJ; Protein 27.2g; Carbohydrate 7.2g, of which sugars 6.2g; Fat 12.8g, of which saturates 2.9g; Cholesterol 75mg; Calcium 29mg; Fibre 3g; Sodium 87mg.
Mussaman Beef Energy 626kcal/2610kJ; Protein 44.6g; Carbohydrate 24.8g, of which sugars 15.4g; Fat 39.3g, of which saturates 22.7g; Cholesterol 98mg; Calcium 74mg; Fibre 1.6g; Sodium 288mg.

Beef Tagine with Sweet Potatoes

This warming dish of tender beef and succulent sweet potatoes is eaten during the winter in Morocco, where it can get surprisingly cold.

Serves 4
675–900g/1½–2lb braising or stewing beef
30ml/2 tbsp sunflower oil
a good pinch of ground turmeric
1 large onion, chopped
1 red or green chilli, seeded and chopped
7.5ml/1½ tsp paprika
a good pinch of cayenne pepper
2.5ml/½ tsp ground cumin
450g/1lb sweet potatoes
15ml/1 tbsp chopped fresh parsley
15ml/1 tbsp chopped fresh coriander (cilantro)
15g/½oz/1 tbsp butter
salt and ground black pepper

1 Cube the beef. Heat the oil in a flameproof casserole and fry the meat, with the turmeric and seasoning, for 3–4 minutes until evenly brown, stirring frequently.

2 Cover the pan with a tight-fitting lid and cook for 15 minutes over a fairly gentle heat, without lifting the lid. Preheat the oven to 180°C/350°F/Gas 4.

3 Add the onion, chilli, paprika, cayenne pepper and cumin to the casserole, with just enough water to cover the meat. Cover tightly and cook in the oven for 1–1½ hours until the meat is very tender, checking occasionally and adding a little extra water to keep the stew moist.

4 Meanwhile, peel the sweet potatoes and slice them straight into a bowl of salted water. Transfer to a pan, bring to the boil and simmer for 3 minutes until just tender. Drain.

5 Stir the herbs into the meat. Arrange the potato slices over the top of the meat and dot with the butter. Cover again and bake for a further 10 minutes.

6 Increase the oven temperature to 200°C/400°F/Gas 6 or heat the grill (broiler). Remove the lid of the casserole and cook in the oven or under the grill for a further 5–10 minutes until the potatoes are golden. Serve immediately.

Spicy Meat Loaf with a Chilli and Egg Topping

This deliciously spicy meat loaf is baked in the oven. It provides a hearty meal for the whole family on a cold winter day.

Serves 4–6
5 eggs
450g/1lb minced (ground) beef
30ml/2 tbsp grated fresh root ginger
30ml/2 tbsp crushed garlic
6 fresh green chillies, chopped
2 small onions, finely chopped
2.5ml/½ tsp ground turmeric
50g/2oz/2 cups fresh coriander (cilantro), chopped
175g/6oz potato, grated
salt
lemon twist, to garnish
salad leaves, to serve

1 Preheat the oven to 180°C/350°F/Gas 4. In a large mixing bowl, beat two eggs until they are fluffy and pour them into a greased 900g/2lb loaf tin (pan).

2 Knead together the meat, ginger and garlic, 4 green chillies, 1 chopped onion, 1 beaten egg, the ground turmeric, fresh coriander, potato and salt.

3 Pack the mixture into the loaf tin, filling the corners, and smooth the surface with a knife. Place in the preheated oven and cook for about 45–50 minutes.

4 Meanwhile, beat the remaining eggs and fold in the remaining green chillies and onion. Remove the loaf tin from the oven and pour the mixture all over the meat.

5 Return the tin to the oven and cook until the eggs have just set. Serve the loaf immediately on a bed of salad leaves, garnished with a twist of lemon.

Cook's Tip
It is always best to buy meat for mincing by the piece if possible so that you can choose lean meat with little fat and remove any remaining fat before you mince it.

Beef Tagine Energy 301kcal/1254kJ; Protein 21.9g; Carbohydrate 12g, of which sugars 3.2g; Fat 18.7g, of which saturates 4.6g; Cholesterol 61mg; Calcium 18mg; Fibre 1.4g; Sodium 67mg.
Spicy Meat Loaf Energy 272kcal/1133kJ; Protein 22.1g; Carbohydrate 7.3g, of which sugars 2g; Fat 17.6g, of which saturates 6.6g; Cholesterol 204mg; Calcium 73mg; Fibre 1.5g; Sodium 129mg.

Green Beef Curry with Thai Aubergines

This is a very quick curry so it is essential that you use good-quality meat. Sirloin is recommended here, but tender rump or even fillet steak could be used instead, if they are available.

Serves 4–6

450g/1lb beef sirloin
15ml/1 tbsp vegetable oil
45ml/3 tbsp Thai green curry paste
600ml/1 pint/2½ cups coconut milk
4 kaffir lime leaves, torn
15–30ml/1–2 tbsp Thai fish sauce
5ml/1 tsp palm sugar (jaggery) or light muscovado (brown) sugar
150g/5oz small Thai aubergines (eggplants), halved
a small handful of fresh Thai basil, roughly chopped
2 fresh green chillies, plus extra Thai basil sprigs, to garnish

1 Trim off any excess fat from the beef. Using a sharp knife, cut it into long, thin strips. This is easiest to do if it is well chilled, so place it into the freezer for about 10 minutes first if you have time. Set it aside while preparing the other ingredients.

2 Heat the oil in a large, heavy pan or wok. Add the curry paste and cook for 1–2 minutes, until it is fragrant.

3 Stir in half the coconut milk, a little at a time. Cook, stirring frequently, for about 5–6 minutes, until an oily sheen appears on the surface of the liquid.

4 Add the beef to the pan with the kaffir lime leaves, fish sauce, sugar and aubergine halves. Cook for 2–3 minutes, then stir in the remaining coconut milk.

5 Bring back to a simmer and cook until the meat and aubergines are tender. Stir in the Thai basil.

6 Prepare the garnish. Slit the fresh green chillies and scrape out the pith and seeds and discard. Shred the chillies finely. Spoon the curry into a heated dish or on to warmed individual plates. Sprinkle the finely shredded chillies over the top of the curry, add the sprigs of basil and serve immediately.

Beef and Aubergine Curry

This slow-cooked creamy curry is full of spicy flavours with an extra chilli kick from the fresh chilli garnish.

Serves 6

120ml/4fl oz/½ cup sunflower oil
2 onions, thinly sliced
2.5cm/1in fresh root ginger, sliced and cut into matchsticks
1 garlic clove, crushed
2 fresh red chillies, seeded and very finely sliced
2.5cm/1in fresh turmeric, crushed, or 5ml/1 tsp ground turmeric
1 lemon grass stem, lower part sliced finely, top bruised
675g/1½lb braising steak, cut in even strips
400ml/14fl oz can coconut milk
300ml/½ pint/1¼ cups water
1 aubergine (eggplant), sliced and patted dry
5ml/1 tsp tamarind pulp, soaked in 60ml/4 tbsp warm water
salt and ground black pepper
finely sliced chilli (optional) and deep-fried onions, to garnish
plain boiled basmati rice, to serve

1 Heat half the oil and fry the onions, ginger and garlic for 3–4 minutes. Add the chillies, turmeric and the sliced lower part of the lemon grass. Push to one side of the pan and then turn up the heat and add the beef, stirring until it changes colour.

2 Add the coconut milk, water, lemon grass top and seasoning. Cover and simmer gently for 1½ hours, or until the meat is tender.

3 Towards the end of the cooking time heat the remaining oil in a frying pan. Fry the aubergine slices until brown all over.

4 Add the browned aubergine slices to the beef curry and cook for a further 15 minutes. Stir gently from time to time. Strain the tamarind and stir the juice into the curry. Taste and adjust the seasoning. Place into a warm serving dish. Garnish with the sliced chilli, if using, and deep-fried onions, and serve immediately with the boiled rice.

Cook's Tip

If you want to make this curry ahead of time, follow the above method to the end of step 2 and finish later.

Green Beef Curry Energy 147kcal/619kJ; Protein 18.2g; Carbohydrate 6.4g, of which sugars 6.3g; Fat 5.6g, of which saturates 1.9g; Cholesterol 38mg; Calcium 36mg; Fibre 0.5g; Sodium 341mg.
Beef and Aubergine Curry Energy 394kcal/1638kJ; Protein 26g; Carbohydrate 12g, of which sugars 10g; Fat 27g, of which saturates 5g; Cholesterol 71mg; Calcium 54mg; Fibre 203g; Sodium 700mg.

Beef Rendang

This spicy dish is slowly simmered on top of the stove and is usually served with the meat quite dry. If you prefer more sauce, add a little more water.

Serves 6–8
2 onions or 5–6 shallots, chopped
4 garlic cloves, chopped
2.5cm/1in piece fresh galangal, peeled and sliced, or 15ml/1 tbsp galangal paste
2.5cm/1in piece fresh root ginger, peeled and sliced
4–6 fresh red chillies, seeded and roughly chopped
lower part only of 1 lemon grass stalk, sliced
2.5cm/1in piece fresh turmeric, peeled and sliced, or 5ml/1 tsp ground turmeric
1kg/2¼lb prime beef, in one piece
5ml/1 tsp coriander seeds, dry-fried
5ml/1 tsp cumin seeds, dry-fried
2 kaffir lime leaves, torn into small pieces
2 x 400ml/14fl oz cans coconut milk
300ml/½ pint/1¼ cups water
30ml/2 tbsp dark soy sauce
5ml/1 tsp tamarind pulp, soaked in 60ml/4 tbsp warm water
8–10 small new potatoes, scrubbed
salt and ground black pepper
deep-fried onions, sliced fresh red chillies and spring onions (scallions), to garnish

1 Put the onions or shallots in a food processor. Add the garlic, galangal, ginger, chillies, sliced lemon grass and turmeric. Process to a fine paste or grind using a pestle and mortar.

2 Cut the meat into cubes using a large, sharp knife, then place the cubes in a bowl. Grind the dry-fried coriander and cumin seeds, then add to the meat with the onion and chilli paste and kaffir lime leaves; stir well. Cover and leave in a cool place to marinate for at least 1 hour.

3 Pour the coconut milk and water into a wok or large pan, then stir in the spiced meat and the soy sauce. Strain the tamarind water and add to the wok or pan. Stir over a medium heat until the liquid boils, then simmer gently, half-covered with a lid, for about 1½ hours.

4 Add the potatoes to the pan and simmer for 20–25 minutes, or until the meat and potatoes are tender. Season and serve, garnished with deep-fried onions, chillies and spring onions.

Balti Beef Curry with Cumin and Fennel Seeds

This simple curry, which can be prepared and cooked in under an hour. Use whatever lean beef is available.

Serves 4
1 red (bell) pepper
1 green (bell) pepper
15ml/1 tbsp vegetable oil
5ml/1 tsp cumin seeds
2.5ml/½ tsp fennel seeds
1 onion, cut into thick wedges
1 garlic clove, crushed
2.5cm/1in piece fresh root ginger, finely chopped
1 fresh red chilli, finely chopped
15ml/1 tbsp curry paste
2.5ml/½ tsp salt
675g/1½lb lean rump (round) or fillet steak (beef tenderloin), cut into thick strips
naan bread, to serve

1 Halve the red and green peppers, discard the seeds and cut the peppers into 2.5cm/1in chunks.

2 Heat the oil in a karahi, wok or frying pan and fry the cumin and fennel seeds for 2 minutes or until they begin to splutter. Add the onion, garlic, ginger and chilli and fry for a further 5 minutes, stirring constantly.

3 Stir the curry paste and salt into the pan and cook for a further 3–4 minutes, stirring constantly.

4 Add the peppers to the pan and toss over the heat for about 5 minutes. Stir in the beef strips and continue to fry for 10–12 minutes or until the meat is tender. Serve from the pan, with warm naan bread.

Variations
• This recipe would also work well with chicken breast fillet in place of the rump (round) or fillet steak.
• You could add mangetouts (snow peas), trimmed and left whole, to the dish for added crunch. As the peas need only the minimum amount of cooking, add them for the last 5 minutes of cooking time only.

Beef Rendang Energy 289kcal/1210kJ; Protein 30.2g; Carbohydrate 15.4g, of which sugars 8.6g; Fat 12.2g, of which saturates 5g; Cholesterol 73mg; Calcium 63mg; Fibre 1.4g; Sodium 465mg.
Balti Beef Energy 374kcal/1556kJ; Protein 39.7g; Carbohydrate 7.8g, of which sugars 6.2g; Fat 20.5g, of which saturates 7g; Cholesterol 98mg; Calcium 43mg; Fibre 2.5g; Sodium 129mg.

Beef and Kidney Curry with Spinach

Here, spinach is coarsely chopped and added towards the end of cooking, which retains the nutritional value of the spinach and gives the curry a lovely appearance.

Serves 4–6

5cm/2in piece fresh root ginger
30ml/2 tbsp vegetable oil
1 large onion, finely chopped
4 garlic cloves, crushed
60ml/4 tbsp mild curry paste, or
   60ml/4 tbsp mild curry powder
1.5ml/¼ tsp ground turmeric
900g/2lb steak and kidney, cubed
450g/1lb fresh spinach, trimmed,
   washed and chopped, or
   450g/1lb frozen spinach,
   thawed and drained
60ml/4 tbsp tomato
   purée (paste)
2 large tomatoes, finely chopped
salt

1 Using a sharp knife or vegetable peeler, remove the skin from the ginger. Grate it on the fine side of a metal grater.

2 Heat the oil in a frying pan, wok or karahi and fry the onion, ginger and garlic, stirring frequently, until the onion is soft and the ginger and garlic turn golden brown.

3 Lower the heat and add the curry paste or powder, turmeric and salt. Add the steak and kidney to the pan and mix well. Cover and cook, stirring frequently to prevent the mixture from sticking to the pan, for 20–30 minutes over a medium heat, until the meat is just tender.

4 Add the spinach and tomato purée and mix well. Cook uncovered until the spinach has softened and most of the liquid in the pan has evaporated.

5 Fold the chopped tomatoes into the pan. Increase the heat, as the tomatoes will have a cooling effect on the other ingredients, and cook the mixture for a further 5–7 minutes, until the tomatoes have turned soft but not too mushy.

6 Spoon into shallow bowls and serve piping hot with a simple accompaniment to offset the rich, gamey flavour of the dish, like plain boiled basmati rice. Go easy on any side portions though, as this is a rich and filling dish.

Stewed Beef Curry

This deliciously aromatic curry uses stewing beef, which is succulent and tender after long, slow simmering in the spicy, fragrant sauce.

Serves 4

900g/2lb lean stewing beef
15ml/1 tbsp vegetable oil
1 large onion, finely chopped
4 cloves
4 green cardamom pods
2 green chillies, finely chopped
2.5cm/1in piece fresh root ginger,
   finely chopped
2 garlic cloves, crushed
2 dried red chillies
15ml/1 tbsp curry paste
10ml/2 tsp ground coriander
5ml/1 tsp ground cumin
2.5ml/½ tsp salt
150ml/¼ pint/⅔ cup beef stock
handful of fresh coriander
   (cilantro) sprigs, to garnish
boiled rice, to serve

1 Trim any visible fat from the beef with a sharp knife and cut the meat into 2.5cm/1in cubes.

2 Heat the oil in a large, heavy frying pan and stir-fry the onion, cloves and cardamom pods for about 5 minutes. Add the fresh green chillies, ginger, garlic and dried red chillies and fry for a further 2 minutes until the spices release their fragrances and the fresh chillies have softened a little.

3 Add the curry paste to the pan and fry for 2 minutes until fragrant. Add the cubed beef and fry for 5–8 minutes until all the meat pieces are lightly browned.

4 Add the coriander, cumin, salt and hot stock. Cover and simmer gently for 1–1½ hours or until the meat is tender. Garnish with fresh coriander sprigs and serve immediately, accompanied by boiled rice.

Cook's Tip
When whole cardamom pods are used as a flavouring in curries, they are not meant to be eaten. In India, they are fished out while eating and left on the side of the plate, along with any bones from the meat in the dish.

Beef Curry Energy 289kcal/1209kJ; Protein 32.6g; Carbohydrate 9.9g, of which sugars 6.9g; Fat 13.5g, of which saturates 4g; Cholesterol 372mg; Calcium 181mg; Fibre 4.5g; Sodium 251mg.
Stewed Beef Curry Energy 442kcal/1840kJ; Protein 52.2g; Carbohydrate 2.8g, of which sugars 0.1g; Fat 24.7g, of which saturates 9g; Cholesterol 131mg; Calcium 25mg; Fibre 0g; Sodium 147mg.

Oxtail in Hot Tangy Sauce

Considered a delicacy in some parts of South-east Asia, oxtail and the tails of water buffalo are generally cooked for special feasts and celebrations. Served with steamed rice, or chunks of fresh, crusty bread, it makes a very tasty supper dish.

Serves 4–6
8 shallots, chopped
8 garlic cloves, chopped
4–6 fresh red chillies, seeded and chopped
25g/1oz fresh galangal, chopped
30ml/2 tbsp rice flour or plain (all-purpose) flour
15ml/1 tbsp ground turmeric
8–12 oxtail joints, cut roughly the same size and trimmed of fat
45ml/3 tbsp vegetable oil
225g/8oz tamarind pulp
400g/14oz can plum tomatoes, drained and chopped
2 lemon grass stalks, halved and bruised
a handful of fresh kaffir lime leaves
30–45ml/2–3 tbsp sugar
salt and ground black pepper
fresh coriander (cilantro) leaves, roughly chopped

1 Using a mortar and pestle or food processor, grind the shallots, garlic, chillies and galangal to a coarse paste.

2 Mix the flour with the ground turmeric and spread it on a flat surface. Roll the oxtail in the flour and set aside.

3 Heat the oil in a heavy pan or flameproof pot. Stir in the spice paste and cook until fragrant and golden. Add the oxtail joints and brown on all sides.

4 Soak the tamarind pulp in 600ml/1 pint/2½ cups water, squeeze it, strain the juice and discard the pulp and seeds. Add the tomatoes, lemon grass stalks, lime leaves and tamarind juice.

5 Pour in enough water to cover the oxtail, and bring it to the boil. Skim off any fat from the surface. Reduce the heat, cover the pan with a lid and simmer the oxtail for 2 hours.

6 Stir in the sugar, season with salt and pepper and continue to cook, uncovered, for a further 30–40 minutes, until the meat is very tender. Sprinkle with the coriander and serve the curry immediately straight from the pan.

Slow-cooked Buffalo in Coconut Milk

Cook this slowly for tender meat and a rich sauce.

Serves 6
1kg/2¼lb buffalo or beef, cubed
115g/4oz fresh coconut, grated
45ml/3 tbsp coconut oil
2 onions, sliced
3 lemon grass stalks, halved
2 cinnamon sticks
3–4 lime leaves
1.2 litres/2 pints/5 cups coconut milk
15ml/1 tbsp tamarind paste dissolved in 90ml/6 tbsp water
15ml/1 tbsp sugar
salt and ground black pepper
15ml/1 tbsp vegetable oil,
6 shallots, carrot strips, cooked rice and a salad, to serve

For the spice paste
8 red chillies, seeded and chopped
8 shallots, chopped
4–6 garlic cloves, chopped
50g/2oz galangal, chopped
25g/1oz fresh turmeric, chopped
15ml/1 tbsp coriander seeds
10ml/2 tsp cumin seeds
5ml/1 tsp black peppercorns

1 First make the spice paste. Grind the chillies, shallots, garlic, galangal and turmeric to a smooth paste. In a frying pan, dry-fry the coriander, cumin and peppercorns for 2–3 minutes. Grind the dry-fried spices to a powder then stir into the spice paste.

2 Put the buffalo or beef in a large bowl and mix in the spice paste. Leave to marinate for at least 2 hours.

3 Dry-fry the coconut in a heavy pan until brown. Grind the coconut in a food processor. Set aside.

4 Heat the oil in a flameproof casserole. Add the onions, lemon grass, cinnamon and lime leaves, and fry for 5 minutes. Add the beef and paste and fry until browned. Add the coconut milk and tamarind juice and bring to the boil. Reduce the heat and simmer gently for 2–4 hours for beef (4 hours for buffalo).

5 Stir in the sugar and coconut, cover and cook for 4 hours if using buffalo and 2–4 hours if using beef, stirring occasionally, until the meat is tender and the sauce is very thick. Season.

6 Fry the shallots in the oil. Spoon the meat on to a serving dish, garnish with the shallots, carrots and serve with rice and a salad.

Oxtail Energy 386kcal/1611kJ; Protein 34.5g; Carbohydrate 11.3g, of which sugars 6.6g; Fat 22.6g, of which saturates 7.7g; Cholesterol 125mg; Calcium 31mg; Fibre 1.2g; Sodium 191mg.
Slow-cooked Buffalo Energy 494kcal/2064kJ; Protein 40.6g; Carbohydrate 20.9g, of which sugars 18.8g; Fat 28.2g, of which saturates 17g; Cholesterol 97mg; Calcium 95mg; Fibre 3.9g; Sodium 335mg.

Red Beef Curry with Tamarind

This delectable red curry can also be made using diced lamb, in which case reduce the cooking time by 30 minutes.

Serves 4–6

400g/14oz canned coconut milk, strained and separated
300ml/½ pint/1¼ cups beef stock
30ml/2 tbsp smooth peanut butter
30ml/2 tbsp tamarind sauce
900g/2lb stewing, chuck, shin or blade steak, cut into 2.5cm/1in dice
350g/12oz new potatoes, peeled and roughly chopped
350g/12oz pumpkin, chopped
200g/7oz canned bamboo shoots, sliced
juice of 2 limes
1 small bunch fresh coriander (cilantro), chopped, to garnish
plain boiled rice, to serve (optional)

For the red curry paste

30ml/2 tbsp coriander seeds
5ml/1 tsp cumin seeds
6 green cardamom pods, seeds only
2.5ml/½ tsp freshly grated nutmeg
1.5ml/¼ tsp ground cloves
2.5ml/½ tsp ground cinnamon
20ml/4 tsp paprika
rind of 1 mandarin orange, chopped
4–5 small red chillies, seeded and finely chopped
25ml/1½ tbsp sugar
2.5ml/½ tsp salt
10cm/4in piece lemon grass, shredded
3 garlic cloves, crushed
2cm/¾in piece galangal or fresh root ginger, peeled and chopped
4 red shallots or 1 medium red onion, finely chopped
2cm/¾in piece shrimp paste
50g/2oz coriander (cilantro), white root or stem, chopped
30ml/2 tbsp vegetable oil

1 Heat all of the thin part and half of the thick part of the coconut milk with the stock, bring to the boil and simmer uncovered for 1 hour. Strain and set aside.

2 Meanwhile make the paste. Dry-fry the seeds in a wok for 1–2 minutes. Process the seeds and the remaining paste ingredients in a food processor or blender.

3 Place a cupful of the coconut milk liquid in a wok. Add 30–45ml/ 2–3 tbsp of the paste. Boil rapidly to reduce slightly then stir in the peanut butter and tamarind sauce. Add the beef, potatoes, pumpkin and bamboo shoots and simmer for 25 minutes. Stir in the remaining coconut milk and the lime juice. Heat through then serve, garnished with the chopped coriander.

Beef Vindaloo

This is a fiery, slow-cooked dish originally from Goa. A vindaloo is made using a unique blend of hot aromatic spices and vinegar to give it a distinctive flavour.

Serves 6

15ml/1 tbsp cumin seeds
4 dried red chillies
5ml/1 tsp black peppercorns
seeds from 5 green cardamom pods
5ml/1 tsp fenugreek seeds
5ml/1 tsp black mustard seeds
2.5ml/½ tsp salt
2.5ml/½ tsp demerara (raw) sugar
60ml/4 tbsp white wine vinegar
30ml/2 tbsp vegetable oil
1 large onion, finely chopped
900g/2lb lean stewing beef, cut into 2.5cm/1in cubes
2.5cm/1in piece fresh root ginger, finely chopped
1 garlic clove, crushed
10ml/2 tsp ground coriander
2.5ml/½ tsp ground turmeric
plain and yellow basmati rice, to serve

1 Put the cumin seeds, chillies, peppercorns, cardamom seeds, fenugreek seeds and mustard seeds into a spice grinder (or a mortar and pestle) and grind to a fine powder.

2 Spoon into a bowl, add the salt, sugar and white wine vinegar and mix to a thin paste. Heat 15ml/1 tbsp of the oil in a large, heavy pan and fry the onion, stirring, for 5 minutes until soft.

3 Put the onion and the spice paste into a food processor or blender and process to a coarse paste.

4 Heat the remaining oil in the frying pan and fry the meat cubes for about 10 minutes until lightly browned all over. Remove with a slotted spoon.

5 Add the ginger and garlic to the oil remaining in the pan and fry for about 2 minutes. Stir in the ground coriander and the turmeric and fry for a further 2 minutes. Add the spice and onion paste to the pan and fry, stirring frequently, for about 5 minutes until fragrant.

6 Return the beef cubes to the pan with 300ml/½ pint/1¼ cups water. Cover and simmer for about 1–1½ hours or until the meat is tender. Serve with plain and yellow basmati rice.

Red Beef Curry Energy 367kcal/1534kJ; Protein 25.5g; Carbohydrate 18.8g, of which sugars 9.3g; Fat 21.7g, of which saturates 5.7g; Cholesterol 54mg; Calcium 57mg; Fibre 2.5g; Sodium 403mg.
Beef Vindaloo Energy 352kcal/1468kJ; Protein 36.5g; Carbohydrate 9.5g, of which sugars 4.2g; Fat 19.2g, of which saturates 6.3g; Cholesterol 87mg; Calcium 44mg; Fibre 0.9g; Sodium 102mg.

Madras Beef Curry

Although Madras is renowned for the best vegetarian food in the country, meat-based recipes such as this beef curry are also extremely popular. This particular recipe is a contribution by the area's small Muslim community.

Serves 4–6

60ml/4 tbsp vegetable oil
1 large onion, finely sliced
3–4 cloves
4 green cardamoms
2 whole star anise
4 fresh green chillies, chopped
2 fresh or dried red
 chillies, chopped
45ml/3 tbsp Madras
 masala paste
5ml/1 tsp ground turmeric
450g/1lb lean beef, cubed
60ml/4 tbsp tamarind juice
sugar, to taste
salt
a few fresh coriander (cilantro)
 leaves, chopped, to garnish
pilau rice and mixed salad,
 to serve

1 Heat the vegetable oil in a wok, karahi or large pan over a medium heat. Add the onion slices and fry for 8–9 minutes, stirring occasionally, until they soften and turn golden brown.

2 Lower the heat, add all the spice ingredients to the pan, and fry for a further 2–3 minutes, stirring constantly, until the spices release their fragrances.

3 Add the beef to the pan and mix well. Cover and cook over a low heat until the beef is cooked through and tender. Cook uncovered on a high heat for the last few minutes to reduce any excess liquid and produce a thicker sauce.

4 Fold in the tamarind juice, sugar and salt. Reheat the dish and garnish with the chopped coriander leaves. Serve with pilau rice and a simple mixed salad.

Cook's Tip

If your beef isn't the leanest, to help tenderize it you can add about 60ml/4 tbsp white wine vinegar in step 2, along with the meat, and omit the tamarind juice.

Curried Meat with Spicy Peas

This spicy dish can be served as a main course, or try mixing it with fried or scrambled eggs for a delicious brunch. It also makes a good pizza topping, and can be used as a filling for samosas.

Serves 4–6

5ml/1 tsp vegetable oil
1 large onion, finely chopped
2 garlic cloves, crushed
5cm/2in piece fresh root
 ginger, crushed
4 green chillies, chopped
30ml/2 tbsp curry powder
450g/1lb lean minced
 (ground) beef
225g/8oz frozen peas, thawed
salt
juice of 1 lemon
a few coriander (cilantro)
 leaves, chopped

1 Heat the vegetable oil in a wok or large frying pan. Add the chopped onion and cook for 2–3 minutes, stirring frequently, until it is just beginning to soften.

2 Add the garlic, ginger and chillies and cook, stirring constantly, for 4–5 minutes until the onion has turned translucent.

3 Turn the heat down to low, add the curry powder to the pan and mix well. Cook for a minute until the curry powder releases its aromatic fragrances.

4 Add the meat to the pan and stir well, pressing the meat down with the back of a spoon. Cook, stirring frequently, for about 8–10 minutes until the meat is just cooked through and evenly browned all over.

5 Add the peas, salt and lemon juice to the pan, mix well, cover and simmer for 4–5 minutes until the peas are tender. Mix in the fresh coriander. Serve immediately.

Variation

This dish is equally delicious if made with minced lean lamb or pork. Simply substitute the same amount of lamb or pork for the minced beef. Or try using half pork and half beef.

Madras Beef Curry Energy 524kcal/2180kJ; Protein 37.6g; Carbohydrate 13.8g, of which sugars 7.4g; Fat 36g, of which saturates 13.8g; Cholesterol 133mg; Calcium 65mg; Fibre 2.6g; Sodium 160mg.
Curried Meat Energy 199kcal/827kJ; Protein 17.5g; Carbohydrate 7.3g, of which sugars 2.7g; Fat 11.3g, of which saturates 4.8g; Cholesterol 58mg; Calcium 40mg; Fibre 2.6g; Sodium 61mg.

Cauliflower, Pea and Potato Curry

This highly spiced vegetable curry is often prepared for religious festivals and other special occasions in India. It also makes a delicious light lunch.

Serves 4
500g/1¼lb potatoes
1 small cauliflower or 350g/12oz cauliflower florets, with outer stalks removed
45ml/3 tbsp sunflower oil or olive oil
1 large onion, finely sliced
5ml/1 tsp ginger purée
5ml/1 tsp garlic purée
2 green chillies, chopped, seeded if preferred
2.5ml/½ tsp ground turmeric
5ml/1 tsp ground coriander
175g/6oz fresh tomatoes, chopped
5ml/1 tsp salt, or to taste
115g/4oz frozen garden peas
15ml/1 tbsp chopped fresh coriander (cilantro), to garnish

1 Halve or quarter the potatoes – the pieces should be quite chunky so that they do not fall apart during cooking.

2 Divide the cauliflower into 2.5cm/1in florets, then blanch them briefly and plunge them in cold water.

3 Heat the oil in a large, non-stick pan over a medium to high heat and brown the potatoes in two to three batches until they are well browned and form a crust on the surface – they will look a little like roast potatoes. Drain them thoroughly on absorbent kitchen paper.

4 In the same oil, fry the onion, ginger, garlic and chillies over a low to medium heat, stirring regularly, for 6–8 minutes or until the mixture begins to brown.

5 Add the ground turmeric and coriander, cook for 1 minute and then add the tomatoes, fried potatoes and salt. Pour in 400ml/14fl oz/1⅔ cups warm water. Bring this to the boil, reduce the heat to low, then cover and cook for 15 minutes.

6 Drain the cauliflower and add to the pan with the coated potato mixture. Add the peas, cook for 5 minutes. Remove from the heat and serve, garnished with coriander.

Curried Stuffed Peppers

These fabulous peppers are served at weddings in India.

Serves 4–6
15ml/1 tbsp sesame seeds
15ml/1 tbsp white poppy seeds
5ml/1 tsp coriander seeds
60ml/4 tbsp desiccated (dry unsweetened shredded) coconut
½ onion, sliced
2.5cm/1in piece fresh root ginger, sliced
4 garlic cloves, sliced
1 bunch of fresh coriander (cilantro), stalks removed, roughly chopped
6 fresh green chillies
60ml/4 tbsp vegetable oil
2 potatoes, boiled and coarsely mashed
2 each green, red and yellow (bell) peppers
30ml/2 tbsp sesame oil
5ml/1 tsp cumin seeds
15ml/1 tbsp tamarind pulp soaked in 45ml/3 tbsp water, pulp and seeds discarded
salt

1 In a frying pan, dry-fry the sesame, poppy and coriander seeds, then add the coconut and continue to roast until the coconut turns golden brown. Add the onion, ginger, garlic, coriander, and two of the chillies, and roast for a further 5 minutes. Cool, and grind to a paste using a mortar and pestle or food processor. Set aside.

2 Heat 30ml/2 tbsp of the oil in a frying pan and fry the ground paste for about 4–5 minutes. Add the potatoes and salt to the pan, and stir well until the spices have blended evenly into the mashed potatoes.

3 Trim the bases of the peppers so that they can stand upright, then slice off the tops and reserve. Remove the seeds and any white pith. Fill the peppers with equal amounts of the potato mixture and replace the tops.

4 Slit the remaining chillies and remove the seeds, if you like. Heat the sesame oil and remaining vegetable oil in a large pan and fry the cumin seeds and the slit green chillies. When the chillies turn white, add the tamarind juice and bring to the boil.

5 Place the peppers over the mixture, cover the pan and cook until the peppers are just tender. Serve immediately.

Cauliflower Curry Energy 276kcal/1153kJ; Protein 9.7g; Carbohydrate 37g, of which sugars 11.6g; Fat 10.9g, of which saturates 1.5g; Cholesterol 0mg; Calcium 89mg; Fibre 6.5g; Sodium 33.8mg.
Curried Stuffed Peppers Energy 267kcal/1116kJ; Protein 13.9g; Carbohydrate 26.1g, of which sugars 15.3g; Fat 12.5g, of which saturates 4.7g; Cholesterol 37mg; Calcium 81mg; Fibre 4.4g; Sodium 84mg.

Hot and Spicy Thai Vegetable Curry

This spicy curry made with coconut milk has a creamy richness that contrasts wonderfully with the heat of the chilli. Thai yellow curry paste is available in supermarkets, but you will really taste the difference when you make it yourself.

Serves 4
30ml/2 tbsp sunflower oil
200ml/7fl oz/scant 1 cup
  coconut cream
300ml/½ pint/1¼ cups
  coconut milk
150ml/¼ pint/⅔ cup vegetable
  stock
200g/7oz green beans, cut into
  2cm/¾in lengths
200g/7oz baby corn
4 baby courgettes (zucchini),
  thickly sliced

1 small aubergine (eggplant),
  cubed or sliced
30ml/2 tbsp Thai
  mushroom ketchup
10ml/2 tsp palm sugar (jaggery)
fresh coriander (cilantro) leaves,
  to garnish
noodles or rice, to serve

For the yellow curry paste
10ml/2 tsp hot chilli powder
10ml/2 tsp ground coriander
10ml/2 tsp ground cumin
5ml/1 tsp turmeric
15ml/1 tbsp chopped fresh
  galangal
10ml/2 tsp finely grated garlic
30ml/2 tbsp finely chopped
  lemon grass
4 red Asian or brown shallots,
  finely chopped
5ml/1 tsp finely chopped
  lime rind

1 To make the curry paste, place all the ingredients in a food processor and blend with 30–45ml/2–3 tbsp of cold water to make a smooth paste. Add a little more water to the paste if the mixture seems too dry.

2 Heat a large wok over a medium heat and add the sunflower oil. When hot add 30–45ml/2–3 tbsp of the curry paste and stir-fry for 1–2 minutes. Add the coconut cream and cook gently for 8–10 minutes, or until the mixture starts to separate.

3 Add the coconut milk, stock and vegetables and cook gently for 8–10 minutes, until the vegetables are just tender.

4 Stir in the mushroom ketchup and palm sugar, garnish with coriander leaves and serve with noodles or rice.

Pineapple and Coconut Curry

This sweet and spicy curry benefits from being made the day before, enabling the flavours to mingle longer. In Indonesia it is often eaten at room temperature, but it is also delicious hot.

Serves 4
1 small, firm pineapple
15–30ml/1–2 tbsp palm or
  coconut oil
4–6 shallots, finely chopped
2 garlic cloves, finely chopped
1 red chilli, seeded and
  finely chopped

15ml/1 tbsp palm
  sugar (jaggery)
400ml/14fl oz/1⅔ cups
  coconut milk
salt and ground black pepper
1 small bunch fresh coriander
  (cilantro) leaves, finely chopped,
  to garnish

For the spice paste
4 cloves
4 cardamom pods
1 small cinnamon stick
5ml/1 tsp coriander seeds
2.5ml/½ tsp cumin seeds
5–10ml/1–2 tsp water

1 First make the spice paste. Using a mortar and pestle or spice grinder, grind all the spices together to a powder. In a small bowl mix the spice powder with the water to make a smooth paste. Set aside.

2 Remove the skin from the pineapple then cut the flesh lengthways into quarters and remove the core. Cut each pineapple quarter widthways into chunky slices and set aside.

3 Heat the oil in a wok or large, heavy frying pan, stir in the shallots, garlic and chilli and stir-fry until fragrant and beginning to colour. Stir in the spice paste and stir-fry for 1 minute. Toss the pineapple slices into the wok, making sure they are well coated in the spicy mixture.

4 Stir the sugar into the coconut milk and pour into the wok. Bring to the boil, reduce the heat and simmer for 3–4 minutes to thicken the sauce, but don't allow the pineapple to become too soft. Season to taste with salt and pepper.

5 Transfer the curry into a warmed serving dish and top with the coriander to garnish. Serve hot or at room temperature.

Hot Thai Curry Energy 279kcal/1161kJ; Protein 9.8g; Carbohydrate 17.4g, of which sugars 13.3g; Fat 19.4g, of which saturates 3.6g; Cholesterol 5mg; Calcium 99mg; Fibre 3.3g; Sodium 824mg.
Pineapple Curry Energy 135kcal/573kJ; Protein 1.6g; Carbohydrate 25.4g, of which sugars 23.6g; Fat 3.8g, of which saturates 0.5g; Cholesterol 0mg; Calcium 87mg; Fibre 2.9g; Sodium 131mg.

Tofu and Vegetable Thai Curry

Coconut milk, chillies, galangal, lemon grass and kaffir lime leaves give this curry a wonderful flavour.

Serves 4

175g/6oz firm tofu, drained
45ml/3 tbsp dark soy sauce
15ml/1 tbsp sesame oil
5ml/1 tsp chilli sauce
2.5cm/1in piece fresh root ginger, finely grated
30ml/2 tbsp vegetable oil
1 onion, sliced
400ml/14fl oz/1⅔ cups coconut milk
150ml/¼ pint/⅔ cup water
1 red (bell) pepper, seeded and chopped
175g/6oz green beans, halved
225g/8oz cauliflower florets
225g/8oz broccoli florets
115g/4oz/1½ cups shiitake or button (white) mushrooms, halved
shredded spring onions (scallions), to garnish
boiled rice or noodles, to serve

For the curry paste

2 fresh green chillies, seeded and chopped
1 lemon grass stalk, chopped
2.5cm/1in piece fresh galangal, chopped
2 kaffir lime leaves
10ml/2 tsp ground coriander
a few sprigs fresh coriander (cilantro), including the stalks

1 Cut the drained tofu into 2.5cm/1in cubes and place in an ovenproof dish. Mix together the soy sauce, sesame oil, chilli sauce and ginger and pour over the tofu. Toss gently, then leave to marinate for 4 hours or overnight, turning occasionally.

2 For the curry paste, place the ingredients and 45ml/3 tbsp water in a food processor and blend for a few seconds.

3 Preheat the oven to 190°C/375°F/Gas 5. Heat the oil in a flameproof casserole. Fry the onion for 7–8 minutes. Add the paste and the coconut milk. Add the water and bring to the boil.

4 Stir in the red pepper, beans, cauliflower and broccoli, then cover and place in the oven.

5 Place the tofu and marinade in the oven for 30 minutes. Stir them into the curry with the mushrooms. Reduce the oven to 180°C/350°F/Gas 4 and cook for a further 15 minutes. Garnish with spring onions and serve with rice or noodles.

Tamarind-laced Vegetables

The flavours in this dish make it popular in southern India.

Serves 4

125g/4½oz green beans, cut into 2.5cm/1in lengths
200g/7oz carrots, cut into 1cm/½in thick circles
225g/8oz potatoes, cubed
1 small aubergine (eggplant), about 200g/7oz, quartered lengthways and cut into 2.5cm/1in pieces
2.5ml/½ tsp ground turmeric
5ml/1 tsp salt or to taste
200g/7oz cauliflower, divided into 1cm/½in florets
10ml/2 tsp cumin seeds
50g/2oz/⅔ cup desiccated (dry unsweetened shredded) coconut
2–3 green chillies, chopped
200ml/7fl oz/¾ cup buttermilk
30ml/2 tbsp tamarind juice
30ml/2 tbsp sunflower oil
2.5ml/½ tsp black mustard seeds
2.5ml/½ tsp cumin seeds
2–3 whole dried red chillies
6–8 curry leaves
1.5ml/¼ tsp asafoetida
15ml/1 tbsp fresh coriander (cilantro), chopped
plain boiled basmati rice, to serve

1 Put the green beans, carrots, potatoes and aubergine into a large pan and add 350ml/12fl oz/1½ cups hot water. Add the turmeric and salt. Bring to the boil, reduce the heat to low and cover the pan. Cook for 5–6 minutes, then add the cauliflower. Cover and cook until the vegetables are tender, but still firm.

2 Meanwhile, heat a small heavy pan over a medium heat. Dry-roast the 10ml/2tsp cumin seeds for 30–40 seconds. Remove from the pan and dry-roast the coconut and green chillies until lightly browned. Allow to cool. Using a mortar and pestle or spice grinder, grind with the roasted cumin seeds until fine.

3 Add the ground roasted ingredients, buttermilk and tamarind juice to the vegetables. Cook gently for 4–5 minutes, then remove from the heat.

4 Heat the oil in a small pan over a medium heat. When hot, but not smoking, add the mustard seeds, followed by the 2.5ml/½tsp cumin seeds, red chillies, curry leaves and asafoetida. Blacken the chillies, then pour the spices over the vegetables. Stir in the chopped coriander and remove from the heat. Stand covered, for 5–6 minutes. Serve with basmati rice.

Tofu Thai Curry Energy 210kcal/873kJ; Protein 11g; Carbohydrate 15.1g, of which sugars 13.3g; Fat 12g, of which saturates 1.8g; Cholesterol 0mg; Calcium 328mg; Fibre 5g; Sodium 927mg.
Tamarind Vegetables Energy 252kcal/1050kJ; Protein 7.55g; Carbohydrate 22.5g, of which sugars 10.7g; Fat 15.5g, of which saturates 7.7g; Cholesterol 1.75mg; Calcium 119mg; Fibre 6.1g; Sodium 57mg.

Spiced Root Vegetable Gratin

This subtle gratin makes a fine supper dish. It also makes a good accompaniment to a vegetable or bean curry.

Serves 4
2 large potatoes, total weight about 450g/1lb
2 sweet potatoes, total weight about 275g/10oz
175g/6oz celeriac
15ml/1 tbsp unsalted butter
5ml/1 tsp curry powder
5ml/1 tsp ground turmeric
2.5ml/½ tsp ground coriander
5ml/1 tsp mild chilli powder
3 shallots, chopped
150ml/¼ pint/⅔ cup single (light) cream
150ml/¼ pint/⅔ cup semi-skimmed (low-fat) milk
salt and ground black pepper
chopped fresh flat leaf parsley, to garnish

1 Thinly slice the potatoes, sweet potatoes and celeriac, using a sharp knife or the slicing attachment on a food processor. Immediately place the vegetables in a bowl of cold water to prevent them discolouring.

2 Preheat the oven to 180°C/350°F/Gas 4. Heat half the butter in a heavy pan, add the curry powder, turmeric and coriander and half the chilli powder. Cook for 2 minutes, then set aside to cool slightly.

3 Drain the vegetables, then pat dry with kitchen paper. Place in a bowl, add the spice mixture and the shallots and mix well.

4 Arrange the vegetables in a lightly greased gratin dish, seasoning between the layers with salt and pepper.

5 Mix together the cream and milk, pour the mixture over the vegetables, then sprinkle the remaining chilli powder on top.

6 Cover the dish with a sheet of baking parchment and bake in the preheated oven for about 45 minutes.

7 Remove the baking parchment, dot the gratin with the remaining butter and bake for a further 50 minutes. Serve immediately, garnished with chopped fresh parsley.

Curried Parsnip Pie

Sweet, creamy parsnips are beautifully complemented by the addition of curry spices and cheese in this delectable pie. It is sure to go down a treat with the whole family.

Serves 4
For the pastry
115g/4oz/½ cup butter
225g/8oz/1 cup plain (all-purpose) flour
5ml/1 tsp dried thyme or oregano
cold water, to mix
salt and ground black pepper

For the filling
8 shallots, peeled
2 large parsnips, thinly sliced
2 carrots, thinly sliced
25g/1oz/2 tbsp butter
30ml/2 tbsp wholemeal (whole-wheat) flour
15ml/1 tbsp mild curry paste
300ml/½ pint/1¼ cups milk
115g/4oz cheese, grated
45ml/3 tbsp fresh coriander (cilantro) or parsley, chopped
1 egg yolk, beaten with 10ml/ 2 tsp water
salt and ground black pepper

1 Make the pastry by rubbing the butter into the flour until it resembles fine breadcrumbs. Season and stir in the thyme or oregano, then mix with enough cold water to make a firm dough.

2 Blanch the shallots with the parsnips and carrots in water for 5 minutes. Drain, reserving 300ml/½ pint/1¼ cups of the stock.

3 In a clean pan, melt the butter, and stir in the flour and curry paste to make a roux. Whisk in the milk until smooth. Simmer for a minute or two. Stir in the cheese and seasoning, then mix into the vegetables with the coriander or parsley. Pour into a pie dish, fix a pie funnel in the centre and allow to cool.

4 Roll out the pastry, large enough to fit the pie dish. Re-roll the trimmings into long strips. Brush the edges of the dish with egg yolk wash and fit on the strips. Carefully lift the rolled pastry over the pie top, pressing it down. Cut off any excess and crimp the edges. Cut a hole for the funnel and make decorations with the trimmings. Brush with egg yolk wash.

5 Place the dish on a baking sheet and chill for 30 minutes while you preheat the oven to 200°C/400°F/Gas 6. Bake the pie for 25–30 minutes until golden brown and crisp on top.

Root Vegetable Gratin Energy 268kcal/1129kJ; Protein 5.8g; Carbohydrate 37.7g, of which sugars 9.8g; Fat 11.6g, of which saturates 7.1g; Cholesterol 31mg; Calcium 127mg; Fibre 3.6g; Sodium 117mg.
Curried Parsnip Pie Energy 411kcal/1721kJ; Protein 5.9g; Carbohydrate 47.4g, of which sugars 24.8g; Fat 23.4g, of which saturates 13.9g; Cholesterol 117mg; Calcium 96mg; Fibre 1.7g; Sodium 106mg.

Malay Vegetable Curry with Coconut

Originally from southern India, this delicious curry has found its way into many Malay homes. Made with firm vegetables, roots and gourds, all cut into long bitesize pieces, it is substantial and flexible – choose your own assortment of vegetables.

Serves 4

2–3 green chillies, seeded and chopped
25g/1oz fresh root ginger, peeled and chopped
5–10ml/1–2 tsp roasted cumin seeds
10ml/2 tsp sugar
5–10ml/1–2 tsp ground turmeric
1 cinnamon stick
5ml/1 tsp salt
2 carrots, cut into bitesize sticks
2 sweet potatoes, cut into bitesize sticks
2 courgettes (zucchini), partially peeled in strips, seeded and cut into bitesize sticks
1 green plantain, peeled and cut into bitesize sticks
a small coil of yard-long beans or a few green beans, cut into bitesize sticks
a handful fresh curry leaves
1 fresh coconut, grated
250ml/8fl oz/1 cup Greek (US strained plain) yogurt
salt and ground black pepper

1 Using a mortar and pestle or food processor, grind the chillies, ginger, roasted cumin seeds and sugar to a paste.

2 In a heavy pan, bring 450ml/15fl oz/scant 2 cups water to the boil. Stir in the turmeric, cinnamon stick and salt. Add the carrots and cook for 1 minute. Add the sweet potatoes and cook for 2 minutes. Add the courgettes, plantain and beans and cook for a further 2 minutes.

3 Reduce the heat, stir in the spice paste and curry leaves, and cook gently for 4–5 minutes, or until the vegetables are tender but not soft and mushy, and the liquid has greatly reduced.

4 Gently stir in half the coconut. Take the pan off the heat and fold in the yogurt. Season to taste with salt and pepper.

5 Quickly roast the remaining coconut in a heavy pan over a high heat, until nicely browned. Sprinkle a little over the curry in the pan, and serve the rest with the curry and flatbread.

Spicy Chickpea and Aubergine Stew

This is a Lebanese dish, but similar recipes are found all over the Mediterranean. The vegetables have a warm, smoky flavour, subtly enriched with spices. Crunchy fried onion rings provide a contrast of taste and texture. Serve the stew on a bed of rice.

Serves 4

3 large aubergines (eggplants), cut into cubes
200g/7oz/1 cup chickpeas, soaked overnight
60ml/4 tbsp olive oil
3 garlic cloves, chopped
2 large onions, chopped
2.5ml/½ tsp ground cumin
2.5ml/½ tsp ground cinnamon
2.5ml/½ tsp ground coriander
3 × 400g/14oz cans chopped tomatoes
salt and ground black pepper
cooked rice, to serve

For the garnish

30ml/2 tbsp olive oil
1 onion, sliced
1 garlic clove, sliced
sprigs of coriander (cilantro)

1 Place the aubergines in a colander and sprinkle them with salt. Sit the colander in a bowl and leave for 30 minutes, to allow the bitter juices to escape. Rinse with cold water and pat dry using a piece of kitchen paper.

2 Drain the chickpeas and put in a pan with enough water to cover. Bring to the boil, reduce the heat and simmer for about 30 minutes, or until tender. Drain.

3 Heat the oil in a large pan. Add the garlic and onions and cook gently until soft. Add the spices and cook, stirring, for a few seconds. Add the aubergine and stir to coat with the spices and onion. Cook for 5 minutes.

4 Add the tomatoes and chickpeas and season with salt and pepper. Cover and simmer for 20 minutes.

5 To make the garnish, heat the oil in a frying pan and, when very hot, add the sliced onion and garlic. Fry until golden and crisp. Serve the stew with rice, topped with the onion and garlic and garnished with coriander.

Malay Curry Energy 419kcal/1753kJ; Protein 9.9g; Carbohydrate 47.7g, of which sugars 19.4g; Fat 23g, of which saturates 16.9g; Cholesterol 0mg; Calcium 176mg; Fibre 9g; Sodium 104mg.
Spicy Chickpea Stew Energy 201kcal/843kJ; Protein 7.1g; Carbohydrate 22.3g, of which sugars 10.4g; Fat 10g, of which saturates 1.4g; Cholesterol 0mg; Calcium 57mg; Fibre 5.9g; Sodium 175mg.

Spicy Chickpea Tagine

This tangy Moroccan tagine features the traditional preserved lemon. The flavour of preserved lemon is wonderful. It adds a real zing to the nuttiness of the chickpeas.

Serves 4

150g/5oz/¾ cup chickpeas, soaked overnight, or 2 x 400g/14oz cans chickpeas, rinsed and drained
30ml/2 tbsp sunflower oil or vegetable oil
1 large onion, chopped
1 garlic clove, crushed (optional)
400g/14oz can chopped tomatoes
5ml/1 tsp ground cumin
350ml/12fl oz/1½ cups vegetable stock
¼ preserved lemon
30ml/2 tbsp chopped fresh coriander (cilantro)
Moroccan bread, to serve

1 If using dried chickpeas, cook them in plenty of boiling water for 1–1½ hours until tender. Drain well.

2 Place the chickpeas in a bowl of cold water and rub them between your fingers to remove the skins.

3 Heat the oil in a pan or flameproof casserole and fry the onion and garlic, if using, for 8–10 minutes, until golden.

4 Add the chickpeas, tomatoes, cumin and vegetable stock to the pan and stir well to combine.

5 Bring to the boil and simmer for 30–40 minutes, until most of the liquid has evaporated.

6 Rinse the preserved lemon and cut away the flesh and pith. Cut the peel into slivers and stir it into the chickpeas together with the coriander. Serve immediately with Moroccan bread.

Cook's Tip
Preserved lemon is popular in North Africa, particularly Morocco, where the distinctive yellow globes in glass jars glimmer like miniature suns in the markets.

Aubergine and Sweet Potato Stew

This aubergine and sweet potato stew cooked in a coconut sauce is scented with fragrant lemon grass, ginger and lots of garlic.

Serves 6

60ml/4 tbsp sunflower oil
400g/14oz baby aubergines (eggplants), halved, or 2 standard aubergines, cut into chunks
225g/8oz red shallots or other small shallots or pickling onions
5ml/1 tsp fennel seeds, crushed
4–5 garlic cloves, thinly sliced
25ml/1½ tbsp finely chopped fresh root ginger
475ml/16fl oz/2 cups vegetable stock
2 lemon grass stalks, outer layers discarded, finely chopped
15g/½oz fresh coriander, stalks and leaves chopped separately
3 kaffir lime leaves, lightly bruised
2–3 small red chillies
45–60ml/3–4 tbsp Thai green curry paste
675g/1½lb sweet potatoes, peeled and cut into thick chunks
400ml/14fl oz/1⅔ cups coconut milk
2.5–5ml/½–1 tsp light muscovado (brown) sugar
250g/9oz mushrooms, sliced
juice of 1 lime, to taste
salt and ground black pepper
18 fresh Thai basil leaves or ordinary basil, to garnish

1 Heat half the oil in a lidded wok or deep frying pan. Cook the aubergines over a medium heat, stirring occasionally, until lightly browned on all sides. Remove and set aside.

2 Slice 4–5 of the shallots or 3–4 onions and set aside. Fry the remaining whole shallots or onions until lightly browned. Set aside. Heat the remaining oil and cook the sliced shallots, fennel seeds, garlic and ginger very gently until soft. Add the stock, lemon grass, coriander stalks and any roots, lime leaves and whole chillies. Cover with a lid and simmer gently for 5 minutes.

3 Stir in 30ml/2 tbsp of the curry paste and the sweet potatoes. Simmer for 10 minutes, then return the aubergines and browned shallots to the pan and cook for 5 minutes.

4 Stir in the coconut milk and the sugar. Season to taste, then stir in the mushrooms and simmer for 5 minutes. Stir in more curry paste and lime juice to taste, followed by the coriander leaves. Serve in warmed bowls, garnished with basil leaves.

Chickpea Tagine Energy 207kcal/871kJ; Protein 9.7g; Carbohydrate 26.4g, of which sugars 7.1g; Fat 7.8g, of which saturates 0.9g; Cholesterol 0mg; Calcium 87mg; Fibre 5.6g; Sodium 56mg.
Aubergine Stew Energy 228kcal/960kJ; Protein 4.3g; Carbohydrate 34g, of which sugars 13.4g; Fat 9.3g, of which saturates 1.2g; Cholesterol 0mg; Calcium 130mg; Fibre 7.2g; Sodium 159mg.

Prawn Pilau

This pilau from Goa combines tasty prawns with a very simple preparation method. A flavoursome meal in itself, the dish also fits easily into a spread that includes meat, poultry and vegetable dishes as well.

Serves 4

275g/10oz/1⅓ cups basmati rice
60ml/4 tbsp sunflower oil or
    olive oil
5cm/2in piece of cinnamon
    stick, halved
6 green cardamom pods, bruised
4 cloves
2 bay leaves, crumpled
1 large onion, finely sliced
10ml/2 tsp ginger purée
1 green chilli, finely chopped, and
    seeded if preferred
5ml/½ tsp ground turmeric
5ml/1 tsp salt, or to taste
15ml/1 tbsp chopped fresh
    coriander (cilantro)
250g/9oz cooked and peeled
    prawns (shrimp)

1 Wash the rice in several changes of cold water and soak for 20 minutes. Leave to drain.

2 In a heavy pan, heat the oil over a low heat and add the cinnamon, cardamom, cloves and bay leaves. Stir-fry the ingredients gently for 25–30 seconds and then add the onion. Increase the heat to medium, and fry until the onion is beginning to brown, around 7–8 minutes, stirring regularly to prevent the spices from burning.

3 Add the ginger purée and chilli to the pan and continue to fry until the onion is well browned.

4 Add the turmeric, salt, chopped coriander, prawns and rice to the pan. Stir gently to mix the ingredients. Stir-fry for about 2–3 minutes, then pour in 475ml/16fl oz/2 cups hot water. Bring the mixture to the boil and let it cook, uncovered, for 2–3 minutes. Reduce the heat to low, cover the pan tightly and cook for a further 7–8 minutes.

5 Remove from the heat and leave to stand for 5–6 minutes to absorb the flavour. Fluff up the pilau with a fork and transfer it to a serving dish.

Prawn and Vegetable Rice

This is an excellent combination of prawns and vegetables, which is lightly flavoured with whole spices, including cardamom, cinnamon and peppercorns. Using a mixture of frozen vegetables speeds up the preparation time. Serve with a cool and refreshing cucumber raita.

Serves 4

300g/11oz/1½ cups
    basmati rice
15ml/1 tbsp vegetable oil
2 medium onions, sliced
3 green cardamom pods
2.5cm/1in cinnamon stick
4 black peppercorns
1 bay leaf
1.5ml/¼ tsp black cumin seeds
2.5cm/1in piece root ginger, grated
2 garlic cloves, roughly chopped
2 green chillies, seeded
    and chopped
30ml/2 tbsp chopped fresh
    coriander (cilantro)
30ml/2 tbsp lemon juice
115g/4oz/1 cup frozen
    vegetables (carrots, beans,
    corn and peas)
175–225g/6–8oz/1½–2 cups
    cooked peeled prawns (shrimp)
475ml/16fl oz/2 cups water
raita, to serve

1 Wash the rice well in cold water and leave it to soak in plenty of water in a bowl for 30 minutes.

2 Heat the oil in a heavy pan and fry the sliced onions, cardamom pods, cinnamon stick, peppercorns, bay leaf, black cumin seeds, ginger, garlic and chillies for about 3 minutes, stirring continuously.

3 Add half the fresh coriander, the lemon juice, mixed vegetables and prawns. Stir for a further 3 minutes.

4 Drain the rice and add it to the pan. Gently stir in the water and bring to the boil.

5 Lower the heat, add the remaining fresh coriander and cook, covered with a lid, for 15–20 minutes or until all the liquid has been absorbed and the rice is cooked.

6 Remove from the heat and leave to stand, still covered, for about 5–7 minutes before serving with raita.

Prawn Pilau Energy 440kcal/1835kJ; Protein 17.9g; Carbohydrate 64.1g, of which sugars 5.6g; Fat 12.4g, of which saturates 1.3g; Cholesterol 122mg; Calcium 94mg; Fibre 1.4g; Sodium 123mg.
Prawn Rice Energy 409kcal/1708kJ; Protein 17.6g; Carbohydrate 73.6g, of which sugars 6.3g; Fat 5g, of which saturates 0.6g; Cholesterol 85mg; Calcium 93mg; Fibre 2.8g; Sodium 89mg.

Prawn Biryani

Fragrant saffron rice and king prawns are combined with button mushrooms, peas and traditional Indian spices for this delicious one-pot meal.

Serves 4–6
2 onions, sliced and boiled
    for 5 minutes
300ml/½ pint/1¼ cups natural
    (plain) low-fat yogurt
30ml/2 tbsp tomato purée (paste)
60ml/4 tbsp green masala paste
30ml/2 tbsp lemon juice
5ml/1 tsp black cumin seeds

5cm/2in piece cinnamon stick
4 green cardamom pods
1.5ml/¼ tsp salt
450g/1lb raw king prawns (jumbo
    shrimp), peeled and deveined
225g/8oz/3 cups button
    (white) mushrooms
225g/8oz/2 cups frozen
    peas, thawed
450g/1lb/generous 2⅓ cups
    basmati rice
300ml/½ pint/1¼ cups water
1 sachet saffron powder mixed
    with 90ml/6 tbsp milk
15ml/1 tbsp vegetable oil, plus
    extra for greasing

1 Mix the onions, yogurt, tomato purée, green masala paste, lemon juice, black cumin seeds, cinnamon stick and cardamom pods together in a large bowl and add salt to taste. Mix the prawns, mushrooms and peas into the marinade and leave to absorb the spices for at least 2 hours.

2 Wash the rice well, cover with boiling water and leave to soak for 5 minutes, then drain.

3 Grease the base of a heavy pan with a little of the oil and add the prawns, vegetables and any remaining marinade juice. Cover with the drained rice and smooth the surface gently with a spoon until you have an even layer.

4 Pour the measured water all over the surface of the rice. Make random holes through the rice with the handle of a spoon and pour in the saffron milk.

5 Sprinkle the oil over the surface of the rice and place a circular piece of foil directly on top. Cover and steam gently over a low heat for 45–50 minutes until the rice is cooked. Gently toss the rice, prawns and vegetables together and serve hot.

Prawns with Mushroom Basmati

Warm spices complement the flavour of mushrooms well in this tasty prawn dish.

Serves 4
150g/5oz/⅔ cup basmati rice
15ml/1 tbsp vegetable oil
1 medium onion, chopped
4 black peppercorns
2.5cm/1in cinnamon stick
1 bay leaf
1.5ml/¼ tsp cumin seeds
2 cardamom pods
5ml/1 tsp crushed garlic
5ml/1 tsp grated fresh
    root ginger

5ml/1 tsp garam masala
5ml/1 tsp chilli powder
7.5ml/1½ tsp salt
115g/4oz/1 cup cooked peeled
    prawns (shrimp)
115g/4oz/1½ cups mushrooms,
    cut into large pieces
30ml/2 tbsp chopped fresh
    coriander (cilantro)
120ml/4fl oz/½ cup natural
    (plain) low-fat yogurt
15ml/1 tbsp lemon juice
50g/2oz/½ cup frozen peas
250ml/8fl oz/1 cup water
1 fresh red chilli, seeded and
    sliced, to garnish

1 Wash the rice well under cold running water and leave to soak in water for 30 minutes.

2 Heat the oil in a heavy pan and add the chopped onion, peppercorns, cinnamon, bay leaf, cumin seeds, cardamom pods, garlic, ginger, garam masala, chilli powder and salt. Lower the heat and stir-fry for 2–3 minutes.

3 Add the prawns to the spice mixture in the pan and cook for about 2 minutes, then add the mushrooms.

4 Stir in the coriander and yogurt, followed by the lemon juice and peas, and cook for 2 more minutes.

5 Drain the rice and add it to the prawn mixture. Pour in the water, cover the pan and cook over a medium heat for about 15 minutes, checking once to make sure that the rice has not stuck to the base of the pan.

6 Remove the pan from the heat and leave to stand, still covered, for about 5 minutes. Transfer to a serving dish and serve garnished with the sliced red chilli.

Prawn Biryani Energy 230kcal/967kJ; Protein 17g; Carbohydrate 33.6g, of which sugars 7.6g; Fat 3.2g, of which saturates 0.5g; Cholesterol 146mg; Calcium 92mg; Fibre 2g; Sodium 161mg.
Prawns with Mushroom Energy 227kcal/951kJ; Protein 12.5g; Carbohydrate 40.3g, of which sugars 5.4g; Fat 2.1g, of which saturates 0.4g; Cholesterol 56mg; Calcium 117mg; Fibre 1.6g; Sodium 85mg.

Kedgeree

This classic dish is best made with basmati rice, which goes well with the mild curry flavour, but other long grain rice will do. For a colourful garnish, add some finely sliced red onion and a little red onion marmalade.

Serves 4
450g/1lb undyed smoked
    haddock fillet
750ml/1¼ pints/3 cups milk
2 bay leaves
½ lemon, sliced

50g/2oz/¼ cup butter
1 onion, chopped
2.5ml/½ tsp ground turmeric
5ml/1 tsp mild curry powder
2 green cardamom pods
350g/12oz/1¾ cups basmati
    or long grain rice, washed
    and drained
4 hard-boiled eggs,
    coarsely chopped
150ml/¼ pint/⅔ cup single
    (light) cream (optional)
30ml/2 tbsp chopped
    fresh parsley, to garnish
salt and ground black pepper

1 Put the haddock in a pan and add the milk, bay leaves and lemon slices. Poach gently for 8–10 minutes, until the haddock flakes easily. Strain the milk into a jug (pitcher), discarding the bay leaves and lemon slices. Remove the skin from the haddock and flake the flesh into large pieces. Keep hot until required.

2 Melt the butter in the pan, add the onion and cook over a low heat for about 3 minutes, until softened. Stir in the turmeric, the curry powder and cardamom pods and cook for 1 minute.

3 Add the rice, stirring to coat it well with the butter. Pour in the reserved milk, stir and bring to the boil. Lower the heat and simmer the rice for 10–12 minutes, until all the milk has been absorbed and the rice is tender. Season to taste.

4 Gently stir in the fish and hard-boiled eggs, with the cream, if using. Sprinkle with the parsley and serve.

> **Variation**
> Use smoked or poached fresh salmon for a delicious change from haddock.

Creamy Fish Pilau

This salmon dish is fusion food at its most exciting – the method comes from India but the creamy wine sauce is French in flavour.

Serves 4–6
450g/1lb fresh mussels, scrubbed
350ml/12fl oz/1½ cups
    white wine
fresh flat leaf parsley sprig
about 675g/1½lb salmon
225g/8oz scallops
about 15ml/1 tbsp olive oil
40g/1½oz/3 tbsp butter

2 shallots, finely chopped
225g/8oz/3 cups button
    (white) mushrooms
275g/10oz/1½ cups basmati
    rice, soaked in cold water for
    30 minutes
300ml/½ pint/1¼ cups fish stock
150ml/¼ pint/⅔ cup double
    (heavy) cream
15ml/1 tbsp chopped fresh parsley
225g/8oz large cooked prawns
    (shrimp), peeled and deveined
salt and ground black pepper
fresh flat leaf parsley sprigs,
    to garnish

1 Preheat the oven to 160°C/325°F/Gas 3. Place the mussels in a pan with 90ml/6 tbsp of the wine and the parsley. Cover and cook for 4–5 minutes until the mussels have opened. Drain, reserving the cooking liquid. Remove the mussels from their shells, discarding any that have not opened.

2 Cut the salmon into bitesize pieces. Detach the corals from the scallops and cut the white flesh into thick, even pieces.

3 Heat half the oil and all the butter and fry the shallots and mushrooms for 3–4 minutes. Transfer to a bowl. Heat the remaining oil and fry the rice for about 2–3 minutes. Spoon into a flameproof casserole.

4 Pour the stock, remaining wine and reserved mussel liquid into a frying pan, and bring to the boil. Off the heat, stir in the cream and parsley. Season lightly. Pour over the rice, then add the salmon and scallop flesh, and the mushroom mixture.

5 Cover and bake for 30–35 minutes, then add the scallop corals, and cook for 4 minutes. Add the mussels and prawns and cook for 3–4 minutes until the seafood is heated through and the rice is tender. Serve garnished with the parsley sprigs.

Kedgeree Energy 320kcal/1336kJ; Protein 15.6g; Carbohydrate 46.6g, of which sugars 0g; Fat 7.6g, of which saturates 3.3g; Cholesterol 149mg; Calcium 39mg; Fibre 0g; Sodium 357mg.
Creamy Fish Pilau Energy 428kcal/1787kJ; Protein 24.2g; Carbohydrate 39g, of which sugars 1.1g; Fat 15.2g, of which saturates 8.7g; Cholesterol 134mg; Calcium 130mg; Fibre 0.8g; Sodium 200mg.

Spiced Fish with Pumpkin Rice

This is a dish of contrasts – the slightly sweet flavour of pumpkin, the mildly spicy fish, and the coriander and ginger mixture that is stirred in at the end – all bound with well-flavoured, tender rice.

Serves 4

450g/1lb sea bass or other firm
   fish fillets, skinned and boned
30ml/2 tbsp plain
   (all-purpose) flour
5ml/1 tsp ground coriander
1.5–2.5ml/¼–½ tsp
   ground turmeric
500g/1¼lb pumpkin flesh
30–45ml/2–3 tbsp olive oil
6 spring onions (scallions),
   sliced diagonally
1 garlic clove, finely chopped
275g/10oz/1½ cups basmati
   rice, soaked and drained
550ml/18fl oz/2½ cups fish stock
salt and ground black pepper
lime or lemon wedges and fresh
   coriander (cilantro) sprigs,
   to serve

For the flavouring mixture

45ml/3 tbsp finely chopped fresh
   coriander (cilantro)
10ml/2 tsp finely chopped fresh
   root ginger
½–1 fresh chilli, seeded and very
   finely chopped
45ml/3 tbsp lime or lemon juice

1 Cut the fish into 2cm/¾in chunks. Mix the flour with the coriander, turmeric and a little salt and pepper and coat the fish. Set aside. Mix all the ingredients for the flavouring mixture.

2 Cut the pumpkin into 2cm/¾in chunks. Heat 15ml/1 tbsp oil in a flameproof casserole and stir-fry the spring onions and garlic for a few minutes until softened.

3 Add the pumpkin to the pan and cook over a fairly low heat, stirring, for about 4–5 minutes.

4 Add the rice and toss over a brisk heat for 2–3 minutes. Stir in the stock. Bring to simmering point, then lower the heat, cover and cook for 12–15 minutes.

5 Heat the remaining oil in a pan and fry the fish for about 3 minutes on each side. Stir the flavouring mixture into the rice and transfer to a serving dish. Lay the fish on top. Serve with the coriander, and lemon or lime wedges for squeezing.

Indonesian Fried Rice

This dish is a marvellous way to use up leftover rice, chicken and meats such as pork or beef.

Serves 4–6

350g/12oz/1¾ cups dry weight
   long grain rice, cooked and
   allowed to go cold
2 eggs
30ml/2 tbsp water
105ml/7 tbsp vegetable oil
225g/8oz pork fillet (tenderloin)
   or fillet of beef
115g/4oz peeled, cooked
   prawns (shrimp)
175–225g/6–8oz cooked
   chicken, chopped
2–3 fresh red chillies, seeded
   and sliced
1cm/½in cube shrimp paste
2 garlic cloves, crushed
1 onion, sliced
30ml/2 tbsp dark soy sauce or
   45ml/3 tbsp tomato ketchup
salt and ground black pepper
celery leaves, fresh coriander
   (cilantro) sprigs, to garnish

1 Fork the cooled rice through to separate the grains and keep it in a covered pan or dish until it is required. Beat the eggs with seasoning and the water and make two or three omelettes in a frying pan, with the minimum of oil. Roll up each omelette and when cold cut into strips. Set aside.

2 Cut the pork or beef into strips. Put the meat, prawns and chicken in separate bowls. Shred one chilli and reserve. Put the shrimp paste, with the remaining chilli, garlic and onion, in a food processor and grind to a paste, or use a pestle and mortar.

3 Fry the paste in the remaining hot oil, without browning, until it gives off a rich, spicy aroma. Add the strips of pork or beef and fry over a high heat to seal in the juices. Stir constantly to prevent the meat sticking to the bottom of the pan.

4 Add the prawns, cook for 2 minutes and then stir in the chicken, cold rice, dark soy sauce or ketchup and seasoning to taste. Stir constantly to keep the rice light and fluffy and prevent it from sticking to the base of the pan.

5 Turn the biryani on to a hot serving platter and garnish with the omelette strips, celery leaves, reserved shredded fresh chilli and coriander sprigs. Serve immediately.

Spiced Fish Energy 436kcal/1825kJ; Protein 27.9g; Carbohydrate 64.2g, of which sugars 3g; Fat 7.2g, of which saturates 1.1g; Cholesterol 52mg; Calcium 101mg; Fibre 2.3g; Sodium 73mg.
Fried Rice Energy 182kcal/764kJ; Protein 6.6g; Carbohydrate 22g, of which sugars 3.1g; Fat 8.2g, of which saturates 1.6g; Cholesterol 127mg; Calcium 45mg; Fibre 0.8g; Sodium 589mg.

Curried Chicken and Rice

This simple meal is made in a single pot, so it is perfect for casual entertaining. It can be made using virtually any meat or vegetables that you have to hand, but chicken is quick and easy to cook and takes extremely well to Indian spicing.

Serves 4
60ml/4 tbsp vegetable oil
4 garlic cloves, finely chopped
1 medium-sized chicken or 1.3kg/3lb chicken portions, skin and bones removed and meat cut into bitesize pieces
5ml/1 tsp garam masala
450g/1lb/2⅔ cups jasmine rice, rinsed and drained
10ml/2 tsp salt
1 litre/1¾ pints/4 cups chicken stock
small bunch fresh coriander (cilantro), chopped, to garnish

1 Heat the oil in a wok or flameproof casserole that has a lid. Add the garlic and cook over low to medium heat until golden brown. Add the chicken pieces to the pan, increase the heat and brown the pieces on all sides.

2 Add the garam masala to the pan, stir well to coat the chicken pieces all over in the spice, then add in the drained rice. Add the salt and stir to mix.

3 Pour in the stock, stir well, then cover the wok or casserole and bring to the boil. Reduce the heat to low and simmer gently for 10 minutes, until the rice is tender.

4 Lift the wok or casserole off the heat, leaving the lid on, and leave for 10 minutes for the flavours to mingle. Fluff up the rice grains with a fork and spoon on to a platter. Sprinkle with the fresh coriander and serve immediately.

Cook's Tip
You will probably need to brown the chicken in a couple of batches. Don't be tempted to add too much chicken to the pan at once, as this will lower the temperature of the oil and the chicken will stew and boil rather than fry.

Chicken Pilau

Like biryanis, pilaus cooked with meat and poultry make a convenient one-pot meal. No accompaniment is really necessary, but for a special meal you could serve the pilau with a vegetable side dish and a raita.

Serves 4
400g/14oz/2 cups basmati rice
75g/3oz/6 tbsp ghee or unsalted butter
1 onion, sliced
1.5ml/¼ tsp mixed onion and mustard seeds
3 curry leaves
5ml/1 tsp grated fresh root ginger
5ml/1 tsp crushed garlic
5ml/1 tsp ground coriander
5ml/1 tsp chilli powder
7.5ml/1½ tsp salt
2 tomatoes, sliced
1 potato, cubed
50g/2oz/½ cup frozen peas, thawed
175g/6oz chicken breast fillets, skinned and cut into bitesize cubes
60ml/4 tbsp chopped fresh coriander (cilantro)
2 fresh green chillies, chopped
700ml/1¼ pints/3 cups water

1 Wash the rice thoroughly under cold running water, then leave to soak in a bowl of water for about 30 minutes. Drain and set aside in a sieve (strainer).

2 In a pan, melt the ghee or butter and fry the sliced onion for 5–6 minutes, stirring frequently, until golden.

3 Add the onion and mustard seeds, the curry leaves, ginger, garlic, ground coriander, chilli powder and salt. Stir-fry for about 2 minutes over a low heat – ground spices require only gentle warmth to release their flavours.

4 Add the sliced tomatoes, cubed potato, peas and chicken and mix everything together well. Add the rice to the pan and stir gently to combine with the other ingredients.

5 Add the coriander and chillies to the pan. Mix well and stir-fry for about 1–2 minutes. Pour in the water, bring to the boil and then lower the heat. Cover and cook for 20 minutes. Remove from the heat and leave the pilau to stand for 6–8 minutes before serving.

Curried Chicken Energy 715kcal/2994kJ; Protein 56.3g; Carbohydrate 89.8g, of which sugars 0g; Fat 13.8g, of which saturates 1.9g; Cholesterol 140mg; Calcium 32mg; Fibre 0g; Sodium 120mg.
Chicken Pilau Energy 649kcal/2713kJ; Protein 33.6g; Carbohydrate 87.3g, of which sugars 15.1g; Fat 18.3g, of which saturates 2.3g; Cholesterol 118mg; Calcium 73mg; Fibre 2.7g; Sodium 1105mg.

Chicken Biryani

Easy to make and very tasty, this chicken rice dish is the ideal one-pot dish for a family supper.

Serves 4

10 green cardamom pods
275g/10oz/1½ cups basmati
    rice, soaked and drained
2.5ml/½ tsp salt
2–3 cloves
5cm/2in cinnamon stick
45ml/3 tbsp vegetable oil
3 onions, sliced
4 skinless chicken breast fillets,
    each about 175g/6oz, cubed
1.5ml/¼ tsp ground cloves
5ml/1 tsp ground cumin
5ml/1 tsp ground coriander
2.5ml/½ tsp ground black pepper
3 garlic cloves, chopped
5ml/1 tsp finely chopped fresh
    root ginger
juice of 1 lemon
4 tomatoes, sliced
30ml/2 tbsp chopped fresh
    coriander (cilantro)
150ml/¼ pint/⅔ cup natural
    (plain) yogurt
4–5 saffron threads, soaked in
    10ml/2 tsp hot milk
150ml/¼ pint/⅔ cup water
toasted flaked (sliced) almonds
    and fresh coriander (cilantro)
    sprigs, to garnish
natural (plain) yogurt, to serve

1 Preheat the oven to 190°C/375°F/Gas 5. Remove the seeds from half the cardamom pods and grind them finely, using a mortar and pestle. Set the seeds aside.

2 Bring a flameproof casserole of water to the boil and add the soaked and drained rice, then stir in the salt, the remaining whole cardamom pods, cloves and cinnamon stick. Boil the rice for 2 minutes, then drain, leaving the whole spices in the rice.

3 Heat the oil in the flameproof casserole and fry the onions for 8 minutes, until soft and browned. Add the chicken and the ground spices, including the ground cardamom seeds. Mix well, then add the garlic, ginger and lemon juice. Stir-fry for 5 minutes.

4 Arrange the sliced tomatoes on top. Sprinkle on the coriander, spoon the yogurt on top and cover with the rice.

5 Drizzle the saffron milk over the rice and add the water. Cover and bake for 1 hour. Garnish with the almonds and coriander and serve with the yogurt.

Madras Meat Curry

Goat or mutton is the traditional choice in this tangy meat curry, but lamb on the bone is also ideal.

Serves 4

675g/1½lb boned leg of lamb, fat
    trimmed and cut into
    2.5cm/1in cubes
30ml/2 tbsp red wine vinegar
5ml/1 tsp ground turmeric
10ml/2 tsp garlic purée
10ml/2 tsp ginger purée
10ml/2 tsp chilli powder
15ml/1 tbsp tomato purée (paste)
5ml/1 tsp salt, or to taste
5ml/1 tsp black peppercorns
5ml/1 tsp coriander seeds
5ml/1 tsp cumin seeds
2.5ml/½ tsp black mustard seeds
1.5ml/¼ tsp fenugreek seeds
20 curry leaves
25g/1oz/⅓ cup desiccated
    (dry unsweetened
    shredded) coconut
60ml/4 tbsp sunflower oil
    or light olive oil
2.5cm/1in piece of cinnamon
    stick, halved
2 black cardamom pods
4 cloves
1 large onion, finely chopped

1 Put the meat in a non-metallic bowl and add the vinegar, turmeric, garlic, ginger, chilli powder, tomato purée and salt. Mix thoroughly, cover the bowl and marinate for 4–5 hours.

2 Put the marinated meat into a heavy pan and add 150ml/ ¼ pint/⅔ cup water, bring it to a slow simmer, cover and cook until the water evaporates. Stir several times during cooking so that the meat does not stick to the bottom of the pan.

3 Preheat a small heavy pan over a medium heat. Reduce the heat to low, add the peppercorns, coriander, cumin, mustard and fenugreek seeds, and the curry leaves. Stir until the spices release their aroma, then add the coconut. Stir-fry until the coconut is lightly browned. Remove the spices from the pan and cool, then grind them until they are a very fine texture.

4 Heat the oil over a medium heat and add the cinnamon, cardamom and cloves. Leave to sizzle for 30 seconds, add the onion and brown. Add the ground ingredients and stir for 1 minute, then add the cooked meat. Add 150ml/5fl oz/⅔ cup warm water, cover and simmer for 10 minutes. Take off the heat and adjust the consistency with a little water. Serve immediately.

Chicken Biryani Energy 563kcal/2359kJ; Protein 45.4g; Carbohydrate 70g, of which sugars 12.5g; Fat 11.3g, of which saturates 1.7g; Cholesterol 105mg; Calcium 152mg; Fibre 3.2g; Sodium 138mg.
Madras Curry Energy 524kcal/2180kJ; Protein 37.6g; Carbohydrate 13.8g, of which sugars 7.4g; Fat 36g, of which saturates 13.8g; Cholesterol 133mg; Calcium 65mg; Fibre 2.6g; Sodium 160mg.

Spicy Lamb and Vegetable Pilau

Tender lamb is served in this dish with basmati rice and a colourful selection of vegetables and cashew nuts. The dish is presented in cabbage leaf 'bowls'.

Serves 4

450g/1lb boned shoulder of
  lamb, cubed
2.5ml/½ tsp dried thyme
2.5ml/½ tsp paprika
5ml/1 tsp garam masala
1 garlic clove, crushed
25ml/1½ tbsp vegetable oil
900ml/1½ pints/3¾ cups stock
large Savoy cabbage leaves,
  to serve

For the rice

25g/1oz/2 tbsp butter
1 onion, chopped
1 medium potato, diced
1 carrot, sliced
½ red (bell) pepper, chopped
1 green chilli, seeded
  and chopped
115g/4oz/1 cup sliced cabbage
60ml/4 tbsp natural (plain) yogurt
2.5ml/½ tsp ground cumin
5 green cardamom pods
2 garlic cloves, crushed
225g/8oz/generous 1 cup
  basmati rice, soaked
  and drained
50g/2oz/½ cup cashew nuts
salt and ground black pepper

1 Put the lamb cubes in a large bowl and add the thyme, paprika, garam masala and garlic, with plenty of salt and pepper. Stir, cover, and leave in a cool place for 2–3 hours.

2 Heat the oil in a pan and brown the lamb, in batches, over a medium heat for 5–6 minutes. Stir in the stock, cover, and cook for 35–40 minutes. Using a slotted spoon, transfer the lamb to a bowl. Pour the liquid into a measuring jug (cup), topping it up with water if necessary to make 600ml/1 pint/2½ cups.

3 Melt the butter in a separate pan and fry the onion, potato and carrot for 5 minutes. Add the red pepper and chilli and fry for 3 minutes more, then stir in the cabbage, yogurt, spices, garlic and the reserved lamb stock. Stir well, cover, then simmer gently for 5–10 minutes, until the cabbage has wilted.

4 Stir the rice into the stew with the lamb. Cover and simmer over a low heat for 20 minutes or until the rice is cooked. Sprinkle in the cashew nuts and season to taste with salt and pepper. Serve hot, cupped in cabbage leaves.

Lamb Curry with Cashew Rice

The lamb and rice in this simple and tasty curry are slowly cooked together in a clay pot.

Serves 4

1 large onion, quartered
2 garlic cloves
1 green chilli, halved and seeded
5cm/2in piece fresh root ginger
15ml/1 tbsp ghee or butter
15ml/1 tbsp vegetable oil
675g/1½lb boned shoulder or leg
  of lamb, cut into chunks
15ml/1 tbsp ground coriander
10ml/2 tsp ground cumin
1 cinnamon stick, in 3 pieces
150ml/¼ pint/⅔ cup thick natural
  (plain) yogurt
150ml/¼ pint/⅔ cup water
75g/3oz/⅓ cup ready-to-eat dried
  apricots, cut into chunks
salt and ground black pepper
1 onion, sliced and fried, and sprigs
  of coriander (cilantro), to garnish

For the rice

250g/9oz/1¼ cups basmati rice
6 cardamom pods, split open
25g/1oz/2 tbsp butter
45ml/3 tbsp toasted cashew nuts
  or flaked (sliced) almonds

1 Soak a large clay pot in cold water for 20 minutes, then drain. Place the onion, garlic, chilli and ginger in a food processor or blender and process with about 15ml/1 tbsp water until a smooth paste forms.

2 Heat the ghee and oil in a pan. Fry the lamb in batches until brown. Remove from the pan, using a slotted spoon, and set aside. Add the paste to the pan, stir in the coriander and cumin, add the cinnamon stick and fry for 1–2 minutes. Return the meat to the pan. Stir in the yogurt and the water, and season. Transfer to the clay pot, cover and place in an unheated oven. Set the oven to 180°C/350°F/Gas 4 and cook for 45 minutes.

3 Meanwhile, place the rice in a bowl, cover with cold water and soak for 20 minutes. Drain and cook in a pan of boiling salted water for 10 minutes. Drain and stir in the cardamom pods.

4 Stir the apricots into the clay pot. Pile the rice on top and dot with the butter. Drizzle over 60ml/4 tbsp water, then sprinkle the cashew nuts or almonds on top. Cover, reduce the oven to 150°C/300°F/Gas 2 and cook for 30 minutes. Fluff up the rice with a fork. Serve with fried onion slices and coriander.

Lamb Pilau Energy 751kcal/3135kJ; Protein 33.7g; Carbohydrate 86.3g, of which sugars 7.3g; Fat 30.1g, of which saturates 11.6g; Cholesterol 102mg; Calcium 88mg; Fibre 2.3g; Sodium 200mg.
Lamb Curry Energy 769kcal/3208kJ; Protein 43.6g; Carbohydrate 67.6g, of which sugars 14.5g; Fat 36.2g, of which saturates 15g; Cholesterol 142mg; Calcium 134mg; Fibre 2.6g; Sodium 252mg.

Lamb Biryani

Serves 4–5

675g/1½lb leg of lamb, cubed
50g/2oz/¼ cup natural (plain) yogurt
5ml/1 tsp salt
75g/3oz ghee
2 large onions, finely sliced
10ml/2 tsp ginger purée
10ml/2 tsp garlic purée

For the ground spice mix

10ml/2 tsp coriander seeds, ground
5ml/1 tsp cumin seeds, ground
2.5cm/1in cinnamon stick, ground
4 cardamom pods, finely ground
4 cloves, finely ground
15ml/1 tbsp poppy seeds, ground
¼ of a whole nutmeg, grated

For the rice

2.5ml/½ tsp saffron, pounded
30ml/2 tbsp hot milk
350g/12oz/1¾ cups basmati
    rice, washed and drained
2.5cm/1in cinnamon stick
4 cardamom pods, bruised
4 cloves
2 star anise
2 whole bay leaves
10ml/2 tsp salt, or to taste
15ml/1 tbsp ghee, melted

1 Put the lamb in a large bowl. Add the yogurt and salt. Mix, and set aside for 20–30 minutes.

2 Melt the ghee over a medium heat and fry the onions. Drain on kitchen paper. Return the pan to the heat and add the ginger and garlic, and fry for 1 minute. Add the ground spice mix and stir-fry for 1–2 minutes. Add the lamb. Stir and cook over a medium heat for 2–3 minutes, then remove from the heat.

3 For the rice, soak the saffron in hot milk and set aside. Preheat the oven to 160°C/325°F/Gas Mark 3. Parboil the rice for 5 minutes in 1.5 litres/2½ pints/6¼ cups water and add the remaining ingredients except the ghee. Boil for 3 minutes, then drain, reserving the spices.

4 Spread the lamb evenly in a heavy, ovenproof pan. Top with half the fried onions and pile the rice on top, with the whole spices. Sprinkle the saffron milk and melted ghee over the top.

5 Seal the pan with a double thickness of foil and cover with the lid. Cook in the oven for 1 hour. Leave to stand for 30 minutes. Stir the biryani with a metal spoon to mix the rice and meat. Transfer to a serving dish and garnish with fried onion.

Beef Biryani

Moguls brought this spicy dry curry to central India.

Serves 4

2 large onions
2 garlic cloves, chopped
2.5cm/1in root ginger, chopped
1 green chilli, seeded and chopped
bunch of fresh coriander (cilantro)
60ml/4 tbsp flaked (sliced) almonds
30–45ml/2–3 tbsp water
15ml/1 tbsp butter, plus 30ml/2
    tbsp butter, for the rice
45ml/3 tbsp sunflower oil
30ml/2 tbsp sultanas (golden raisins)
500g/1¼lb braising steak, cubed
5ml/1 tsp ground coriander
15ml/1 tbsp ground cumin
2.5ml/½ tsp ground turmeric
2.5ml/½ tsp ground fenugreek
good pinch of ground cinnamon
175ml/6fl oz/¾ cup natural
    (plain) yogurt
275g/10oz/1½ cups basmati rice
1.2 litres/2 pints/5 cups stock
salt and ground black pepper
2 hard-boiled eggs, chopped, to
    garnish

1 Chop 1 onion. Place in a food processor with the garlic, ginger, chilli, coriander, half the almonds and water and process to a paste. Slice the remaining onion into rings. Heat half the butter and oil in a flameproof casserole and fry the onion for 10–15 minutes. Transfer to a plate. Fry the rest of the almonds and set aside, then fry the sultanas until they swell. Transfer to the plate.

2 Heat the remaining butter in the casserole with 15ml/1 tbsp of the oil. Fry the meat, in batches, until brown and set aside. Heat the remaining oil and pour in the spice paste. Stir-fry for 2–3 minutes. Stir in all the spices, season and cook for 1 minute. Lower the heat, then stir in the yogurt. Add the meat. Stir to coat, cover tightly and simmer for 45 minutes until the meat is tender.

3 Soak the rice in a bowl of cold water for 15 minutes. Preheat the oven to 160°C/325°F/Gas 3. Drain the rice, place in a pan and add the stock. Bring to the boil, cover and cook for 6 minutes. Drain the rice and mound on top of the meat in the casserole.

4 Using a spoon handle, make a hole through the rice and meat mixture, to the bottom. Sprinkle with fried onions, almonds and sultanas and dot with butter. Cover with a lid. Cook in the oven for 30–40 minutes. To serve, place on a warmed serving plate and garnish with the eggs. Serve immediately.

Lamb Biryani Energy 769kcal/3208kJ; Protein 43.6g; Carbohydrate 67.6g, of which sugars 14.5g; Fat 36.2g, of which saturates 15g; Cholesterol 142mg; Calcium 134mg; Fibre 2.6g; Sodium 252mg.
Beef Biryani Energy 778kcal/3240kJ; Protein 40g; Carbohydrate 70.4g, of which sugars 13.4g; Fat 37.4g, of which saturates 11.8g; Cholesterol 94mg; Calcium 164mg; Fibre 2.3g; Sodium 183mg.

Steamed Rice

Good-quality rice should have a visible sheen, and the grains will be free from scratches and blemishes.

Serves 4
400g/14oz/2 cups short grain
    white rice or pudding rice
a drop of sunflower oil

1 Rinse and drain the rice in cold water four or five times. Place the rice in a heavy pan and add cold water to about 5mm/¼in above the level of the rice.

2 Add one drop of sunflower oil to give the rice a lustrous shine, and then cover with a lid and bring to the boil.

3 Lower the heat and leave the rice to steam. Do not remove the lid during the cooking process.

4 After 12–15 minutes turn off the heat and leave the rice, still covered, to steam for a further 5 minutes.

Bamboo-steamed Sticky Rice

Sticky rice is available in Chinese and Asian stores.

Serves 4
350g/12oz/1¾ cups sticky rice

1 Put the rice into a large bowl and fill the bowl with cold water. Leave the rice to soak for at least 6 hours, then drain, rinse thoroughly, and drain again.

2 Fill a wok or heavy pan one-third full with water. Place a bamboo steamer, with the lid on, over the wok or pan and bring the water to the boil.

3 Uncover the steamer and place a damp piece of muslin (cheesecloth) over the rack. Spread the rice out in the middle.

4 Fold the muslin over the rice, cover and steam for about 25 minutes until the rice is tender but firm. The measured quantity of rice grains doubles when cooked.

Five-grain Rice

The extra ingredients in this rice give more of a crunch to the dish's texture, and impart exotic combinations of flavours.

Serves 4
40g/1½oz/generous ¼ cup dried
    black beans

50g/2oz/¼ cup barley
50g/2oz/¼ cup millet
50g/2oz/¼ cup brown rice
50g/2oz/¼ cup sorghum
    or lentils
200g/7oz/1 cup short grain
    white rice
salt

1 Soak the beans, barley, millet, brown rice and sorghum or lentils in cold water for 24 hours.

2 Add the white rice to the soaked grains and black beans. Drain and rinse well in cold running water.

3 Place the rice in a heavy pan and add water to about 5mm/¼in above the level of the rice.

4 Add a generous pinch of salt to the rice, then cover the pan with a lid and bring to the boil.

5 Lower the heat and leave to steam. Do not remove the lid during cooking. After 12–15 minutes turn off the heat and leave the grains, still covered, to steam for a further 5 minutes.

> **Variations**
> *Other ingredients can be added in place of the grains or beans. Soya beansprouts and chestnuts are popular.*

> **Cook's Tip**
> *Any leftover rice can be stored in the refrigerator. Ensure it is well wrapped with clear film (plastic wrap) to help preserve the moisture. Don't keep rice in the refrigerator for more than two days, reheat thoroughly, and don't reheat more than once.*

Steamed Rice Energy 202kcal/845kJ; Protein 4.2g; Carbohydrate 44.9g, of which sugars 0g; Fat 0.3g, of which saturates 0g; Cholesterol 0mg; Calcium 11mg; Fibre 0g; Sodium 0mg.
Sticky Rice Energy 314kcal/1314kJ; Protein 7g; Carbohydrate 66g, of which sugars 0g; Fat 1g, of which saturates 0g; Cholesterol 0mg; Calcium 14mg; Fibre 0g; Sodium 0mg.
Five-grain Rice Energy 299kcal/1252kJ; Protein 6.9g; Carbohydrate 65.2g, of which sugars 9.9g; Fat 1g, of which saturates 0.2g; Cholesterol 0mg; Calcium 34mg; Fibre 2.4g; Sodium 348mg.

Caramelized Basmati Rice

This dish is the traditional accompaniment to a dhansak curry. The sugar is caramelized in hot oil before the rice is added, along with whole spices.

Serves 4

225g/8oz/generous 1 cup basmati rice

45ml/3 tbsp vegetable oil
20ml/4 tsp sugar
4 or 5 green cardamom pods, bruised
2.5cm/1in piece cinnamon stick
4 cloves
1 bay leaf, crumbled
2.5ml/½ tsp salt
475ml/16fl oz/2 cups hot water

1 Wash the rice under cold running water until the water runs clear. Put it in a large bowl and pour over cold water to cover. Leave to soak for 20 minutes.

2 Drain the rice thoroughly in a sieve (strainer), shaking it a little as you do so. Run the washed grains through your fingers to check that there is no excess water trapped between them. Set aside while you cook the other ingredients.

3 In a large pan, heat the vegetable oil over medium heat. When the oil is hot, sprinkle the sugar over the surface and wait until it has caramelized. Do not stir.

4 Reduce the heat to low and add the spices and bay leaf. Allow to sizzle for 15–20 seconds, then add the rice and salt. Fry gently, stirring, for 2–3 minutes.

5 Pour in the water and bring to the boil. Let it boil steadily for 2 minutes then reduce the heat to very low. Cover the pan with a tight-fitting lid and cook for 8 minutes.

6 Remove the rice from the heat and leave to stand for 6–8 minutes. Fluff up the rice with a fork and serve.

> **Cook's Tip**
> *Watch the sugar carefully so that it does not burn.*

Festive Jasmine Rice

This pretty rice dish is traditionally shaped into a cone and surrounded by a variety of accompaniments before being served.

Serves 8

450g/1lb/2⅔ cups jasmine rice
60ml/4 tbsp vegetable oil
2 garlic cloves, crushed
2 onions, thinly sliced
2.5ml/½ tsp ground turmeric

750ml/1¼ pints/3 cups water
400ml/14fl oz can coconut milk
1–2 lemon grass stalks, bruised

For the accompaniments
omelette strips
2 fresh red chillies, seeded and shredded
cucumber chunks
tomato wedges
deep-fried onions
prawn (shrimp) crackers

1 Put the jasmine rice in a large sieve (strainer) and rinse it thoroughly under cold running water. Drain well.

2 Heat the oil in a frying pan with a lid. Cook the garlic, onions and turmeric over low heat for 2–3 minutes, until the onions have softened. Add the rice and stir well to coat in oil.

3 Pour the water and coconut milk into the pan and add the lemon grass. Bring to the boil, stirring. Cover the pan with a tight-fitting lid and cook gently for 12 minutes, or until all the liquid has been absorbed by the rice.

4 Remove the pan from the heat and lift the lid. Cover with a clean dish towel, replace the lid and leave to stand in a warm place for about 15 minutes.

5 Remove the lemon grass, mound the rice mixture in a cone on a warmed serving platter and garnish with the accompaniments, then serve immediately.

> **Cook's Tip**
> *Jasmine rice is widely available in most supermarkets and Asian stores. It is also known as Thai fragrant rice. It has a delicately scented, almost milky, aroma.*

Caramelized Rice Energy 324kcal/1353kJ; Protein 4.1g; Carbohydrate 56.4g, of which sugars 12.5g; Fat 9.1g, of which saturates 1.1g; Cholesterol 0mg; Calcium 17mg; Fibre 0g; Sodium 1mg.
Festive Rice Energy 303kcal/1263kJ; Protein 6.4g; Carbohydrate 49.5g, of which sugars 4.2g; Fat 8.6g, of which saturates 2g; Cholesterol 53mg; Calcium 41mg; Fibre 0.5g; Sodium 212mg.

Tricolour Pilau Rice

Most Indian restaurants in the West serve this popular vegetable pilau, which has three different vegetables. The effect is easily achieved with canned or frozen vegetables, but for entertaining or a special occasion dinner, you may prefer to use fresh produce.

Serves 4–6
30ml/2 tbsp vegetable oil
2.5ml/½ tsp cumin seeds
2 dried bay leaves
4 green cardamom pods
4 cloves
1 onion, finely chopped
1 carrot, finely diced
225g/8oz/1 cup basmati rice, rinsed and soaked for 30 minutes
50g/2oz/½ cup frozen peas, thawed
50g/2oz/⅓ cup frozen corn, thawed
25g/1oz/¼ cup cashew nuts, lightly fried
475ml/16fl oz/2 cups water
1.5ml/¼ tsp ground cumin
salt

1 Heat the oil in a wok, karahi or large pan over medium heat, and fry the cumin seeds for 2 minutes.

2 Add the bay leaves, cardamoms and cloves to the pan, and fry gently for about 2 minutes more, stirring the spices from time to time so they do not catch on the pan base.

3 Add the chopped onion to the pan and fry for about 5–6 minutes until lightly browned. Stir in the diced carrot and cook, stirring, for a further 3–4 minutes.

4 Drain the soaked basmati rice and add to the contents of the pan. Stir well to combine the ingredients. Add the peas, corn and fried cashew nuts.

5 Pour the measured water into the pan and add the ground cumin. Season with salt to taste. Bring to the boil, cover with a lid and simmer for 15 minutes over low heat until all the water is absorbed.

6 Leave the rice to stand, still covered, for 10 minutes. Transfer to a warmed serving dish and serve.

Red Fried Rice

This vibrant rice dish owes its appeal as much to the bright colours of its ingredients – red onion, red pepper and cherry tomatoes – as it does to their flavours.

Serves 2
130g/4½oz/¾ cup basmati rice
30ml/2 tbsp vegetable oil
1 small red onion, finely chopped
1 red (bell) pepper, seeded and chopped
225g/8oz cherry tomatoes, cut into halves
2 eggs, beaten
salt and ground black pepper
chopped fresh coriander (cilantro), to garnish

1 Wash the rice several times under cold running water until the water runs clear. Drain well and set aside.

2 Bring a large pan of water to the boil. Add the basmati rice and cook for 10–12 minutes.

3 Meanwhile, heat the oil in a wok or large, heavy pan until it is very hot. Add the onion and red pepper to the pan and stir-fry for about 2–3 minutes.

4 Add the cherry tomatoes to the pan and continue cooking for 2 minutes more, stirring frequently.

5 Pour the beaten eggs into the pan all at once. Cook for about 30 seconds without stirring, then stir to break up the egg as it just begins to set.

6 Drain the cooked rice thoroughly. Add to the pan and toss it over the heat with the vegetables and egg mixture for about 3 minutes. Season with salt and ground black pepper to taste, sprinkle with the coriander and serve immediately.

Variation
To add even more colour to this bright dish, you could replace the red (bell) pepper with an orange or green variety.

Tricolour Pilau Rice Energy 221kcal/922kJ; Protein 4.9g; Carbohydrate 35.5g, of which sugars 1.8g; Fat 6.5g, of which saturates 0.9g; Cholesterol 0mg; Calcium 18mg; Fibre 0.8g; Sodium 36mg.
Red Fried Rice Energy 437kcal/1821kJ; Protein 12.6g; Carbohydrate 57.4g, of which sugars 10.5g; Fat 17.6g, of which saturates 3.1g; Cholesterol 190mg; Calcium 62mg; Fibre 3g; Sodium 85mg.

Persian Rice with Fried Onions

Malay Yellow Rice

Persian cuisine is exotic and delicious, with intense flavours. This dish forms a lovely crust on the bottom.

Serves 6–8
450g/1lb/2¹⁄₃ cups basmati rice, soaked and drained
150ml/¹⁄₄ pint/²⁄₃ cup sunflower oil
2 garlic cloves, crushed
2 onions, 1 chopped, 1 sliced
600ml/1 pint/2¹⁄₂ cups stock

150g/5oz/²⁄₃ cup green lentils, soaked
50g/2oz/¹⁄₃ cup raisins
10ml/2 tsp ground coriander
45ml/3 tbsp tomato purée (paste)
1 egg yolk, beaten
10ml/2 tsp natural (plain) yogurt
75g/3oz/6 tbsp melted butter
a few saffron strands, soaked in a little hot water
salt and ground black pepper

1 Cook the rice in boiling salted water for 10–12 minutes. Drain. Heat 30ml/2 tbsp of the oil in a large pan and fry the garlic and chopped onion for 5 minutes. Stir in the stock, lentils, raisins, coriander and tomato purée. Bring to the boil, lower the heat, cover and simmer for 20 minutes.

2 Mix the egg yolk and yogurt in a bowl. Spoon in about 120ml/4 fl oz/¹⁄₂ cup of the cooked rice and mix thoroughly. Season. Heat about two-thirds of the remaining oil in a large pan and sprinkle the egg and yogurt rice over the bottom.

3 Place a layer of rice in the pan, then a layer of lentils. Build up the layers in a pyramid shape away from the sides. Finish with a layer of plain rice. With a wooden spoon handle, make three holes down to the bottom of the pan; drizzle over the melted butter. Bring to a high heat, then wrap the pan lid in a wet dish towel and place on top. When the rice is steaming well, lower the heat and cook slowly for about 30 minutes.

4 Fry the onion slices in the remaining oil until browned and crisp. Drain. Remove the rice pan from the heat, and dip the base into cold water to loosen the crust. Strain the saffron water into a bowl and stir in a few spoons of cooked rice. Toss the rice and lentils together in the pan and spoon on to a serving dish. Sprinkle the saffron rice on top. Break up the crust and place around the mound. Top with the onions and serve.

This is a delicately flavoured rice dish, made with long grain rice that is coloured yellow by vibrant turmeric powder. This simple rice curry is cooked in the same way as plain steamed rice, using the quick and easy absorption method.

Serves 4
30ml/2 tbsp vegetable oil or sesame oil
3 shallots, finely chopped

2 garlic cloves, peeled and finely chopped
450g/1lb/generous 2 cups long grain rice, thoroughly washed and drained
400ml/14fl oz/1²⁄₃ cups coconut milk
10ml/2 tsp ground turmeric
4 fresh curry leaves
2.5ml/¹⁄₂ tsp salt
ground black pepper
2 red chillies, seeded and finely sliced, to garnish

1 Heat the vegetable or sesame oil in a heavy pan and stir in the shallots and garlic. Just as they begin to colour, stir in the rice until the grains are coated in the oil.

2 Pour the coconut milk into the pan, along with about 450ml/³⁄₄ pint/scant 2 cups water, the ground turmeric, curry leaves, salt and ground black pepper.

3 Bring the mixture to the boil, then turn down the heat and cover the pan tightly with a lid. Cook gently for 15–20 minutes, until all the liquid has been absorbed.

4 Turn off the heat and leave the rice to steam in the pan for 10 minutes. Fluff up the rice with a fork and serve immediately garnished with the sliced red chillies.

> **Cook's Tips**
> • Regular long grain rice, or other types such as jasmine rice, short grain or sticky rice, can all be used for this recipe.
> • This rice is often served at Malay festivals. It is also one of the popular dishes at Malay and Indonesian stalls, where it is served with a variety of meat and vegetable dishes.

Persian Rice Energy 398kcal/1658kJ; Protein 6.5g; Carbohydrate 69.9g, of which sugars 0.1g; Fat 9.7g, of which saturates 5.9g; Cholesterol 24mg; Calcium 19mg; Fibre 0g; Sodium 559mg.
Malay Yellow Rice Energy 481kcal/2011kJ; Protein 8.8g; Carbohydrate 95.9g, of which sugars 5.8g; Fat 6.4g, of which saturates 0.9g; Cholesterol 0mg; Calcium 54mg; Fibre 0.2g; Sodium 356mg.

Chillies with Green Gram and Rice

Basmati Rice with Potato

The whole spices in this tasty dish are edible, although it is advisable to warn the diners about them to avoid any unexpected surprises.

Serves 4–6
60ml/4 tbsp ghee
1 onion, finely chopped
2 garlic cloves, crushed
2.5cm/1 in piece fresh root
   ginger, grated
4 green chillies, chopped
4 whole cloves
2.5cm/1 in cinnamon stick
4 whole green cardamoms
5ml/1 tsp turmeric
350g/12oz patna rice, washed
   and soaked for 20 minutes
175g/6oz split green gram,
   washed and soaked for
   20 minutes
600ml/1 pint/2½ cups water
salt

1 Gently heat the ghee in a large heavy pan with a tight-fitting lid. Fry the onion, garlic, ginger, chillies, cloves, cinnamon, cardamoms, turmeric and salt until the onion is beginning to turn soft and translucent.

2 Drain the rice and the green gram, and then add them to the spices in the pan and fry for 2–3 minutes.

3 Add the water to the pan and bring to the boil. Reduce the heat, cover and simmer for about 20–25 minutes, or until all the water has been absorbed.

4 Take the pan off the heat and leave to rest for 5 minutes. Gently toss the mixture together until the ingredients are well combined and serve immediately.

Cook's Tip
Ghee is a clarified unsalted butter widely used in Indian cooking. It has a nutty, caramel flavour and aroma and is made by simmering the butter until all water has boiled off and the milk solids have settled to the bottom. The lack of water and solids mean that it has a longer life and a higher smoking point than normal butter.

Rice is eaten at all meals in Indian and Pakistani homes. There are several ways of cooking rice, and mostly whole spices are used. Always choose a good-quality basmati rice.

Serves 4
300g/11oz/1½ cups basmati rice
15ml/1 tbsp vegetable oil
1 small cinnamon stick
1 bay leaf
1.5ml/¼ tsp black cumin seeds
3 green cardamom pods
1 medium onion, sliced
5ml/1 tsp grated fresh root ginger
5ml/1 tsp crushed garlic
1.5ml/¼ tsp ground turmeric
7.5ml/1½ tsp salt
1 large potato, roughly diced
475ml/16fl oz/2 cups water
15ml/1 tbsp chopped fresh
   coriander (cilantro)

1 Wash the rice well under cold running water and leave it to soak in water for 20 minutes.

2 Heat the oil in a heavy pan, add the cinnamon, bay leaf, black cumin seeds, cardamom pods and onion and cook for about 2 minutes, stirring constantly.

3 Add the ginger, garlic, turmeric, salt and potato to the pan, and cook for a further 1 minute.

4 Drain the rice thoroughly. Add it to the potato and spices in the pan and stir well to combine the ingredients.

5 Pour the water into the pan and then stir in the coriander. Cover the pan with a lid and cook for 15–20 minutes.

6 Remove the pan from the heat and leave to stand, still covered, for 5–10 minutes before serving.

Cook's Tip
It is important to observe the full standing time for this dish before serving. Use a slotted spoon to serve the rice and potato mixture and handle it carefully to avoid breaking or damaging the delicate grains of rice.

Chillies with Rice Energy 397kcal/1662kJ; Protein 11.6g; Carbohydrate 63.8g, of which sugars 1.3g; Fat 10.7g, of which saturates 4.8g; Cholesterol 0mg; Calcium 31mg; Fibre 1.6g; Sodium 12mg.
Basmati Rice with Potato Energy 355kcal/1483kJ; Protein 7.2g; Carbohydrate 70.5g, of which sugars 1.5g; Fat 4.8g, of which saturates 0.6g; Cholesterol 0mg; Calcium 28mg; Fibre 0.7g; Sodium 745mg.

Naan

Probably the most popular bread enjoyed with an Indian curry is naan, which was introduced from Persia. Traditionally, naan is not rolled, but patted and stretched until the teardrop shape is achieved. You can, of course, roll it out to a circle, then gently pull the lower end, which will give you the traditional shape.

Makes 3

225g/8oz/2 cups unbleached strong white bread flour
2.5ml/½ tsp salt
15g/½ oz fresh yeast
60ml/4 tbsp milk, heated until lukewarm
15ml/1 tbsp vegetable oil
30ml/2 tbsp natural (plain) yogurt
1 egg, beaten
30–45ml/2–3 tbsp melted ghee or butter, for brushing

1 Sift the flour and salt together into a large bowl. In a smaller bowl, cream the yeast with the milk. Set aside for 15 minutes.

2 Add the yeast and milk mixture, vegetable oil, yogurt and egg to the flour. Combine the mixture using your hands until it forms a soft dough. Add a little lukewarm water if the dough is too dry.

3 Turn the dough out on to a lightly floured surface and knead it for about 10 minutes, or until it feels smooth. Return the dough to the bowl, cover and leave in a warm place for about 1 hour, or until it has doubled in size. Preheat the oven to its highest setting – it should not be any lower than 230°C/450°F/Gas 8.

4 Turn out the dough back on to the floured surface and knead for a further 2 minutes. Divide into three equal pieces, shape into balls and roll out into teardrop shapes 25cm/10in long, 13cm/5in wide and 5mm–8mm/¼–⅓in thick.

5 Preheat the grill (broiler) to its highest setting. Meanwhile, place the naan on preheated baking sheets and bake for 3–4 minutes, or until puffed up.

6 Place under the hot grill for a few seconds until the tops brown. Brush with ghee or butter and serve warm.

Spiced Naan

Another excellent recipe for naan bread, this time it features the aromatic fennel seeds, onion seeds and cumin seeds.

Makes 6

450g/1lb/4 cups strong white bread flour
5ml/1 tsp baking powder
2.5ml/½ tsp salt
1 sachet easy-blend (rapid-rise) dried yeast
5ml/1 tsp caster (superfine) sugar
5ml/1 tsp fennel seeds
10ml/2 tsp onion seeds
5ml/1 tsp cumin seeds
150ml/¼ pint/⅔ cup hand-hot milk
30ml/2 tbsp vegetable oil, plus extra for brushing
150ml/¼ pint/⅔ cup natural (plain) yogurt
1 egg, beaten

1 Sift the flour, baking powder and salt into a mixing bowl. Stir in the yeast, sugar, fennel seeds, onion seeds and cumin seeds. Make a well in the centre. Stir the hand-hot milk into the flour mixture, then add the oil, yogurt and beaten egg. Mix to form a ball of dough.

2 Transfer the dough on to a lightly floured surface and knead it for 10 minutes until smooth. Return to the clean, lightly oiled bowl and roll the dough to coat it with oil. Cover the bowl with clear film (plastic wrap) and set aside in a warm place until the dough has doubled in bulk.

3 Put a heavy baking sheet in the oven and preheat the oven to 240°C/475°F/Gas 9. Also preheat the grill (broiler). Knead the dough again lightly and divide it into six pieces. Keep five pieces covered while working with the sixth. Quickly roll the piece of dough out to a teardrop shape, brush lightly with oil and slap the naan on to the hot baking sheet. Repeat with the remaining dough.

4 Bake the naan in the preheated oven for about 3 minutes or until they have puffed up, then place the baking sheets under the grill for about 30 seconds or until the naan are lightly browned. Serve hot or warm as an accompaniment to an Indian curry.

Naan Energy 315kcal/1334kJ; Protein 9.4g; Carbohydrate 58.5g, of which sugars 1.5g; Fat 6.5g, of which saturates 1.1g; Cholesterol 63mg; Calcium 123mg; Fibre 2.3g; Sodium 356mg.
Spiced Naan Energy 311kcal/1319kJ; Protein 11g; Carbohydrate 63.8g, of which sugars 4.9g; Fat 3.2g, of which saturates 0.9g; Cholesterol 34mg; Calcium 197mg; Fibre 2.3g; Sodium 211mg.

Chapatis

A chapati is an unleavened bread that is made from chapati flour, a wholemeal flour known as atta, which is finer than the Western equivalent. An equal quantity of standard wholemeal flour and plain flour will also produce satisfactory results, although chapati flour is widely available from Indian grocers.

This is the everyday bread of the Indian home.

Makes 8–10
225g/8oz/2 cups chapati flour
   or an equal quantity of
   wholemeal (whole-wheat) flour
   and plain (all-purpose) flour
2.5ml/½ tsp salt
175ml/6fl oz/¾ cup water

1 Sift the flour and salt into a large mixing bowl. Make a well in the centre and gradually stir in the water, mixing it well with your fingers.

2 Form a supple dough and knead for 7–10 minutes. Ideally, cover with clear film (plastic wrap) and leave to one side for 15–20 minutes to rest.

3 Divide the dough into eight to ten equal portions. Roll out each piece to a circle on a well-floured surface.

4 Place a tava (chapati griddle) or heavy frying pan over high heat. When steam rises from it, lower the heat to medium and add the first chapati to the pan.

5 When the chapati begins to bubble, carefully turn it over. Press down with a clean dish towel or a flat spoon and turn the chapati over once again.

6 Remove the cooked chapati from the pan and keep warm in a piece of foil lined with kitchen paper while you cook the other chapatis.

7 Repeat the process until all the dough has been used up. Serve immediately.

Red Lentil Pancakes

This is a type of *dosa*, which is essentially a pancake from southern India, but it is used in a similar fashion to north Indian bread.

Makes 6
150g/5oz/¾ cup long
   grain rice

50g/2oz/¼ cup red split lentils
250ml/8fl oz/1 cup warm water
5ml/1 tsp salt
2.5ml/½ tsp ground turmeric
2.5ml/½ tsp ground black pepper
30ml/2 tbsp chopped fresh
   coriander (cilantro)
vegetable oil, for frying
   and drizzling

1 Place the rice and lentils in a large bowl, cover with the warm water, cover and soak for at least 8 hours or overnight.

2 Drain off the water and reserve. Place the rice and lentils in a food processor or blender and blend until smooth. Blend in the reserved soaking water. Scrape into a bowl, cover tightly with clear film (plastic wrap) and leave in a warm place to ferment for about 24 hours.

3 Stir the salt, turmeric, black pepper and coriander into the rice mixture. Heat a heavy frying pan over medium heat for a few minutes until hot. Smear the pan with oil and add about 30–45ml/2–3 tbsp of the batter mixture.

4 Using the rounded base of a soup spoon, gently spread the batter out, using a circular motion, to make a pancake that is about 15cm/6in in diameter.

5 Cook in the pan for 1½–2 minutes, or until set. Drizzle a little oil over the pancake and around the edges. Turn over and cook for about 1 minute, or until golden brown. Keep the cooked pancakes warm in a low oven or on a plate over simmering water while cooking the remaining pancakes. Serve warm.

> **Variation**
> Add 60ml/4 tbsp grated coconut to the batter just before cooking to create a richer flavour.

Chapatis Energy 99kcal/421kJ; Protein 3.7g; Carbohydrate 19.9g, of which sugars 0.5g; Fat 1.1g, of which saturates 0.2g; Cholesterol 0mg; Calcium 38mg; Fibre 1.9g; Sodium 165mg.
Red Lentil Pancakes Energy 153kcal/641kJ; Protein 4.1g; Carbohydrate 25.1g, of which sugars 0.3g; Fat 4.1g, of which saturates 0.4g; Cholesterol 0mg; Calcium 21mg; Fibre 0.7g; Sodium 333mg.

Parathas

Making paratha is similar to making flaky pastry, although paratha can be handled freely, unlike flaky pastry.

Makes 12–15

350g/12oz/3 cups chapati flour or an equal quantity of wholemeal (whole-wheat) flour and plain (all-purpose) flour

50g/2oz/½ cup plain (all-purpose) flour for dusting work surfaces
50g/2oz/½ cup plain (all-purpose) flour
5ml/1 tsp salt
40g/1½oz/3 tbsp ghee or unsalted butter

1 Sift the flours and salt into a bowl. Make a well in the centre and add 10ml/2 tsp melted ghee or butter. Fold it into the flour to make a crumbly texture.

2 Gradually add water to the flour and ghee or butter in the bowl to make a soft, pliable dough. Knead until the dough is smooth. Cover and leave to rest for 30 minutes.

3 Heat the remaining ghee or butter in a small heavy pan over low heat until fully melted. Divide the dough into about 12–15 equal portions and keep covered.

4 Take one portion at a time and roll out on a lightly floured surface or chopping board to about 10cm/4in in diameter.

5 Brush the dough with a little of the melted ghee or butter and sprinkle with flour.

6 With a sharp knife, make a straight cut from the centre to the edge of the dough, then lift a cut edge and roll the dough into a cone shape. Lift it and flatten it again into a ball.

7 Roll the dough out again on a lightly floured surface or chopping board until it is about 18cm/7in wide.

8 Heat a griddle and cook one paratha at a time, placing a little of the remaining ghee along the edges. Cook on each side until golden brown. Serve immediately while hot.

Tandoori Rotis

Roti means bread, and it is the most common food in central and northern India. For generations, roti has been made with just wholemeal flour, salt and water, although the art of making rotis is generally more refined these days.

Makes 6

350g/12oz/3 cups 139 flour or wholemeal (whole-wheat) flour
5ml/1 tsp salt
250ml/8fl oz/1 cup water
30–45ml/2–3 tbsp melted ghee or unsalted butter, for brushing

1 Sift the flour and salt into a large mixing bowl. Add the water to the bowl and mix it with your hands or a wooden spoon until a soft, pliable dough forms.

2 Knead the dough on a lightly floured work surface for about 3–4 minutes until smooth.

3 Place the dough in a lightly oiled bowl, cover with lightly oiled clear film (plastic wrap) and leave to rest for 1 hour.

4 Turn out the dough on to a lightly floured surface. Divide the dough into six even pieces and shape each into a ball with your hands. Press out into a larger round with the palm of your hand, cover with a piece of lightly oiled clear film and leave to rest for about 10 minutes.

5 Meanwhile, preheat the oven to 230°C/450°F/Gas 8. Place three baking sheets in the oven to heat.

6 Roll the rotis into 15cm/6in rounds, place two on each baking sheet and bake for 8–10 minutes. Brush with melted ghee or butter and serve warm.

Cook's Tip
Tandoori rotis are traditionally baked in a tandoor, or clay oven, but they can also be made successfully in an electric or gas oven set at the highest setting.

Parathas Energy 108kcal/456kJ; Protein 2.3g; Carbohydrate 19.2g, of which sugars 0.4g; Fat 3g, of which saturates 1.3g; Cholesterol 0mg; Calcium 35mg; Fibre 0.8g; Sodium 132mg.
Tandoori Rotis Energy 244kcal/1030kJ; Protein 5.5g; Carbohydrate 45.3g, of which sugars 0.9g; Fat 5.8g, of which saturates 2.5g; Cholesterol 0mg; Calcium 82mg; Fibre 1.8g; Sodium 329mg.

Pooris

These delicious little deep-fried breads, shaped into discs, make it very easy to overindulge.

Makes 12
115g/4oz/1 cup unbleached plain (all-purpose) flour
115g/4oz/1 cup wholemeal (whole-wheat) flour
2.5ml/½ tsp salt
2.5ml/½ tsp chilli powder
30ml/2 tbsp vegetable oil
100–120ml/3½–4fl oz/ scant ⅓ – ½ cup water
vegetable oil, for frying

1 Sift the flours, salt and chilli powder, if using, into a mixing bowl. Add the vegetable oil then add sufficient water to mix to a dough. Turn out on to a lightly floured surface and knead for 8–10 minutes until smooth. Place in an oiled bowl and cover with oiled clear film (plastic wrap). Leave for 30 minutes.

2 Turn out on to the floured surface. Divide the dough into 12 equal pieces. Keeping the rest of the dough covered, roll one piece into a 13cm/5in round. Repeat with the remaining dough. Stack the pooris, layered between sheets of lightly oiled clear film, to keep them moist.

3 Pour the oil for frying to a depth of 2.5cm/1in in a deep frying pan and heat it to 180°C/350°F. Lift one poori and gently slide it into the oil; it will sink but will then return to the surface and begin to sizzle. Gently press the poori into the oil. It will puff up. Turn the poori over after a few seconds and allow it to cook for a further 20–30 seconds.

4 Remove the poori from the pan and pat dry with kitchen paper. Place the cooked poori on a large baking tray, in a single layer, and keep warm in a low oven while you cook the remaining pooris. Serve immediately while warm.

> **Variation**
> For spinach-flavoured pooris, thaw 50g/2oz frozen spinach, drain, and add to the dough with a little grated fresh root ginger and 2.5ml/½ tsp ground cumin.

Bhaturas

These leavened and deep-fried breads are from Punjab, where the local people enjoy them with a bowl of chickpea curry.

Makes 10
15g/½oz fresh yeast
5ml/1 tsp sugar
120ml/4fl oz/½ cup lukewarm water
200g/7oz/1¾ cups plain (all-purpose) flour
50g/2oz/½ cup semolina
2.5ml/½ tsp salt
15g/½oz/1 tbsp ghee or butter
30ml/2 tbsp natural (plain) yogurt
vegetable oil, for frying

1 Mix the yeast with the sugar and water in a jug (pitcher). Sift the flour into a large mixing bowl and stir in the semolina and salt. Rub in the ghee or butter.

2 Add the yeast mixture and yogurt to the bowl and mix to a dough. Turn out on to a lightly floured surface and knead for about 10 minutes until smooth and elastic.

3 Place the dough in an oiled bowl, cover with oiled clear film (plastic wrap) and leave to rise, in a warm place, for about 1 hour, or until doubled in size.

4 Turn out on to a lightly floured surface and knock back (punch down). Divide into ten equal pieces and shape each into a ball. Flatten into discs with the palm of your hand. Roll out on a lightly floured surface into 13cm/5in rounds.

5 Heat oil to a depth of 1cm/½in in a deep frying pan and slide in one bhatura. Fry for 1 minute, turning over after 30 seconds, then drain on kitchen paper. Keep warm in a low oven while frying the remaining bhaturas. Serve immediately, while hot.

> **Cook's Tip**
> Ghee is available from Indian stores and some supermarkets but is easy to make at home. Melt unsalted butter over low heat. Simmer gently until the residue becomes light golden, then leave to cool. Strain through muslin (cheesecloth).

Pooris Energy 120kcal/501kJ; Protein 2.1g; Carbohydrate 13.5g, of which sugars 0.3g; Fat 6.7g, of which saturates 0.8g; Cholesterol 0mg; Calcium 17mg; Fibre 1.2g; Sodium 164mg.
Bhaturas Energy 141kcal/590kJ; Protein 2.6g; Carbohydrate 19.7g, of which sugars 0.5g; Fat 6.3g, of which saturates 1.3g; Cholesterol 0mg; Calcium 35mg; Fibre 0.7g; Sodium 102mg.

Thin and Crispy Flat Bread

Thin and crispy, this flat bread is universally eaten throughout the Middle East. It's ideal for serving with soups and appetizers.

Makes 10
275g/10oz/2½ cups unbleached strong white bread flour
175g/6oz/1½ cups wholemeal (whole-wheat) flour
5ml/1 tsp salt
15g/½oz fresh yeast
250ml/8fl oz/1 cup lukewarm water
60ml/4 tbsp natural (plain) yogurt or milk

1 Sift the flours and salt together into a large bowl and make a well in the centre. Mix the yeast with half the lukewarm water until creamy, then stir in the remaining water.

2 Add the yeast mixture and yogurt or milk to the centre of the flour and mix to a soft dough. Turn out on to a lightly floured surface and knead for 8–10 minutes until smooth and elastic. Place in a lightly oiled bowl, cover with lightly oiled clear film (plastic wrap) and leave to rise, in a warm place, for about 1 hour, or until doubled in bulk. Knock back (punch down) the dough, re-cover and leave to rise for 30 minutes.

3 Turn the dough back out on to a lightly floured surface. Knock back gently and divide into ten equal pieces. Shape into balls, then flatten into discs with the palm of your hand. Cover and leave it to rest for 5 minutes.

4 Meanwhile, preheat the oven to the maximum temperature – it should be at least 230°C/450°F/Gas 8. Place three or four baking sheets in the oven to heat.

5 Roll the dough as thinly as possible, then lift it over the backs of your hands and stretch and turn the dough. Leave to rest in between rolling for a few minutes if necessary to avoid tearing.

6 Place four on the baking sheets and bake for 6–8 minutes, or until starting to brown. Stack the remaining rolled dough, layered between clear film to keep moist. Transfer to a wire rack to cool and cook the remaining breads. Serve hot.

Syrian Onion Bread

The basic Arab breads of the Levant and Gulf have traditionally been made with a finely ground wholemeal flour similar to chapati flour, but now are being made with white flour as well. This Syrian version has a tasty, aromatic topping.

Makes 8
450g/1lb/4 cups unbleached strong white bread flour
5ml/1 tsp salt
20g/¾oz fresh yeast
280ml/9fl oz/scant 1¼ cups lukewarm water

For the topping
60ml/4 tbsp finely chopped onion
5ml/1 tsp ground cumin
10ml/2 tsp ground coriander
10ml/2 tsp chopped fresh mint
30ml/2 tbsp olive oil

1 Lightly flour two baking sheets. Sift the flour and salt together into a large mixing bowl and make a well in the centre. Cream the yeast with a little of the water in a small bowl, then mix in the remaining yeast until well combined.

2 Add the yeast mixture to the centre of the flour and mix to a firm dough. Turn out on to a lightly floured surface and knead for 8–10 minutes until smooth and elastic.

3 Place the dough in a lightly oiled bowl, cover with lightly oiled clear film (plastic wrap) and leave to rise, in a warm place, for about 1 hour, or until doubled in size.

4 Knock back (punch down) the dough and turn out on to a lightly floured work surface. Divide the dough into eight equal pieces and roll into 13–15cm/5–6in rounds. Make them slightly concave. Prick all over with a fork and space well apart on the baking sheets. Cover with lightly oiled clear film and leave to rise for about 15–20 minutes.

5 Meanwhile, preheat the oven to 200°C/400°F/Gas 6. Mix the chopped onion, ground cumin, ground coriander and chopped mint in a bowl. Brush the breads with the olive oil for the topping, sprinkle them evenly with the spicy onion mixture and bake for 15–20 minutes. Serve the onion breads warm.

Flat Bread Energy 108kcal/456kJ; Protein 2.3g; Carbohydrate 19.2g, of which sugars 0.4g; Fat 3g, of which saturates 1.3g; Cholesterol 0mg; Calcium 35mg; Fibre 0.8g; Sodium 132mg.
Syrian Bread Energy 220kcal/932kJ; Protein 5.5g; Carbohydrate 44.4g, of which sugars 1.3g; Fat 3.5g, of which saturates 0.5g; Cholesterol 0mg; Calcium 85mg; Fibre 1.9g; Sodium 248mg.

Balti Baby Vegetables with Chilli and Chickpeas

There is a wonderful selection of baby vegetables available these days, and this simple recipe does full justice to their delicate flavour and attractive appearance. Serve as part of a main meal or even as a light appetizer.

Serves 4–6
10 new potatoes, halved
12–14 baby carrots
12–14 baby courgettes (zucchini)
30ml/2 tbsp corn oil
15 baby onions
30ml/2 tbsp chilli sauce
5ml/1 tsp crushed garlic
5ml/1 tsp grated fresh root ginger
5ml/1 tsp salt
400g/14oz/scant 3 cups drained canned chickpeas
10 cherry tomatoes
5ml/1 tsp crushed dried red chillies, seeds removed
30ml/2 tbsp sesame seeds

1 Bring a medium pan of salted water to the boil and add the new potatoes and baby carrots. Cook for 12–15 minutes.

2 Add the courgettes, and boil for a further 5 minutes or until all the vegetables are just tender. Take care not to overcook the vegetables, as there will be additional cooking time later. Drain the vegetables well and put them in a bowl. Set aside.

3 Heat the corn oil in a karahi, wok or deep frying pan and add the baby onions. Fry over a medium heat until the onions turn golden brown, stirring frequently.

4 Lower the heat and add the chilli sauce, garlic, ginger and salt, taking care not to burn the mixture.

5 Stir in the chickpeas and stir-fry over a medium heat until the moisture has evaporated.

6 Add the cooked vegetables and cherry tomatoes, and stir over the heat with a slotted spoon for about 2 minutes.

7 Sprinkle the crushed red chillies and sesame seeds evenly over the vegetable mixture and serve.

Vegetables with Almonds and Indian Spices

Natural yogurt is added to the vegetables towards the end of the cooking time, which not only gives this dish a tangy note but also makes it creamy.

Serves 4
30ml/2 tbsp vegetable oil
2 medium onions, sliced
5cm/2in piece fresh root ginger, grated
5ml/1 tsp black peppercorns, roughly crushed
1 bay leaf
1.5ml/¼ tsp turmeric
5ml/1 tsp ground coriander
5ml/1 tsp salt
2.5ml/½ tsp garam masala
175g/6oz/2½ cups mushrooms, thickly sliced
1 medium courgette (zucchini), thickly sliced
50g/2oz green beans, sliced into 2.5cm/1in pieces
15ml/1 tbsp roughly chopped fresh mint
150ml/¼ pint/⅔ cup water
30ml/2 tbsp natural (plain) low-fat yogurt
25g/1oz/¼ cup flaked (sliced) almonds, to garnish

1 In a wok or deep frying pan, heat the vegetable oil and fry the sliced onions with the ginger, crushed black peppercorns and bay leaf for 3–5 minutes.

2 Lower the heat and add the turmeric, ground coriander, salt and garam masala, stirring occasionally.

3 Gradually add the mushrooms, courgette, green beans and the mint. Stir gently so that the vegetables retain their shapes.

4 Pour the measured water into the pan and bring to the boil, then lower the heat and simmer gently until all the water has evaporated.

5 In a bowl, beat the yogurt with a fork, then pour on to the vegetables and mix together well.

6 Cook the vegetables for a further 2–3 minutes until everything is warmed through, stirring occasionally. Serve immediately garnished with the flaked almonds.

Balti Baby Vegetables Energy 221kcal/929kJ; Protein 9g; Carbohydrate 32.5g, of which sugars 11g; Fat 7.1g, of which saturates 0.9g; Cholesterol 0mg; Calcium 90mg; Fibre 6.5g; Sodium 174mg.
Vegetables with Almonds Energy 182kcal/754kJ; Protein 6.7g; Carbohydrate 14.7g, of which sugars 7.7g; Fat 11.4g, of which saturates 1.3g; Cholesterol 0mg; Calcium 97mg; Fibre 3.1g; Sodium 17mg.

Indian Spiced Okra with Almonds and Paprika

Okra pods have a ridged skin and a tapered, oblong shape. Firm, brightly coloured pods are well suited to cooking with spices.

Serves 2–4
225g/8oz okra
50g/2oz/½ cup blanched almonds, chopped
25g/1oz/2 tbsp butter
15ml/1 tbsp sunflower oil or vegetable oil
2 garlic cloves, crushed
2.5cm/1in piece fresh root ginger, grated
5ml/1 tsp cumin seeds
5ml/1 tsp ground coriander
5ml/1 tsp paprika
salt and ground black pepper

1 Trim just the tops of the okra stems and around the edges of the stalks. They have a sticky liquid which oozes out if prepared too far ahead, so only trim them immediately before they will be cooked.

2 In a large pan, fry the almonds in the butter until they are lightly golden, then remove.

3 Add the sunflower or vegetable oil to the pan and fry the okra, stirring constantly, for 2 minutes.

4 Add the garlic and ginger and fry for a minute, then add the spices and cook for another minute or so, stirring all the time.

5 Pour in about 300ml/½ pint/1¼ cups water. Season well with salt and ground black pepper, cover the pan with a lid and simmer for about 5 minutes or so until the okra feel just tender. Finally, mix in the fried almonds and serve hot.

> **Variation**
> Try okra sliced, fried in garlic and spices, then stirred into a pilaff of basmati rice with cauliflower florets and carrots. This makes a colourful and delicious dish – especially when topped with crushed grilled poppadums.

Okra with Green Mango and Lentils

If you like okra, you'll love this spicy and tangy dish. The green mango adds a delicious tartness that is a perfect complement to the nuttiness of the lentils and the kick from the red chillies and chilli powder.

Serves 4
115g/4oz/⅔ cup chana dhal (yellow lentils)
45ml/3 tbsp corn oil
2.5ml/½ tsp onion seeds
2 medium onions, sliced
2.5ml/½ tsp ground fenugreek
5ml/1 tsp grated fresh root ginger
5ml/1 tsp crushed garlic
7.5ml/1½ tsp chilli powder
1.5ml/¼ tsp turmeric
5ml/1 tsp ground coriander
1 green (unripe) mango, peeled and sliced
450g/1lb okra, cut into 1cm/½in pieces
7.5ml/1½ tsp salt
2 fresh red chillies, seeded and sliced
30ml/2 tbsp chopped fresh coriander (cilantro)
1 tomato, sliced

1 Wash the lentils thoroughly and put in a pan with enough water to cover. Bring to the boil and cook for about 15 minutes or until soft but not mushy. Drain and set to one side.

2 Heat the oil in a wok, deep frying pan or a karahi and fry the onion seeds until they begin to pop.

3 Add the onions to the pan and fry over a medium heat for 5–7 minutes until golden brown.

4 Lower the heat and add the ground fenugreek, ginger, garlic, chilli powder, turmeric and ground coriander to the pan. Cook for 1–2 minutes, stirring frequently.

5 Add the mango slices and the okra. Stir well and add the salt, red chillies and fresh coriander. Stir-fry for about 3 minutes or until the okra is well cooked.

6 Finally, add the cooked lentils and sliced tomato and cook for a further 3 minutes. Serve hot.

Indian Spiced Okra Energy 211kcal/873kJ; Protein 5g; Carbohydrate 6.3g, of which sugars 5.2g; Fat 18.7g, of which saturates 7.1g; Cholesterol 0mg; Calcium 246mg; Fibre 7.6g; Sodium 15mg.
Okra with Mango Energy 253kcal/1063kJ; Protein 11.3g; Carbohydrate 31.6g, of which sugars 13.7g; Fat 10.1g, of which saturates 1.4g; Cholesterol 0mg; Calcium 220mg; Fibre 8.2g; Sodium 25mg.

Winter Melon Pachadi

In India, there are a variety of pachadi and raita dishes designed to cool the palate and aid digestion when eating spicy food. These are made with yogurt and cooling vegetables and herbs, such as winter melon, okra, courgette, spinach, pumpkin, and cucumber with mint.

Serves 4

225g/8oz winter melon, peeled, seeded and diced
5ml/1 tsp ground turmeric
5ml/1 tsp red chilli powder
300ml/½ pint/1¼ cups Greek (US strained plain) yogurt
2.5ml/½ tsp salt
2.5ml/½ tsp sugar
15g/½oz fresh root ginger, peeled and grated
1 green chilli, seeded and finely chopped
15ml/1 tbsp vegetable oil
1.5ml/¼ tsp ground asafoetida
5ml/1 tsp brown mustard seeds
8–10 dried curry leaves
1 dried red chilli, seeded and roughly chopped

1 Put the winter melon in a heavy pan with the turmeric and chilli powder and pour in enough water to just cover. Bring to the boil and cook gently, uncovered, until the winter melon is tender and all the water has evaporated.

2 In a bowl, beat the yogurt with the salt and sugar until smooth and creamy. Add the ginger and green chilli, and fold in the warm winter melon.

3 Heat the oil in small heavy pan. Stir in the asafoetida and the mustard seeds. As soon as the mustard seeds pop, stir in the curry leaves and dried chilli. When the chilli darkens, add the spices to the yogurt and mix well. Serve at room temperature.

> **Cook's Tip**
> In Malaysia and Singapore cooling Indian dishes like pachadi are often served at the Indian and Malay stalls and coffee shops to balance the hot curries and spicy grilled dishes. In many Indian households, the pachadi is made a day or two in advance, so that the flavours mingle.

Cucumber and Pineapple Sambal

Sambals are the little side dishes served at almost every Malay meal. In poorer societies, a main meal may simply be a bowl of rice and a sambal made from pounded shrimp paste, chillies and lime juice: the sambal is poured over the rice to give it flavour. This recipe is known as sambal nanas. Use sparingly, as it is quite fiery.

Serves 8–10

1 small or ½ large fresh ripe pineapple
½ cucumber, halved lengthways
50g/2oz dried shrimps
1 large fresh red chilli, seeded and roughly chopped
1cm/½in cube shrimp paste, prepared
juice of 1 large lemon or lime
soft light brown sugar, to taste (optional)
salt

1 Cut off the top and the bottom of the pineapple. Stand it upright on a board, then slice off the skin from top to bottom, cutting out the spines. Slice the pineapple, removing the central core. Cut into thin slices and set aside.

2 Trim the ends from the cucumber and slice thinly. Sprinkle with salt and set aside. Place the dried shrimps in a food processor and chop finely. Add the chopped red chilli, prepared shrimp paste and lemon or lime juice, and process again until a coarse paste has formed.

3 Rinse the cucumber, drain and dry on kitchen paper. Mix with the pineapple and chill. Just before serving, spoon in the spice mixture with sugar to taste, if liked. Mix well and serve.

> **Cook's Tip**
> The pungent shrimp paste, also called blachan and terasi, is popular in many South-east Asian countries, and is available in Asian food markets. Since it can taste a bit raw in a sambal, dry-fry it by wrapping it in foil and heating it in a frying pan over a low heat for 5 minutes, turning from time to time. If the shrimp paste is to be fried with other spices, this preliminary cooking can be eliminated.

Melon Pachadi Energy 127kcal/527kJ; Protein 5.1g; Carbohydrate 5.3g, of which sugars 5.3g; Fat 10.5g, of which saturates 4.2g; Cholesterol 0mg; Calcium 120mg; Fibre 0.2g; Sodium 316mg.
Cucumber Sambal Energy 105kcal/446kJ; Protein 13.3g; Carbohydrate 11.9g, of which sugars 11.9g; Fat 0.8g, of which saturates 0.1g; Cholesterol 114mg; Calcium 298mg; Fibre 1.5g; Sodium 1715mg.

Spinach and Mushroom Curry

A tasty vegetable that is often overlooked, spinach is highly nutritious. Cooked in this way it tastes wonderful. Serve with chapatis.

Serves 4

450g/1lb fresh or frozen spinach, thawed
30ml/2 tbsp vegetable oil
2 medium onions, diced
6–8 curry leaves
1.5ml/¼ tsp onion seeds
5ml/1 tsp crushed garlic
5ml/1 tsp grated fresh root ginger
5ml/1 tsp chilli powder
5ml/1 tsp salt
7.5ml/1½ tsp ground coriander
1 large red (bell) pepper, seeded and sliced
115g/4oz/1½ cups mushrooms, roughly chopped
225g/8oz/1 cup low-fat fromage frais or ricotta cheese
30ml/2 tbsp fresh coriander (cilantro) leaves

1 If using fresh spinach, blanch it briefly in a pan of boiling water and drain thoroughly. If using frozen spinach, drain well. Set aside while you cook the other ingredients.

2 Heat the oil in a karahi, wok or heavy pan and fry the onions with the curry leaves and the onion seeds for 1–2 minutes. Add the garlic, ginger, chilli powder, salt and ground coriander. Stir-fry for a further 2–3 minutes.

3 Add half the red pepper slices and all the mushrooms and continue to stir-fry for 2–3 minutes.

4 Add the spinach and stir-fry for 4–6 minutes, then add the fromage frais or ricotta and half the fresh coriander, followed by the remaining red pepper slices. Cook for 2–3 minutes before serving, garnished with the remaining coriander.

Cook's Tip
Whether you use fresh or frozen spinach, make sure it is well drained, otherwise the stir-fried mixture will be too wet when you add the fromage frais or ricotta. Transfer the spinach into a colander, and press it against the sides of the colander with a wooden spoon to extract as much liquid as possible.

Curried Winter Vegetables

A mixture of chunky mashed root vegetables, such as carrots, parsnips and turnips or swedes, makes a wonderfully warming winter side dish.

Serves 4–6

225g/8oz carrots, chopped
225g/8oz parsnips, chopped
1 small swede (rutabaga), chopped
25g/1oz/2 tbsp butter
10ml/2 tsp mild curry paste
115g/4oz/½ cup fromage frais or ricotta cheese
15ml/1 tbsp fresh chives, finely chopped
salt and ground black pepper

1 Boil the carrots, parsnips and swede in a large pan with plenty of lightly salted water for about 6–8 minutes, or until they are just tender but not soft.

2 Drain the vegetables then return them to the pan with the butter, curry paste and seasoning.

3 Mash the vegetables lightly with a fork or potato masher so that you end up with a chunky purée; you want to retain a good coarse texture with plenty of chunks.

4 Stir the fromage frais or ricotta cheese and chopped chives into the pan. Check the seasoning, adding more if needed, and serve immediately while hot. This is a good dish to prepare in advance and reheat when required.

Cook's Tip
Vegetable purées are a popular accompaniment with any dish which could be a little on the dry side, providing a good contrast of textures and colours.

Variation
Other vegetables work well in this dish: try pumpkin, sweet potatoes, potatoes, peas, broccoli or leeks.

Spinach and Mushroom Energy 225kcal/933kJ; Protein 10.8g; Carbohydrate 10g, of which sugars 6.2g; Fat 16.2g, of which saturates 6.1g; Cholesterol 24mg; Calcium 215mg; Fibre 3.4g; Sodium 164mg.
Curried Vegetables Energy 268kcal/1129kJ; Protein 5.8g; Carbohydrate 37.8g, of which sugars 9.8g; Fat 11.6g, of which saturates 7.1g; Cholesterol 31mg; Calcium 127mg; Fibre 3.6g; Sodium 117mg.

Potatoes in Chilli Tamarind Sauce

In this favourite potato dish from southern India, the combination of chilli and tamarind awakens the taste buds immediately. This version adapts the classic recipe slightly, to reduce the pungency and enhance the fiery appearance.

Serves 4–6

450g/1lb small new potatoes, washed and dried
25g/1oz whole dried red chillies
7.5ml/1½ tsp cumin seeds
4 garlic cloves
90ml/6 tbsp vegetable oil
60ml/4 tbsp thick tamarind juice, made by mixing tamarind paste with warm water
30ml/2 tbsp tomato purée (paste)
4 curry leaves
5ml/1 tsp sugar
1.5ml/¼ tsp asafoetida
salt
coriander (cilantro) sprigs and lemon wedges, to garnish

1 Cook the potatoes in a large pan of salted water for about 12–15 minutes, or until they are just cooked, ensuring they do not break. To test, insert a thin sharp knife into the potatoes. Drain the potatoes and place in a bowl of iced water to cool them down and prevent further cooking.

2 Soak the chillies for 5 minutes in warm water. Drain and grind with the cumin seeds and garlic to a coarse paste either using a mortar and pestle or in a food processor.

3 Heat the oil in a wok or deep frying pan and fry the spice paste, tamarind juice, tomato purée, curry leaves, salt, sugar and asafoetida until the oil separates from the spice paste.

4 Drain the the potatoes and add to the pan. Reduce the heat to low, cover the pan with a lid and simmer the potatoes for 5 minutes. Garnish with coriander and lemon wedges and serve immediately.

Variation
Chunks of sweet potatoes can be used as an alternative to new potatoes in this dish, if you prefer.

Cauliflower and Potatoes with Indian Spices

Cauliflower and potatoes are encrusted with Indian spices in this delicious curry. It is a popular side dish or can be served as a main course with other dishes such as a salad, spicy dhal or simply with Indian breads.

Serves 4

450g/1lb potatoes, cut into 2.5cm/1in chunks
30ml/2 tbsp vegetable oil
5ml/1 tsp cumin seeds
1 green chilli, finely chopped
450g/1lb cauliflower, broken into florets
5ml/1 tsp ground coriander
5ml/1 tsp ground cumin
1.5ml/¼ tsp chilli powder
2.5ml/½ tsp ground turmeric
2.5ml/½ tsp salt
chopped fresh coriander (cilantro), to garnish
tomato and onion salad and pickle, to serve

1 Par-boil the potatoes in a large pan of boiling water for 10 minutes. Drain well and set aside.

2 Heat the oil in a wok or large frying pan and fry the cumin seeds for about 2 minutes, until they begin to splutter and release their fragrance. Add the chilli to the pan and fry, stirring constantly, for a further 1 minute.

3 Add the cauliflower florets to the pan and fry, stirring constantly, for about 5 minutes.

4 Add the potatoes, the ground spices and salt and cook for 7–10 minutes, or until both the vegetables are tender.

5 Garnish with fresh coriander and serve immediately with a tomato and onion salad and pickle.

Variation
Try using sweet potatoes instead of ordinary potatoes for an alternative curry with a sweeter flavour. The cauliflower could also be replaced with the same amount of broccoli.

Potatoes in Tamarind Sauce Energy 90kcal/379kJ; Protein 2.7g; Carbohydrate 19.5g, of which sugars 5.7g; Fat 0.7g, of which saturates 0.1g; Cholesterol 0mg; Calcium 30mg; Fibre 1.9g; Sodium 12mg.
Cauliflower and Potatoes Energy 181kcal/759kJ; Protein 6.7g; Carbohydrate 23.2g, of which sugars 4.3g; Fat 7.5g, of which saturates 1.1g; Cholesterol 0mg; Calcium 40mg; Fibre 3.2g; Sodium 24mg.

Spiced Potatoes and Carrots with Fresh Herbs

Ready prepared 'parisienne' vegetables have recently become available in many supermarkets. These are simply root vegetables that have been peeled and cut into perfectly spherical shapes. This dish looks extremely fresh and appetizing and is equally as delicious.

Serves 4

175g/6oz carrots parisienne
175g/6oz potatoes parisienne
115g/4oz runner (green)
    beans, sliced
75 g/3 oz/6 tbsp butter
15ml/1 tbsp corn oil
1.5ml/¼ tsp onion seeds
1.5ml/¼ tsp fenugreek seeds
4 dried red chillies, seeded and
    roughly chopped
2.5ml/½ tsp mustard seeds
6 curry leaves
1 medium onion, sliced
5ml/1 tsp salt
4 garlic cloves, sliced
4 fresh red chillies, sliced
15ml/1 tbsp chopped fresh
    coriander (cilantro)
15ml/1 tbsp fresh mint leaves,
    finely chopped
mint sprig, to garnish

1 Place the carrots, potatoes and runner beans into a large pan of boiling water, and cook for about 7–8 minutes, or until they are just tender but do not let them become overcooked. Drain thoroughly and set to one side.

2 Heat the butter and oil in a wok, deep frying pan or a large karahi and add the onion seeds, fenugreek seeds, dried red chillies, mustard seeds and curry leaves. Stir-fry over a medium heat for 2 minutes until they release their fragrances.

3 Add the sliced onion to the pan with the spices and fry for about 3–5 minutes, stirring frequently.

4 Add the salt, garlic and fresh chillies to the pan, followed by the cooked vegetables, and cook for about 5 minutes, over a medium heat, stirring gently.

5 Add the fresh coriander and mint to the pan and serve immediately garnished with a sprig of mint.

Potatoes in Spicy Yogurt Sauce

Tiny potatoes cooked with their skins on are delicious in this fairly spicy yet tangy yogurt sauce. Serve with any meat or fish dish or just with hot chapatis.

Serves 4

12 small new or salad
    potatoes, halved
300ml/ pint/1¼ cups natural
    (plain) low-fat yogurt
300ml/½ pint/1¼ cups water
1.5ml/¼ tsp turmeric
5ml/1 tsp chilli powder
5ml/1 tsp ground coriander
2.5ml/½ tsp ground cumin
5ml/1 tsp salt
5ml/1 tsp light soft brown sugar
30ml/2 tbsp vegetable oil
5ml/1 tsp white cumin seeds
15ml/1 tbsp chopped fresh
    coriander (cilantro)
2 fresh green chillies, sliced
1 coriander (cilantro) sprig,
    to garnish (optional)

1 Cook the potatoes in their skins in boiling salted water until just tender, then drain and set aside.

2 Place the yogurt, water, turmeric, chilli powder, ground coriander, ground cumin, salt and sugar in a bowl. Mix well until all the ingredients are combined. Set aside.

3 Heat the vegetable oil in a medium pan over a medium-high heat and stir in the white cumin seeds.

4 Reduce the heat to medium, and stir the prepared yogurt mixture into the pan. Cook the sauce, stirring continuously, for about 3–5 minutes until heated through and bubbling.

5 Add the fresh coriander, green chillies and potatoes to the sauce. Mix well and cook for 5–7 minutes, stirring occasionally. Transfer to a serving dish, garnish with the coriander sprig, if you wish, and serve immediately.

> **Cook's Tip**
> If new or salad potatoes are unavailable, use 450g/1lb large potatoes instead, but choose a waxy not a floury variety. Peel them and cut into large chunks, then cook as described above.

Spiced Potatoes Energy 252kcal/1044kJ; Protein 3.5g; Carbohydrate 16.1g, of which sugars 5.7g; Fat 19.9g, of which saturates 10.4g; Cholesterol 40mg; Calcium 72mg; Fibre 3g; Sodium 628mg.
Potatoes in Yogurt Sauce Energy 161kcal/677kJ; Protein 5.9g; Carbohydrate 24.7g, of which sugars 7g; Fat 5.1g, of which saturates 1g; Cholesterol 1mg; Calcium 154mg; Fibre 1.1g; Sodium 73mg.

Mango Chutney

No Indian meal would be complete without this classic chutney, which is ideal for making in a slow cooker. Its gloriously sweet, tangy flavour is the perfect complement to warm spices.

Makes 450g/1lb
3 firm mangoes
120ml/4fl oz/½ cup cider vinegar
200g/7oz/scant 1 cup light muscovado (brown) sugar
1 small red finger chilli or jalapeño chilli, split
2.5cm/1in piece fresh root ginger, peeled and finely chopped
1 garlic clove, finely chopped
5 cardamom pods, bruised
1 bay leaf
2.5ml/½ tsp salt

1 Peel the mangoes and cut out the stone (pit), then cut the flesh into small chunks or thin wedges.

2 Put the chopped mangoes in the ceramic cooking pot of the slow cooker. Add the cider vinegar, stir briefly to combine, and cover the slow cooker with the lid. Switch the slow cooker to the high setting and cook for about 2 hours, stirring the chutney halfway through the cooking time.

3 Stir the sugar, chilli, ginger, garlic, bruised cardamom pods, bay leaf and salt into the mango mixture, until the sugar has dissolved completely.

4 Cover and cook for 2 hours, then uncover and let the mixture cook for a further 1 hour, or until the chutney is reduced to a thick consistency and no excess liquid remains. Stir the chutney every 15 minutes during the last hour.

5 Remove and discard the bay leaf and the chilli. Spoon the chutney into hot sterilized jars and seal. Store for 1 week before eating and use within 1 year.

Cook's Tip
To make a more fiery chutney, seed and slice two green chillies and stir into the chutney mixture with the other spices.

Hot Coconut Chutney with Onion

Serve this exotic chutney as an accompaniment for Indian curries or with a raita and other chutneys and poppadums as an interesting start to a meal.

Serves 4–6
200g/7oz fresh coconut, grated
3–4 fresh green chillies, seeded and chopped
20g/¾oz fresh coriander (cilantro), chopped
30ml/2 tbsp chopped fresh mint
30–45ml/2–3 tbsp lime juice
about 2.5ml/½ tsp salt
about 2.5ml/½ tsp caster (superfine) sugar
15–30ml/1–2 tbsp coconut milk (optional)
30ml/2 tbsp groundnut (peanut) oil
5ml/1 tsp kalonji
1 small onion, very finely chopped
fresh coriander (cilantro) sprigs, to garnish

1 Place the coconut, chillies, coriander and fresh mint in a food processor or blender. Add 30ml/2 tbsp of the lime juice, then process until thoroughly chopped.

2 Scrape the mixture into a bowl and add more lime juice to taste. Add salt and sugar to taste. If the mixture is dry, stir in 15–30ml/1–2 tbsp coconut milk.

3 Heat the groundnut oil in a small heavy pan and fry the kalonji until they begin to pop, then reduce the heat and add the onion. Fry, stirring frequently, for about 4–5 minutes, until the onion softens but does not brown.

4 Add the onion mixture to the coconut mixture. Stir well to combine the two and leave to cool. Garnish with fresh coriander sprigs before serving.

Cook's Tips
• *Kalonji are small black seeds which have a slightly bitter, yet pleasant, taste. They are fried to release their flavour.*
• *Use more chillies in step 1 to make the paste if you prefer a chutney with a hotter flavour.*

Mango Chutney Energy 1045kcal/4465kJ; Protein 4.1g; Carbohydrate 272.5g, of which sugars 271.1g; Fat 0.9g, of which saturates 0.5g; Cholesterol 0mg; Calcium 908mg; Fibre 11.7g; Sodium 1002mg.
Coconut Chutney Energy 145kcal/596kJ; Protein 1.6g; Carbohydrate 2.8g, of which sugars 2.5g; Fat 14.2g, of which saturates 9.3g; Cholesterol 0mg; Calcium 40mg; Fibre 3.3g; Sodium 11mg.

Sesame Seed and Chilli Chutney

This is an extremely versatile Indian chutney, which doubles as a delicious dip for poppadums, pakora or bhajias. It also makes a tasty sandwich filling with cucumber.

Serves 4
175g/6oz sesame seeds
5ml/1 tsp salt
120–150ml/4–5fl oz/1/2–2/3 cup water
2 green chillies, seeded and diced
60ml/4 tbsp chopped fresh coriander (cilantro)
15ml/1 tbsp chopped fresh mint leaves
15ml/1 tbsp tamarind paste
30ml/2 tbsp sugar
5ml/1 tsp corn oil
1.5ml/1/4 tsp onion seeds
4 curry leaves
6 onion rings, 1 green chilli, seeded and sliced, 1 red chilli, seeded and sliced, and 15ml/1 tbsp fresh coriander (cilantro) leaves, to garnish

1 Dry-roast the sesame seeds and leave to cool. Place them in a spice grinder and grind to a grainy powder, or grind the seeds using a mortar and pestle.

2 Transfer the sesame powder to a bowl. Add the salt, water, diced chillies, coriander, mint, tamarind paste and sugar and, using a fork, mix everything together.

3 Taste and adjust the seasoning if necessary: the mixture should have a sweet-and-sour flavour.

4 Heat the oil in a heavy pan and fry the onion seeds and curry leaves, stirring constantly, for 2–3 minutes until the seeds begin to splutter and release their fragrances.

5 Add the sesame seed paste to the pan and fry the mixture for about 45 seconds, stirring constantly to avoid it sticking to the base of the pan and burning. Transfer the mixture to a warmed serving dish.

6 Garnish the chutney with onion rings, sliced green and red chillies and the fresh coriander leaves. If it is not to be eaten immediately, cover the chutney tightly and store it in the refrigerator until it is required.

Tomato and Fresh Chilli Chutney

This fresh-tasting and invigorating chutney is the perfect partner to liven up a simple curry or dhal.

Makes about 475ml/ 16fl oz/2 cups
1 red (bell) pepper
4 tomatoes, chopped
2 fresh green chillies, chopped
1 garlic clove, crushed
1.5ml/1/4 tsp salt
2.5ml/1/2 tsp sugar
5ml/1 tsp chilli powder
45ml/3 tbsp tomato purée (paste)
15ml/1 tbsp chopped fresh coriander (cilantro)

1 Halve the red pepper and remove the core and seeds. Roughly chop the red pepper halves into chunks.

2 Process the pepper with the tomatoes, chillies, garlic, salt, sugar, chilli powder, tomato purée and coriander with 30ml/ 2 tbsp water in a food processor until smooth. Transfer to a sterilized jar, cover and chill until needed.

Mint and Coconut Chutney

This chutney is made using fresh mint leaves and desiccated coconut, all bound together with yogurt.

Makes about 350ml/ 12fl oz/1 1/2 cups
50g/2oz fresh mint leaves
90ml/6 tbsp desiccated (dry unsweetened shredded) coconut
15ml/1 tbsp sesame seeds
1.5ml/1/4 tsp salt
175ml/6fl oz/3/4 cup natural (plain) yogurt

1 Finely chop the fresh mint leaves, using a sharp kitchen knife or a specialist herb chopper.

2 Put the mint with the coconut, sesame seeds, salt and yogurt into a food processor or blender and process until smooth.

3 Transfer the chutney to a sterilized jar, cover and chill in the refrigerator until needed.

Tomato and Chilli Chutney Energy 187kcal/794kJ; Protein 9.7g; Carbohydrate 33.2g, of which sugars 30g; Fat 2.5g, of which saturates 0.5g; Cholesterol 0mg; Calcium 175mg; Fibre 7.5g; Sodium 157mg.
Mint and Coconut Chutney Energy 753kcal/3117kJ; Protein 18.6g; Carbohydrate 21.7g, of which sugars 18.9g; Fat 66.6g of which saturates 50.2g; Cholesterol 2mg Calcium 559mg Fibre 13.5g Sodium 181mg.
Sesame Chutney Energy 303kcal/1256kJ; Protein 8.5g; Carbohydrate 8.6g, of which sugars 8.4g; Fat 26.3g, of which saturates 3.7g; Cholesterol 0mg; Calcium 327mg; Fibre 4.2g; Sodium 506mg.

Fruit Raita

Refreshing yogurt raitas are not just made with vegetables, they can also be made with almost any fruit. For this version, grapes and bananas are used.

Serves 4
350ml/12fl oz/1½ cups natural (plain) yogurt

75g/3oz seedless grapes
50g/2oz shelled walnuts
2 firm bananas, sliced
5ml/1 tsp sugar
5ml/1 tsp freshly ground cumin seeds
salt
1.5ml/¼ tsp freshly roasted cumin seeds, and chilli powder, to garnish

1 Put the yogurt, grapes and walnuts in a large mixing bowl. Fold in the banana slices.

2 Stir in the sugar, ground cumin and salt. Chill and sprinkle on the roasted cumin seeds and chilli powder before serving.

Spiced Yogurt

This refreshing yogurt accompaniment features whole and ground spice seeds as well as a slight kick from the dried red chilli and curry leaves.

Makes 450ml/¾ pint/scant 2 cups
450ml/¾ pint/scant 2 cups

natural (plain) yogurt
2.5ml/½ tsp freshly ground fennel seeds
2.5ml/½ tsp sugar
60ml/4 tbsp vegetable oil
1 dried red chilli
1.5ml/¼ tsp mustard seeds
1.5ml/¼ tsp cumin seeds
4–6 curry leaves
a pinch each of asafoetida and ground turmeric

1 Mix together the yogurt, fennel seeds and sugar, and add salt to taste. Chill in the refrigerator.

2 Heat the oil and fry the remaining ingredients. When the chilli turns dark, pour the oil and spices over the yogurt and mix. Cover and chill before serving.

Cucumber Raita

Raitas are slightly sour, yogurt-based accompaniments that have a cooling effect on the palate when eaten with spicy foods. They help to balance out the flavours of an Indian meal. This is the cucumber version, which is one of the most popular varieties.

Makes about 600ml/1 pint/ 2½ cups
½ cucumber
1 fresh green chilli, seeded and chopped
300ml/½ pint/1¼ cups natural (plain) yogurt
1.5ml/¼ tsp salt
1.5ml/¼ tsp ground cumin

1 Dice the cucumber finely and place in a large mixing bowl. Sprinkle over the chopped green chilli and mix well to combine it with the cucumber.

2 Place the natural yogurt in a bowl and beat it with a fork until it becomes smooth, then stir it into the cucumber and chilli mixture in the large bowl.

3 Stir the salt and ground cumin into the yogurt mixture. Cover the bowl with clear film (plastic wrap) and chill in the refrigerator for at least 30 minutes before serving.

Cook's Tip
The cucumber can be sprinkled with 5ml/1 tsp salt and left in a sieve (strainer) to release any excess moisture, if you prefer, although this isn't necessary. If you do salt the cucumber, ensure that it is well rinsed and squeezed dry afterwards.

Variations
• *Instead of using cucumber in this raita, use two skinned, seeded and chopped tomatoes and about 15ml/1 tbsp chopped fresh coriander (cilantro).*
• *If you prefer, the cucumber can be grated, rather than diced, before adding to the yogurt.*

Fruit Raita Energy 202kcal/847kJ; Protein 7.2g; Carbohydrate 23.2g, of which sugars 21.5g; Fat 9.8g, of which saturates 1.2g; Cholesterol 1mg; Calcium 186mg; Fibre 1.1g; Sodium 75mg.
Spiced Yogurt Energy 441kcal/1842kJ; Protein 25.2g; Carbohydrate 41.6g, of which sugars 36.4g; Fat 21.5g, of which saturates 4.3g; Cholesterol 6mg; Calcium 884mg; Fibre 0g; Sodium 379mg.
Cucumber Raita Energy 31kcal/131kJ; Protein 2.8g; Carbohydrate 4.2g, of which sugars 4g; Fat 0.6g, of which saturates 0.3g; Cholesterol 1mg; Calcium 104mg; Fibre 0.2g; Sodium 141mg.

Tomato Relish

This is a simple relish that can be served with most meals. It provides a contrast to hot curries, with its crunchy texture and refreshing ingredients.

Serves 4–6

2 small fresh green chillies
2 limes
2.5ml/½ tsp sugar, or to taste
2 onions, finely chopped
4 firm tomatoes, seeded and
    finely chopped
½ cucumber, finely chopped
a few fresh coriander (cilantro)
    leaves, chopped
salt and ground black pepper
a few fresh mint leaves,
    to garnish

1 Using a sharp knife, cut both the green chillies in half. Scrape out the seeds and discard, then chop the chillies finely and place them in a small bowl.

2 Squeeze the limes. Pour the juice into a glass bowl and add the sugar, with salt and pepper to taste. Set aside until the sugar and salt have dissolved, stirring the mixture occasionally.

3 Add the chopped chillies to the bowl, with the chopped onions, tomatoes, cucumber and fresh coriander leaves. Mix well to combine the ingredients.

4 Cover the bowl with clear film (plastic wrap) and place in the refrigerator for at least 3 hours, so that the flavours blend. Just before serving, taste the relish and add more salt, pepper or sugar if needed. Garnish with mint and serve.

Cook's Tip
If you find that preparing chillies irritates your skin then wear a pair of kitchen gloves or cover your hands with a plastic bag.

Variation
For a milder-flavoured relish, use just one chilli, or dispense with them altogether and substitute with a green (bell) pepper.

Bombay Duck and Chilli Pickle

The bummalo fish is found off the west coast of India during the monsoon season. It is salted and dried in the sun and is characterized by a strong smell and distinctive piquancy. How this fish acquired the name Bombay duck in the West is far from certain.

Serves 4–6

6–8 pieces bummalo (Bombay
    duck), soaked in water for
    5 minutes
60ml/4 tbsp vegetable oil
2 fresh red chillies, crushed
15ml/1 tbsp sugar
450g/1lb cherry tomatoes, cut
    in half
115g/4oz fried onions

1 Pat the soaked fish dry with kitchen paper. Heat the oil in a frying pan and fry the fish pieces for about 30–45 seconds on both sides until crisp. Be careful not to burn them as they will taste bitter. Drain well on kitchen paper. When cool enough to handle, break the fish into small pieces.

2 To the same oil, add the chillies and fry, stirring constantly, for about 2–3 minutes, until the chillies release their aromas.

3 Add the sugar, cherry tomatoes and fried onions to the pan and mix well to combine the ingredients. Continue to cook, stirring frequently, until the tomatoes become pulpy and the mixture is blended into a fairly thick sauce.

4 Fold the fish pieces into the tomato sauce and cook for a minute until all the ingredients are heated through. Serve immediately if eating hot, or it will be equally delicious if left to cool before eating cold.

Cook's Tip
The origin of the term 'Bombay duck' is uncertain. Some believe that, during the British Raj, the dried fish was often transported on the railway and that the mail carriages of the train (dak means 'mail' in Hindi) would smell of the fish, consequently leading the British to refer to the pungent smell of the fish as the 'Bombay dak', which became 'duck'.

Tomato Relish Energy 530kcal/2262kJ; Protein 3.7g; Carbohydrate 134.1g, of which sugars 134.1g; Fat 1.4g, of which saturates 0.5g; Cholesterol 0mg; Calcium 93mg; Fibre 4.5g; Sodium 2012mg.
Bombay Duck Pickle Energy 156kcal/652kJ; Protein 11.8g; Carbohydrate 5g, of which sugars 4.2g; Fat 10g, of which saturates 1.9g; Cholesterol 22mg; Calcium 22mg; Fibre 1.4g; Sodium 141mg.

Pineapple Pickle

This sweet-and-sour pickle is ideal as an accompaniment to curries.

Serves 6–8

15ml/1 tbsp brown mustard seeds
2 dried chillies, soaked in water, seeded, and squeezed dry
15g/½oz fresh root ginger, chopped
1 garlic clove, chopped
5ml/1 tsp ground turmeric
200ml/7fl oz/scant 1 cup white wine vinegar or rice vinegar
15ml/1 tbsp palm sugar (jaggery)
1 pineapple, cored and diced
salt

1 Dry-roast the mustard seeds until they pop. Using a mortar and pestle or food processor, grind the chillies, ginger and garlic to a paste. Stir in the mustard seeds and ground turmeric. Add the vinegar and sugar, stirring until the sugar has dissolved.

2 Put the pineapple in a bowl and pour over the sauce. Add salt to taste. The pickle will keep for 3 days in the refrigerator.

Chilli Strips with Lime

This fresh, tangy relish is made with strips of fresh chilli, lime juice and onion. It is ideal for serving with curries, stews, rice dishes or bean dishes.

Makes about 60ml/4 tbsp

10 fresh green chillies
½ white onion
4 limes
2.5ml/½ tsp dried oregano
salt

1 Roast the chillies in a griddle pan over a medium heat until the skins are charred and blistered but not blackened. Place the chillies in a plastic bag and tie the top. Set aside for 20 minutes.

2 Meanwhile, slice the onion very thinly and put it in a bowl. Squeeze the limes and add the juice to the bowl, with any pulp that gathers. Stir in the oregano.

3 Peel the chillies. Slit them, scrape out the seeds, then cut the chillies into long strips. Add to the onion mixture and season with salt. Cover and chill for 1 day before serving.

Onion Relish

This fiery side dish from Mexico is particularly good served with chicken, turkey or fish dishes.

Makes 1 small jar

2 fresh red fresno chillies
5ml/1 tsp allspice berries
2.5ml/½ tsp black peppercorns
5ml/1 tsp dried oregano
2 white onions
2 garlic cloves, peeled
100ml/3½fl oz/⅓ cup white wine vinegar
200ml/7fl oz/scant 1 cup cider vinegar
salt

1 Spear the fresno chillies on a long-handled metal skewer and roast them over the flame of a gas burner until the skins blister. Take care not to let the flesh burn. Alternatively, dry-fry them in a griddle pan until the skins are scorched. Place the roasted chillies in a strong plastic bag and tie or twist the top. Set aside for 20 minutes.

2 Meanwhile, place the allspice, black peppercorns and oregano in a mortar or food processor. Grind slowly by hand with a pestle or process until coarsely ground.

3 Cut the onions in half and slice them thinly. Put them in a bowl. Dry-roast the garlic in a heavy frying pan until golden, then crush and add to the onions in the bowl.

4 Remove the chillies from the bag and peel off the skins. Slit the chillies, scrape out the seeds, then chop them.

5 Add the ground spices to the onion mixture, followed by the chillies. Stir in both vinegars. Add salt to taste and mix thoroughly. Cover the bowl and chill in the refrigerator for at least 1 day before serving.

Cook's Tip
White onions have a pungent flavour and are good in this relish. Spanish (Bermuda) onions can also be used, and shallots also make an excellent pickle.

Pineapple Pickle Energy 56kcal/238kJ; Protein 0.7g; Carbohydrate 12.5g, of which sugars 12.2g; Fat 0.2g, of which saturates 0g; Cholesterol 0mg; Calcium 20mg; Fibre 1.3g; Sodium 4mg.
Chilli Strips with Lime Energy 49kcal/204kJ; Protein 3.9g; Carbohydrate 7g, of which sugars 5.7g; Fat 0.7g, of which saturates 0g; Cholesterol 0mg; Calcium 52mg; Fibre 0.9g; Sodium 10mg.
Onion Relish Energy 173kcal/721kJ; Protein 6.3g; Carbohydrate 35.1g, of which sugars 22.4g; Fat 2.1g, of which saturates 0.2g; Cholesterol 0mg; Calcium 118mg; Fibre 5.6g; Sodium 15mg.

Pickled Onions

The English love of pickled onions is famous, and at the time of the Raj the popular pickle was introduced into India. The onions should be stored in a cool, dark place for at least 6 weeks before being eaten.

Makes 3 or 4 450g/1lb jars
1kg/2¼lb pickling onions
115g/4oz/½ cup salt
750ml/1¼ pints/3 cups
    malt vinegar
15ml/1 tbsp sugar
2 or 3 dried red chillies
5ml/1 tsp brown mustard seeds
15ml/1 tbsp coriander seeds
5ml/1 tsp allspice berries
5ml/1 tsp black peppercorns
5cm/2in piece fresh root
    ginger, sliced
2 or 3 blades of mace
2 or 3 fresh bay leaves

1 Trim off the root end of each onion, but leave the onion layers attached. Cut a thin slice off the top (neck) end of each onion. Place the onions in a bowl, then cover with boiling water. Leave to stand for about 4 minutes, then drain. Peel off the skin from each onion with a small, sharp knife.

2 Place the peeled onions in a bowl and cover with cold water, then drain the water off and pour it into a large pan. Add the salt and heat slightly to dissolve it, then cool before pouring the brine over the onions. Cover the bowl with a plate and weigh it down slightly so that all the onions are submerged in the brine. Leave the onions to stand in the salted water for 24 hours.

3 Pour the vinegar into a large pan. Wrap all the remaining ingredients, except the bay leaves, in a piece of muslin (cheesecloth) or sew them into a filter paper for coffee. Add to the vinegar with the bay leaves. Bring to the boil, simmer for 5 minutes, then remove from the heat. Leave overnight so that the flavours have time to combine.

4 Drain the onions, rinse and pat dry. Pack them into sterilized jars. Add some or all of the spice from the vinegar, but not the ginger slices. The pickle will get hotter if you add the chillies. Pour the vinegar over the onions to cover and add the bay leaves. Cover the jars with non-metallic lids.

Hot Pickled Shallots

Pickling shallots in this way demands some patience while the vinegar and spices work their magic, but the results are worth the wait.

Makes 2–3 jars
5 or 6 small red or green bird's
    eye chillies
500g/1¼lb Thai pink
    shallots, peeled
2 large garlic cloves, peeled,
    halved and any green
    shoots removed

For the vinegar
40g/1½oz/3 tbsp sugar
10ml/2 tsp salt
5cm/2in piece fresh root
    ginger, sliced
15ml/1 tbsp coriander seeds
2 lemon grass stalks, cut in
    half lengthways
4 kaffir lime leaves or pared
    strips of lime rind
600ml/1 pint/2½ cups
    cider vinegar
15ml/1 tbsp chopped fresh
    coriander (cilantro)

1 The chillies can be left whole, or halved and seeded. The pickle will be hotter if you leave the seeds in. If leaving the chillies whole, prick them several times with a cocktail stick (toothpick). Bring a large pan of water to the boil.

2 Add the chillies, shallots and garlic. Blanch for 1–2 minutes, then drain. Rinse all the vegetables under cold water. Drain again.

3 Prepare the vinegar. Put the sugar, salt, ginger, coriander seeds, lemon grass and lime leaves or lime rind in a pan, pour in the vinegar and bring to the boil.

4 Reduce the heat to low and simmer the spiced vinegar for about 3–4 minutes to allow the flavours to mingle. Remove from the heat and set aside to cool.

5 Remove and discard the ginger from the pan, then bring the vinegar back to the boil. Add the fresh coriander, chillies, shallots and garlic, and cook for 1 minute.

6 Pack the shallots into sterilized jars, distributing the lemon grass, lime leaves, chillies and garlic among them. Pour over the hot vinegar. Set aside to cool, then seal and store in a cool, dark place for 2 months before eating.

Hot Pickled Shallots Energy 127kcal/536kJ; Protein 2.3g; Carbohydrate 30.4g, of which sugars 26.5g; Fat 0.4g, of which saturates 0g; Cholesterol 0mg; Calcium 52mg; Fibre 2.7g; Sodium 7mg.
Pickled Onions Energy 109kcal/454kJ; Protein 3.1g; Carbohydrate 24.5g, of which sugars 18.6g; Fat 0.5g, of which saturates 0g; Cholesterol 0mg; Calcium 67mg; Fibre 3.6g; Sodium 8mg.

Korean Cucumber Namul

This sautéed dish retains the natural succulence of the cucumber, while also infusing the recipe with a pleasantly refreshing hint of garlic and fresh chilli.

Serves 2

200g/7oz cucumber
15ml/1 tbsp vegetable oil

5ml/1 tsp spring onion (scallion),
  finely chopped
1 garlic clove, crushed
5ml/1 tsp sesame oil or
  groundnut (peanut) oil
sesame seeds, and seeded
  and shredded red chilli,
  to garnish
salt

1 Thinly slice the cucumber and place in a colander over a bowl. Sprinkle with about 5ml/1 tsp salt, then leave to stand in a cool place for at least 10 minutes.

2 Drain off any excess liquid from the cucumber slices and transfer them to a clean bowl.

3 Coat a frying pan or wok with the vegetable oil, and heat it over a medium heat. Add the spring onion, garlic and cucumber to the pan, and quickly stir-fry together for about 2–3 minutes.

4 Remove the pan from the heat, add the sesame or groundnut oil and toss lightly to blend all the ingredients. Place the salad in a shallow serving dish and garnish with the sesame seeds and shredded red chilli before serving.

Cook's Tip
Take care when handling chillies that you don't touch other sensitive parts of your body afterwards otherwise the chilli oil from your fingers will cause irritation. Wash your hands well.

Variation
Replace the chilli with thin strips of shredded red (bell) pepper if you prefer a version with less heat.

Green Mango Salad

Green mangoes have light green flesh and go well with prawns (shrimp) or beef.

Serves 4

450g/1lb green mangoes
rind and juice of 2 limes
30ml/2 tbsp sugar

30ml/2 tbsp nuoc cham
  (Vietnamese fish sauce)
2 green Thai chillies, seeded and
  finely sliced
1 small bunch fresh coriander
  (cilantro), stalks removed,
  finely chopped
salt

1 Peel, halve and stone (pit) the mangoes, then slice into strips.

2 In a bowl, mix together the lime juice and rind, sugar and nuoc cham. Add the mango strips with the chillies and coriander. Add salt to taste and set aside for 20 minutes before serving.

Rocket and Coriander Salad

Rocket leaves have a wonderful, peppery flavour and, mixed with coriander, make a delicious salad. You may need extra spinach to pad this salad out unless you have a big supply of rocket.

Serves 4

115g/4oz or more rocket
  (arugula) leaves

115g/4oz young spinach leaves
1 large bunch (about 25g/1oz)
  fresh coriander
2–3 fresh parsley sprigs
1 garlic clove, crushed
45ml/3 tbsp olive oil
10ml/2 tsp white wine vinegar
pinch of paprika
salt
cayenne pepper

1 Wash the rocket and spinach, pat dry, then place in a salad bowl. Chop the herbs and add to the salad.

2 In a small jug (pitcher), blend together the garlic, olive oil, vinegar, paprika, salt and cayenne pepper.

3 Pour the dressing over the salad in the bowl. Toss with your hands to coat the salad in the dressing and serve immediately.

Korean Namul Energy 74kcal/304kJ; Protein 0.8g; Carbohydrate 1.7g, of which sugars 1.6g; Fat 7.1g, of which saturates 0.9g; Cholesterol 0mg; Calcium 20mg; Fibre 0.7g; Sodium 4mg.
Green Mango Salad Energy 92kcal/391kJ; Protein 1g; Carbohydrate 22g, of which sugars 15g; Fat 0g, of which saturates 0g; Cholesterol 0mg; Calcium 32mg; Fibre 33g; Sodium 0.5mg.
Rocket Salad Energy 68kcal/280kJ; Protein 2g; Carbohydrate 1.3g, of which sugars 1.2g; Fat 6.1g, of which saturates 0.9g; Cholesterol 0mg; Calcium 123mg; Fibre 1.8g; Sodium 85mg.

Cambodian Soya Beansprout Salad

Unlike mung beansprouts, soya beansprouts are slightly poisonous raw and need to be par-boiled before using. Tossed in a salad and served with noodles and rice they make a perfect light meal.

Serves 4
450g/1lb fresh soya beansprouts
2 spring onions (scallions),
  finely sliced

1 small bunch fresh coriander
  (cilantro), stalks removed

For the dressing
15ml/1 tbsp sesame oil
30ml/2 tbsp light soy sauce
15ml/1 tbsp white rice vinegar
10ml/2 tsp palm sugar (jaggery)
1 fresh red chilli, seeded and
  finely sliced
15g/¹⁄₂oz fresh young root ginger,
  finely shredded

1 To make the dressing, in a bowl, beat the sesame oil, soy sauce and rice vinegar with the palm sugar, until it dissolves. Stir in the sliced red chilli and ginger and set the bowl aside for about 30 minutes to let the flavours develop.

2 Bring a pan of salted water to the boil. Drop in the beansprouts and blanch for a minute only. Drain and refresh under cold water until cool. Drain again and put them into a clean dish towel. Shake out the excess water.

3 Put the beansprouts into a bowl with the spring onions. Pour over the dressing and toss well. Garnish with the coriander leaves and serve immediately.

Fennel Coleslaw

Another variation on traditional coleslaw in which the flavour of fennel plays a major role in creating this delectable salad.

Serves 4
175g/6oz fennel
2 spring onions (scallions)
175g/6oz white cabbage
115g/4oz celery

175g/6oz carrots
50g/2oz/scant ¹⁄₂ cup sultanas
  (golden raisins)
2.5ml/¹⁄₂ tsp caraway
  seeds (optional)
15ml/1 tbsp chopped
  fresh parsley
45ml/3 tbsp extra-virgin olive oil
5ml/1 tsp lemon juice
strips of spring onion (scallion),
  to garnish

1 Using a sharp knife, cut the fennel and spring onions into thin slices. Place in a serving bowl.

2 Slice the cabbage and celery finely and cut the carrots into fine strips. Add to the fennel and spring onions in the serving bowl. Add the sultanas and caraway seeds to the bowl, if using, and toss lightly to mix through.

3 Stir the chopped parsley, olive oil and lemon juice into the bowl and mix all the ingredients very thoroughly.

4 Cover the bowl with clear film (plastic wrap) and chill in the refrigerator for about 3 hours to allow all the flavours of the coleslaw to mingle together. Serve the coleslaw immediately, garnished with strips of spring onion.

Fruit and Raw Vegetable Gado-Gado

Banana leaves are often used as wrappers in which to cook small parcels of food, but if you are serving this salad for a special occasion, you could use a large single banana leaf instead of the mixed salad leaves to line the platter.

Serves 6
¹⁄₂ cucumber
2 pears (not too ripe) or
  175g/6oz wedge of
  yam bean
1–2 eating apples
juice of ¹⁄₂ lemon
mixed salad leaves or
  1–2 banana leaves
6 tomatoes, seeded and cut
  into wedges

3 fresh pineapple slices, cored
  and cut into wedges
3 hard-boiled eggs, quartered
175g/6oz egg noodles, cooked,
  cooled and chopped
deep-fried onions, to garnish

For the peanut sauce
2–4 fresh red chillies, seeded and
  ground, or 15ml/1 tbsp hot
  tomato sambal
300ml/¹⁄₂ pint/1¹⁄₄ cups
  coconut milk
350g/12oz/1¹⁄₄ cups crunchy
  peanut butter
15ml/1 tbsp dark soy sauce or
  dark brown sugar
5ml/1 tsp tamarind pulp, soaked
  in 45ml/3 tbsp warm water
coarsely crushed peanuts
salt

1 Make the peanut sauce. Put the ground chillies or hot tomato sambal in a pan. Pour in the coconut milk, then stir in the peanut butter. Heat gently, stirring, until well blended.

2 Simmer the sauce gently until it begins to thicken, then stir in the soy sauce or sugar. Strain in the tamarind juice, discarding the seeds and pulp, add salt to taste and stir well. Spoon into a bowl and sprinkle with coarsely crushed peanuts.

3 To make the salad, core the cucumber and peel the pears or yam bean. Cut the flesh into fine matchsticks. Finely shred the apples and sprinkle them with the lemon juice. Spread a bed of mixed salad leaves on a flat platter and pile the cucumber, pears or yam bean, apples, tomatoes and pineapple on top.

4 Add the quartered eggs and the noodles and garnish with the deep-fried onions. Serve with the peanut sauce.

Cambodian Salad Energy 95kcal/396kJ; Protein 4.5g; Carbohydrate 8.4g, of which sugars 5.6g; Fat 5.6g, of which saturates 0.5g; Cholesterol 3mg; Calcium 54mg; Fibre 2.4g; Sodium 79mg.
Fennel Coleslaw Energy 145kcal/604kJ; Protein 1.9g; Carbohydrate 15.6g, of which sugars 15.3g; Fat 8.7g, of which saturates 1.2g; Cholesterol 0mg; Calcium 70mg; Fibre 3.8g; Sodium 46mg.
Fruit Gado-Gado Energy 577kcal/2411kJ; Protein 21.2g; Carbohydrate 46.3g, of which sugars 21g; Fat 35.5g, of which saturates 8.4g; Cholesterol 95mg; Calcium 88mg; Fibre 6.8g; Sodium 482mg.

Curried Chicken Salad with Green Beans and Penne

This mildly spicy sauce goes well with lean chicken.

Serves 4

2 cooked chicken breast portions, skinned and boned
175g/6oz green beans
350g/12oz multi-coloured penne
150ml/¼ pint/⅔ cup natural (plain) yogurt
5ml/1 tsp mild curry powder
1 garlic clove, crushed
1 fresh green chilli, seeded and finely chopped
30ml/2 tbsp chopped fresh coriander (cilantro) and a few extra leaves to garnish
4 firm ripe tomatoes, skinned and seeded, and cut into strips
salt and ground black pepper

1 Cut the chicken into strips. Cut the green beans into 2.5cm/1in lengths and cook in boiling water for 5 minutes. Drain and rinse under cold water.

2 Cook the pasta in a large pan of lightly salted boiling water according to the packet instructions. Drain and rinse thoroughly.

3 To make the sauce, mix the yogurt, curry powder, garlic, chilli and chopped coriander together in a bowl. Stir in the chicken pieces and leave to stand for 30 minutes.

4 Transfer the pasta to a large serving bowl and toss with the beans and tomatoes. Spoon the chicken mixture on top. Garnish with the coriander leaves and serve immediately.

Variations
• This salad becomes the perfect lunchbox treat, delicious, filling and healthy, if you simply toss the pasta, beans and tomatoes in with the chicken, so that all the ingredients have a light coating of curry sauce. It's also a good way to use up left-over roast chicken – just omit step one.
• The salad also works well with boiled and sliced waxy salad potatoes or white rice instead of the pasta. Simply add chopped red (bell) pepper for colour.

Rice Vermicelli and Fried Pork Salad

Fragrant pork tossed with beansprouts and fine noodles is a winning dish.

Serves 4

225g/8oz lean pork
2 garlic cloves, finely chopped
2 slices fresh root ginger, peeled and finely chopped
30–45ml/2–3 tbsp rice wine
45ml/3 tbsp vegetable oil or sunflower oil
2 lemon grass stalks, finely chopped
10ml/2 tsp curry powder
175g/6oz/¾ cup beansprouts
225g/8oz rice vermicelli, soaked in warm water until soft then drained
½ lettuce, finely shredded
30ml/2 tbsp fresh mint leaves
lemon juice and Thai fish sauce, to taste
salt and ground black pepper
2 spring onions (scallions), chopped, and 25g/1oz/¼ cup toasted peanuts, chopped, to garnish

1 Cut the pork into thin strips. Place in a shallow dish with half the garlic and ginger. Season with salt and pepper, pour over 30ml/2 tbsp rice wine and set aside to marinate for 1 hour.

2 Heat the oil in a frying pan. Add the remaining garlic and ginger and fry for a few seconds until fragrant. Stir in the pork, with the marinade, and add the lemon grass and curry powder. Fry on a high heat until the pork is golden and cooked through, adding more rice wine if the mixture seems too dry.

3 Place the beansprouts in a sieve (strainer) and lower into a pan of boiling water for 1 minute, then drain and refresh under cold running water. Drain again. Using the same water, cook the rice vermicelli for 3–5 minutes, until tender. Drain and rinse.

4 Drain the vermicelli well and put in a large bowl. Add the beansprouts, shredded lettuce and mint leaves. Season with lemon juice and fish sauce to taste. Toss lightly.

5 Divide the vermicelli mixture between individual serving plates and top with the pork. Garnish with spring onions and peanuts, and serve immediately.

Chicken Salad Energy 430kcal/1828kJ; Protein 32.1g; Carbohydrate 72.5g, of which sugars 9.8g; Fat 3.4g, of which saturates 0.7g; Cholesterol 53mg; Calcium 128mg; Fibre 4.8g; Sodium 94mg.
Fried Pork Salad Energy 409kcal/1705kJ; Protein 20.8g; Carbohydrate 48.7g, of which sugars 2.8g; Fat 14.5g, of which saturates 2.4g; Cholesterol 35mg; Calcium 68mg; Fibre 2.4g; Sodium 60mg.

Cucumber and Shallot Salad

In Malaysia and Singapore, this light, refreshing salad is served with Indian food almost as often as the cooling mint-flavoured cucumber raita. The Malays also enjoy this salad with many of their spicy fish and grilled meat dishes. It can be made ahead of time and kept in the refrigerator. Serve it as a salad, or a relish.

Serves 4
1 cucumber, peeled, halved
  lengthways and seeded
4 shallots, halved lengthways and
  sliced finely along the grain
1–2 green chillies, seeded and
  sliced finely lengthways
60ml/4 tbsp coconut milk
5–10ml/1–2 tsp cumin seeds,
  dry-roasted and ground to
  a powder
salt
1 lime, quartered, to serve

1 Slice the cucumber halves finely and sprinkle with a little salt. Set aside for about 10–15 minutes to draw out any excess moisture. Rinse well and drain off any excess water.

2 Put the cucumber, shallots and chillies in a salad serving bowl. Pour in the coconut milk and toss well. Sprinkle most of the roasted cumin seeds over the top.

3 Just before serving, toss the salad again, season with salt, and sprinkle the rest of the roasted cumin seeds over the top. Serve with lime wedges to squeeze over the salad.

Orange and Red Onion Salad

Cumin and mint give this refreshing, quick-to-prepare salad a very Middle Eastern flavour. Small, seedless oranges are most suitable, if available.

Serves 6
6 oranges
2 red onions

15ml/1 tbsp cumin seeds
5ml/1 tsp coarsely ground
  black pepper
15ml/1 tbsp chopped
  fresh mint
90ml/6 tbsp olive oil
salt
fresh mint sprigs and black
  olives, to garnish

1 Slice the oranges thinly, catching any juices. Holding each orange slice in turn over a bowl, cut round with scissors to remove the peel and pith. Reserve the juice.

2 Slice the red onions thinly and as evenly as possible. Separate each of the slices into rings.

3 Arrange the orange and onion slices in layers in a shallow dish, sprinkling each layer with cumin seeds, ground black pepper, chopped mint, olive oil and salt to taste. Pour over the reserved orange juice.

4 Leave the salad in a cool place or in the refrigerator for a minimum of 2 hours but no longer than about 4 hours.

5 Sprinkle over the fresh mint sprigs and black olives to garnish, and serve immediately.

Vietnamese Table Salad

The Vietnamese table salad can vary from a bowl of fresh, leafy herbs to a more tropical combination of beansprouts, water chestnuts, mangoes, bananas, star fruit, peanuts and rice noodles. The arrangement of a salad is simple and attractive.

Serves 4–6
1 crunchy lettuce, individual
  leaves separated
half a cucumber, peeled and
  thinly sliced

2 carrots, peeled and
  finely sliced
200g/7oz/scant 1 cup
  beansprouts
2 unripe star fruit (carambola),
  finely sliced
2 green bananas, finely sliced
1 firm papaya, cut in half,
  seeds removed, peeled and
  finely sliced
1 bunch each fresh mint and
  basil, stalks removed
1 lime
dipping sauce, to serve

1 Arrange all the ingredients, except the lime and sauce, on a large serving plate, with the lettuce leaves placed on one side so that they can be used as wrappers.

2 Squeeze the lime and pour the juice all over the sliced fruits, particularly the bananas to help them retain their colour and avoid discoloration from contact with the air.

3 Place the salad on the serving plate in the middle of the table. Serve immediately with a dipping sauce in a separate bowl so that diners can help themselves.

> **Cook's Tips**
> • When this Vietnamese table salad, known as sa lach dia, is served on its own, the vegetables and fruit are usually folded into little packets using lettuce leaves or rice wrappers, and then dipped in a sauce, or added bit by bit to bowls of plain boiled rice or noodles.
> • Choose a lettuce with crisp, crunchy leaves such as iceberg, Little Gem (Bibb), cos or romaine.

Cucumber Salad Energy 17kcal/68kJ; Protein 0.7g; Carbohydrate 3.3g, of which sugars 2.7g; Fat 0.1g, of which saturates 0g; Cholesterol 0mg; Calcium 19mg; Fibre 0.7g; Sodium 15mg.
Orange Salad Energy 199kcal/825kJ; Protein 1.6g; Carbohydrate 11.5g, of which sugars 11.3g; Fat 16.6g, of which saturates 2.4g; Cholesterol 0mg; Calcium 68mg; Fibre 2.3g; Sodium 7mg
Vietnamese Salad Energy 108kcal/455kJ; Protein 4g; Carbohydrate 21g, of which sugars 12g; Fat 1g, of which saturates 0g; Cholesterol 0mg; Calcium 110mg; Fibre 42g; Sodium 20mg.

Index